W9-BCV-814

3-28-00

WITHDRAWN
NDSU

MICROFORMS IN
LIBRARIES

MICROFORMS IN LIBRARIES
A Reader

Edited by
ALBERT JAMES DIAZ

WITHDRAWN
NDSU

MICROFORM REVIEW INC.
Weston, Conn.

Z
692
m5
m53

Library of Congress Cataloging in Publication Data
Main entry under title:

Microforms in libraries.

Bibliography: p.
1. Libraries--Special collections--Microforms--
Addresses, essays, lectures. I. Diaz, Albert James.
Z692.M5M53   025.17'9   75-6666
ISBN 0-913672-03-3

Original material copyright © 1975 by Albert James Diaz

All rights reserved. No part of this publication may be reproduced
in any form without permission from the publisher,
except by a reviewer who may quote brief passages in review.

ISBN for Mansell edition 0 7201 0536 6

Microform Review Inc.
P.O. Box 1297
Weston, Conn. 06880
Printed in United States of America

Published outside North and South America by
Mansell Information/Publishing Limited, 3 Bloomsbury Place,
London, WCIA 2QA, England.

To Kotchie

CONTENTS

MICROFORMS IN LIBRARIES

INTRODUCTION

Background

It might have been better for microfilm if those often cited carrier pigeons had not flown from Paris to Bordeaux during the Franco-Prussian War carrying dispatches[1] on microfilm. As Rolland Stevens notes, for over fifty years "microfilming was regarded more as a stunt or a curiosity than a method for promoting scholarly, or, other serious activities."[2]

In addition to being looked upon as curious, microforms have also been regarded as mysterious which is odd when one considers the general acceptance of photography; somehow, when a page is reproduced on a frame of 35mm film, it's mysterious; when a person's likeness is reproduced on the same frame, it isn't. The latter process may not be understood but it's accepted.

Similarly, when 35mm film contains images of people, places, or events, it's simply a roll of film but when it contains images of pages, it's a roll of microfilm, even though the size of the film hasn't changed.

Microforms have also suffered from overly enthusiastic promoters touting low cost as an absolute whereas microforms are low in cost when compared to other methods of reproduction *provided that the number of copies to be distributed is low*. As the number of copies increase, the price advantage of microforms decreases. This can be seen without elaborate computations by comparing the price of a paperback against the price of a book of similar length in microform. This is, of course, a simplistic comparison but nevertheless a legitimate one from the consumer standpoint as it compares actual prices rather than theoretical ones. As Dan Lacy points out, "It [cost of printing, paper, binding] is also a cost subject to rather sharp reduction in long runs, as the cost of photographically reproduced microfiche is not. In fact the per-copy cost of printing and binding a mass-market paperback is considerably less than that of reproducing the same images in microfiche."[3]

Espousers of microforms' "low cost" often tend to overlook composition and marketing costs and the fact that the cost of printing, paper, and binding (the costs microforms replace), "are among the smaller costs of publication, and will usually be no more than 15-to-20 percent of the retail cost of the book."[4]

"Hence," according to Lacy, "micropublishing in itself offers no prospect of significant savings as an alternative method of publishing individual books. The low price of most microfiche is derived not primarily from economies inherent in the micropublishing process, but from the fact that the materials micropublished exist in reproducible form in the public domain and therefore involve no royalties, editing or plant costs. The low price is also derived from the fact that micropublished products are usually large collections, series, or periodical sets sold as a unit and thereby avoiding the marketing costs of selling individual titles."[5]

Another myth, apparently due to the fact that many writers about microforms know little or nothing about libraries, is that microforms in libraries are held to be in dead storage and that scholarly research is somehow an inactive endeavour in contrast to, say, looking up insurance policies which is considered an "active" use of microforms. One writer, for example, notes, "By the 1950s, there was a widespread realization that microfilm could be used not only for the preservation of backfiles and oversized documents but as an integral part of *active* information systems as opposed to archival storage."[6] Needless to say, if libraries only stored microforms they wouldn't be concerned with such things as cataloging, organization, reading equipment, user reactions, and the other topics discussed in this book, nor would scholars care about indexing and bibliographic control.

Hopefully this book will dispel some myths and shed some light on problems encountered by librarians and scholars in dealing with microforms.

Scope and Purpose

This book, compiled for librarians, deals with the traditional use of microforms in libraries—the publishing of scholarly and research materials. It does not cover newer uses such as library catalogs on microfilm or the utilization of computer output microfilm (COM). Nor does it cover ultrafiche as the two major efforts to date (NCR's PCMI Library Collections and Library Resources, Inc.'s, Microbook, have not been successful in the marketplace and it appears that ultrafiche will have no significant impact upon library microforms).[7] As Frederick Lynden has noted, "the response of the library community to published microform libraries employing high reduction film seems to signal slow progress towards the use of ultrafiche."[8]

The purpose of the book is to give both students and practicing librarians a basic understanding of all aspects of micropublishing as it applies to libraries. The emphasis is on library usage rather than microform technology, on the practical rather than the theoretical, on the present rather than the past. Most articles have been written in recent years. Some older ones have been included because of their importance in understanding today's problems.

Six major topics are covered: (1) Introduction to Microforms, which includes a brief history of micropublishing, microform orientation, and some articles on micropublishing; (2) Organizing the Microform Collection, which has sub-chapters on operational problems—acquisitions, cataloging, organization, hardware and storage; (3) Bibliographic Control, perhaps the overriding microform problem at the present time; (4) Applications; (5) Standards and Specifications, which includes a descriptive article on the importance of standards and two filming specifications, one for books/pamphlets and the other for newspapers; (6) User Reactions, an area overlooked in the past but one to which much attention has been paid of late.

Role of Microforms

Before proceeding it might be worthwhile to give consideration to some general aspects of the use of microforms by libraries.

Why do libraries use microforms? According to a 1974 survey by a micropublisher, saving space was the reason given by most respondents. Holmes, on the other hand, found, "to acquire materials not otherwise available,"[9] as the major reason. Others include: (1) Instead of binding serials (journals are retained unbound for two to three years after publication, the period of heaviest use, and are then discarded and replaced by microform versions;[10] (2) To preserve deteriorating materials; (3) Easing access to bulky materials such as newspapers; (4) To provide working copies of materials too delicate for continued use such as rare books; (5) To save money—in most cases the cost of an out-of-print set or serial backfile will be substantially less in microform than the cost of a full-size reprint or the cost of the original on the used book market; (6) Ease of acquisition—i.e., acquiring materials which would otherwise be difficult to acquire; (7) Mutilations reduced.

Among the emerging and future uses of microforms by libraries four stand out: (1) to replace book or card catalogs; (2) for preservation purposes as part of a systematic approach to preserving materials printed on poor paper which in time will deteriorate; (3) in non-circulating libraries where the collection is on fiche and duplicate copies are made and sold (or given away) by the library in lieu of circulating; (4) to replace inter-library loan—instead of lending, the material is filmed and the film sold or given to the requesting library.

Problems Unique to Microforms

What problems do microforms present to libraries? (1) They require read-ing machines and patrons need to be instructed in the use of these ma-chines; (2) Machines require maintenance; (3) Open access presents prob-lems especially with microfiche; (4) It is difficult to place ownership iden-tification on microforms; (5) Difficulties with cataloging, bibliographic control; (6) Microforms are more easily damaged in normal use than are full size library materials; (7) Difficulties in inspecting microforms to de-termine completeness, adherence to standards, etc.; (8) Too many formats, sizes, necessitating many different reading machines; (9) Books and other materials to be filmed vary in size from the pocket size book to the daily newspaper and type sizes from footnote to display making standards diffi-cult to develop; (10) No agreement as to how microforms are to be counted for statistical purposes.

What problems do microforms present to students, scholars, and re-searchers? (1) They require reading machines which among other things tie the user down to a particular location; (2) Often reading machines are placed in undesirable locations—as Holmes notes, "reading machines are often placed in stack aisles where their users are often interrupted by other library patrons . . . dust and dirt are so bad in some cases that dam-age to both microforms and reading machines is commonplace,"; [11] (3) Eye strain, although this appears more imagined than real—"Most complaints are made by the casual user. Experienced microform users sel-dom complain.";[12] (4) Underlining or marginal notes are not possible; (5) Browsing is considered difficult; (6) Use of more than one book at a time (i.e., referring back and forth) is difficult; (7) Charts, maps, and illustra-tions often difficult to read.

The Investment in Microforms

How much are libraries spending on micropublications and how large are libraries' microform holdings? According to Yerkes writing in 1972, "the number of libraries with microform collections is high but the collection sizes are low compared to the hardcopy volumes in these same libraries."[13] He estimates that by page count 4.5 percent of the collections of college and university libraries are in microform, 1.9 percent of public libraries serving populations over 25,000, and 5 percent of special libraries. Reichmann and Tharpe found a much higher ratio for university libraries—"A substantial part of the holdings in United States libraries is on microform. The median ARL library in 1970 has 1,268,159 books and 355,490 units on microform. Thus, for every 100 printed books, the library had 28 microforms a ratio of less than four to one." [14] 1972-73 statistics for 2,550 colleges and universities show 425 million volumes, 10 million microfilm reels, and 97 million other microform units for a total of 107 million microform units resulting in a similar four to one ratio. [15] Reichmann and Tharpe expect the number of microforms issued to reach parity with printed books in the very near future; Holmes found an average growth rate of microform collections of 10 percent to 15 percent. [16] According to the college and university library statistics we have cited, libraries added 600,000 reels of microfilm and one million other microform units to their collections between 1971-72 and 1972-73. Assuming an average price per reel of $20.00 and an average price per unit of $.60 for "other microform units" this would make the higher education micropublishing market $18 million or approximately 5.7 percent of the $315 million spent on books and other library materials, a percentage which I think is too low. According to Miller, "Academic libraries are now [1972] spending between $25 million and $40 million per year on microforms." [17] My own educated guess would place the annual dollar volume for micropublications sold to all libraries at $35 to $45 million.

Which is better, positive or negative? This is one of those questions that I do not think can be answered definitively; it appears to be an entirely subjective matter. Positive microforms (black text, white background) outsell negatives in the library market. They resemble the printed page and are definitely better for photographs. Proponents of negative microforms feel that white images on a black background reduce glare and therefore eye fatigue. Scratches show up less on negative microforms. At one time reader-printers reversed polarity (a negative microform gave a positive print-out and vice-versa) so that if much enlarged copy was to be made, negative microforms were recommended, but now most reader-printers can go from negative to negative or positive to positive.

Which is the best microform? Again, there is no clear cut answer. Holmes found that, "a very large majority believed that roll microfilm should be used for miniaturizing serials, monographs, and manuscripts. These respondents also thought that microfiche was ideal for miniaturizing report literature. There was a general consensus that roll film, installed in cassettes for use in a suitable reading machine, would be highly desirable if the cost were not prohibitive." [18]

One thing that is clear is that no microform has been put completely out of business by another microform with the possible exception of the photographic micro-opaque, which has been largely supplanted by microfiche. This is unusual, as in similar circumstances the marketplace in time generally makes a choice. In the late 40s, for example, competing approaches to the record album market, which until then had utilized 78 rpm records, came out. One used a 10″ or 12″ disc revolving at 33 1/3 rpm and the other used a smaller disc revolving at 45 rpm. Within a short time the marketplace clearly chose 33 1/3 rpm for albums; 45 rpm became the medium for singles and 78 rpm disappeared. But this has not happened with microforms apparently because the marketplace considers them equal (I use the "marketplace" because I trust it much more as an expression of sentiment than surveys). Even the often repeated view that roll film is good for serials and fiche for reports (i.e., one report per fiche) and that fiche present problems of file integrity does not hold up as a substantial number of serials and other long-run materials have been successfully sold on fiche. What you seem to find is vocal adherents to every microform, but an insufficient number for any one microform to become predominant.

References

1. What was on the film, from where the pigeon flew, and its destination varies depending on whom you read.

2. Stevens, Rolland E., "The Microform Revolution," *Library Trends*, 19: 380 (January 1971).

3. Lacy, Dan, "A Book Publisher Looks at Micropublishing," National Microfilm Association, *Proceedings, 1972*. Silver Springs, Md.: National Microfilm Association, 1972, p. II-14.

4. *Ibid.*, p. II-14.

5. *Ibid.*, p. II-14.

6. Gaddy, Dale, *A Microform Handbook*. Silver Springs, Md: National Microfilm Association, 1974, p. 6.

7. The following articles will be of value to persons interested in the library use of ultrafiche: Evans, Charles W., "High Reduction Microfiche for Libraries: an Evaluation of Collections from the National Cash Register Company and Library Resources, Inc.," *Library Resources and Technical Services*, 16: 590-94 (Winter 1972), Grieder, E. M., "Ultrafiche Libraries: A Librarian's View," *Microform Review*, 1: 85-97 (April 1972), Hawken, William R., "Systems Instead of Standards," *Library Journal*, 98: 2515-25 (September 15, 1973), Lawrence, Larry L., "The Library of English Literature/Review Article," *Microform Review*, 2: 111-13 (April 1973), Linford, J. E., "Books in English," *Microform Review*, 1: 207-13 (July 1972), Napier, Paul, "The Library Resources Inc., *Library of American Civilization* Demonstration at the George Washington University Library," *Microform Review*, 3: 158-76 (July 1974), Rebuldela, Harriet K., "Ultrafiche Libraries: A User Survey of the Library of American Civilization," *Microform Review*, 3: 178-88 (July 1974), and "Ultrafiche Libraries: the Publishers Respond," *Microform Review*, 1:101-11 (April 1972). Consists of responses to Grieder's article by Treadwell Ruml (Library Resources) and Charles C. Goldman and Henry Grinberg (NCR) and a rejoinder by Grieder.

8. Lyndon, Frederick, "Replacement of Hard Copy by Microforms," *Microform Review*, 4: 17 (January 1975).

9. Holmes, Donald C., *Determination of User Needs and Future Requirements for a Systems Approach to Microform Technology*. July 19, 1969, ERIC ED 029 168, p. 6.

10. For a discussion of binding costs vs. replacement by microforms see Lynden, op cit, pp. 18-19. The sources he cites give binding costs as ranging from $3.85 to $7.88 per volume and the preparation cost as $2.75 per volume.

11. Holmes, *op cit.*, p. 7.

12. *Ibid.*, p. 13.

13. Yerkes, Charles P., "Micropublishing Market," National Microfilm Association, *Proceedings, 1972*. Silver Springs, Md.: National Microfilm Association, 1972, p. II-29.

14. Reichmann, Felix, and Tharpe, Josephine, *Bibliographic Control of Microforms*. Westport: Greenwood, 1972, p. 4. Yerkes compared pages whereas Reichmann/Tharpe compared books to microform units, however, when the Reichmann/Tharpe figures are translated into pages the ratio remains four to one.

15. *The Bowker Annual of Library and Book Trade Information, 1973.* New York: Bowker, 1973, p. 299. It should be noted that comparing books to microform units is a poor comparison especially when "other microform units" are treated as equivalent to reels. The number of pages on a reel of microfilm varies considerably depending upon the size of the original material, the filming mode, and the reduction ratio, but I think a figure of 2500 pages is acceptable for calculations and this is substantially greater than the number of pages in most books. The number of pages on "other microform units," excluding ultrafiche, varies from approximately forty to 112, with seventy a reasonable figure to use for calculations and this is substantially less than the number of pages in most books.

16. Holmes, *op cit.*, p. 10.

17. Miller, Edward A., *Determination of the Administrative and Functional Characteristics of a National Microform Agency.* Washington: Association of Research Libraries, 1972, p. 14.

18. Holmes, *op cit.*, p. 9.

INTRODUCTION TO MICROFORMS

INTRODUCTION

This chapter orients the reader to the history, language (i.e., jargon), and scholarly uses of microforms.

Veaner's article gives a thumbnail sketch of the history of micropublishing which is amplified by Stevens', "Microform Revoltuion." Excluding the early, conceptual period, we find 35mm microfilm being used in the middle to late thirties for the reproduction of scholarly materials by individuals, libraries, and commercial firms. Following the Second World War, two other forms appear: Microprint (a 6" × 9" opaque card containing micro-images reproduced through offset lithography) and Microcard (a 3" × 5" opaque card with images reproduced through photographic processes). In the early 60s, the microfiche, a format that had been in use in Europe for several years, is adopted by the federal government for reproducing technical and other reports and its use subsequently becomes widespread. Another form, 16mm microfilm, which libraries had rejected, regains popularity as cartridges and cassettes enable users to load and unload film easily. The introduction of the reader-printer enables users to make an immediate, full-size copy of any page on a microform. In the 70s, a new microform, the ultrafiche, which allows several thousand pages to be reproduced on 4" × 6" fiche.

Fiche and Reel, a very useful work issued by Xerox University Microfilms, describes the technical side of microforms. Bernhardt's article discusses the pros and cons of the various formats.

The two articles by Stevens give an overview of how microforms have been used by detailing the development of the scholarly micropublishing concept and the use of microforms to conserve storage space ("The Microform Revolution") and by describing various microform projects ("Resources in Microform").

Born's article, which originally appeared in *PMLA* in 1964 was subsequently reprinted in *Microform Review* in 1972, reviews scholarly micropublishing, with particular emphasis on archival and manuscript materials, comments on the "randomness with which scholarly resources on the North American continent have been enriched by photofacsimile," calls for "being more systematic in the employment of funds available for microfilming projects," and concludes with five important recommendations.

HISTORY OF
MICROPUBLISHING

by Allen B. Veaner

Stevens (1968) reports that microwriting was known to the ancients. Excavations at Nineveh conducted by Layard are said to have revealed clay cylinders containing minute inscriptions, but they are not so small that a magnifier is required to read them. Robert Hooke (1665) discusses the application of miniaturized handwriting for the transmission of secret messages:

> If this manner of small writing were made easie and practicable (and I think I know such a one, but have never yet made tryal of it, whereby one might be inabled to write a great deale with much ease, and accurately enough in a very little roome) it might be of very good use to convey secret intelligence without any danger of discovery or mistrusting.

But it was the achievement of practical photography by Niepce, Daguerre, and others which laid the foundations for modern microreproduction. Ardern (1960) has recounted the work of the Englishman, John Benjamin Dancer, who manufactured microreproduced novelty texts and illustrations in the middle of the last century. Luther (1959) has carefully documented the story of Dagron's pigeon-carried microtexts during the siege of Paris in 1871, a story that has been referenced innumerable times.

The earliest known suggestion of using micropublication for scholarly purposes is contained in an exchange of correspondence between Sir John

Reprinted from "Micropublication," *Advances in Librarianship*, 2: 173-76 (1971) by permission of the author and publisher. Copyright © 1971 by Seminar Press, Inc.

Herschel and his brother-in-law, John Stewart (Herschel and Stewart, 1853). Herschel wrote to the editor of the *Athenaeum* on July 6:

Your insertion of the annexed letter from my brother-in-law, Mr. John Stewart, of Pau, will much oblige me. The utility of this mode of reproduction seems indisputable. In reference to its concluding paragraph, I will only add, that the *publication* of concentrated microscopic editions of works of reference—maps, atlases, logarithmic tables, or the concentration for pocket use of private notes and MSS., &c. &c. and innumerable other similar applications—is brought within the reach of any one who possesses a small achromatic object-glass of an inch or an inch and a half in diameter. . . .

Stewart, after recounting the difficulties of making the original master copy, goes on talking like the modern micropublisher:

Thus, by the simultaneous action, if necessary, of some hundreds of negatives, many thousand impressions of the same picture may be produced in the course of a day.

Stewart concludes on the point Herschel seized on:

Should your old idea of preserving public records in a concentrated form on microscopic negatives ever be adopted, the immediate positive reproduction on an enlarged readable scale, without the possibility of injury to the place, will be of service.

Even the microfiche is not a newcomer; its current design and format were proposed two thirds of a century ago by Goldschmidt and Otlet (1906).

The concepts originated by Herschel, Stewart, Goldschmidt, and Otlet had to await modern technology. It was not until 1928 that practical microphotography became commercially available; it was in that year that George McCarthy, a bank executive, convinced the Eastman Kodak Company to market his Checkograph—a camera designed to microfilm cancelled checks as a deterrent to fraud. Kodak formed a wholly owned subsidiary, the Recordak Corporation, to develop and market microfilm products and services under the tradename Recordak.

By 1935 Recordak had perfected the 35mm microfilm camera, and a few sporadic attempts were made to micropublish newspapers. In fact, the Recordak organization itself, with the aid and advice of the New York Public Library, filmed and published a substantial file of the *New York Times*, and for a while it looked as though Recordak would become the nation's principal micropublisher.

But the real beginning of micropublication occurred in 1938, which was marked by two major events: commencement of the Foreign Newspaper Microfilm Project by Harvard University Library and the founding of University Microfilms by Eugene Power, a former member of Edwards

Brothers, a publishing firm. Both enterprises were founded upon the idea of disseminating research materials on demand from a central repository. Weber (1956) has recounted the origin and history of the Foreign Newspaper Microfilm Project, now a continuing effort of the Association of Research Libraries. Newspapers were of interest because the originals were space consuming, expensive to maintain, unhandy to use, and deteriorated rapidly. University Microfilms concentrated upon hard-to-obtain rare books and doctoral dissertations which could not be mass marketed by conventional publishing techniques.

Following the Second World War, micropublication made little further progress until five new developments occurred. First, the Microcard Corporation was established in an attempt to fulfill the ideas conceived by Fremont Rider (1944). Second, a variety of standards efforts were initiated—by the Association of Research Libraries (1950), the American Library Association's Board on Resources of American Libraries (1953), and the Association's Committee on Photoduplication and Multiple Copying Methods (1955). These efforts culminated in the publication of *Specifications for Library of Congress Microfilming* (1964) and *Microfilm Norms* (American Library Association, 1966). Third, the Department of Defense established an engineering drawing microreproduction program which stimulated the creation of new hardware, films, and quality control procedures. Fourth, the United States Navy contracted with Xerox (then the Haloid Company) for development of the Copyflo dry enlarger. Fifth, a variety of government agencies (the Atomic Energy Commission, the Department of Defense, NASA, ERIC, and the Clearinghouse for Federal Scientific and Technical Information) agreed to promote the dissemination of technical reports on 4" × 6" microfiche. From that point on, a major influx of federal dollars to aid higher education stimulated very rapid growth in micropublication.

[More information on the early history of microphotography is obtainabe from Luther (1959). Recent history is available from the *Journal of Documentary Reproduction*, published from 1938 to 1942 by the American Library Association.]

References

American Library Association. Board on Resources of American Libraries (1953). Proposed statement of principles to guide large scale acquisition and preservation of library materials on microfilm. *College & Research Libraries* 14, 288-291, 302.
American Library Association. Committee on Photoduplication and Multiple Copying Methods (1955). "A Guide to Microfilming Practices." American Library Association, Chicago, Illinois.
American Library Association. Resources & Technical Services Division (1966). Microfilm Norms. American Library Association, Chicago, Illinois.
American National Standard PH5.3-1967. "Specifications for 16mm and 35mm Silver Gelatine Microfilms for Reel Applications." American National Standards Institute, New York.
American National Standard PH5.9-1969. "Specifications for Microfiches." American National Standards Institute, New York.

Applebaum, E. L. (1965). Implications of the National Register of Microform Masters as part of a national preservation program. *Library Resources & Technical Services* 9, 489-494.
Ardern, L. L. (1960). "John Benjamin Dancer: The Originator of Microphotography." The Library Association, London.
Association of Research Libraries. Committee on Photographic Reproduction of Research Materials (1950). A proposed standard for the microphotographic reproduction of newspapers. *American Documentation* 1, 46-50.
Bookmaking news; microfiche inserts may be useful in book publishing (1970). *Publishers' Weekly* 197, (June 29) 97.
Canning, R. (1969). A case for involvement? *EDP Analyzer* 7, No. 12, 8-9.
Clapp, V. W. (1964). "The Future of the Research Library;" p. 19. University of Illinois Press, Urbana, Illinois.
Forbes, E. J., and Bagg, T. C. (1966). "Report of a Study of Requirements and Specifications for Serial and Monograph Microrecording for the National Library of Medicine." National Bureau of Standards, Washington, D.C. (NBS Report 9446).
Goldschmidt, R., and Otlet, P. (1906). "Sur une forme nouvelle du Livre—Le Livre Microphotographique." Institut International de Bibliographie, Bruxelles. (Institut International de Bibliographie, Publication No. 81).
Gregory, R. (1970). Acquisition of microforms. *Library Trends* 18, 373-384.
"Guide to Microforms in Print" (1961-   ). NCR Microcard Editions, Washington, D.C.
Hawken, W. R., Klessig, K. K., Nelson, C. E., and Kristy, N. F. (1970). Microbook publications—a new approach for a new decade. *Journal of Micrographics* 3, 188-193.
Herschel, J. F. W., and Stewart, J. (1853). New photographic process. *Athenaeum* No. 1341, p. 831.
Holmes, D. C. (1969). The needs of library microform users. *National Microfilm Association Proceedings* 1969, 256-261.
Hooke, R. (1665). "Micrographia." Printed by Martyn and Allestry, London.
International Filmbook Corporation (1937). (Advertisement). *Microfilm, a Journal Published by Microfilm Publishing Corporation* 1, No. 1, 24-25.
Journal of Documentary Reproduction (1938-1942). American Library Association, Chicago, Illinois.
Library of Congress (1964). "Specifications for Library of Congress Microfilming." Library of Congress, Washington, D.C.
Luther, F. (1959). "Microfilm: A History, 1839-1900." National Microfilm Association, Annapolis, Maryland.
Microreproduction vs. the regional warehousing of research materials (1953). *In* "Microtext in the Management of Book Collections, a Symposium." *College & Research Libraries* 14, 292-298.
Myers, W. C. (1970a). Remote viewing and printing of graphic materials. *Journal of Micrographics* 3, 173-178.
Myers, W. C. (1970b). Micropublishing roundup. *Micrographics News & Views* 1, 1,5.
National Register of Microform Masters (1965-   ). (Compiled by the Library of Congress with the Cooperation of the American Library Association and the Association of Research Libraries, Washington, D.C.) (Included in a subscription to the *National Union Catalog* and also separately available.)
New York Times on microfilm (1968). *Choice* 5, 1276-1277.
Orne, J. (in press). Microforms and the research library. *National Microfilm Association Proceedings.*
Philadelphia Bibliographical Center and Union Library Catalogue (1961). "Union List of Microfilms; Cumulation 1949-1959." J. W. Edwards, Ann Arbor, Michigan.
Rider, F. (1944). "The Scholar and the Future of the Research Library." Hadham Press, New York.
Schwegmann, G. A. (1960). The bibliographical control of microforms. *Library Trends* 8, 380-390.
Simonton, W. (1962). The bibliographical control of microforms. *Library Resources & Technical Services* 6, 29-40.
Stevens, G. W. W. (1968). "Microphotography—Photography and Photofabrication at Extreme Resolution." John Wiley, New York.
Sullivan, R. C. (1970). Developments in reproduction of library materials, 1969. *Library Resources & Technical Services* 14, 189-230.
Veaner, A. B. (in press). "The Technical Evaluation of Micropublications; A Handbook for Librarians." (Tentative title.) Library Technology Program, Chicago, Illinois.

Weber, D. C. (1956). The foreign newspaper microfilm project, *Harvard Library Bulletin* 10,
   275-281.
Williams, B. J. S. (1970). "Miniaturised Communications—A Review of Microforms." The Library
   Association, London.
Wooster, H. (1969). "Microfiche 1969—A User Survey." National Technical Information Service,
   Springfield, Virginia (AD 695 049).

FICHE
AND REEL

by E. Stevens Rice

Microfilm

Microfilm is black and white photographic film with a much reduced
image on it. Every time you "snap" a picture with your 35mm camera you
are exposing microfilm of a sort. There are three main differences between
professionally produced microfilm for libraries and your snapshot. First,
the microfilm is meant to be intellectually valuable whereas your snapshot
is generally meant to be aesthetically valuable. Second, the emulsion, or
image-producing material used for microfilm, is formulated to produce
high contrasts, with deep blacks on a (nearly) clear background, whereas
the emulsion of standard photographic films is formulated to produce low
contrasts with many shades of grey from the deepest blacks to the clearest
whites. Accordingly we say that the microfilm is a high contrast film with
a short tonal range, whereas your snapshot film is a low contrast film with
a long tonal range. Third, negative microfilm is generally printed to film,
whereas your snapshot is printed to photographic paper.

The term *microfilm* is somewhat misleading, since the film used in
microphotography is no more "micro" than the 35mm film you use in
your hand camera. It is the image, rather than the film size, which is small.
There are many different sizes, forms and shapes of *microfilms*, the generic
term for microimages produced in useful formats.

The film used in microform photography consists of a clear, pliant base,
coated with a photosensitive emulsion. When the photosensitive material in

Excerpted from the pamphlet *Fiche and Reel* by E. Stevens Rice. (Ann Arbor, Michigan: Xerox
University Microfilms, 1972). Reprinted by permission of the author. Copies of the pamphlet are
available from Xerox University Microfilms, 300 North Zeeb Road, Ann Arbor, Michigan 48106.

the emulsion consists of silver halides, the film is a silver film. This is the most common type of film and is the kind you use in your hand camera. Other photosensitive materials are in use, however, and will be mentioned briefly later.

Negatives and Positives

The photosensitive material exposed in a microfilm camera is silver film because it is very sensitive to light and can be correctly exposed with little light and/or a shutter speed of short duration. After exposure to light in a camera the film has on it a latent image which must be chemically developed to be made visible. This image will have tonal values just opposite to those in the object photographed, so it is called a negative. If it is a book page that has been photographed, the negative image will have white (clear) letters against a black page. Film exposed in a camera is a *camera negative*, or first generation microfilm. Unexposed film can now be exposed or printed from this negative by being held in contact with it in front of a light source. When properly developed, the newly-exposed and processed film will be a positive, second generation print with black letters on a white background just like the original book page. This procedure can go on for many generations: negative to positive to negative to positive. . . , but each successive generation is a little poorer in quality. There are also direct imaging materials which yield a negative from a negative and a positive from a positive, and each process and material has its own advantages and disadvantages.

Film Materials

The camera negative used for microphotography is usually silver film because of its high sensitivity to ordinary light. Other kinds of photosensitive materials require longer exposures, more light, or both. None of these alternatives is attractive to the professional microphotographer.

It is common, however, to print to other photosensitive materials from silver film. Some of the materials in everyday use are diazo, vesicular materials like Kalvar and Xidex, and photochromic like PCMI materials manufactured by the National Cash Register Company. These are developed by light, heat, or chemicals, depending on the type of film.

Sizes

Silver film is manufactured in wide webs which are later slit to practical sizes. Beginning with the smallest, common widths are 8mm (5/16 in.),

16mm (5/8 in.), 35mm (1-3/8 in.), 70mm (2-3/4 in.), and 105mm (4-1/8 in.). (Inch equivalents are approximations. One millimeter measures 0.03937 inches.) Film for professional microphotographic use is often sold in 1000 foot lengths as a matter of convenience for large scale production, but films can be cut to any reasonable length. Microfilms in libraries are usually 100 feet or less in length. The first modern microfilm was 16mm wide when used for commercial records and 35mm wide when used for library materials, since these sizes accepted the low reductions (a larger image on the film) needed for quality which the narrower films would not. Seventy millimeter film was used for engineering drawings for a time, for the same reason, but is not much used for this purpose now. Standard microfiches are approximately 4 X 6 inches, and are made from 105mm film.

Formats

A negative film can be printed to a positive film which has been formed into any one of several different sizes and shapes to make reference copies suited to the needs of the user, although the images usually remain the same size. Thirty-five millimeter film may be printed to 35mm rollfilm, but it can just as easily be made up as filmcards or fiches, or be cut apart into separate exposures and inserted into aperture cards, or be cut into short pieces and inserted into transparent jackets. There are many variations in final forms but most formats begin as 16mm or 35mm rollfilm.

There are four rollfilm image placements in common use: 1A, 2A, 1B and 2B. In the A positions the lines of type run across the width of the film, while in the B positions the lines of type lie parallel to the length of the film; the numbers refer to the number of pages photographed in each exposure. Sometimes these positions are called ciné (for the A positions) and comic (for the B).

Microfiches

Standard microfiches are 105 X 148mm (approximately 4 X 6 in.) in size, upon which microimages have been arranged in 7 rows and 14 columns for a maximum 98 pages per fiche. This American National Standard has been approved by the National Microfilm Association and has been adopted by most micropublishers for many of their publications.

While reduction ratios for images on 16 and 35mm rollfilm are determined by the kind and condition of the material to be photographed and the system to be used—especially the camera and enlarging device—in the standard microfiche, the maximum size of the image has been specified without regard to the amount of reduction necessary to fit the image into the 10 X 12.5mm space allotted. An 8.5 by 11 in. document (approximately 216 X 279mm) will fit the space easily at 1/24 original size. A larger document, say 10 X 12 in. microfilmed at 1/24 would not fit. Many viewer lenses are made to enlarge 24 diameters so if we must use a higher reduction than 1/24 to make the image fit the available space, the size of this image on such a viewer will be smaller than the original document page. In the example given, the difference is so trifling as to be scarcely noticeable, but clearly the standard was not meant for pages larger than this on the one hand, nor for pages much smaller than 8.5 X 11 in. on the other, since a typical 6 X 9 in. book page would be wasteful of space at 24X and there would be no point in making the image larger to "fill up the frame."

An alternative is to select a reduction ratio commensurate with the enlargement to be used and suitable to the materials photographed. In general, reductions to 1/12 for color, 1/24 for most library materials and 1/48 for closed systems in which standards can be controlled carefully seem to be reasonable reductions for microfiche projects.

Among the proposals for unusual fiche formats is the proposal that the text of a book (or other material) be in continuous columns rather than in page form. Information arranged in continuous columns takes only about a third of the space required for pages, with their waste space (as far as information is concerned) in margins, etc., at a reduction of 24X. Reading is easier too, as one needs to guide the fiche carrier in only one direction most of the time, and the eyes make fewer movements. There are some drawbacks as well, such as the difficulty of finding one's place.

In cooperation with the Air Force, James Kottenstette, Research Engineer at Denver Research Institute, has developed an unusual format to be used in teaching airmen, in which the information is so arranged on the fiche that a student can review material already studied, can work additional problems, read supplementary information, or can consider a different aspect of a point in question by following different paths on the fiche. In this novel arrangement of information the fiche has become a programmed instruction device.

In these two examples, the innovators have made the fiche a valuable carrier of information because they have been able to turn to good advantage the fact that it *is* a fiche. That the formats do not correspond to the standard is of no importance in these cases.

Additional schemes for formatting fiches for maximum utility are made easier through COM (Computer Output Microform) devices that permit information to be manipulated in a computer, then imaged directly onto microfilm without intermediate printing steps. The information-bearing characters are displayed on a cathode ray tube in one version of COM, and exposed to microfilm which may then be made up into fiche format. While at present there are more applications for COM in business and industry than for libraries and academic institutions, some interesting COM publishing projects are beginning to emerge. One of these is MEMEM: Michigan Early Modern English Materials, a kind of scholar's dictionary of the English language at a particular period in its development. Information concerning this fiche publication may be obtained from Professor Richard W. Bailey, Department of English Language and Literature, University of Michigan, Ann Arbor.

Another non-standard format is occasioned by the extremely high reductions of ultrafiche, by means of which some 3000 book pages at about 150X may be put on one standard size fiche. With such small images (almost 29 per square centimeter in one example) the ever-present possibility of scratches in the emulsion represents a serious threat to legibility, so manufacturers have laminated the emulsion side of their ultra-high reduction fiche to prevent scratching of the emulsion in normal use. Scratches on this protective layer do not show on the viewer screen because they are not in the focusing field of the emulsion and so are not visible.

Ultra-high reduction fiches are those made at reductions greater than 100. They are usually made in two steps: materials are first photographed at, say, 1/10 original size, then the film is again photographed at perhaps 15X to achieve a final reduction of 1/150 original size.

Micro-Opaques

When a negative is printed to photographic paper rather than to film, the paper is called a *micro-opaque*, or sometimes a *micropaque*. The 3 X 5 inch Microcard is a micro-opaque. Another opaque microform is the Microprint card. Although these begin as microfilm, the Microprint cards themselves are printed by offset lithography by the Readex Microprint Company. They have an interesting indexing feature in that each card is printed with 100 pages arranged in 10 rows and 10 columns so that it is easy to find any given page by its location on the card. Special viewers must be used for the micro-opaques, since the enlarged image is formed by reflected rather than by transmitted light.

Viewing and Printing

Every microimage must be enlarged to eye-legible size for reading, and there are two ways commonly used to do this: first, a shadow image is formed on the glass or opaque screen of a microform viewer. Dozens of different makes and models are available, but the optical principles are the same regardless of the outward appearance of the apparatus. In a typical viewer for transparencies, light from a light source is intensified by condenser lenses, is directed through the microimage, which is then enlarged by another lens system, and finally the image is displayed in approximately the size of the object photographed. The image may be reflected from mirrors inside the viewer to allow the equipment to be of smaller size than would otherwise be possible. Many modern viewers will accept either 16mm or 35mm rollfilm interchangeably, as well as standard size microfiches, although in some a special attachment must be used when changing from one microform to another. Special purpose viewers accept only a particular film size or shape. Some viewers have lenses of different powers to enable the user to read films made at different reductions.

The second common way to make a microimage useful is to capture the enlarged image by some photographic process on photosensitive paper or by xerography on ordinary paper. Since a microfilm which displays a positive image on the screen yields a negative image on photographic paper, negative film is used when positive prints on photographic paper are to be made. Viewers which will enlarge microimages onto a screen and will also make prints from them are called reader-printers. They are made by several manufacturers to accept various formats and to print out on different kinds of photographic stock.

The librarian should choose the viewers which will best accommodate the film in the library's collection. An ideal viewer for most library collections would be one having lenses which enlarge 20X, 24X, and 40X and will accept microfiches as well as 16mm and 35mm rollfilm.

At least one reader-printer should be provided for all but the smallest collections. The one which yields the clearest prints and is most versatile should be chosen.

For trouble-free viewers, preventive maintenance procedures following manufacturers' recommendations should be followed. Since dust is the great enemy of film and optical systems alike, the most important aspect of maintenance is cleanliness. The film transport mechanism and the screen should be given special attention. Sparce amounts of lens cleaner and lens tissues should be used on the optical system.

The librarian who knows how to keep the viewers clean and who can change bulbs, should have trouble-free viewing for a long time. Service men should be called for more complicated maintenance unless the library is blessed with a good mechanic.

Reduction Ratios

Microimages are reduced a greater or lesser amount by varying the distance of the camera from the book being photographed; the farther away the camera, the smaller the image and the greater the reduction.

Reductions are usually expressed as a ratio between the size of the object, which is always one, and the proportionate size of the microimage.

For example, a 9 × 12 inch book page photographed at a reduction ratio of 1/12 (or 12×) would form an image on the film 3/4 inch by 1 inch, or 1/12 of the linear measure of each dimension.

As technology has improved the reduction ratios have become greater. Thirty years ago a reduction to 1/10 or 1/12 of the original size was common, but today such low reductions are not much used; 1/20 is more common for library materials. A reduction of 1/24 to 1/40 would not be thought excessive for some types of material, and some library materials are being reduced as much as 80 diameters (to 1/80 of the size of the objective). Despite the demonstrated capability of techniques which permit photographing in the ultra high ranges of 100 or 200 diameters, these are not yet much used for microfilming library materials.

A reduction ratio should be chosen on the basis of the size of type in the original document, the way in which the microforms will be used, and the enlarging power of the equipment which will enlarge the image to readable size once more. All of the factors of reducing, enlarging, sorting, finding and retrieving individual frames must be taken into consideration when planning a microform collection.

Retrieval

To make their microforms more useful, some manufacturers code frames, or other units, so they can be retrieved easily and quickly. The simplest code mark is a line, or blip, centered at the botton of each page to facilitate automatic page counting for reference. When a predetermined number of blips have been counted, the film is stopped and the correct frame is displayed on the screen of a viewer. Manufacturers use many different types of codes, ranging from simple to complex.

To utilize coding systems to the fullest it is best to use a viewer which transports the film at high speeds with the help of a small electric motor. Speed is especially helpful when many files are to be searched consecutively.

Quality

Since microfilming involves the reduction of the image of an original down to a very small size, and later enlarging that reduced image back up to a readable, useful size, the quality of the image is very important. The prime factors which determine quality are density, contrast and resolution. The ultimate goal in microfilming is maximum contrast without loss of resolution. Too much contrast gives a generally weak, washed out appearance to the entire image.

Density and Contrast

Density is the extent to which the dark areas of the microfilm are truly opaque (that is, will not transmit light). When light strikes an object, it is either:

REFLECTED,
ABSORBED, or
TRANSMITTED.

When a document is being recorded with a microfilm camera, most of the light striking the white areas is reflected, while most of the light striking the dark areas is absorbed, but some of the light is transmitted through the document onto the copy table.

Again, when light strikes a frame of negative microfilm (as during an enlargement) most of the light falling on the opaque areas will be absorbed, most of the light falling on the clear areas is transmitted; some of the light, however, is reflected from the surface of the film.

To ensure the best quality of enlarged reproductions from microfilm, regardless of the reproduction method used, the dark areas should be as opaque as possible, and the light areas as clear as possible. This is another way of saying that we look for density in the opaque areas, and contrast between the opaque and clear areas in our striving to achieve the maximum of both density and contrast without loss of resolution.

Density is an expression of the amount of silver deposited in a given area, in terms of the amount of light that it will absorb. Or, more simply, it is a measure of the light-stopping power of a negative.

Density is defined by professionals as the logarithmic value of the reciprocal of the transmittance. Material which permits the transmission of 50 percent (1/2) of the source light is said to have an opacity of 2 (the reciprocal of 1/2). The logarithm of 2 is 0.3, so a material that transmits half the light striking it has a density of 0.3. Some other values are shown in the table:

% of light transmitted	% represented as fraction	Opacity	Density (log of opacity)
50	1/2	2	0.3
25	1/4	4	0.6
12.5	1/8	8	0.9
6.25	1/16	16	1.2
3.125	1/32	32	1.5

Contrast is the difference in density between the opaque areas and the clear areas of a microfilm image. You can not obtain good contrast without high density. It would be simple to obtain it if all documents to be photographed consisted of jet black, matte-textured lines on pure white backgrounds. Such backgrounds would reflect light very well, thus yielding very dense opaque areas on the film. The black lines would absorb virtually all of the light striking them, and thus yield clear areas on the film. With correct exposure and proper processing, such originals would yield images of the highest quality, having proper density and contrast. The microphotographer must compensate with his skill and experience for the many variations from this ideal that he finds in his daily work.

Resolution

Resolution is the measure of the ability of a film, a lens, or a complete photographic system to faithfully reproduce closely spaced fine lines and maintain distinguishable separation between them. The measure is the number of lines per millimeter that can be distinguished or resolved.

The tests are made by photographing resolution charts which have been carefully and accurately made to exacting standards. Test patterns are placed at each corner and in the center of the exposure area, so that maximum over-all resolution can be determined. The best resolution will be obtained at the center, since lenses tend to be more nearly optically perfect at the center than towards their outer edges. The resolution for any particular exposure is read from the most poorly resolved pattern in that frame.

Resolution charts consist of a series of evenly spaced horizontal and vertical lines. All lines in a given group are of the same thickness, with the space between the lines equal to that thickness. The groupings become progressively smaller, with each succeeding group of lines made up of smaller (finer) lines with equally smaller spaces between the lines. Beside each group of lines is a number that indicates the number of lines per millimeter in that group.

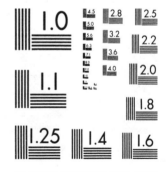

MICROCOPY RESOLUTION TEST CHART
NATIONAL BUREAU OF STANDARDS-1963-A

Lines are said to be resolved when they can be seen as distinct lines and spaces, and their direction and number can be determined, when the microfilm is enlarged under a microscope.

Resolution is usually expressed as a power obtained by multiplying the number of the highest numbered line grouping that can just be resolved, by the reduction factor used when photographing the resolution test chart. Suppose the group with the number 6.3 can just be resolved under a microscope on microfilm made at a reduction of 20X (1/20). Multiply 6.3 by 20 to obtain the resolving power of 126.

Making Microfilm

In a microfilm laboratory, typical manufacturing procedures occur in this order:

a. editing of incoming materials,
b. photographing,
c. processing the negative,
d. inspecting and correcting the negative,
e. printing the positive,
f. processing the positive,
g. labeling, packaging,and shipping the positive film, and
h. storing the negative.

Every step is important to the quality of the completed film and its subsequent value to the librarian and those he serves.

In editing, material coming into the laboratory is collated, then checked for completeness. Titles are prepared and specifications are set. The materials should be ready for photographing without further work by the camera operator.

In the larger laboratories the film is processed on continuously running processing machines which guide the film through successive chemical baths which develop, clear and harden, then wash and dry the film in one continuous process. Film quality depends on the careful control of time, temperature, and the strength of the chemicals used.

Archival quality film contains less than .005mg. thiosulfate per square inch of black and white processed film. Thiosulfate is the chemical which clears the film, and makes the images permanent. It is sometimes called hypo. Librarians can not test accurately for residual hypo, since such tests must be made soon after processing. Hypo remaining in the film after processing tends to diminish with time, so only very excessive amounts at time of processing would show as exceeding the standard for archival film at a later time.

Careful inspection takes as much time as photography, as every frame should be carefully looked at to make sure that editorial instructions have been followed, targeting is correct, and all pages have been well photographed, for once a perfect negative has been prepared, positive copies made from it are pretty sure to be good ones. Any errors found are corrected at this time.

Satisfactory negative is sent to the printing department so that positive distribution copies can be printed and processed. The processing steps for positive microfilm are the same as those for negative film. Positive film copies going out to purchasers are given a quick, final inspection as they are placed on reels and packaged, or in fiche envelopes.

Having served its purpose for the time being, the negative is stored in such a way that it can readily be found when needed again. Micropublishers generally store master films in vaults especially constructed for keeping films safe.

Microform for Libraries

Properly prepared microfilm of good quality, having good density, contrast and resolution, is of the utmost importance no matter what physical form the microimages may take. But with so many formats and reduction ratios and photosensitive materials, how can one know what microforms to purchase for the library?

The wise librarian will purchase only from those micropublishers whose reputations assure him that they will stand behind the quality of their products, but it is helpful in choosing among the products of several companies to consider factors other than quality as well.

The microfilm industry has not set up standard formats for different kinds of printed, typed and drawn materials, and until they do the librarian will have to choose those which are most practical for his library, and will probably be strongly guided by formats already in the collection, provided he can get the materials he needs in this form.

For example, microfiches might be chosen for a collection of monographs if only one or two fiches are used for each title. Or one might choose fiche when he expects to replace all or part of the file periodically, or when a file must be rearranged according to subject, or geographical location, or date, etc., in order to be most useful to different people or to meet the needs of different situations.

If pages must be retained in sequence to be most easily retrieved, as the pages of a long serial run, then probably rollfilm will be chosen. Formats should be chosen with a view to the way in which the microform will be used.

During the past few years 16mm film has become increasingly popular, especially for scientific and technical periodicals. One reason for this popularity is its availability in cassettes or cartridges. These give a certain amount of protection to the film and at the same time reduce the threading of the microfilm viewer to almost nothing. Rollfilm in cartridges manufactured by different producers may not fit the machines of competitors.

Unless a coded retrieval system is used, the library probably does not need to be equipped with motorized viewers. It takes about 30 seconds to wind 100 feet of film from beginning to end manually, but since the page one is looking for is as likely to be one place as another, the average time necessary to turn to a given page on a full roll of film is 15 seconds. The added convenience of a motorized viewer is worth its additional cost to most librarians only when large numbers of reels of film are to be searched.

Reduction ratio, as well as kind of film and image placement, is also important. The advantages of higher reduction are in the amount of space saved and in the ability to get a complete bibliographic unit on one piece of film. However, the convenience of having all film in one or two formats at the same range of reductions must be weighed against the advantages of special-purpose formats, each of which may have advantages for the material concerned, but may also require special viewers and other devices for display and reproduction.

Most important to every library is the intellectual content of the film, which takes precedence over the format or reduction or any other technical feature, providing it is consonant with library viewing equipment. If formats become standardized to the extent that the information the librarian wants will be in a variety of formats, then it will be possible for him to choose the intellectual content in the format best suited to the needs of his library.

Storage in the Library

The maintenance of technical standards is of special importance for all archival microfilm, and the responsibility is a dual one. Proper manufacture is the responsibility of the supplier, but proper care thereafter is the responsibility of the owner. Ideal storage conditions are seldom present, but care of materials may make the difference between satisfaction and dissatisfaction in their use.

The revised ANSI Standard for "Practice for Storage of Processed Silver-Gelatin Microfilm" sponsored by the American Library Association, reads as follows:

> The stability of photographic records depends on the physical and chemical nature of the film, how it is processed, and the conditions under which the records are stored.
>
> The important storage elements affecting preservation of processed microfilm are the level of humidity and temperature of the air and cycling of these factors, as well as the hazards of fire, water, fungal growth, contact with certain chemicals in solid, liquid, or gaseous form, and physical damage.
>
> With the exception of high humidity, a condition outside the specified ranges for humidity and temperature does not necessarily mean an unsuitable storage condition. The extent to which humidity or temperature or variations of both can be

permitted to reach beyond recommended limits without producing adverse effects
will depend upon the duration of exposure, on biological conditions conducive to
fungal growth on the gelatin, and on film processing technique.

For housing the film, the committee recommends steel cabinets, where
a separate vault or room is not provided. Where conditions of high humidity are present, the cabinets would be separately air conditioned or be
placed in an air conditioned room. It is recommended that the relative
humidity not exceed 40 percent, and that the temperature not exceed
70° F. for archival storage standards. In Appendix A to the Standard, the
committee goes on to say:

> Humidity essentially above the limits specified in the Standard has a deleterious
> effect to a much greater extent than humidity below the optimum range. Prolonged
> exposure to conditions above 60 percent relative humidity will tend to damage or
> destroy the gelatin of the film, due to growth of fungus, and will eventually cause
> sticking of emulsion and buckling of the film base. Storage at low humidities not
> only avoids fungal growth but reduces the rate of chemical degradation.
>   An important aspect of temperature is its effect on relative humidity. Low
> temperature in storage will raise the humidity of a storage area which is not
> humidity controlled, causing conditions beyond the range of recommended humid-
> ities for proper storage of film in unsealed containers.

It is apparent that the committee has, quite rightfully, set up ideal conditions for storage, but University Microfilms has received few reports of
film deteriorating even when it is stored under unfavorable conditions.
In general and in summary, prolonged high humidity and high temperature
may promote the growth of fungus on film gelatins (the emulsion) but
generally speaking, storage conditions favorable to the storage of books
are safe for photographic films.

Project Design

In a well-designed microform project, the knowledgeable reader will have
an accurate reproduction of the original document and will know exactly
what document he has, from information given him by the editor of the
film project. At the same time, the general reader will not be given so
much information that he will become confused or annoyed by having
every picayune deviation from a rigid standard pointed out to him.

Notes in microforms are called "targets," and are clearly identified to
the reader as information pertaining to the document photographed, but
not an integral part of the document itself.

A target at the beginning of the reel, or deck of fiche-cards, lists important bibliographic information such as:

a. author,
b. title,
c. imprint,
d. micropublisher and date of publication,
e. owner of the material photographed,
f. other pertinent bibliographic information that aids identification of the exact work, or helps the reader in some further way.

If there are several items on one reel or set of cards, each item should have its individual title-target, and the reel or deck target then becomes a table of contents which helps the user find the items on the film and outlines the plan of the project.

In addition to the title target, a ruler should be placed on a blank page at the beginning of the book (as a fly leaf) at the time the document is being photographed, so that an accurate measure of the size of the original can be determined. The reduction ratio used may also be given, but the rule is a more accurate measure provided it is in an exposure with a book page rather than with a target.

Targets interspersed throughout the text as necessary alert the reader to departures from what would generally be considered a normal text. Targets of this type include:

a. BEST COPY. This target indicates that the photographer has faithfully reproduced an original document that was poor copy to begin with: a typewritten carbon copy, a yellowed newspaper, a foxed book page, etc.
b. PHOTOGRAPHED AS BOUND. This target indicates that the pages in the original were bound out of order, and the photographer has photographed them in the order in which he found them.
c. PAGES LACKING. This target indicates that pages were lacking in the original document and for some reason were not secured from a different file.
d. PAGES MISNUMBERED. This target indicates that pages were misnumbered, although the text may follow logically from one page to another, indicating that all pages are included.

It is the duty of the publisher to draw the attention of the reader to matters such as these so that the reader will know exactly what he has. Targets are the way publishers put "footnotes" in microforms to explain the text to readers.

In large projects, additional information about the extent of the project, the plan, and other information of value is given to the interested researcher in a printed guide to the film. This guide, which may also serve as a table of contents or index to the project, can be a very useful informational piece in itself.

FORMATS

by Homer I. Bernhardt

There are a wide variety of sizes, shapes, and configuragions within the physical formats of microforms.

MICROFILM: It is generally available in 8mm, 16mm, 35mm, 70mm, and 105mm sizes, and the usual length of a roll of film is 100 feet, although thinner film bases can provide longer lengths on the same size reel. Only 16mm and 35mm have gained any amount of common acceptance thus far. There is some work being done on 8mm films in the European countries.

Advantages:
1. Much material is supplied in this format by commercial producers.
2. A master copy can be produced economically.
3. Secondary distribution is economical.
4. The file is easy to maintain and lends itself to self-service.
5. Containers can be coded to facilitate retrieval from the file, and individual reels indexed to speed up searching within.
6. The film, itself, can be coded for very fast retrieval.
7. It can be viewed on a variety of economical readers.
8. Hard copy prints are commonly available on reader-printers now in use in many libraries.
9. It can be shelved with hard copy, i.e., on bound journal shelves with or in lieu of the hard copy.

Disadvantages:
1. It is difficult to update, i.e., insert revisions to documents already filmed.
2. Film to film copies of individual documents are not easily made.
3. The use of one roll can tie up hundreds of documents.

Reprinted from Homer I. Bernhardt, *An Overview of Microforms: a Report on the Role of Microforms in the University of Pittsburgh Libraries.* Pittsburgh: University of Pittsburgh, Graduate School of Library and Information Science, 1972, pp. 2-6, by permission of the author. Copyright © 1972 by Homer I. Bernhardt.

4. Special containers are needed for mailing.
5. Once removed from their boxes, the reels' contents are difficult to identify.
6. It presents problems in interfiling related documents, since sequential filming is not always possible due to publishing schedules and/or receipt of material.
7. It is not economical to distribute individual documents.
8. Field duplication (film to film) is not economical.

MICROFICHE: Sizes range from the 3X 5" to 8X 6" with each having a variety of their own row and column configurations. The Federal Government has accepted the COSATI (Committee on Scientific and Technical Information) standard which is approximately 4X 6" with 60 images on the initial fiche and 72 on trailers. The N.M.A. (National Microfilm Association) has adopted a similar sized fiche which uses a higher reduction ratio, and consequently it contains 98 images. Quite a bit of material is still being published on the 3X 5" size, while the Europeans generally use the 3-1/2X 4-3/4" fiche.

Advantages:
1. Fiche offer a unit record approach, use of one fiche does not tie up other documents.
2. Fiche to fiche copies are quite economical and can be produced in the field on inexpensive equipment.
3. They are the only media (outside of special systems) which lend themselves to totally automated retrieval systems.
4. Documents are easily updated and revised.
5. Fiche are easy and economical to mail, and special packing is not needed.
6. Through the use of microfiche jackets, various sizes of film can be interchanged. This is important when text may accompany large drawings.
7. Secondary distribution is economical.
8. Eye-readable headings identify individual fiche.
9. When coordinately indexed, specific images can be located with speed.
10. Much free (depository) and inexpensive material from federal agencies (AEC, DDC, ERIC, NASA, and the National Technical Information Service) come in this format.
11. Fiche can be viewed on a variety of economical readers.
12. Hard copy prints are commonly available on reader-printers now in use in many libraries.

Disadvantages:
1. The master is costly to produce.

2. Unless automated, the microfiche file is difficult to maintain: however, automated files are limited in storage capacity.
3. The larger the file, the more difficult it is to locate specific fiche.
4. The file must be serviced by library personnel to insure a maximum amount of file integrity.
5. Misfiled fiche are difficult to recover.
6. Fiche are very susceptible to theft and souveniring.
7. The configurations of the images on present day fiche (left to right, left to right, etc.) cause needless shuffling back and forth to obtain the correct image.
8. There is a loss of detail (resolution) when making fiche to fiche copies of microfiche in jackets.
9. It is difficult to keep the initial fiche and trailer fiche together unless envelopes are used.

MICRO-OPAQUES: There are several sizes which are identified by their trade names: (1) The Microcard in 3X 5" and 4X 6" sizes; (2) The Microprint which measures 6X 9"; (3) The Microlex which is 6-1/2X 8-1/2", and (4) The Mini-Print at 6X 9".

Advantages:
1. Opaques offer a unit record approach, use of one opaque does not tie up other documents.
2. Unless automated, the micro-opaque file is difficult to maintain.
3. The larger the file, the more difficult it is to locate specific opaques.
4. The file must be serviced by library personnel to insure a maximum amount of file integrity.
5. Misfiled opaques are difficult to recover.
6. They are susceptible to theft and souveniring.
7. The configurations of the images on present day opaques (left to right, left to right, etc.) causes needless shuffling back and forth.
8. There is a very limited selection of readers (only one for 6X 9" micro-opaques).
9. Opaque to opaque copies cannot be made.
10. Opaques are limited to the lower reduction ratios.
11. There is only one hard copy printer for printing copies of micro-opaques.

APERTURE CARDS: This format offers standardization, since it evolves around the standard tab card (3-1/4X 7-3/8") which is used by many companies for data processing. This card has a slot in it in which a micro image is placed. It is usually one frame of a 35mm microfilm, although larger sizes (70mm) have been used in a few instances. The tab card, itself, is usually coded to facilitate retrieval and/or lend itself to topical searches.

Advantages:
1. Aperture cards offer a unit record approach, use of one aperture card does not tie up other documents.
2. Secondary distribution is economical.
3. Eye-readable headings (to some extent) identify individual cards.
4. Documents are easily updated and revised.
5. Aperture cards are easy and economical to mail, and special packing is not needed.
6. The file is machine searchable, although as the size of the file increases, so does the search time.
7. Film to film copies are economical.
8. The image size is ideal for large materials such as engineering drawings.
9. A variety of economical aperture-card readers are available.
10. Hard copy prints are commonly available on reader-printers now in use in many libraries.

Disadvantages:
1. The coded master is somewhat costly to produce.
2. They have low storage density (maximum of 8 images per unit).
3. Their basic use is for engineering drawings, and not for the wide variety of material in libraries.
4. The file is inoperative when the equipment is not functioning.
5. Unless automated, the file is difficult to maintain.
6. The equipment to run the automated file is costly.

OTHER FORMATS: There are several other formats that microforms come in such as film chips, film strips, etc., but which evolve around systems that have been specifically built to handle that form and that form alone. Their lack of flexibility in the utilization of any other type of microform is a severe limitation. Although their data bases can be totally automated, they are more suited to the needs of smaller collections, and as a consequence it is unnecessary to discuss them here.

THE MICROFORM
REVOLUTION

by Rolland E. Stevens

Librarians have tried replacing some of their books and journal files with microfilm copies or other microforms in order to save valuable space in the bookstacks, instead of or in addition to extension of the stack area, decentralization, compact shelving, separate storage warehouse, or any of the other solutions to the storage problem. Although the distinct forms will not often be designated, "microform" is used here to mean the four forms most common in the United States: 35mm. roll microfilm, microfiche (now standardized in the United States and Great Britain at 4 by 6 inches) and the two micro-opaque forms—3 by 5 inch Microcard, and 6 by 9 inch Microprint.

Library materials in microform are acquired for a variety of reasons: 1) to obtain rare books, journals, manuscripts, archives, and other needed information sources that are either unobtainable or prohibitively expensive in their original form; 2) to replace items that are printed or written on badly deteriorating paper; 3) to furnish a working copy of rare and fragile books; 4) to replace large, bulky volumes such as newspaper volumes with a compact form that is easier to handle and to use; or 5) to replace printed sources with copies in microform in order to save stack space. Each of these is a separate and distinct purpose, yet the librarian is seldom motivated by one of them alone. Usually the acquiring of microform materials is intended to answer several of these purposes, even in the case of a single title. Microfilm copies of newspapers already owned by the library are usually substituted for ease of use, for saving of shelf space, and to replace originals on deteriorating paper. Working copies of fragile books are acquired both to prolong the life of the original work as long as possible, and as a safeguard against the day of its final crumbling. British sessional papers may be purchased in microform both because of their relative scarcity and, therefore the expense of getting a complete file in its original form, and in order to save shelf space. Insofar as possible,

Reprinted from *Library Trends*, 19: 379-95 (January 1971) by permission of the author and publisher. Copyright © 1971 by the University of Illinois.

this paper will concern itself only with the space-saving aspect of acquiring materials in microform.* While it is recognized that motives other than this are usually present, no examples will be used in which the motive of space saving is not the primary reason for microform acquisition.

Saving of shelving space has not always been one of the motives for reducing books to microform. Microphotography was invented by J.B. Dancer in England in 1839, when he produced the first microphotographs at a reduction of 160:1.[1] The invention suffered the fate of most new ideas for which a social need is not yet well developed, however, in not being taken up either by librarians or individual collectors for many years. Interestingly, microfilmed dispatches were flown into news-hungry Paris by carrier pigeon during the war of 1870.[2] Other than this, or probably including this use, microfilming was regarded more as a stunt or a curiosity than as a method for promoting scholarly or other serious activities. Not until the 1920s was microfilm taken up for serious purposes. By this time a pressing need, essential for the development of an invention, was arising, and cameras and other equipment adapted to microfilming had been produced. The Leica camera, marketed in 1924, is mentioned as especially valuable for this purpose.[3] The great impetus for the development of microfilming at this time and especially in the 1930s was from the scholar, who now found that he could microfilm manuscripts, archives, and other needed records in much less time, with less effort, and most important, with greater accuracy than by his previous method of copying extracts by hand. This was especially important to him because the libraries in which these documents were kept frequently permitted only severely limited hours of use. When in the same decade the largest research libraries began to purchase microfilms and to produce their own, they used the method for acquiring information sources that could not be purchased in original form or for preparing microfilm copies for other libraries from this kind of research material held in their own stock.[4]

Not until the following decade was there a concern for microforms of library materials as a means of reducing the storage space needed. In 1944, Fremont Rider published *The Scholar and the Future of the Research Library, a Problem and Its Solution.*[5] In it he called attention, in his characteristically dramatic style, to the exponential rate of growth of the nation's research libraries and extrapolated from statistics of growth over the past century to indicate the probable size of the largest ones by the end of another century. Yale, for example, in the year 2040 would have about 200 million volumes occupying more than six thousand miles of shelves; its catalog would cover eight acres of floor space, and cataloging of the twelve million volumes acquired annually would require a cataloging staff of more than six thousand persons.[6] Rider then went on to propose the following solution to this problem of growth:

*EDITOR'S NOTE: This article appeared in an issue of *Library Trends* devoted to storage.

the entire book collection of the research library would be microfilmed and photographically printed on micro-cards.* These were 3 by 5 inch opaque cards of which the front was a standard catalog card plus an abstract of the work; the reverse side contained the complete text of the book at a reduction of about 20X to a maximum of 250 pages. No book-stack would be needed in this library of the future since the entire contents of the collection, excepting perhaps a few of the more frequently used reference books, would be on the back of the micro-cards, filed in the card catalog in the usual dictionary arrangement. When a reader wished to use a book, he would remove the micro-card from the catalog, leaving in its place a call slip, and charge out the micro-card for home use. Or he could make his own copy of the micro-card in a coin-operated camera.[7] † The saving in space, as Rider pointed out, would be 100 percent, since the bookstack would be completely eliminated.[8]

Rider's book had little practical effect on libraries. No library converted any significant part of its collection to micro-cards. Microcards, containing the text of rare, out-of-print, and little-used research materials, such as accounts of early travel in the United States, theses, and other unpublished papers began to be produced commercially. Such research materials had been issued on a subscription basis in the form of microfilm since at least 1937, when University Microfilms began to distribute its Short Title Catalogue series, and since 1950 on Microprint when the Readex Microprint Corporation began publishing its famous series of scarce research sources. But purchases of these series by libraries have been for the purpose of adding otherwise unobtainable titles to the collection, not for saving space. Again in 1951, Rider urged librarians to consider the great saving in space and therefore in cost, of substituting micro-cards for books in their original form. In this article he no longer considers the earlier idea of converting the entire book collection to micro-card form and filing these in the card catalog. Only the infrequently used books will be converted. Presumably these micro-cards would be housed in cabinets in or near the conventional bookstacks, would be represented by conventional catalog cards in the catalog, and would be charged out for home use in the same manner as regular books, rather than being duplicated by camera.[9] As far as using this method primarily for space saving, librarians paid no more attention to Rider's reminder than they did to his initial proposal seven years earlier.

In the same issue of *American Documentation* as the article just referred

---

* Rider was the first to use this term, hyphenated and uncapitalized, as used here. The currently used Microcard is a trade name.

† The caption under the frontispiece illustration of a micro-card reads in part, "This photogravure reproduction of the original micro-text is merely an attempt to show the general appearance of the card; for, being a reproduction of a reproduction, it is *not* readable." He does not explain, however, why the reproduction of a micro-card made in a coin-operated camera would be more readable.

to, there appeared an article by Eugene Power, president of University Microfilms, pointing out the economy of substituting microfilm copies of older files of periodicals for bound volumes.[10] He sought to demonstrate mathematically that the cumulated difference in annual storage cost between bound volumes and microfilm copies in several years would be about equal to the difference in cost of binding and microfilming and that thereafter the saving in storage cost for the microfilm copy would be actual saving to the library. The details of these mathematics need not occupy us here, since they are taken up at more length below. The point is that this, together with Rider's publication of the micro-card idea, is the earliest consideration of microforms purely from the viewpoint of saving storage cost. Since that time there have been several other papers on the subject, but this aspect of microform acquisitions has never ranked foremost with the average librarian, certainly not with those in large public and research libraries.

The purchase of microforms for the main purpose of conserving storage space has been favored more by librarians in the largest and best high school libraries and in small junior college and college libraries than by those in public, university, or research libraries. Even among the former group, the practice is by no means universal or even common. The writer is informed by University Microfilms that the largest proportion of its current periodicals service is to college libraries, followed by university libraries, with high school libraries and public libraries using the service less.[11] A recent trend is observed in technical libraries, where bound volumes of journals are being replaced, in order to conserve space, with 16mm. film in cartridges for use in motor-driven reader-printers. Users find the ease of loading cartridges, the speed of searching the film, and the convenience of getting an immediate, take-home copy of any desired page preferable to using the original bound journal.[12]

The kind of microform material that is most often used for conserving shelving space is back files of periodicals and newspapers on microfilm. Libraries which do not retain back files of periodicals and newspapers, such as the average school library or small public library, would, of course, have no need for such files on microfilm. On the other hand, libraries in which back files are not only kept but also frequently used do not want the inconvenience of microfilm copies, even though they may need to conserve shelving space. The latter group would include large public and college libraries and all university and research libraries.

In order to partially solve the storage problem by substituting microform copies for the original form of infrequently used materials, the librarian has several alternative methods. He may make his own microforms of materials in his own collection. He may send his volumes or papers to a commercial firm to have microforms made. He may share the cost with a certain number of other librarians, each of whom will then receive a microform copy. Or he may purchase microform copies of certain journals, theses, or other works, which are offered for sale by a commercial producer on a mass basis. In general, the larger the number of microform copies made of the same material, the lower the cost of each copy, since the most expensive part of the process is making the initial microform. For microfilm the initial negative costs at least five times as much as each copy made from that negative. If one hundred microfilm copies were made of a book, each would cost only a little more than one-fifth the cost of a single copy. The best buy in microfilm or some other microform, then, is a title that many other libraries will also be interested in acquiring in that form. Thus, the kind of library material for which microform is most often acquired in place of the original, which the library either has already or could easily get is the general journal or newspaper, such as *Atlantic Monthly, Christian Century, Current History, Harper's, Life,* or the *New York Times.* These and similar titles, both back runs and recent volumes, are not infrequently purchased in microfilm copies by strong high school libraries and some junior college and college libraries for three reasons: 1) a substantial saving in storage space can be realized by the substitution for the original volumes, 2) microfilm of these runs is relatively inexpensive, and 3) in these libraries, back files of such journals are needed but are not used with great frequency. With respect to the second reason, a check of several general periodical titles shows that the cost of microfilm is about the same as the cost of binding for current volumes and even lower than binding costs for earlier volumes. In elaboration of the third reason, practices vary among libraries as to the length of back run to be acquired, if any. High school libraries may not have a need for purchasing any back runs, although they would keep the microfilms they acquired on standing order; college libraries usually need good files of most journals.

Whether or not the library purchases back files of these commonly held journals on microfilm, it may want to subscribe to a microfilm of the current year, to be sent soon after the volume is complete. The library retains the unbound issues as long as they are heavily used and discards them when use has decreased sufficiently. The cost of the microfilm is usually no greater than binding the volume would be. The publishers of such general journals expect libraries to subscribe to the journal and not to get the microfilm copy in place of the journal itself; the microfilming firm, therefore, requires evidence that the library does subscribe to the journal.[13]

When a librarian determines to save storage space by substituting microforms for the original bound volumes, the kind of library materials which are considered first are these standard, general periodicals and newspapers. The writer is not aware of any other category of library materials which is widely converted to microform primarily to save storage space. The purchase of microfilm or microfiche technical reports and scientific or technical journals in place of original format is sometimes done in the special library in order to save space.[14] A detailed examination of several studies of the cost of microfilming printed matter, outlined below, will make clear why the general periodical or newspaper is the favored material for this purpose. Up to the present time, furthermore, the substitution of microform is the least used method of solving the storage problem. What factors must the librarian consider in reaching a decision about microfilming or going to one of the other microforms for this purpose? David Peele listed the following factors to be considered in deciding whether to bind and keep periodicals in their original form or to substitute microfilm copies: 1) The likelihood of theft or mutilation of the material if left in its original form. 2) The nature of the material. Is it an abstract index or other reference work which would be unsatisfactory on microfilm? Does it have many color illustrations which would make black and white microfilm unsatisfactory? Does it have ads and text on the same page, which would make binding expensive, since ads cannot be removed? 3) The user. Is he a high school student to whom microfilm may be an adventure, or is he a college professor, to whom it is a pain in the neck? 4) Cost.[15]

Admittedly, the decision to bind or microfilm is not quite the same as the one we are considering in this paper; the likelihood of theft and mutilation does not enter into the latter decision as it does in the former. But the other three factors can be examined further here. The cost factor is the one most often considered by librarians in the past. Rider's and Power's articles on this aspect have already been mentioned. Rider's exaggerated claim for the economy of substituting micro-cards for the original volumes was pure gobbledegook. He maintained that the library would realize a substantial saving of money by discarding bound volumes of little-used sets and purchasing micro-cards in their place. In order to prove his case he contrasts the cost of micro-carding with the capital investment needed, from which the annual interest would pay the storage cost of the bound volumes. This seems fair enough. But what he neglects to draw attention to, although he does not actually hide the detail, is that his estimates of the cost of preparing micro-cards are based on the agreement of about one hundred libraries to purchase micro-cards of the same titles and to share the cost. Nowhere in his estimates does Rider include the cost of cabinets for storing the micro-cards, of machines for reading the micro-cards, of maintaining and replacing these reading machines, or of the additional space required for the reading machines.

The analysis by Power is much more realistic than that by Rider. It shows that the cost of microfilming an average city newspaper is less than half the cost of binding and shelving the bound volumes for fifty years. If two libraries share the cost of microfilming, each receiving a print, the cost to each library would be about the same as binding and shelving the bound volumes for ten years. Beyond ten years, the cost of storing the bound volumes would be substantially higher than storing the microfilm copy. Power's formula does not include the costs of reading machines. But he acknowledges that these costs should be included in the librarian's estimates and even suggests the number of machines required and the probable replacement costs, although his prediction that reading machines will have a useful life of twenty years now seems optimistic.

Several thorough studies of the economy of microfilming in place of conventional storage have been made since the one by Power. Alan B. Pritsker and J. William Sadler reported a study they had made in the Columbia University School of Engineering storage library.[16] They stated that many undesirable economies would have to be made in order to bring the cost of microfilming down to a comparable level with that of storing the original books. These economies included cutting the bindings off the books to be filmed, thus removing the possibility of reducing the cost by selling the volumes after they were filmed; the use of the faster rotary camera, although it results in poorer quality filming than that possible with a planetary camera; elimination of final editing of the film for pages missing or mutilated in the original or illegible in the film; and, worst, the use of the master negative as the working copy. "If a positive copy of the film is required," they report, "the cost of microfilm storage is prohibitive."[17] But by making these economies, they were able to get a microfilming cost of the order of one-tenth and even one-twentieth the amount charged by commercial firms. Pritsker and Sadler, however, considered only the case where a single library bears the cost of microfilming. Six years earlier, Dallas Irvine had reported that a study made by the U.S. National Archives showed "that micro-reproduction is not a generally applicable means of reducing the costs of storing records. For records that are not to be preserved beyond thirty years and for records that cannot be microfilmed at a very low cost, it is simply cheaper to provide suitable warehousing."[18]

More recently, Verner W. Clapp and Robert T. Jordan sought to re-examine the comparative cost question, by considering the sharing of the cost of microfilming among several libraries.[19] They were able to reach somewhat more favorable conclusions than Pritsker and Sadler. By assuming twenty libraries to share the cost, each of whom would receive a positive print of the film, they could match the cost of conventional shelving without making any of the sacrifices required in the earlier study except that of shearing the backs off the volumes before filming. With fewer than twenty libraries, the cost of microfilming in their plan would be higher than the cost of storing the bound volumes; with more than twenty libraries participating, it would be cheaper to microfilm and discard the original volumes. Their proposal would allow both pre-inspection of the books and post-inspection of the film, use of the higher quality planetary camera, color filming where required, and retention of the negative as a master copy, from which further positives could be made on demand. If the participating libraries would be satisfied with the product of the faster rotary camera and/or with all black and white film, further economies could be realized. This study was limited to storage and microfilming costs; it did not consider binding costs, on one hand, nor reading-machine costs, on the other. Nor did it take into account building maintenance, servicing, or altering catalog records, each of which would be different for the two methods of storage.

It now becomes clear, since the cost of microfilming can be comparable to the cost of conventional storage only when a number of libraries share in the cost of filming, why librarians wishing to save space acquire microfilm of general periodicals and newspapers rather than infrequently used monographs, archives, manuscripts, local reports, and other research materials that are not commonly held. The latter represents the type of library material which Rider supposed would be appropriate for microcarding. But the former are the serials that are widely needed; therefore, the kind of material for which there would be more demand. Only microfilm has been considered in these studies of cost, except by Rider. The reason for this seeming neglect of the other microforms is that the micro-opaque forms, of which Microcards and Microprint are considered in this paper, cannot be produced economically in small editions. From the cost standpoint, Microcards should be made in editions of no less than twenty-five, although in large editions they can become cheaper than microfilm.[20] Microprint requires a still larger edition and is even cheaper in large editions than Microcard. Even in these larger (and cheaper) editions, however, there are deterrents to the use of micro-opaques. The chief problems are the number of pages of original text that will fit on a single card and the optical problems of the opaque card. A double-sided Microcard or a single-sided Microprint card will hold about 100 to 120 pages of the original text; a 100-foot microfilm roll will hold about 1,200 to 1,500 pages. The Microcard has the advantage for pamphlets and small booklets, but to reproduce a typical 400-page volume of a periodical on four separate cards has come drawback. More serious are the optical problems of the micro-opaques, for which reading machines have never been as satisfactory as those developed for transparencies and for which no feasible reader-printer has ever been developed. The fourth form mentioned at the beginning of this paper, microfiche, also suffers from the first disadvantage, but not from the second. Furthermore, it has so many advantages, mainly its ease of handling, that it is soon likely to supplant the microfilm roll as the most widely used microform in this country. That it has not done so already is most likely the result of our brief experience with it and the caution with which we cling to old and familiar habits. It is no credit to librarians or the microform industry that we were so slow in the United States in adopting this form, which Europe has long used successfully, and which has long been acknowledged to be superior to roll film.[21]

In addition to these considerations of cost, however, are the far more important, and too often neglected factors of the material involved and of the user's convenience. Reference books are rarely, and never should, be issued in microform. Even the reference features of non-reference books, such as the index, are more and more frequently issued in original size, when the text is reduced to microform. The *New York Times* on microfilm with its *Index* in bound form is a familiar example of this. A more recent example is the "dual media" proposal by the United States Historical Documents, Inc., to issue the various series of the proceedings of the U.S. Congress on microfilm with index volumes in bound form.[22] Other kinds of library material which are least suitable in microform, if original form is available, are texts which must be compared with other similar texts for the purpose of collating or editing, early printed books which are to be studied in their original state for the placement of watermark or the positioning of separate pages, books of art reproductions or other books in which the quality of illustrations are important, reserve books, and other books which are used frequently. Often these books are not available in original format and must be acquired in microform or not at all. Such use of microform, however, is not the subject of this paper.

Even more important than the nature and probable use of the material is the convenience of the user. The reluctance of most readers to use microfilm or other microform is too well known to argue.[23] Those who seldom need to use it waste time learning how to use the reading machine; those who must frequently use it complain about eyestrain. Criticisms from both groups of users are mostly well founded. Physical discomfort of using microfilm for long hours comes not only from eyestrain but also from sitting and holding the head in the same position for an extended period in order to get the best possible view of the projected image. Both sources of difficulty in the use of microfilm can be corrected on the basis of our present knowledge. The difficulty of inserting the roll microfilm in the reading machine is overcome by the use of cartridge film and microfiche. The difficulty of readily finding the desired frame can be solved by coding the frames and using an automatic reader, such as Eastman's Lodestar. Eight years ago, L. E. Walkup and his colleagues at Battelle Memorial Institute experimented with different levels of magnification, definition, page brightness, ambient light, and other factors that affect reading ease.[24] They were able to identify the features that should be incorporated into a microfilm reader in order to promote optimum ease of use, and they constructed a breadboard model of this ideal reader. The model was made to simulate ordinary reading of a book by projecting the image onto a gray opaque reading surface held in the lap; the projector was light and small enough to enable the user to change his position and even to move about the room while reading. Testing of the model showed that a user could read microfilm for long periods of time with no more discomfort than he would experience in reading a book.[25] It is interesting to note that the investigators worked only with transparencies because of "the projection difficulties encountered with opaque microimages."[26] Unfortunately, the study, which was implemented by a grant of the Council on Library Resources, Inc.,[27] was never followed up and the indicated microfilm reader was never commercially developed.

It was noted above that if storage space is conserved by substituting microfilm copies for the original volumes, they are usually general periodicals and newspapers rather than little-used monographs or other kinds of library material, even though these would seem to be good candidates for microfilming. It was further noted that this general practice results from the duplication of these periodicals and newspapers in most libraries and, therefore, from the potential market for microfilm copies of them. But we know that there is also high duplication of monographs among libraries of the same type: high school, public, college, and university libraries. A study of duplication among collections of members of the Association of Research Libraries made in 1942 by the late LeRoy C. Merritt showed a duplication among these libraries averaging between 15 percent and 25 percent. This study included monographs and serials alike and indicated a core of titles held commonly by most of the libraries.[28] A more recent study of a highly homogeneous group of smaller university libraries showed an average duplication of monographs of 40 percent to 45 percent.[29] There seems to be no reason, then, why agreement might not be reached among a hundred or more libraries of like type on the infrequently used monographs they would buy on microfilm or microfiche to replace the original bound volumes. In the light of past experience, however, the move will come probably not from librarians but from microform publishers, who will offer a compact package library on film or fiche.

At this time no counterpart of the current periodicals system has been offered for monographs; that is, one in which microform copies are purchased by the library to replace the bound volumes, which can then be discarded in order to save space. A number of "package libraries" have been offered on microform, since University Microfilms began to distribute the Short Title Catalogue microfilm in 1937, as mentioned earlier. Typical projects have been "Russian Historical Sources," "Three Centuries of English and American Plays," and "British Sessional Papers" on Microprint, titles from Clark's *Travels in the Old South*, on Microcard, and "American Periodical Series," on microfilm. When a library subscribed to these, it was almost always to acquire texts of sources not generally available in original form; saving space by discarding bound volumes and substituting microform copies was not a motive in this acquisition. The market for these source collections was usually the research library. In the present year, several package libraries on microform are being offered to a different market—the new junior college library or college library which must quickly build a collection to support undergraduate study. What is needed in these libraries is a collection of 50,000 to 100,000 or more volumes on various subjects in the sciences, social sciences, and humanities. Only a small part of these needed books will be in print and readily available. Current titles must be backed up with a large collection of books considered standard sources in various fields. Such collections, selected by subject specialists or from standard bibliographies, are now being offered in microform. The collections range from several hundred to several thousand volumes on a related subject field such as American civilization, British history, Black studies, Shakespeare, etc. Two such projects are now being offered in a new microform that has not yet been tested outside the industrial field. The original, patented name of this microform is PCMI, for photochromic micro-image, a process developed by the National Cash Register Company (NCR) about 1960. Essentially, the technique is to microfilm a text at the conventional ratio of 15X to 20X, then to reduce it further onto a grain-free coating that allows high resolution at linear reductions of 200:1, or area reductions of 40,000:1. The photochromic coating has certain properties different from those of conventional microfilm, which are not important for this paper but which make feasible the storage of a 300-page book on a single square inch of film.[30] The National Cash Register Company is producing a series of PCMI Library Collections, with initial delivery date announced for fall, 1970. Each collection will consist of one hundred 4 by 6 inch transparencies containing the text of seven to ten books on closely related subjects. The National Cash Register Company has already developed a reading machine for PCMI fiches made at 150:1 reduction.[31] It is in use at many Ford Motor Company service departments for consulting the Ford parts catalogs, which have been issued on PCMI fiches. The image projected on this reader is sharp and clear although refocusing is frequently necessitated in moving from page to page. Loading the fiche and moving to the desired frame are easy and fast. The vertical position of the screen may lead to discomfort in long hours of reading. This reader is also capable of producing hard copy, although the writer has not seen an example. Library Resources, Inc., a division of Encyclopaedia Britannica Company, has also announced a series of Microbook Libraries on a similar micro-format, which will be a 3 by 5 inch fiche containing a maximum 1,000 pages, but no more than a single title. These will be made at a variable reduction up to 90X, depending on the size of the original book. Library Resources does not yet have a reading machine in production, but promises a table reader and a smaller lap reader early in 1971, when the first shipments of Microbooks will be made to libraries. A reader-printer is promised later. The first Microbook will be the Library of American Civilization, consisting of over 12,000 fiches. It will contain the texts of books on politics and government, foreign affairs, military government, science and technology, and other aspects of American life. Later libraries offered by Library Resources will include the Library of European Civilization, the Library of English Literature, the Library of the History of Art, and the Library of the History of Philosophy.[32] Most titles in the series of both firms will be out of print and very difficult to find in original form, although the National Cash Register Company says that about 10 percent of its PCMI titles are still under copyright.[33]

New projects of this type are being announced more and more frequently, some, like the Newberry project, being directed primarily at the large research library; others, like the two described above and NCR's *Books for College Libraries*, appealing more to the new junior college or college library. While it cannot be claimed that any of these are acquired primarily in order to conserve space, they have been described because they approach the "all microform" library, which has for some years been a predicted form of the future library. Probably the ancestor of this idea was a classical paper by Vannevar Bush, in which he proposed the ideal scholar's library, a "memex," as he called it.[34] This would be the size of a desk; in it would be reels of microfilm on which were reproduced all of the papers and books of even potential interest to the scholar. Each document would be coded for its subjects. The user would merely tap out subjects of his immediate interest on a keyboard on top of the desk; this would cause each pertinent document to be displayed on a screen, and hard copy could be produced of any document at will. Furthermore, memex could record an associative trail among the documents, as the scholar threaded his way from one subject to a related one, so that any of these search trails could be called up in the future. Ralph Shaw, then librarian of the United States Department of Agriculture, developed a working model based on this idea; he called it the Rapid Selector,[35] although it seems never to have been produced commercially.

These, however, were specialized collections and led to a number of information retrieval systems, based on microfilm storage, in industry and in government.[36] Of the all-microform library in a more general sense, Verner Clapp, then President of the Council on Library Resources, Inc., explored the possibilities and obstacles in his 1963 Windsor lecture at the University of Illinois.[37] By all-microform library in this general sense should be understood one in which most of the collection has been miniaturized, but reference books and other materials that need to be used frequently and quickly would remain in easier to use form. Several years before that, L. B. Heilprin, then a senior staff member of the Council on Library Resources, Inc., had gone considerably more deeply into the concept of a D-library, that is, a duplicating-library. This kind of library never circulates its books but duplicates them on demand. The library copy of the book remains in the store, where it is immediately available for the next request. The stored master copy may be a microfilm negative or another form which can be duplicated quickly and cheaply. The duplicate copy may be kept by the user and need not be returned to the library. This concept has been a familiar one, of course, for about a decade in construction firms, architectural firms, map services, and similar very specialized uses, where the drawing, blueprint, or map is copied for the user and

and refiled for other requests. In the D-library there is no need for loan records, overdue notices, or fines. No books are mutilated, lost, at the bindery, or charged out. Heilprin faced but did not solve, the problem of copyright.[38] If microfilm negatives are used as master copies, it is because they are easy to handle and make inexpensive, high quality copies. It must be admitted again that this proposed all-microform library is not strictly within the scope of this paper, since saving space is not its principal purpose. Compactness, however, is valued for reasons other than saving space. Most readers would prefer to use a microfilm of a 1915 newspaper than the heavy, dirty, crumbling bound volume. Also, in the all-microform library, manipulating, retrieving, copying, replacing, and inventorying are much easier with microfilm copies than with originals.

Do we have in Heilprin's D-library a model for the future library? Peter Scott, in a flight of fancy but one based on present technical capability, has given a vision of the information center in a university library of the near future. It is Vannevar Bush's memex multiplied many times to accommodate a number of users simultaneously. This is a search room, where the reader can retrieve and display by computer all documents pertinent to his needs, following associative trail patterns worked out over the years by some of the best thinkers of our time. In the adjacent reading room, to which the user had retired with the titles of the documents he needed, were the newest and best reading machines. These had screens adjustable for magnification, background color, and orientation of position, all of which help to eliminate reading fatigue. Loading of film in the machines was completely automatic. Even in this library, the user observes, about half the collection was still in book form, but with a rapidly increasing ratio of film to paper.[39]

The kind of library envisioned by Scott is no more science fiction than the atom bomb or moon travel was when the writer used to read about such fantasies some forty years ago in *Amazing Stories*. We can perform now all of the operations and make all of the equipment required in Scott's dream library. There are, in fact, libraries making use of coded microfilm on rolls or micro-chips in specialized information retrieval systems.[40] Further development both of coding systems and of equipment to extend these techniques to the general library may require another twenty-five years, or about the length of time it took to adopt microfiche in this country following its widespread, successful use in Europe. But there is no real obstacle to this development, and there are apparently many advantages that are either not possible or very difficult with the book in its traditional form. Space saving will not be the principal motive in conversion to an all-microform library, but the value and uses of such a compact library will be evident.[41]

References

1. Luther, Frederic. *Microfilm: A History 1839-1900.* Annapolis, Md., National Microfilm Associaiton, 1959, p. 16.

2. *Ibid.,* pp. 70-82.

3. Günther, Alfred. "Microphotography in the Library," *Unesco Bulletin for Libraries,* 16:1, Jan.-Feb. 1962; and Hawkins, Reginald. *Production of Microforms* (The State of the Library Art. Vol. 5, pt. 1). New Brunswick, N.J., Graduate School of Library Service, Rutgers, The State University, 1960, pp. 6-7.

4. Hawkins, *op. cit.,* p. 8; and Johnson, Amandus. "Early Experiences in Microfilming." *In* National Microfilm Association. *Proceedings.* Vol. 8. Annapolis, Md., 1959, pp. 70-75.

5. Rider, Fremont. *The Scholar and the Future of the Research Library, a Problem and Its Solution.* New York, Hadham Press, 1944.

6. *Ibid.,* p. 12.

7. *Ibid.,* pp. 168-70.

8. *Ibid.,* pp. 101-02.

9. Rider, Fremont. "Microcards vs. the Cost of Book Storage," *American Documentation,* 2:39-44, Jan. 1951.

10. Power, Eugene. "Microfilm as a Substitute for Binding," *American Documentation,* 2:33-39, Jan. 1951.

11. Farr, Rick. Letter dated June 8, 1970.

12. Starker, Lee N. "User Experiences with Primary Journals on 16-mm Microfilm," *Journal of Chemical Documentation,* 10:6, Feb. 1970.

13. University Microfilms, Ann Arbor, Mich. *Serials on Microfilm, 1970.* Ann Arbor, Mich., University Microfilms, 1970, p. v.

14. Lyon, Cathryn C. "Some Current Uses of Microform for Scientific and Technical Research Information," *NMA Journal,* 2:129-31, Summer 1969.

15. Peele, David. "Bind or Film: Factors in the Decision," *Library Resources & Technical Services,* 8:168-71, Spring 1964.

16. Pritsker, Alan B., and Sadler, J. William. "An Evaluation of Microfilm as a Method of Book Storage," *College & Research Libraries,* 18:290-96, July 1957.

17. *Ibid.,* p. 296.

18. Irvine, Dallas. "Storage Problems and Micro-Reproduction," *American Documentation,* 2:86, Spring 1951.

19. Clapp, Verner W., and Jordan, Robert T. "Re-evaluation of Microfilm as a Method of] Book Storage." *College & Research Libraries,* 24:5-15, Jan. 1963.

20. Günther, *op. cit.,* p. 9; and Davison, G. H. "Microcards and Microfiches, History and Possibilities," *Library Association Record,* 63:69-78, March 1961.

21. Hawkins, *op. cit.,* pp. 56-60.

22. Advertisement in *Library Journal,* 95:1419-22, April 15, 1970.

23. Walkup, L. E., *et al.* "The Design of Improved Microimage Readers for Promoting the Utilization of Microimages." *In* National Microfilm Association. *Proceedings.* Vol. 11. Annapolis, Md., 1962, p. 285.

24. *Ibid.,* pp. 283-310.

25. *Ibid.,* p. 299.

26. *Ibid.,* p. 287.

27. Council on Library Resources. *Report.* 6th. Washington, D.C., 1962, p. 24.

28. Merritt, LeRoy C. "Resources of American Libraries: A Quantitative Picture." *In* Robert B. Downs, ed., *Union Catalogs in the United States.* Chicago, ALA, 1942, pp. 74-77.

29. Nugent, William R. "Statistics of Collection Overlap at the Libraries of the Six New England State Universities," *Library Resources & Technical Services,* 12:31-36, Winter 1968.

30. Tauber, A. S., and Myers, W. C. "Photochromic Micro-Images: A Key to Practical Micro-document Storage and Dissemination." *In* National Microfilm Association. *Proceedings.* Vol. 11, Annapolis, Md., 1962, pp. 257-69.

31. "NCR's Answer to the Problems of Printing and Distributing Vast Amounts of Information: PCMI Ultrafiche," Manufacturer's brochure, [1970] ; Manufacturer's advertisement in *Library Journal,* 95:2062-63, June 1, 1970, and elsewhere; "In One Standard-Size File Drawer Your Library can Hold . . .," Manufacturer's brochure, [n.d.] ; and other advertising matter.

32. "The Microbook Library Series," Manufacturer's brochure, [n.d.] ; and Ruml, Treadwell. Letter dated April 20, 1970.
33. Goldman, C. C. Letter dated May 18, 1970.
34. Bush, Vannevar. "As We May Think," *Atlantic Monthly*, 176:106-07, July 1945.
35. Shaw, Ralph. "The Rapid Selector," *Journal of Documentation*, 5:164-71, Dec. 1949.
36. Bagg, Thomas C., and Stevens, Mary E. *Information Selection Systems Retrieving Replica Copies: A State-of-the-Art Report* (National Bureau of Standards. Technical Note 157). Washington, D.C., U.S. Dept. of Commerce, National Bureau of Standards, 1961.
37. Clapp, Verner W. *The Future of the Research Library* (Phineas L. Windsor Lectures in Librarianship, No. 8). Urbana, University of Illinois Press, 1964, pp. 18-30.
38. Heilprin, L. B. "The Economics of 'On-Demand' Library Copying." *In* National Microfilm Association. *Proceedings*. Vol. II. Annapolis, Md., 1962, pp. 311-39.
39. Scott, Peter. "Scholars and Researchers and Their Use of Microfilms," *NMA Journal*, 2:121-26, Summer 1969.
40. Bagg and Stevens, *op. cit.*
41. "News: Outer Space Microfilm Library Included in World's Fair Exhibit," *Library Journal*, 89:1700+, April 15, 1964.

RESOURCES
IN MICROFORM FOR
THE RESEARCH LIBRARY

by Rolland E. Stevens

Microforms serve several functions in libraries. They (1) permit acquisition of rare books, journals, manuscripts, archives, and other information sources that are either unobtainable or prohibitively expensive in their original form; (2) replace items that are printed or written on badly deteriorating paper; (3) furnish a working copy of rare and fragile records; (4) replace large newspapers and other bulky volumes with a compact form that is easier to handle and use; or (5) replace printed materials, thereby saving stack space. Although the librarian who acquires microforms might act from a single motive, in acquiring even one title in microform he is probably fulfilling several of the above functions. A newspaper file is acquired on microfilm to replace a deteriorating copy, to save the user the pain of handling a bulky, dirty, crumbling volume, and to save shelf space. One of these functions can hardly be said to take precedence over the others and is probably not even considered apart from the others.

Reprinted from *Microform Review*, 1: 9-18 (January 1972) by permission of the publisher. Copyright © 1972 by Microform Review Inc.

Nevertheless, in writing about the use of microform in the library, it is convenient to treat these several purposes separately. In a previous article, [1] the author discussed the microform as a means of saving shelf space in the library. In this article, the emphasis will be on the research materials that are obtainable in microform, problems associated with their production, efforts to improve and coordinate their production, and the prospects for improved and increased research materials in these forms.

Microphotography was developed in England before 1840, but was regarded more as a curiosity than a useful technique for nearly a hundred years. [2] In the early part of this century, scholars who were working with archives and manuscripts began to experiment in microfilming their papers, using homemade equipment. [3] Not until George McCarthy developed a camera for microfilming canceled bank checks in 1928 did the potentialities of microphotography for business and libraries become apparent. About 1935, transcripts of the hearings of the National Recovery Administration and of the Agricultural Adjustment Agency, amounting to some 300,000 pages, were microfilmed by the federal government for several libraries desiring a copy. [4] It was this early microfilming project that initiated a train of copying programs for research libraries: Eugene Power learned of the possibilities of this new copying medium when Doctor T. R. Schellenberg, then secretary of the Joint Committee on Materials for Research and intimately associated with the NRA and AAA filming projects, explained its economies for the reproduction of scholarly material in small quantities on his visit to Ann Arbor in February 1935. Several months after this discussion, Power took a movie camera adapted for microfilming to the British Museum and began filming books printed in English before 1550. [5] This was the start of the *Short Title Catalogue* series, the earliest of the large, well-planned projects aimed at securing for libraries copies of rare and relatively unobtainable research materials. The value of having a photographic copy of every extant book listed in Pollard and Redgrave's *Short Title Catalogue* had been pointed out years before by Andrew Keough, librarian of Yale University; the means of doing this economically enough to be feasible was not seen until Schellenberg had provided microfilm prints of the NRA and AAA records to about a dozen libraries, sharing the cost among them. [6] In this way a new dimension was added to microcopying services: formerly the technique had been used for making a single copy of selected manuscripts or archives for the immediate need of an individual scholar; now texts of a large but related group of books or manuscripts, not needed immediately but of potential research value, might be made for a number of subscribing libraries. These libraries would share the costs of the initial microfilming and a positive print for each subscriber.

When Eugene Power began microfilming pre-1550 English books in the British Museum, he was in the employ of Edwards Brothers, Inc., Ann Arbor, Michigan, whose business was publication of scholarly books by

offset. The special requirements of microfilming as to equipment, expertise, and management soon became apparent, and a division was established
within the firm under the name of University Microfilms. In 1938 the division separated from Edwards Brothers and thereafter operated independently. [7] In the same year, University Microfilms instituted its service of
microfilming dissertations, publishing their abstracts in *Dissertation Abstracts*, and providing a positive microfilm copy to a purchaser on request.
This innovation added still another dimension to the service provided to a
research library by microcopying. It was an easy and inexpensive means of
providing worldwide dissemination of the research buried in unpublished
dissertations, replacing traditional requirements that the doctoral candi-
date publish his complete dissertation in a minimum-sized edition, or at
least a summarizing article in a national journal. [8]

Several years later a new microform was developed which was to become important in offering unavailable research materials to the library. In
1940 the Readex Microprint Corporation announced manufacture of a
6 × 9-inch opaque microform carrying normally 100 pages of text. This
medium was planned by the head of the firm, Albert Boni, for publishing
the texts of rare research materials needed in large libraries. The microform, later patented as Microprint, is a calendered paper on which the
texts have been printed by offset at a reduction of 12 to 18 diameters.
Calendered paper is necessary, for its surface is smooth enough to register
clearly the highly reduced letters. It is not a photographic print although
it resembles a print of photographic paper. It cannot be produced economically in a very small edition, but for an edition of at least twenty-five, it
is the cheapest of the microforms to manufacture. [9] This requirement—
an edition that will appeal to a number of libraries—has probably been the
motivating factor behind some of the most imaginative and useful of the
projects offered in microform. When the process was announced, reference was made to "an extensive publishing program which is now under
way." [10] Specific series were not named, but the *British Sessional Papers* and *Three Centuries of English and American Plays, 1500-1800*, were
the first sets published.

Besides these pioneering projects, a large number of important monographs, journals, manuscripts, and archives have been made available in
microform. These materials, which are invaluable for research in a wide
number of disciplines, are often rare or unobtainable in their original form.
Some examples of the resources that can be acquired in microform by any
library are described in the following paragraphs. But it must be recognized
that not every significant microform project can be treated here; the attempt is simply to be representative of what is available. Furthermore, the
emphasis is on the materials needed in advanced research, not on the out-
of-print books offered to new colleges and junior colleges, such as items
from *Books for College Libraries* offered by NCR Microcard Editions; the
PCMI Library Collections, also from NCR; or the Microbook Libraries,

being issued in the ultramicrofiche format by Library Resources, Inc., a division of Encyclopedia Britannica. These are interesting and possibly of importance to the new, small academic library but are out of scope for this article.

General

The University Microfilms project for filming as many of the books listed in Pollard and Redgrave's *Short Title Catalogue* as could be located has been mentioned already. Eleven libraries had sufficient interest in having these books on microfilm to subscribe to the project at its beginning. A companion project conducted by Xerox University Microfilms, filming extant books from Wing's *Short Title Catalogue*, 1641-1700, has been sought equally. Students of the history and literature of England are helped frequently by being able to refer to these texts in their own library. Even when the title is held in original form by the library, its handling can be avoided in many cases by use of the film copy. A related microform project that is too general to be treated under one subject heading is the Microprint edition of available books listed in Charles Evans's *American Bibliography*, offered by Readex in 1955. This series, giving immediate access to American imprints from the *Bay Psalm Book*, 1640, to the *Catalogue of the Members of Yale College*, 1800, answered needs of many research libraries. So evident was a demand for this or a similar series that two competing microform projects emerged almost simultaneously with that offered by Readex Microprint. One was the set of selected Evans imprints on Microcard begun in 1954 and announced in 1956. [11] The other consisted of selected Evans titles on microfilm as part of University Microfilm's *American Culture Series*. [12] The latter was a counterpart to the firm's *American Periodical Series*, featuring runs of such nineteenth-century periodicals as *Columbian Magazine* and the *American Magazine*. Perhaps the several series of United States government publications and United Nations documents available in microform are acquired primarily to save space and to have the documents in a conveniently organized form. Miscellaneous titles from the collection of the New York Public Library are offered on microfilm by 3M-IM (International Microfilm) Press. Surveys of outstanding collections in various subject fields have repeatedly shown New York Public Library to be one of the outstanding libraries in the country. Sampled rare titles from its collections made available in microform are useful to other research libraries.

Religion

Several series of source materials pertaining to early and medieval Christianity have been offered. The texts of writings of the early church fathers, edited by Migne, are held by many libraries in the book form—Latin Fathers: 221 volumes (1844-1864); Greek Fathers: 161 volumes (1857-1887). For those libraries that do not have this set, NCR Microcard Editions offers both the Latin and Greek series in microcard or microfiche. The *Corpus Scriptorum Ecclesiasticorum Latinorum* is another set of texts available in microform to those libraries that do not have the printed edition of 1866-1913. It is published in both microcard and microfiche by NCR Microcard Editions. This set includes writings of Latin church fathers up to the seventh century, reprinted in many cases from better manuscripts than those in Migne. Another set offered by NCR Microcard Editions is the *Analecta Hymnica Medii Aevi*, a collection of medieval Latin hymns of the Christian liturgy. The published edition of 1886-1922, in 55 volumes, is complete in less than thirty libraries of the United States and Canada. The complete works of John Calvin, 1863-1900 edition, 59 volumes, are also available from NCR Microcards in both microfiche and microcards. Another series issued in the same form is the *Acta Sanctae Sedis*, a file of the monthly journal published by the Vatican from 1865 to 1909 containing the principal official documents of those years. Only about twenty libraries in the United States and Canada hold the complete set in the printed edition.

History

Writings of Byzantine scholars and chroniclers, published from 1828 to 1897 in the series *Corpus Scriptorum Historiae Byzantinae*, 50 volumes, are available from NCR Microcards. The same firm offers the complete *Rolls Series* of 254 volumes, editions of the medieval chroniclers of England and Ireland. Copies in either opaque- or transparent-card form of *French Revolutionary Pamphlets*, from the collection at New York Public Library, are also on sale by NCR Microcards. The Lost Cause Press has copied on micro-opaque cards the texts of selected titles from Sabin, *Dictionary of Books Relating to America*. Lost Cause has also issued as many of the books as they could find from several bibliographies of early travels in the south and west: Coulter's *Travels in the Confederate States*, Thomas Clark's *Travels in the New South* and *Travels in the Old South*. Texts from *Travels in the West and Southwest* are being issued.

Black studies

The recent interest in black studies and out-of-print histories, autobiographies, and other books in this field has stimulated several series and projects within a few years. The famed Schomburg Collection of the New York Public Library has been microfilmed by 3M-IM Press. The

Trevor-Arnett Library at Atlanta University, containing 7,000 books and pamphlets on slavery and the Negro in history, has been microfilmed by The Micropublishers, a division of Bell and Howell. NCR Microcard Editions has issued a collection of 18 Negro periodical runs of 1825 to 1960, including some rare issues. Lost Cause has published a collection of about 2,500 antislavery pamphlets at Oberlin College and a pot-pourri of 5,000 volumes called *Black Studies Materials*, many of which have been collected from its previously issued series.

Literature

In literature a number of series have been offered. Three by NCR Microcard Editions are the volumes of *Early English Text Society Publications*, *Scottish Text Society Publications*, and *Sociètè des anciens textes français Bulletin*. These sets, held by many libraries in printed form, are reprints of medieval chronicles and other writings that were available only in manuscript until they were issued in collected editions. Now, in microform, they are accessible to many libraries that cannot fill in the printed edition. *Three Centuries of English and American Plays* and *English and American Plays of the 19th Century* are available from Readex Microprint. The first series includes texts of more than 5,000 plays of 1500 to 1800, many no longer available in a printed edition. The second series is in progress and the total number of plays to be included is not yet determined. The resources of any research library acquiring these Microprint series are thus significantly enriched. *English Literary Periodicals of the 17th and 19th Centuries* filmed by Xerox University Microfilms include such magazines of this era as *Critical Review*, 1756-1817, *Examiner*, 1808-1881, *London Magazine*, 1732-1785, and many shorter, scarce holdings. Lost Cause is publishing as many titles as it can locate from Wright's *American Fiction*, but only one edition of each title. A recent offering of literary texts is the Readex Microprint edition of titles from Blanck's *Bibliography of American Literature*, literary works of major American authors. Thus far this definitive bibliography has been completed only through Longfellow, but early printings of the titles it lists are frequently rare and unavailable to research libraries.

Area studies

Outstanding series offered in this field are the two issued by Readex Microprint: *Russian Historical Sources*, I and II. The sources offered in this form include the stenographic reports of the Imperial Dumas of 1906 to 1917 and of the Communist Party of 1923 to 1939, long runs of several vital historical journals, and many other archives and publications. Most of these are today unavailable in printed form. NCR Microcard Editions also offers *Slavic Materials*, a collection of journals, transactions, and documents of the same period.

The projects described here are only representative of the many sets available in microform that add immeasurably to the resources available to the scholar or other research worker. Most are in the humanistic disciplines. Before the microform revolution of the late 1930s scholars had to spend time, energy, and money locating these works in the great libraries of the United States and Europe, using them as they could gain access to them. Now available in microform, these materials can be acquired by any research library in which they are needed. Complaints about the difficulty of using microfilm and other microforms are rarely expressed by those who heretofore had so much trouble finding and using these resources in their published form.

The important series mentioned above represent only a few of the commercial producers of microforms. The difficulties and problems of issuing a body of research materials in microform and selling sufficient copies to meet costs are not attractive to many businessmen. Those who have been successful in this branch of publishing have been imaginative and sometimes venturesome. But their most important attribute has been an interest in scholarly activity and an ability to judge the practicality of a scholar's wants. It was from Keough that the filming of *Short Title Catalogue* books drew its idea. And probably the plan to issue the *British Sessional Papers and Russian Historical Sources* in Microprint and to copy other collections had their beginnings in conversations with professors, whether remembered or not. But it was the director of the micropublishing firm—Albert Boni of Readex Microprint and Eugene Power of University Microfilms, among others—who decided whether the scholar's dream could be translated into the hard terms of profit and loss. The cost of microfilming the extant books listed in the *Short Title Catalogue* would be prohibitively high if borne by only one or a few libraries. But if fifteen or twenty libraries can share the cost, although still expensive it can be undertaken, and the important resources made available. The producer, then, like any publisher, has to weigh the total cost of the project against the income it is likely to bring. But instead of a market of 5,000 or more, he is working with a market of a hundred or less; instead of a price of several dollars, he is estimating a price in hundreds or thousands of dollars. The break-even edition for microfilm and other microforms is low, however, from one for microfilm to twenty-five for microprint and somewhere between for other micro-opaque forms. And a research library, which will not hesitate to pay $30 to $40 for a volume of scholarly journal, will not scruple to spend $1,250 for half-a-million pages of Russian historical sources in microform. For example, if the Schomburg Collection is to be brought out in microfilm edition, the publisher has to estimate whether he can interest enough libraries in purchasing this collection at a price sufficient to cover his costs of microfilming, advertising, distributing, and overhead, and to allow a small profit. His potential market consists entirely of libraries, almost entirely of research libraries. If the contemplated project is large and costly, e.g., *Short Title Catalogue* texts or *American Bibliography* texts, and one that might, therefore, interest only a few of the largest libraries, there is a further risk that the publisher has to take into account: that the few potential buyers, or at least those potential buyers who share their resources through a research center or other form of cooperation, will decide to buy only one subscription for the group, further reducing the market. Also, the microfilm publisher must be careful not to violate copyright, since he is often copying books that have been previously published. Usually, he films only books on which the copyright has expired. Otherwise he gets permission to copy from the copyright owner. Another hazard faced by book publishers as well as by producers of microforms is that a competitor may be offering a similar collection. An example of this occurred in the mid-1950s, when titles from Evan's *American Bibliography* were offered simultaneously in three competing microforms. Another example today is the ultrafiche library, in which two firms are competing for the same potential customer. A similar publishing problem is the competition of the reprint publisher, who also seeks to fill the need for rare and out-of-print source material in research libraries. One way to meet this competition is for the microform publisher to enter the reprint field, as Xerox University Microfilms has done both with OP books and its facsimile reprints.

These problems are not seen as serious enough to inhibit or limit the industry. On the contrary, new firms do enter the field from time to time. Judging from recent advertisements in library journals, there are still a number of unexploited research collections which libraries will buy in microform. As soon as a new interest is apparent, several new collections will be advertised by competing producers. The interest in black studies a few years ago brought forth the three or four projects named above. One indictment of the industry today is that, like most commercial ventures, its concern for showing a profit and its caution about risking capital on any untested innovation are only too evident. This was not at all true of the pioneers, Power and Boni and others, who launched imaginative series in new microforms and "got the bugs out" as they went along. But since then the industry has become much more profit-conscious and reluctant to try something new until the break occurs, and each firm must quickly adapt to the competition. An example is the suddenness with which the producers of micro-opaque forms began to offer their titles on microfiche, after they had been ignoring for years the advantages of fiche. The federal defense agencies NASA and AEC were the pioneers in the use of fiche in this country about 1960, but most people in the field had known of their use in Europe for years, and of their obvious superiority over both roll microfilm and opaque cards. [13] Apparently it was only after their

successful adoption by NASA and AEC and their demonstrated advantages
that the industry was willing to try them. That innovations have been
made by the industry from time to time is not denied. Outstanding developments over the years were the opaque card, whether printed photographically or by photo-offset, the microfiche, and PCMI. In readers, principal improvements have been the reader-printer, the magazine load with
automatic threading, motorized transport, and film indexing. But the last
three innovations were necessitated by the persistent use of roll microfilm
in long rolls. Why has this form, adopted in the 1930s because it was then,
as motion picture stock, the most available kind of film, [14] persisted to
this day? Francis Wolek has observed that the engineer/designer in general
seeks to improve on earlier designs, but not too much. [15] The same ob-
servation can be applied to the microform industry. When a breakthrough
is finally made, competition forces the other firms to bring out a version
of the innovation. It was the Armed Forces Medical Library that contracted for a reader-printer in 1953. [16] But when the first commercial
reader-printer was marketed in 1958 by Minnesota Mining and Manufacturing Company, [17] it was quickly followed by reader-printers from
other manufacturers. Another criticism of the microform industry by the
library profession is that improvements and gadgets are designed for business offices, not for libraries which are only a small part of the market.
This fault is not peculiar to producers of microforms, any more than is
the lethargy in retooling for innovations until forced to do so. Catering to
needs of the business office is most evident in a related field, full-size
copying. Most copying machines are made for single sheets and only a few
for bound volumes. Less evident an example is the use of position-finding
marks on microfilm. These are adapted primarily for rapid location of a
piece of correspondence or other record on a microfilm roll; libraries
rarely can make use of this device, but it can indicate the break between
the volumes of a journal. Another example of the attention paid to the
needs of business rather than to the needs of libraries is in the design of
microfilm readers. Almost all of them emphasize compactness, portability,
ease of loading, and factors other than the ease of reading. In office procedures, reading microfilm is minimal; once the desired page is found a
printout is usually made. In the library a user may read microfilm for
hours. Yet out of approximately seventy readers described in Hubbard
Ballou's *Guide to Microreproduction Equipment*, only one projects the
image onto an opaque surface parallel to the desk top, a much more comfortable reading position than the vertical screen through which the others
project the image. Lack of standardization is another serious complaint
against the industry, and like the others is an indictment of industry in
general, not only of the microform industry. One of the few achievements
here—the recently adopted international size standards for microfiche—grew from an agreement in 1964 among the four government
agencies that produced the most microfiche, NASA, AEC, DOD, and OTS,

not from industry leadership. [18] Not only does industry fail to press for standardization, it usually opposes it, each company preferring that only its own parts or products be used in machines of its manufacture.

The problems of the industry and the charges against it are not applicable to noncommercial agencies engaged in microform projects. Some of the earliest and most ambitious microfilming programs have been undertaken by the United States government and other nonprofit organizations. As early as 1927, the Foreign Copying Program of the Library of Congress reproduced manuscripts and archives relating to American and European libraries, first by photostat and later by microfilm. [19] Government documents and official papers of Germany and Japan for the period preceding World War II have been filmed under sponsorship of the Library of Congress. It has also copied the papers of the presidents of the United States in its collections. Extensive filming of its own collections has been undertaken by the National Archives. From the master negatives of these projects, kept in the Library of Congress and National Archives respectively, libraries may order prints of any portions wanted. Recently, National Archives has been depositing copies of its film in eleven archives branches across the nation. [20] Other noteworthy copying programs by the Library of Congress were carried out in Greece and the Middle East during 1949-1950 and 1952-1953. Manuscripts selected for their importance to research were microfilmed in the monasteries of Jerusalem, St. Catherine on Mount Sinai, and Mount Athos. These monasteries contain thousands of valuable and beautifully illuminated manuscripts which had not been easily available to scholars before this project. The famed *Codex Sinaiticus*, now in the British Museum, was discovered accidentally in St. Catherine monastery in the nineteenth century. The projects by the Library of Congress in Greece and the Middle East were undoubtedly spurred in part by a realization of the destruction of less fortunate libraries in World War II and an effort to safeguard the content of the remaining monasteries. The same motives may be attributed to two large microfilming projects since 1950 in Europe. About 30,000 selected manuscript codices of the Vatican Library, along with numerous manuscript finding lists and catalogs, were microfilmed from 1951 to 1957 under the sponsorship of the Knights of Columbus. These are not available for purchase by other libraries but can be used at the Pius XII Library of the St. Louis University, where they are housed. A similar project is the extensive microfilming of manuscripts kept in Benedictine monasteries of Italy, Austria, Switzerland, and Germany. This program, sponsored by the Louis and Maude Hill Family Foundation, is still in progress, and the film is housed in the St. John's Monastic Microfilm Library in Collegeville, Minnesota. A final project to be mentioned in this selective listing is the filming of archives and manuscripts in European libraries pertaining to the Reformation. These films are kept at the Foundation for Reformation Research in St. Louis.

With so many programs being undertaken by commercial and non-commercial organizations, some kind of coordination and regulation is desirable. Several agencies have been established to try to effect organization and coordination of microcopying projects. One of these is the Subcommittee on Micropublishing Projects, Resources Committee, Resources and Technical Services Division, American Library Association. This subcommittee was appointed in 1958, when the waste of having the same works from Evans's *American Bibliography* offered to libraries in three different microforms became apparent to the profession, and especially when it seemed that the three suppliers were not even aware of the activities of the others. The subcommittee was appointed "to serve as a coordinating body to which publishers who wish to inaugurate micropublishing projects may turn for advice from librarians and to which librarians may turn for advice when they are considering purchasing proposed micropublishing projects." [21]

Another agency for the dissemination of information about projects and effecting coordination among them grew out of a study made by the American Council of Learned Societies. The amended report of this study, published in 1964, urged better coordination of projects:

> There is, first, an obvious need for much greater coordination of what is copied by different organizations and institutions. Even though satisfying or profitable for the undertakers, it is difficult to see how scholarship is served by having the same American public documents available in both microfilm and micro-opaque forms, or by having new commercial photocopies made of material copied nearly twenty years ago in the American Council of Learned Societies' British Manuscript Project, or by having first the Library of Congress, then a state university, and finally the same state's historical society—each unknown to the others—copy the same archives. Such duplication in the past was understandable, if regrettable. But it is a luxury in which humanistic scholars, to whom financial resources are not easily available, can ill afford to indulge in the future. Coordination is needed not only to avoid duplication of effort but to concentrate resources on projects of genuine and general value to American scholars. [22]

Probably as a direct result of this recommendation, a Center for the Coordination of Foreign Manuscript Copying was established in the Library of Congress in the summer of 1965. In the first issue of its *News from the Center*, Spring 1967, the following statement of purpose was made:

> The Center is seeking to coordinate photocopying projects conducted in foreign libraries and archives by American scholars and institutions and to avoid duplication of effort and expense through cooperative planning. With the cooperation of American libraries, universities, learned societies, and Government agencies, the Center (1) identifies extensive photocopying projects which have been completed, are underway, or are planned; (2) records the location of copies of foreign collections in this country; (3) assists American institutions in learning which

manuscript collections can be photocopied in foreign libraries and archives; and (4) disseminates this information to the scholarly community.

News from the Center, published semiannually from spring 1967 to spring 1970, carried information about current microfilming projects of foreign manuscript materials and about collections of foreign archives suitable for future copying. Only projects being carried on by noncommercial organizations were described, but the news about these was sufficient both to keep the scholarly world informed and to prevent unnecessary duplication by two or more groups. The Center, which had been supported by grants from the Council on Library Resources, Inc., for five years, ceased to exist in 1970, when these funds were no longer available. Today there is no agency expressly committed to the coordination and dissemination of information about microform projects, either commercial or noncommercial, although the staff of the Manuscript Division of the Library of Congress continues to perform a portion of the work formerly done by the center. This coordination and efforts to improve both equipment and the technical aspects of microcopying are most needed if libraries are to benefit fully from the wealth of research resources available from this source. The *Microform Review* will perform a valuable service to the profession if, through its articles and features, it can exert an influence on the microcopying industry and noncommercial agencies to plan projects intelligently and cooperatively. Libraries and the scholarly community must insist on improvements in equipment and standardization to make handling and reading microforms as easy as handling and reading books. We are still far from this millenium, but when it arrives we shall find that we can manipulate, store, retrieve, transport, read, and copy from microforms much more easily than is possible today with books and other printed material of various shapes and sizes.

References

1. Stevens, Rolland E. "The Microform Revolution," *Library Trends*, 19:379-395, January, 1971.

2. Luther, Frederic. *Microfilm: A History 1839-1900* (Annapolis, Md., National Microfilm Association, 1959), p. 16.

3. Johnson, Amandus. "Some Early Experience in Microphotography, 1910-1938," *Journal of Documentary Reproduction* 1:9-19, Winter, 1938.

4. Raney, M. Llewellyn. "Microphotography—A Lay Appraisal," *Journal of Documentary Reproduction* 1:23, Winter, 1938; Power, Eugene B. "University Microfilms," *Journal of Documentary Reproduction* 2:21, Winter, 1938.

5. Power, *op. cit.*, p. 21-22.

6. *Ibid.*, p. 21.

7. *Ibid.*, p. 23.

8. *Ibid.*, p. 25-28.

9. Tennant, John. "Readex Microprints," *Journal of Documentary Reproduction* 3: 66-70, March, 1940.

10. *Ibid.*, p. 66.

11. Wyllie, J. C.   "The Louisville Microcard Project," *Library Journal*, 81:894-895, April 15, 1956.

12. Weimer, David R.   "Microfilm and Bibliography: American Civilization to 1876," *Library Journal*, 80:2072-4, October 1, 1955.

13. Warheit, I. A.   "The Microfiche," *Special Libraries*, 51:65, February, 1970; Bennett, Ralph D.   "Sheet Microfilm," *Journal of Documentary Reproduction* 3:39-41, 1940.

14. Hawkins, Reginald.   *Production of Microforms*, The State of the Library Art, vol. 5, pt. 1 (New Brunswick, N. J., Graduate School of Library Service, Rutgers, The State University, 1960), p. 54.

15. Wolek, Francis W.   "The Engineer: His Work and Needs for Information," in *Proceedings of the American Society for Information Science*, thirty-second Annual Meeting, San Francisco, October 1-4, 1969, vol. 6 (Westport, Conn., Greenwood Publishing Corp., 1969), p. 473.

16. Bull, C. D.   "Instrumentation," *Library Trends* 2:105, July, 1953.

17. Hawken, William R.   Enlarged Prints from Library Microforms; a Study of Processes, Equipment, and Materials (Chicago, American Library Association, 1963), pp. iii, 14.

18. Day, Melvin S.   "The NASA Microform Concept," *National Microfilm Association Proceedings* 13:284-285, 1964.

19. Most of the information in this paragraph concerning microfilming projects by noncommercial agencies has been taken from Born, Lester K.   "Planning for Scholarly Photocopying; a Report Prepared for the American Council of Learned Societies," *PMLA* 79:1-14, September, 1964.

20. *College and Research Libraries News* no. 7 pp. 209-210, July/August, 1971.

21. *American Library Association Bulletin* 52:603-604, September, 1958.

22. Born, Lester K.   "Planning for Scholarly Photocopying . . . " *PMLA* 79:10-11, September, 1964.

PLANNING FOR
SCHOLARLY PHOTOCOPYING

by Lester K. Born

Foreword

To flourish, scholarship must have at hand in copious supply the recorded materials which advance its studies. The history of scholarship is consequently in large measure a history of the diffusion of the materials for scholarly research.

The invention of printing is of course the event which most dramatically accelerated this diffusion. But in our own day microphotography has had an effect of comparable importance. Because of microfilm and the

Reprinted from *PMLA*, 79, pt. 2: 77-90 (September 1964) by permission of the publisher. Copyright © 1964 by the Modern Language Association.

related microphotographic processes any scholar or scholarly community may now have at hand at moderate expense what was previously reserved to a few, or—even more significant—what until recently was not conveniently accessible to any scholar no matter how great his independent means nor how ancient and rich his institution. Unpublished manuscripts scattered in dozens of repositories; printed works long out of print, unprocurable and dispersed; other sources so impermanent that deterioration erases them within a generation—for all of these microphotography has provided a means of diffusion for scholarly purposes where even printing has failed, and which is in some respects even superior to printing.

Microforms have now been employed in the service of research for a third of a century, but we are still learning to live with them. We have not yet found adequate solutions for many of the problems relating to their physical characteristics, their bibliographic control and their use by the individual worker; or to the efficient exploitation of their potentialities for assembling and diffusing the resources for learning.

It is the last of these problems which is the subject of the investigation reported here. After the *Guide to Photocopied Historical Materials in the United States and Canada*[1] showed not only the extent but also the randomness with which scholarly resources on the North American continent have been enriched by photofacsimile, it was felt that the time was appropriate to explore the possibilities of being more systematic in the employment of funds available for microfilming projects. Is the randomness of photocopying, reflecting the variety of individual and institutional interest, which the *Guide* so often portrays, a necessary condition, or can microfilming projects be so planned as to serve more widely and usefully the research interests of large numbers of members of the various disciplines? Might such planning promote, better than the methods now followed, the development of a rational and systematic enrichment of the resources available to American scholarship? Might the very existence of such a plan attract to the work funds which the lack of a plan now fails to elicit?

These questions seemed, to representatives of some of the groups principally concerned,[2] to justify an inquiry. At their urging the American Council of Learned Societies agreed to sponsor an investigation and named an Advisory Committee to oversee it.[3] Dr. Lester K. Born, a scholar on the staff of the Library of Congress who has long been concerned with the planning and the results of microcopying projects, accepted the assignment of making the study. The present report, which is based on Dr. Born's study, is the result. Of necessity, it must be considered only as a basis for planning and consequently a preliminary to next steps.

Frederick Burkhardt

I. The Past as Prologue

The extensive use of photocopying in its several forms[4] is barely a generation old; but it has already become a major library instrument and thus,
necessarily, a matter of growing importance to the scholars who use
libraries. As has been noted more than once, photocopying has come to
serve a variety of ends: it is used for taking notes, saving space, preserving
against damage, publishing, editing, circulating on interlibrary loan, and
acquiring new or otherwise unavailable material. It is this last function—
photocopying as a means of acquisition—that is of primary concern here.
Although it is not always possible to separate acquisition sharply from
other functions of photocopying, it is to be problems raised by the growing number of acquisition programs, particularly those involving unprinted
material, that this report is directed.

In the past three decades acquisition projects have mushroomed. Some
are large, some are small; some relate to printed materials, some to manuscripts; some are domestic, some inter-national; some are intramural, some
are cooperative; some are institutionally supported, some are commercial;
some have been carefully organized from their inception, and some, alas,
have just grown. The proliferation of such projects has presented librarians, scholars, and foundations with problems for which solutions have yet
to be devised. The librarian must catalogue and service an ever-growing
mass of microforms; the scholar gropes, often half-blindly, to learn what
has been copied and where it is; at times the foundation director has voted
subsidies only to discover that the material copied is virtually unusable or
unused. Few can any longer question the benefits which photocopying
can provide, but few would argue that those benefits have yet been fully
realized.

A résumé of some of the more significant projects may help to point
up these problems more concretely. What follows makes no pretense at
being an exhaustive history of the subject: its purpose is to focus attention on the problems raised by scholarly photocopying and to emphasize
"the large intellectual effort necessary for its effective use."[5]

Archives and Manuscripts

The most varied photocopying programs, and probably the mose useful
from the point of view of acquisition, are those involving the reproduction of archival or manuscript materials.

The oldest and largest of these is the Foreign Copying Program of the
Library of Congress, which has involved several distinct but related projects. Project A—unimaginatively named but imaginatively conceived and
executed—was financed by a gift of $490,000 from John D. Rockefeller,
Jr., and covered the years 1927-35. Coming as it did at the point of

transition from the use of handwritten transcripts and photostats. Project A may properly be regarded as the first copying project to make substantial use of microfilm. Since the Library of Congress had been engaged in copying materials abroad since 1905, the project was preceded by a general survey of the large collections of transcripts already at hand and by the formulation of a consistent, ordered plan for selection and acquisition. It was further distinguished by the employment of competent field directors (initially Professor Samuel Flagg Bemis) who selected the material and supervised the copying. By its conclusion, over 3,000,000 pages of material relating to America had been copied from the principal European, and several American, archives and manuscript collections. The material copied has been much used, but, after a lapse of nearly thirty years, still lacks adequate published guides.[6]

Not too dissimilar, except in its scope and in its limitation to material in Europe, is the work done by the Library of Congress since 1925 with the Wilbur Fund. A staff member, who searched out and recommended materials, and arranged for their copying after the selection was made in Washington, was resident in London for some years before World War II and again from 1949 to 1952. This Fund, though smaller than that provided by the Rockefeller grant, is perpetual, and work has been almost continuous for over 35 years. Again, however, there is no complete and printed guide.

By contrast, there is an elaborate 800-page guide, published within a short time after filming was completed, for the State Records Microfilm Project, a joint effort of the Library of Congress and the University of North Carolina.[7] The material was filmed between 1941 and 1950 (with an interruption due to the War) and involved extensive travel to copy the documents, both printed and unprinted, in repositories scattered across the country. Only after the completion of the microfilming was the material organized by bringing together the separate "units" which form each reel—a costly, though possibly unavoidable, feature of the project.

Failure to organize the material in advance of copying has not been characteristic of the Virginia Colonial Records Project, which has been described as "quite unique in its utilization of modern methods to achieve maximum results."[8] The project was planned in advance and abundantly financed. A permanent representative was stationed in London to examine and report material concerning Virginia. His "Survey Reports," in effect brief calendars of the documents filmed, were circulated to interested libraries, and, thus, serve both as a guide to the original material and as a record of what has been copied. The combining of the preparation of the microfilms has been one of the most useful aspects of this project.

Somewhat comparable in that they deal with particular areas are the microfilms relating largely to western America and Latin America collected by the Bancroft Library of the University of California. The copying, for which a preliminary guide was issued in 1955,[9] has been privately financed and the Library has periodically maintained a representative in Spain since the Second World War.

Broader than any of these in geographic scope, but much more restricted in the kind of material copied, is the genealogical project of the Church of Jesus Christ of Latter Day Saints. There is adequate money; there is a large editorial staff in Utah; there are numerous camera teams and directors in the field. The effectiveness of bibliographical control is demonstrated by the extensive listing of material in the *Guide to Photocopied Historical Materials*. The films, however, are not available on interlibrary loan.

Documents relating to the Second World War, and otherwise inaccessible documents made available by the fortunes of that War, have been the object of several important projects. Under official diplomatic auspices a team of American, British, and French scholars have worked for a number of years to publish material from the German foreign office on the coming of the War. At the same time they compiled on microfilm an extensive selection of documents for the years 1920-45. In this instance, microfilming was designed to aid editing of the published volumes and was undertaken hurriedly and in an atmosphere of crisis.[10] As a result, the material on the films is poorly arranged and the collection (in the British Public Record Office and United States National Archives) difficult to use. The recent appearance of the first volume of a catalogue[11] will, it is hoped, help scholars to find their way through the maze created by the size of the collection and the haste of its compilation.

The non-diplomatic material of the era of the Third Reich and pre-1920 German diplomatic archives have fared rather better, largely because there has been less urgency in their filming, more time to spend on the production of finding-aids, and possibly more involvement by the historical profession. Under the auspices of the American Historical Association's Committee for the Study of War Documents a series of guides to the captured German documents in the United States, with brief notes indicating the contents of specific files, has steadily appeared since 1958.[12] Similarly, the scattered and uncoordinated projects of universities, government agencies, and some individuals for microfilming German diplomatic documents of the 1867-1920 period have been brought together in a single finding-aid by the same group.[13]

Numerous Japanese documents—both those brought to the United States and those made available by the Allied occupation of Japan—have also been placed on microfilm. A cooperative Library of Congress-State Department team filmed the records of the ministry of Foreign Affairs in Japan in 1949-51. Military and naval records were hurriedly and incompletely filmed in Washington by an inter-university group with foundation support in 1957.[14]

The most extensive domestic undertaking intended for general use is the Microfilm Publication Program of the National Archives which has been in continuous operation since 1941. In 1948 a grant of $20,000 from the Rockefeller Foundation accelerated the program and insured its continuation through the establishment of a revolving fund. Microfilm negatives, intended solely as master copies from which reproductions of the many different groups of records can be made on demand, are prepared in anticipation of use by scholars. The materials filmed have been copied in accordance with the Archives' excellent standing instructions for preparing material for filming. The 260 microfilm publications, on more than 12,000 reels, provide basic documentation for research in American history, but include material on European, Far Eastern, and Latin American history as well as on local history and genealogy. For about 70 of the publications separate pamphlets have been issued in which are reproduced the introductions to the films, the contents, and any indexes or lists that would be helpful.[15]

Also operating on Federal funds, in this case especially appropriated by Congress for the project, is the Presidential Papers Program of the Library of Congress, in which the papers of the Presidents of the United States held by the Library are copied on a master negative from which positive copies are made on demand and sold. A printed index is available separately as well as with the film order, so that scholars may use it independently as an aid to research.[16]

Separate projects dealing exclusively or primarily with manuscripts or codices (as distinct from archival records) have been fewer and less extensive.

The Rotograph (later microfilm) Project of the Modern Language Association, which ran for more than 25 years before it was terminated in 1952, was intended to provide the individual scholar with sources in the form of manuscripts and rare books.[17] Shorter lived, cooperatively planned, and financed by the Rockefeller Foundation was the British Manuscripts Project of the American Council of Learned Societies. Some five million pages were copied on 2600 reels of film by a commercial contractor working in collaboration with a committee in the United States on the selection of material during the difficult years 1941-45. That so much of value was selected and copied under such trying conditions is a tribute to the project's originators. But the work was done in great haste and inadequate measures of bibliographic control were used. The finished product was thus marred by poor arrangement of material and, until the Library of Congress at its own expense prepared a check-list,[18] no guide to the documents was provided. It is one of the symptomatic ironies of scholarly photocopying that these British manuscripts are so little known or used.

The most extensive project to concentrate on codices is that of the Foundation for the Preservation of Historic Documents in the Vatican

Library, centered at St. Louis University and financed by the Knights of Columbus. Approximately 30,000 codices and many hundreds of manuscript catalogues, indexes, and inventories, as well as 250,000 cards from the card catalogue of the Vatican Library were copied in 1951-57.[19] The films can be used, however, only in the St. Louis University Library.

Three projects executed by the Library of Congress in collaboration with scholars from cooperating institutions also deal with medieval manuscripts. In 14 months during 1949-50 more than 2700 carefully selected manuscripts, some 1700 firmans, and nearly 2500 illuminations were copied in the libraries of the Greek and Armenian patriarchates in Jerusalem and in the monastery of St. Catherine on Mount Sinai. A third rich center of manuscript collections, the many monasteries on Mount Athos, was the object of another Library of Congress project for a six-month period in 1952-53. Selection was made by a competent scholar whose expenses were paid by a Fulbright grant; the expense of camera, film, and publication were borne by the Library. Checklists for all three projects have been issued.[20]

Government Documents

The official publications of governments, both American and foreign, have been in sufficient demand to attract commercial photocopyists.[21] Microcard Editions, Inc., has produced, among other things, portions of the debates of both the French Chamber of Deputies and the German Reichstag. University Microfilms, Inc., supplies the successive series of American Congressional debates since 1789. Readex Microprint Corporation provides various American and United Nations' serial collections as well as a collection of basic British public documents—the "sessional Papers," the *Parliamentary Debates*, and the *Journal of the House of Commons*.

Not all copying of government publications can be commercially profitable or "self-liquidating," however. The project, begun several years ago at the New York Public Library, to microfilm the more than 350 national and local gazettes, originated with the Association of Research Libraries. Processed lists have appeared several times in an effort to keep the interested consumer abreast of copying schedules for the future. The Library of Congress copied the official gazettes of the Mexican states between November 1948 and June 1951 at its own expense. A checklist was published in 1953 as a 36-page supplement to the *Microfilming Clearing House Bulletin*.[22] The copying was done by a staff member of the Library based at the Benjamin Franklin Library in Mexico City.

Periodicals

Periodicals are likewise primarily, but not exclusively, the target for commercial copying. Examples are found in the *Cumulative List of Periodical Titles* issued by University Microfilms, Inc., which includes current materials and back files. The academic hand may be seen behind some of the work of this same company. Richmond P. Bond of the University of North Carolina, with the aid of a committee, prepared the bibliography upon which the series of English literary periodicals was based. The project for American periodicals of the eighteenth and nineteenth centuries was sponsored by the William L. Clements Library and the Department of English at the University of Michigan. Long runs of general periodicals, foreign and domestic, in almost all subject fields are also found in the micro-opaque format.[23]

The Jewish periodicals microfilmed for the American Jewish Periodical Center are listed in a catalogue published in 1957 and since supplemented.[24] Southern Methodist University copied the *Christian Advocate* and *Zion's Herald* some twelve years ago. The Hoover Institute has filmed a number of its serials; the New York Public Library has copied a number of periodicals of different types; the Wisconsin State Historical Society has filmed many labor journals; the Library of Congress has copied a number of Chinese journals; and the Historical Commission of the Southern Baptist Convention includes periodicals in its program for copying Baptist materials. These examples, picked at random from the *Microfilm Clearing House Bulletin*, illustrate the noncommercial aspects of periodical copying projects.

Newspapers

Newspapers do not lend themselves to the opaque medium: Readex Microprint Corporation lists none, and the project to put the Louisville *Courier-Journal* on microcard has ceased. By contrast, the number of newspaper titles offered by such commercial microfilming firms as Micro Photo, Inc., of Cleveland, Ohio (now filming the *Courier-Journal*) and University Microfilms, Inc., of Ann Arbor, Michigan, is very considerable. These lists, however, are as nothing when compared with the truly formidable operations in the states. Universities, state libraries, and state historical societies are the principal sponsors of newspaper copying projects. A glance at the *Microfilming Clearing House Bulletin*, however, will show that statewide projects are not yet general throughout the United States, although the geographical distribution is wide.

In addition to the lists appearing in the *Bulletin*, there are cumulative guides: the Library of Congress' *Newspapers on Microfilm*, the list of *Canadian Labour Papers Available on Microfilm*, the *Union List of*

Canadian Newspapers on Microfilm, Micro Photo, Inc.'s *Newspapers on Microfilm*, University Microfilms, Inc.'s special catalogue of newspapers, Microfilm Service and Sales Co.'s *Newspaper Film Catalog*, the State Historical Society of Wisconsin's *Labor Papers on Microfilm*, Universal Microfilming Corporation's *List of Newspapers and Periodicals available on Microfilm*, and *Negro Newspapers on Microfilm* prepared at the Library of Congress for a project sponsored by the American Council of Learned Societies.

Foreign producers of newspapers on microfilm are not lacking, although most are known through notices in periodicals or similar media rather than through lists. Helsinki University is copying Finnish newspapers. Commercial firms are copying newspapers in Sweden, South Africa, Germany, and Denmark. The International Documentation Center in Stockholm is copying on microfiche all articles indexed in 70 Swedish daily newspapers. Japanese newspapers are being copied by the National Diet Library, and the Union of German Newspaper Publishers recommends that its members film every issue and store the negatives in the Deutsche Bibliothek at Frankfurt am Main. The National Microfilm Service of Spain has a large collection of newspapers of film in the Hemeroteca, while the French Association for Conservation and Photographic Reproduction of the Press is copying on a priority basis those newspapers already in the national collections, and is systematically filming the main current French newspapers. The British Museum is copying newspapers both current and old.

There is no ready means of checking on the foreign activity, although it is obviously increasing rapidly. The domestic scene—wherein University Microfilms, Inc., has copied all major Irish newspapers, the Midwest Interlibrary Center is continuing the project for copying foreign newspapers established at Harvard University some 25 years ago, quantities of Latin American newspapers have been copied by numerous agencies, and current issues (since 1954) of some 80 Oriental vernacular newspapers are being filmed at the Library of Congress—is a readily documented complement to foreign activity. The 1953 edition of *Newspapers on Microfilm* contained 3412 titles of domestic newspapers and 673 foreign titles, whereas the 1957 edition contained approximately 8,000 titles of which about 1650 were foreign. The fifth edition, published in 1963, lists some 16,000 titles of which 4,000 are foreign.

Rarities and Miscellany

Micro-opaques come into their own with out-of-print books and series, although microfilms are by no means excluded. Varied legal series are published by the Microlex Corporation and Matthew Bender and Company, Inc. The Godfrey Memorial Library supplies microcard reprints of genealogical works; the Lost Cause Press has reprinted a great number of eighteenth- and nineteenth-century books, principally relating to America; and the University of Rochester Press has done the same with rare musical writings.

In microfilm form, University Microfilms, Inc., with its general and special catalogues, is the largest single producer of serials, books, and quasi-books (theses and dissertations). Books by the thousands have been copied, usually for individual scholars, on an *ad hoc* basis. A listing of these titles undoubtedly would be useful in avoiding duplication of effort in the future. However, neither the *Union List of Microfilms* nor the *Microfilming Clearing House Bulletin* provides coverage for these personal copies of films.

A variety of rarities has been filmed by others. Some were copied in the Modern Language Association's Rotograph Project. The Library of Congress has reproduced the first editions of Ronsard, and keeps the films as a unit, but has issued no special list. The same is true of the Chinese books from the National Library of China that were copied (with the consent of the owners, of course) while they were stored at the Library of Congress for safe-keeping during the Second World War. By contrast, the project conducted jointly by the library of Brown University and the John Carter Brown Library for copying Latin American imprints listed in the Medina bibliographies is doubly provided with a listing: once the checklist issued by Brown University,[25] and again through the printed cards prepared by the Library of Congress which are included in the Library's book-form catalogues. Similarly, the American Antiquarian Society-Readex Microprint Corporation copies of "Early American Imprints" are accessible through printed cards as well as through the Evans' bibliography on which they were based. Other printed rarities have been photocopied by the Speech Association of American and University Microfilms, Inc., the latter of which is engaged in reproducing the many works listed in the *Short Title Catalogues* of Pollard and Redgrave and of Wing.

Card files, which can be considered bibliographical works not yet set up on pages, have likewise been copied, and so have typewritten dissertations which are books not yet printed. The first group is illustrated by the Bibliography of Cartography, a file of about 45,000 cards at the Library of Congress that complements Phillips' *List of Geographical Atlases in the Library of Congress*. Another illustration is the card file in the Archabbey at Beuron, Germany, containing some 600,000 quotations from the Betus Latina Bible. Both have been microfilmed, and complete copies of the second are at the Catholic University in Washington and at the University of Notre Dame. Dissertations are now microfilmed by the majority of Ph.D.-granting universities, while *Dissertation Abstracts* incorporates summaries of many of them.

Foreign Activities

This review of past experience in microcopying has been largely confined to the domestic scene. Photocopying, however, is an international enterprise and some note should thus be taken of a few major foreign sources of microcopies in bulk.[26] The French Institut de Recherche et d'Histoire des Textes and the Belgian Commission Interuniversitaire du Microfilm both publish lists of films available, as does the Spanish Servicio Nacional de Microfilm. The Polish National Library has, since 1949, set up a central file of microfilm of valuable Polish collections on film and has issued a printed list since 1951.

The Arab League, through its Institute of Arab Manuscripts, has copied more than 15,000 manuscripts in a little more than 10 years. It is cataloguing collections not yet catalogued, and has published several catalogues for materials filmed. Less extensive is the filming by the University of Leiden of some 500 of its 15,000 western and oriental manuscripts, and the filming by the National Library of Hungary of its oriental manuscripts. The Italian government is said to have embarked on a large-scale program for microfilming manuscripts in order to preserve them. The National Library of Ireland has assembled Irish materials from most countries of Europe; the Union of South Africa is copying material relating to it in other countries including the United States; the government of India is copying Indian records located in England; and the Canadian National Archives, with a program similar to that of the Library of Congress, continues to assemble material from England and France.

The UNESCO Mobile Microfilm Unit has worked in Latin American and the Middle East. A duplicate negative of the Latin American films will be deposited with the History Commission of the Pan-American Institute of History and Geography which will publish lists and make copies on demand through its headquarters in Mexico City. The plan agreed upon in the Cultural Committee of the Council of Europe to microfilm unpublished finding-aids in member countries and exchange them on a demand basis has, unfortunately, not been fully carried out. As a guide to such world-wide activities UNESCO has begun the publication of a list of micro-editors (book publishers who also do micropublishing), libraries, societies, and institutions producing microforms.[27]

Although information on photocopying abroad is not easily obtained, it is clear that there has been a steady and large growth of such activities in the last decade.

Some Conclusions

As these examples of photocopying projects suggest, the number of items already copies (or being copied) in one form or another is incalculable.

Scholarly photocopying is the major preoccupation not only of countless technicians and of some commercial entrepreneurs, but of a number of archivists, librarians, and scholars as well. The history of their projects suggests some conclusions pertinent to any future projects or to any national plan for photocopying.

1. All types of material of American origin and certain kinds of non-American printed material (notably newspapers and government documents) have been extensively copied. Except for serials and rare books, much of this has been listed in one or another published bibliographical work. By contrast, foreign archival and manuscript material has been less satisfactorily covered and largely unrecorded. There is still much to be done to make material of all kinds more easily available through photocopying, but the need is greatest for foreign unprinted sources.

2. Projects should be carefully and completely planned in advance. Material should be selected and organized before any copying begins and no project should be considered finished until it has made the material copied available through adequate finding-aids. The copying of material which has already been copied, the accumulation of photocopies for which there are no finding-aids provided, and the large-scale copying of material for which users will be few and infrequent are clear wastes of resources of both men and money.

3. Adequate financing of programs is essential and more permanent financing is desirable. Except for government publications and certain periodicals, few large photocopying projects can pay their own way by the sale of the finished project. Moreover, the short-term financing of a number of projects—the fact that a lump sum has been provided for a limited number of years—has frequently led to hastily devised plans and uncompleted projects.

4. Greater coordination of information on photocopying projects—and, indeed, greater coordination of the projects themselves—is necessary. Bibliographic control, in the form of published guides, must be established over the major bodies of photocopied material—especially foreign manuscripts and archival records—in America. Only in this way can the community of scholars make the greatest use of photocopied material, and only in this way will wasteful duplication of effort and money be avoided.

5. There is a need for even greater involvement of working scholars themselves in copying projects. Like war, photocopying is too important a matter to be left to technical experts. Projects should involve, so far as possible, the close collaboration of individual scholars on a full-time basis and of representatives from learned societies with archivists, librarians, and technicians.

The history of scholarly photocopying over the last generation is one of trial and error and of mistakes honestly made, as well as of the collection of a great deal of useful material. New errors may be made, but there is no reason to repeat those of the past.

II. What Scholars Want

American scholars have never been loath to indicate their desires for material in microform. Either individually, through organized committees of scholarly associations, or in collaboration with libraries they have produced want lists in a number of different areas. In general, however, such lists have come into existence only in response to, or in anticipation of, some very specific need. In nature, scope, and value they vary considerably. A few examples should suffice to illustrate this diversity.

As a preliminary to the Association of Research Libraries' newspaper microfilming project operated by the Midwest Inter-Library Center, the Library of Congress prepared a working paper containing reasoned recommendations, on a priority basis, for some 1200 newspapers published in 170 countries and dependencies throughout the world. A list of Slavica, intended to fill a more or less general gap in American academic library holdings, was prepared by Fred S. Rodkey and executed by the Readex Microprint Corporation. An overall plan to secure early medical literature, both manuscript and printed, led to the preparation of something unique among lists, a notwant list. This was a microfilm record of what was already available in the Armed Forces Medical Library (now the National Library of Medicine) and taken abroad on a purchasing expedition by the then head of the Historical Division, so that he would know at a glance what not to buy.

The various *Short Title Catalogues* are good examples of prefabricated want lists for great numbers of books that are out-of-print. The heterogeneous list prepared by a committee for the American Council of Learned Societies' British Manuscript Project, using hundreds of suggestions received from many scholars, is an example of cooperative planning in an emergency. The numerous country lists, prepared in considerable detail over a longer period of time by the American Historical Association's Committee on Documentary Reproduction, together with the cost figures worked out, is an example of what the concentrated effort of specialists can produce. *Ad hoc* lists prepared, necessarily in haste, by scholars working against time as they searched vast quantities of captured German and Japanese documents that were scheduled for early return to the country of origin illustrate still another type.

More formal want lists, prepared in advance and ready for implementation as soon as money would be available for copying, likewise exist. In 1953 the Library of Congress published a *Selected List of United States Newspapers Recommended for Preservation by the ALA Committee on Cooperative Microfilm Projects*. Approximately 1000 titles, totaling an estimated 100,000,000 pages, were included. Two years later the same institution published a *List of Spanish Residencies in the Archives of the Indies, 1516-1775*, with the idea of furnishing a base on which cooperative microfilming programs by interested institutions in the United States could be planned and executed. In 1959 the Library of Congress published a list of Russian periodicals found in the Helsinki University Library and to a great extent not available in the United States. This work was part of the result of a study of catalogues of Slavica in European libraries conducted by the Library of Congress and the Joint Committee on Slavic Studies of the American Council of Learned Societies and the Social Science Research Council with funds provided by the Ford Foundation.

One of the most ambitious want lists was the proposal brought to the attention of the Library of Congress in 1955 to microfilm the combined resources of the Library of Congress, the National Library of Medicine, and the specialized collections in the Department of Agriculture Library, and to make the films available in one or more lending copies. A working paper showed that the cost of preparing a single negative on 35mm film of the holdings of the Library of Congress alone would generously exceed $60,000,000. Understandably, the project was not undertaken.

Want lists of finding-aids have also been provided. In 1952 the Library of Congress published a list of over 300 *Unpublished Bibliographical Tools in Certain Archives and Libraries of Europe*. Its compiler proposed a much more extensive and elaborate list in 1956.[28] Another and very extensive list of desirable finding-aids in Paul Kristeller's *Latin Manuscript Books before 1600, A List of the Printed Catalogues and Unpublished Inventories of Extant Collections* (New York, 1960).

It is unnecessary to extend the number of examples of previous want lists. They are numerous and diverse. They are also, on the whole, limited to rather specific areas of scholarly interest. To supply one less limited, and directed more specifically towards overall national planning for photocopying, a want list was compiled for the present report. It rests on interviews and correspondence with librarians and faculty members in 69 selected colleges and universities scattered across the country. For obvious reasons large universities with robust graduate programs predominate, but certain other institutions were also selected. The faculty members questioned were those in English, history, languages, and (where possible) those in art history, musicology, and certain area studies programs. Their views, it was felt, would be representative of the desires of the principal scholarly users of photocopied material. The categories of material (which inevitably overlap in some cases) are listed in the order of priority, from those for which participants expressed the most desire to those for which they evinced the least.

Priorities of Material for Photocopying
Wanted by American Scholars

1. *Foreign Archival Materials*, especially those of Western and Southern Europe and of Latin America.

2. *Out of Print Works*, particularly reference books, collected sets, and literary and classical texts.
3. *Periodicals*, with emphasis on general and foreign periodicals of the eighteenth and nineteenth centuries.
4. *Newspapers*, principally pre-1900.
5. *Manuscripts and Codices*, especially English and French.
6. *Finding-Aids*, primarily those to archives and manuscript collections, whether published or unpublished.
7. *Personal Papers*, especially English and French, and of intellectuals as well as of office holders.
8. *Russian Material*, Czarist and Soviet alike, with emphasis on reference works and official publications.
9. *Publications of Academics and Societies*.
10. *Musicological Material*, such as autograph scores and libretti.
11. *Dissertations and Theses*, particularly from European institutions.
12. *Pamphlets*, such as the Thomason Tracts or those on the French Revolution in the Bibliotheque Nationale.
13. *Drama Material*, such as unpublished plays and theater archives.
14. *Drawings*, architectural and artistic.
15. *Parliamentary Papers*, principally Western European.
16. *Asiatic Material*, with emphasis on periodicals and government documents.
17. *Legal Material*, such as session laws, Central and Eastern European codes.
18. *Africana*, particularly archival material, government publications, and newspapers.
19. *Local American Directories and Guides*.
20. *Graphic Art Finding-Aids*.

Taken collectively, American scholars seem to want everything copied. As this list shows, however, their main desires are for material which is unpublished, rare, or foreign. The primacy of foreign archival material and the high places of foreign collections of manuscripts and personal papers (together with their guides) suggest that American scholars see the bringing of the resources of the Old World to the New as the principal role for scholarly photocopying. The emphasis on foreign material in periodicals and newspapers, the high place of out-of-print works (including incunabula and classical texts), and the surprisingly high priority for musical material bear this out. That Russian material is in such demand may be due to its being singled out in the questionnaire, though it undoubtedly also reflects the contemporary interest in Russian studies in the United States. Conversely, the much lower priorities for Asian and African material, which were also specifically asked about, probably shows nothing more than that scholars in these fields are relatively fewer than in others. The relatively low places of parliamentary debates and legal material—both of which are largely in print—suggests that the photocopyists of such material are already doing the job well enough.

Any want list is bound to be selective and open to debate. The above is no exception. Moreover, like most want lists, it takes no account of the practical difficulties presented by copyright laws, by institutional (or governmental) reluctance to destroy the uniqueness of their collections, or by the costs of photocopying in relation to the material's probable use. But, in spite of all qualifications, the size and diversity of scholarly demand indicated by the above list suggests both an awareness of the potentialities of scholarly photocopying and the need for its better coördination.

III. Towards a National Program

Photocopying in America must now come of age. In the last thirty years it has grown from a virtual novelty to a major instrument for the collection of scholarly resources in great quantities. It promises to grow even larger and more rapidly in the future. However, the great expectations and splendid zeal of its pioneers have produced mixed results. The happy dream that "the whole archives of a nation might be packed away in a snuff box"[29] has not, of course, been fulfilled. But even less hyperbolic hopes have been disappointed. The plain truth is that we have accumulated scattered, incomplete, and almost random collections to which there are few guides and of which there is insufficient use. Like the comic hero, photocopying has ridden madly off in all directions; if dissipation of resources is not to continue it must now be systematically ordered.

American experience with scholarly photocopying has made certain essential requirements quite clear.

There is, first, an obvious need for much greater coördination of what is copied by different organizations and institutions. Even though satisfying or profitable for the undertakers, it is difficult to see how scholarship is served by having the same American public documents available in both microfilm and micro-opaque forms, or by having new, commercial photocopies made of material copied nearly twenty years ago in the American Council of Learned Societies' British Manuscript Project, or by having first the Library of Congress, then a state university, and finally the same state's historical society—each known to the others—copy the same archives. Such duplication in the past was understandable, if regrettable. But it is a luxury in which humanistic scholars, to whom financial resources are not easily available, can ill afford to indulge in the future. Coordination is needed not only to avoid duplication of effort but to concentrate resources on projects of genuine and general value to American scholars.

Second it is essential that bibliographic control be maintained over the material copied. This has already been the subject of a separate report,[30] whose recommendations should be better known and more widely followed, but it needs reiteration here. Without better knowledge of what is already available, the coördination of photocopying enterprises is difficult, and duplication of effort will continue. In addition, until scholars can obtain such information more rapidly, the full potentialities of photocopied material will not be realized. It is not enough just to make photocopies. The material copied must be recorded in published bibliographies and, where necessary, equipped with more detailed finding-aids so as to make it truly useful for American scholarship.

Third, it is clear that the problems involved in scholarly photocopying are not equally serious for all kinds of material copied. The area in which the need for both coördination and bibliographical control is most critical is in the reproduction of archival and manuscript materials, particularly those abroad. Printed works—whether books, newspapers, or public documents—are by their nature multiple; few indeed are those which cannot be found somewhere in America. But unprinted public records and personal manuscripts are unique, and those most wanted are outside the United States. In addition, though it is far from complete, a fair degree of bibliographical control has already been attained over photocopies of printed works through the National Union Catalogue, the Microfilm Clearing House, and such published works as *Newspapers on Microfilm*. Such control over photocopies of unprinted works is, by contrast, almost nonexistent. The problems of copying manuscript and archival material lie at the heart of the photocopying tangle; their solution would do more than anything else to make photocopying the true servant of scholars.

Above all, of course, it is necessary that there be a national plan for scholarly photocopying in the areas in which the problems are greatest. Neither expressions of concern nor statements of general desire are, by themselves, enough. What is wanted is a workable program capable of enlisting the support and cooperation of scholars, librarians, and foundations. This is not a wholly new proposal: something like it was urged at least a dozen years ago.[31] Nor is it unprecedented, for it is in many ways an enlargement of the kind of planning and cooperation that has gone on for many years among libraries and within some scholarly organizations. What is new is the urgency.

A detailed national program cannot be fashioned quickly. The range of interests involved and the need to achieve a reasonable consensus of views preclude this. But against the background of the history of photocopying, the desires of American scholars, and the problems in obvious need of solution, it is possible to formulate the criteria which should guide such a plan and to recommend the main features and general machinery for its operation.

Criteria

It should be recognized at the outset that no national plan can satisfy the wants of all scholars. Those wants are so numerous and so diverse that any national program directed to ¦satisfying the individual research needs of the individual scholar is bound to fail. The underlying criterion of national planning—and of future photocopying projects themselves—must be the usefulness of the material copied to the largest possible number of American scholars. There is, for example, no doubt that the desires of several American scholars could be met by microfilming the thousands of friendly society rules in the British Public Record Office. The cost and labor involved, however, would be incommensurate with the results in comparison with the number of scholars who would be served by copying a like amount of British or French diplomatic records. There is, unfortunately, no easy way to reckon the intrinsic research value of a collection, and no way at all to foresee which of today's scholarly frontiers will become the settled land of tomorrow. The individual researcher should still be able to obtain the smaller grants needed to meet his individual research needs. But for large-scale projects the rule must be the greatest good of the greatest number. This will not produce universal happiness, but it should prevent widespread disappointment.

At the same time that we recognize usefulness as the criterion for planning, we must keep in mind certain other practicalities. For one, photocopying can be deceptively inexpensive: in the wish to obtain great quantities of rare or unique material at what seem bargain-basement prices, the full costs of copying projects have too often been overlooked or underestimated. These are not limited to the mere repetitive and mechanical pressing of the shutter-control of a camera, but include in addition the training of competent personnel, the selection and arrangement of the materials to be copied, the preparation of precisely-worded "targets" to be copied with the materials so as to identify them accurately, and—later—the preparation and publication of catalogues and guides to the copied material. Because of failure to take these costs into consideration, photocopying projects have too often been undertaken naively or left uncompleted—or both. In the financing of future programs more emphasis should be given to long-term, continuous, and complete projects in which the disastrous results of haste can be minimized. In addition, it is a simple fact, all too frequently ignored, that not all that should be ideally copied is really available for copying. Owners of rare or unique works and directors of archives or manuscript repositories—particularly abroad—are often unwilling to permit their treasures to be copied. Want lists can represent an ideal. Projects, and any national program, must be guided by an appreciation of what is realistically possible.

Finally, it must be recognized that scholarly photocopying presents problems (and potential blessings) not only to scholars or librarians, or foundations or government, but to all these. The machinery for a national photocopying program must, thus, involve the collaboration of all four. National planning must possess a breadth of vision capable of transcending the parochialism of individual disciplines and of different professions.

Recommendations

The needs of scholarly photocopying rehearsed above and the suggested criteria for a national photocopying program lead to the following proposals:

1. *There should be established at the earliest opportunity a national committee on the photocopying of foreign manuscript and archival material needed by American scholars.* The committee should provide national leadership in this area and assist in the correlation of scholarly wants, available funds, and satisfactory bibliographical control. It should formulate overall national policies, discuss and sanction proposed projects, seek the active cooperation of foundations in the allocation of resources to worthwhile photocopying ventures, oversee the work of the proposed national foreign copying center, and, through that center, several national bibliographical centers, of material copied. The committee's membership should be composed of the chief executive officers (or other representatives) of such organizations as the American Council of Learned Societies, the Social Science Research Council, the Association of Research Libraries, the Society of American Archivists, the American Association for State and Local History, and the National Historical Publications Commission, together with the Librarian of Congress. It is contemplated that such a committee might have an existence independent of the sponsoring agencies, yet reporting to them. To initiate the committee, a joint invitation might be addressed to the others by the organizations which participated in the planning of the present inquiry.

2. *There should be established as soon as possible a national foreign copying center to coördinate projects engaged in the photocopying of foreign archival records and manuscripts, along with the unpublished guides to their use.* The center should operate under the guidance of the national committee mentioned above, for which it should also serve as a secretariat. It should work closely with the committees or sub-committees on photocopying of the various learned societies in formulating priorities of research needs, and, through contact with foreign libraries and archives, assist American scholars in learning what realistically is available for photocopying. In addition, it should cooperate with the National Union Catalogue of Manuscript Collections and the Microfilm Clearing House to assure more adequate reporting of previous and current photocopying enterprises.[32] The initial establishment of such a center will undoubtedly

require foundation support, though, in time, the center should be made permanent and receive permanent financing.

3. *Each learned society concerned with unpublished source material in photocopy should appoint a permanent working committee (or subcommittee of an existing committee on research needs) to evolve a set of realistic priorities for photocopying in its field.* Each committee should cooperate with the national foreign copying center in developing its priorities and in determining the feasibility of copying desired material, and, through the national committee, should relate its wants to those of other disciplines and to the probable sources and extent of funds.

4. *Foundations should insist that any photocopying projects they underwrite should be thoroughly planned in advance, should demonstrate the utility to large numbers of American scholars of the material to be copied, should be satisfactorily coördinated with other projects (past or present), and should involve the adequate reporting of the material copied.* Foundations should be able to call upon the proposed national committee, the proposed national foreign copying center, and the other central agencies involved in scholarly photocopying for advice on specific project proposals. Foundations should also give serious consideration to the permanent financing of select photocopying programs.

5. *The work of the principal centers for external bibliographical control of microforms should be given the full support of scholars, librarians, and foundations.* The Microfilm Clearing House should be regarded as the reporting center for photocopies of published material and of current projects; the National Union Catalogue of Manuscript Collections, as the reporting center for photocopies of manuscript material. Each should cooperate with the proposed national committee and national foreign copying center in devising techniques for more effective dissemination of information on existing photocopies and for more certain reporting of future photocopies.

In terms of machinery, what is thus envisioned will be neither elaborate nor inordinately expensive: a national committee to provide leadership, a national foreign copying center to coördinate projects in the most crucial area, organized groups of scholars to suggest scholarly needs, cooperative foundations, and better-supported bibliographical centers. No machinery can solve the problems of scholarly photocopying overnight. But, given the cooperation of those involved, the agencies proposed above can ultimately bring order to the present chaos and help make the scholar the master of his resources.[33]

References

1. Ed. Hale, Jr., Richard W. (Ithaca, N.Y.: Cornell University Press for American Historical Association, 1961).

2. Dr. William S. Dix for the Association of Research Libraries, Dr. Boyd C. Shafer for the American Historical Association, and Dr. George Winchester Stone, Jr., for the Modern Language Association.

3. Dr. Waldo G. Leland, Director Emeritus of the American Council of Learned Societies, Chairman; Dr. W. Kaye Lamb, Dominion Archivist and National Librarian of Canada; Dr. Stephen A. McCarthy, Librarian of Cornell University; Boyd C. Shafer, Executive Secretary of the American Historical Association; Dr. George Winchester Stone, Jr., Executive Secretary of the Modern Language Association of America; and Dr. Louis B. Wright, Director of the Folger Shakespeare Library.

4. "Photocopying" as used in this report refers principally to micro-transparencies and micro-opaques; other photoduplication processes are involved only incidentally.

5. Wilson, William J., "A Plan for a Comprehensive Medico-Historical Library: Problems of Scope and Coverage," *Library Quarterly*, XXI (October 1951), 249.

6. An exception is Grace Gardner Griffin. *A Guide to Manuscripts Relating to American History in British Depositories Reproduced for the Division of Manuscripts of the Library of Congress* (Washington, D.C., 1946). This work includes the Project A material together with the transcripts which preceded Project A and other microfilming which followed it.

7. *A Guide to the Microfilm Collection of Early State Records*, comp. William Sumner Jenkins, ed. Lillian A. Hamrick (Washington, D.C., 1950), and *Supplement* (Washington, D.C., 1951).

8. Boyd, Julian P., "A New Guide to the Indispensable Sources of Virginia History," *William and Mary Quarterly*, 3rd ser., XV (January 1958), 5.

9. *Preliminary Guide to the Microfilm Collection in the Bancroft Library*, comp. Mary Ann Fisher (Berkeley, Calif., 1955).

10. Sontag, Raymond J. "The German Diplomatic Papers: Publication After Two World Wars," *American Historical Review*, LXVIII (October 1962), 63-68, both explains and criticizes the program.

11. United States, Department of State, Historical Office, *A Catalogue of Files and Microfilms of the German Foreign Ministry Archives, 1920-1945*, comp. and ed. George O. Kent (Stanford, Calif., 1962).

12. *Guides to German Records Microfilmed at Alexandria, Va.* (Washington, 1958-). To date 37 guides have appeared.

13. *A Catalogue of Files and Microfilms of the German Foreign Ministry Archives, 1867-1920* (Washington, D. C., 1959).

14. Guides to these are: Uyehara H. Cecil, comp., *Check-list of Archives in the Japanese Ministry of Foreign Affairs, Tokyo, Japan, 1868-1945, Microfilmed for the Library of Congress, 1949-1951* (Washington, D.C., 1954); John Young, comp., *Checklist of Microfilm Reproductions of Selected Archives of the Japanese Army, Navy, and Other Government Agencies, 1868-1945* (Washington, D.C., 1959).

15. *List of National Archives Microfilm Publications* (Washington, D.C., 1961), pp. 211-218. For a résumé of archival microfilming activities in the states, see Dorothy K. Taylor, "State Microfilming Programs," *American Archivist*, XXII (January 1959), 59-82.

16. The papers of 11 Presidents have so far been filmed; the printed indexes for 9 are available.

17. "Reproductions of Manuscripts and Rare Printed Books," *PMLA*, LXV (April 1950), 289-338, lists material copied to 1 January 1950.

18. *British Manuscripts Project: A Checklist of the Microfilms Prepared in England and Wales for the American Council of Learned Societies, 1941-1945*, comp. Lester K. Born (Washington, D.C., 1955).

19. Since 1957 lists of material copies have appeared in *Manuscripta*.

20. *Checklist of Manuscripts in the Libraries of the Greek and Armenian Patriarchates in Jerusalem, Microfilmed for the Library of Congress, 1949-50* (Washington, D.C., 1953); *Checklist of Manuscripts in St. Catherine's Monastery, Mount Sinai, Microfilmed for the Library of Congress, 1950* (Washington, D.C., 1952); *A Descriptive Checklist of Selected Manuscripts in the Monasteries of Mount Athos Microfilmed for the Library of Congress and the International Greek New Testament Project 1952-1953* . . . comp. Ernest W. Saunders (Washington, D.C., 1957).

21. All commercial photocopyists issue catalogues or sales lists. Convenient summaries are in the *Guide to Microforms in Print* (Washington, D.C., 1961) and the *Subject Guide to Microforms in Print, 1962-63* (Washington, D.C., 1962), both edited by Albert James Diaz and published by Microcard Editions, Inc.

22. The *Bulletin*, in turn, is an irregular appendix to the Library of Congress *Information Bulletin*. To date over 80 numbers have appeared, covering a wide range of photocopied material.

23. Tilton, Eva M., *A Union List of Publications in Opaque Microforms* (New York, 1959) and *Supplement* (New York, 1961) provide the widest coverage of micro-opaques.

24. *Jewish Newspapers and Periodicals on Microfilm, Available at the American Jewish Periodical Center* (Cincinnati, Ohio, 1957); *Supplement* (Cincinnati, Ohio, 1960).

25. *List of Latin American Imprints Before 1800, Selected from Bibliographies of Jose Toribio Medina, Microfilmed by Brown University* (Providence, R.I., 1952).

26. The *UNESCO Bulletin for Libraries* is the most useful source for information on photocopying activities abroad.

27. "List of Micro-Publishers," *UNESCO Bulletin for Libraries*, XVI (July-August 1962), 198-205

28. Born, Lester K., "Universal Guide to Catalogs of Manuscripts and Inventories of Archival Collections: A Proposal for Cooperative Listing," *College and Research Libraries*, XVII (July 1956), 322-329.

29. *Photographic News*, 1859, quoted in Frederic Luther, *Microfilm, A History, 1839-1900* (Annapolis, Md., 1959), p. 23.

30. Simonton, Wesley, "The Bibliographical Control of Microforms," *Library Resources and Technical Services*, VI (Winter 1962), 29-40.

31. Born, Lester K., "A National Plan for Extensive Microfilm Operations," *American Documentation*, I (April 1950), 66-75.

32. Since the inception of the present study the need for such a center has been emphasized by a Conference on Copying European Manuscript Sources for American History held in April 1961. The Conference recommended the establishment of a center at the Library of Congress. An advisory committee has since elaborated certain of such a center's functions and operations in greater detail.

33. The preparation of the present report and its distribution were made possible by a grant to the American Council of Learned Societies from the Council on Library Resources, Inc.

ADDITIONAL READINGS

Bernhardt, Homer I., *An Overview of Microforms: A Report on the Role of Microforms in the University of Pittsburgh Libraries*. Pittsburgh: University of Pittsburgh, Graduate School of Library and Information Sciences, 1972. 34p.

Crawford, Franklin D., *The Microfilm Technology Primer on Scholarly Journals*. Princeton, N.J.: Princeton Microfilm Corp., 1969. 32p. (free).

Gaddy, Dale, *A Microform Handbook*. Silver Springs, Md.: National Microfilm Association, 1974. 116p.

Luther, Frederick. *Microfilm: A History, 1839-1900*. Annapolis, Md.: National Microfilm Association, 1959. (Out-of-print but available on 35mm microfilm from the Frederick Luther Co., Indianapolis, Inc.).

National Microfilm Association, *Glossary of Micrographics*. Silver Springs, Md.: National Microfilm Association, 1971. (MS100-1971) 72p.

National Microfilm Association, *Introduction to Micrographics*. Silver Springs, Md.: National Microfilm Association, 1973. 28p.

Nemeyer, Carol A., *Scholarly Reprint Publishing in the United States*. New York: Bowker, 1972. 262p.

Spigai, Frances G., *The State of the Art of Microform and a Guide to the Literature*. March, 1973. ERIC ED 75 029. 31p.

Veaner, Allen B., "Reprography and Microform Technology," *Annual Review of Information Science and Technology*, 4:175-201 (1969).

Veaner, Allen B., "Micropublication," *Advances in Librarianship*, 2:165-86 (1971).

Veenstra, John G., "Microimages and the Library," *Library Journal*, 95:3443-7 (October 15, 1970).

Veit, F., "Microforms, Microform Equipment, and Microform Use in the Educational Environment," *Library Trends*, 19:447-66 (April 1971).

Williams, Bernard J.S., *Miniaturized Communications: A Review of Microforms*. London: The Library Association, 1970. 190p.

ORGANIZING THE MICROFORM COLLECTION

ACQUISITIONS

Introduction

Persons involved in acquisitions are fortunate in having available to them a work specifically addressed to the buying of microforms. This is Allen Veaner's, *The Evaluation of Micropublications*,[1] which in some fifty odd pages presents comprehensive background information on microforms and micropublishing and then goes on to give evaluation procedures.

Another major tool for acquisitions librarians is the quarterly journal, *Microform Review*,[2] which began publication in 1972. A typical issue contains several articles dealing with microforms, reviews of micropublications, previews of forthcoming publications, and a clearinghouse, or listing, of recent microform projects. Reviews deal primarily with content but technical aspects are also considered and are followed by a "Microform Evaluation" which gives specifics such as format, quantity, film type, reduction ratio, polarity, external finding aids, internal finding aids, sequence, and replacement policy.

In selecting the material that follows an attempt has been made to complement Veaner's recommendations which, even if followed minimally, will require intellectual, financial, and technical evaluations that go beyond the traditional functions of an acquisitions department, especially with respect to evaluations based on laboratory tests.

The Gregory article provides general guidelines and follows a premise that "No library has the staff time to check incoming microforms"—a view in opposition to Veaner's which is that librarians *must* take the time and trouble. This does not necessarily mean there is disagreement but rather that Veaner offers an optimum view while Gregory offers guidelines based on limited staff/funds/time.

The California State University and Colleges, *Criteria for Procurement,* a first of its kind, goes beyond general guidelines to specifics governing the purchase of both equipment and publications, putting the burden on the micropublisher by requiring that he guarantee various aspects of the publication and its indexing. In addition, certain microforms are to be phased out (16mm, micro-opaques) and others avoided (ultrafiche).

My own essay is a bibliographical review of sources of information about micropublications.

Veaner's work and the articles in this section will expose readers to various approaches to the acquisition of microforms and hopefully will help them develop their own procedures and requirements.

References

1. Veaner, Allen B., *The Evaluation of Micropublications*. Chicago: American Library Association, 1971. (LTP Publication No. 17. 59p.)
2. *Microform Review*, P.O. Box 1297, Weston, Conn. 06880.

ACQUISITION
OF MICROFORMS

by Roma S. Gregory

Since microfilm first appeared on the library scene, it and its relatives have been hailed as everything from salvation to damnation by librarians and users alike. They save space and are inexpensive; they require expensive equipment and are an eye-straining nuisance to the user. Acquisitions librarians attempting a satisfactory compromise must perfect a balancing act that would bring a green glint of envy to the eye of an accomplished acrobat.

But why get it at all in this day of the ubiquitous copying machine and the gratifying increase of reprint publications? Librarians are thoroughly familiar with the rewards available in low cost acquisition and storage. The user is not impressed. He can occasionally resign himself to a microform if it is pointed out to him that paper prints can easily be made from

Reprinted from *Library Trends*, 18: 373-80 (January 1970) by permission of the publisher. Copyright © 1970 by the University of Illinois.

transparencies and that the Xerox Corporation has recently developed a copier-enlarger which will print from opaque microforms. Further, the national, not to say international, sores of microform reproductions make acquisition increasingly quick and easy. Low cost can sometimes be palatably presented as a means of broadening acquisition capability. The reluctant user can also see some point in acquiring, or even producing, microforms as reserve or back-up copies of valuable, fragile or vulnerable publications. Even in the face of the completely obstinate user, the librarian must sometimes decide to acquire microforms of particularly vulnerable or very seldom-used material. To date no one has reported the removal of pages from a microfilm. And, finally, microform provides a means by which reproductions of manuscripts, early American imprints, rare legislative reports, and other unique or unobtainable items may be obtained.

Types of Materials Available

Any copyable publication or manuscript can be acquired in microform. But in spite of recent advertisements to the contrary, few libraries want everything in miniprint. There are some very bulky publications, printed originally on poor paper, consulted seldom but of vital importance to research collections which come easily to the attention of acquisitions librarians. Among these are newspapers, journals and government documents. Libraries collecting large numbers of U.S. government-supported research reports can acquire them on microfiche through the ERIC (Educational Resources Information Center), and the Clearinghouse for Federal Scientific and Technical Information.

These and dissertations, many of them no longer available on interlibrary loan, are available on microfilm either from University Microfilms or from the library having the original copy.

In selected cases "binding" copies of journals can be acquired on microfilm. It must be noted here that almost always these must be second copies, since publishers understandably require that libraries subscribe to the original publication. There is also a considerable lag (up to six months) in the production on a journal volume on film.

Certain of the large producers have developed microform projects by which new libraries or libraries developing retrospective research collections can acquire large quantities of publications in microform. Usually these are based on well-known standard bibliographies.

The Formats

It is not the purpose of this paper to explore the technical aspects of either the formats or the equipment required for reading and storing microform. The acquisitions librarian, however, must know enough about them and their differences to make intelligent choices or to recommend the acquisition of necessary equipment if a new format is vital to a collection. Having decided *for* some variety of microform, perhaps in spite of the availability of reprints, the next set of decisions involves the specific form to be chosen.

Some publications have been reproduced in more than one microform with reduction ratios of 15:1 to 25:1. The availability of reading (or enlarging) equipment needed for use may determine the format although most research libraries find it necessary to own equipment capable of accommodating all of the formats. Comparatively small amounts of space are required to store microforms, but seldom can they be satisfactorily housed on book shelves. Most of the formats call for specially designed storage units. An important point to bear in mind is the cost of this equipment; it can cut sharply into the money saved by the low cost of the microforms themselves.

The 1969 edition of *Guide to Microforms in Print* lists ten different transparent or opaque formats. The transparencies include rolls of microfilm in either 16 m.m. or 35 m.m. sizes and microfiche (a sheet of microfilm) in several sets of dimensions. Sizes appear to have been standardized, at least for the moment, on 35 m.m. for roll microfilm and four by six inches for microfiche. A relative newcomer to the transparent scene is the PCMI (photochromic microimage) ultra-high reduction process which uses a reduction ratio of 200:1. One publisher, Encyclopedia Britannica, Inc., has already announced a series of subject collections to be available on four by six inch ultramicrofiche beginning in the fall of 1970. A different breed of readers and reader-printers will have to be used. Theoretically the transparencies may be available in either negative (white print on dark background) or positive (dark print on white background) film. In practice, and if no specification is made, libraries usually receive positive film, especially from commercial producers. The opaque forms are represented by four sizes: three by five inches, six by nine inches, five by eight inches, and four by six inches.

Selection

There are no selection guides for micropublications.[1] The editor of *Choice* has promised microform reviews and hopes that they "will provide a sense of sanity in a confusing field of acquisition."[2] *These reviews will, of necessity, be primarily concerned with the technological reproduction of publications already reviewed for literary content, authority, scope, etc. As Veaner points out in an admirable list of "Criteria for Evaluation,"[3] there is more to it than technology. The producer has copied the original publication, using, perhaps, more than one copy of the original in pursuit of perfection. The prospective buyer of the micro-publication is concerned with the success of the producer's work, including fidelity to the original, the identity of the original and the standards used to control the quality of the product.

Another very important consideration, particularly where a bulk of publication is involved, is the control which provides access to the photographed material. Some of the publishers have arranged for sets of catalog cards, others for printed indexes or bibliographies, still others depend on existing indexes or bibliographies. These are external controls and at least have the advantage of being readable by the naked eye although the quality of them varies widely. Those systems or projects which include internal controls or controls also in microform are less satisfactory for the user who, on the whole, resents having to use a reader for any part of his work.

Where no review or evaluation can be located, the prospective buyer can insist that the publisher cite the technological standards he has maintained, such as those of the United States of American Standards Institute.[4] If his prospectus or catalogs do not make any statement regarding production standards, inquiries are in order. No library has the staff time to check incoming microforms, not to say periodic checks on the state of preservation of earlier purchases.

Since new micropublishing projects abound, as do young and rapidly developing libraries, there is enormous temptation in the "comprehensive" microform subject collections. These represent, at least theoretically, publications long out of print and probably not heavily in demand. If the project is based on a standard and well-known bibliography such as the Readex Microprint Corporation's effort to photograph every publication listed in Charles Evans' *American Bibliography*, a library feels relatively safe in indulging. But what of the new and unknown company proposing to supply thousands of volumes of classics at relatively low cost per volume? It sounds good; the prospectus glows but lacks a few basic facts. To whom does the wary acquisitions librarian turn for advice?

The American Library Association in 1958 established the Micropublishing Projects Subcommittee of the RTSD Resources Committee† to serve as a coordinating agency for both libraries and publishers of microforms,

---

* EDITOR'S NOTE: At the time this article was written neither *The Evaluation of Micropublications* nor *Microform Review* had been published.
† EDITOR'S NOTE: This is now the Micropublishing Projects Committee, Resources Section, Resources and Technical Services Division, ALA.

to advise on the desirability of proposed publishing projects, to recommend micropublishing projects and to keep an eye on the quality of the photography and the bibliographic controls. An acquisitions librarian with serious doubts about a purchase under consideration may address an inquiry to the Subcommittee. He may also recommend it for review in *Choice.*

The Sources

It would be convenient indeed, if purchase orders for microforms could be enclosed in the same envelope with the purchase orders for books. To date few such possibilities exist; indeed, there are not even jobbers who will take on all of the microforms. The acquisitions librarian must go to the producers and these are many. Often one must locate a copy of the publication needed and order a microfilm from the owning library. Since a large number of books and journals have already been copied by commercial microform producers, however, it is easiest to try these sources first.

Although there are various union lists and continuing effort is producing more and better central controls, no microform acquisition program can do without a file of publishers' or producers' catalogs. The list of more than fifty publishers represented in *Guide to Microforms in Print* is an excellent one although it includes only American producers and not all of them. Acquisitions librarians are well advised to send for the catalogs of these publishers and request representation on their mailing lists.

The catalogs must be carefully read. A producer may make a blanket statement about incomplete runs of a journal rather than list the exact contents for each title. If excessively brief bibliographic listings are given, inquiries may be necessary. Occasionally a producer does not list prices. The reasons can be several including a "not yet published" status or requirement of the owner of the original that individual permission to reproduce be given.

Foreign sources are not so easy to identify* but methodical perusal of lists of new publications in library journals often brings to light new sources and lists. Foreign book and serials dealers will occasionally acquire microforms for regular customers. If they are unable to supply, they are good about referring purchasers to a better source.

Since the bulk of the material required by American research libraries is already in at least one American library, a copy of *Directory of Library Photoduplication Services* is indispensable. This handbook, used in conjunction with *National Register of Microform Masters* and the *National Union Catalog*, often turns up either a microform master or a copy of the publication which can be photographed.

*EDITOR'S NOTE: Foreign micropublications are listed in a new annual, *International Microforms in Print, 1974/75-*, available from Microform Review Inc.

It is incorrect, however, to leap to the conclusion that copying automatically follows location of the publication. Copying processes are hard on books and an owner may consider that his book is too fragile or too tightly bound to be copyable. Or he may simply want to preserve its uniqueness. In the case of exceptionably valuable materials not available on interlibrary loan and owned by a library without copying equipment, once again a prospective purchaser must do without.

If the owner is willing to have his book photographed and does not have the equipment to make the copy, an acquisitive library has three choices: 1) it can arrange to borrow the book on interlibrary loan, with permission to copy clearly given, and make its own copy, 2) it can place a purchase order with a commercial firm such as University Microfilms or MicroPhoto, informing them of the location of the book, or, 3) it can request the aid of a research library with photoduplication facilities and also near the owner of the publication.

Acquisitions Procedures

Placement of orders for microcopies can be done in several ways. It is not unusual for correspondence, perhaps between interlibrary loan librarians, to precede preparation of a purchase order. It may take place when an original to be copied is sought. Appeal to the National Union Catalog division of the Library of Congress for help in locating a copy, assuming one cannot be found in a nearer source, is quite in order. Since copies of publications are often sent in lieu of originals, microforms may be acquired through interlibrary loan, either on the standard "Interlibrary Photoduplication Order Form." Both of these ALA designed forms are available from library supply firms. Acquisitions librarians will probably prefer their own purchase order forms. Some libraries with large photoduplication departments such as the Library of Congress or the Library of the British Museum, have work order forms which they request purchasing libraries to use. Their use does not preclude the preparation of the purchaser's own purchase order.

Whatever form is used, the supplier must be told what format (if there is a choice) is expected and, in the case of transparencies, whether a negative or positive is wanted. For the most part, unless a negative is specified, a positive will be supplied. If the publication has never before been photographed, the purchaser requesting a positive may have to bear the cost of two films but probably will receive only the requested positive. Commercial firms accumulating a bank of negatives usually do not charge for the negative. Publications listed for sale in a producer's catalog are made from master negatives which are retained by the owner. If the purchaser insists on a negative, as he may if he wants to make prints, he will probably get a third generation copy, which may lack clarity since there is some loss in definition as copying moves further from the original.

Every acquisitions librarian is familiar with the anxious user who, suffering from the conviction that librarians do not really understand the exquisite proportions of research, have indulged in lengthy and detailed correspondence with the owner of an obscure manuscript or set of a rare journal. Indeed, the librarian may only be handed the bill to pay—or even be asked to arrange for reimbursement of the scholar who has not dared to trust. This is not all bad, especially if the owner of the publication is a private individual or a very small and special foreign library not yet caught up in the clutches of mass-produced collections. Careful and painstaking correspondence, preferably in the language of the owner, is sometimes the only way to successful acquisition. Faculty members ready and able to write, giving the detailed explanation of his research, as is sometimes required, are to be welcomed by the acquisitions librarian. Presentation of an American purchase order form, most especially one of the nasty little three by five inch multiple forms with cryptic abbreviations and incomprehensible directions, if unaccompanied and unheralded by appropriately respectful correspondence, is quite likely to be ignored. Sometimes, after agonizing delay, a letter of inquiry will result reflecting puzzlement and a degree of indignation which could have been avoided by a little diplomacy.

This kind of purchase may require prepayment, or sometimes American publications are specified as payment. The invoices may be presented by a commercial firm to which the copying work has been given and it may be especially difficult to relate the invoice to the product.

If the scholar does bring to the acquisitions librarian a citation in a 1912 journal to a manuscript held in a library which was destroyed in 1942, tracking down the manuscript (which may very well have been saved) can be an interesting task. Getting it photographed, once it is located, is another challenge. Appeal to a large research library in the country of the owner may be extremely helpful and is usually more successful than an arrangement made by the purchaser with a commercial firm.

In the course of correspondence with owning libraries to discuss ways and means of having a copy made, a precise cost quotation may be requested and given, prepayment may be required, or the purchasing library may be specifically requested to pay only on receipt of an invoice.

The correspondence may also bring out facts about the condition of the original publication which would make a copy unsatisfactory, or at least not of high quality. This is often the case with very old books, tightly bound books, manuscripts and stained or otherwise damaged material. In this connection it is perhaps well to point out that, having been warned and having, in any case, ordered a "custom" job, the purchasing library may not return a copy or refuse to pay for it. Responsible craftsmen, either in library photoduplication departments or commercial firms may be expected to replace poor workmanship and, if there is any question about the reasons for poor work, inquiry should be made.

On occasion a library will want to acquire a copy of a publication protected by copyright. In the case of a commercial firm which offers the copy for sale, it may be assumed·that release from the copyright holder has been secured. If in doubt, however, inquire. Libraries asked to make copies either refuse or request the purchaser to get permission to copy.

Earlier mention has been made of microform projects, the big commercial productions coming out over a period of years and intended to supply basic research material not available or terribly space-consuming in the original. As in the case of subscriptions to periodicals in microform, standing orders may be placed for these or, if the project is completed, arrangements can be made to spread payments over a period of years.

Libraries with large photoduplication departments and correspondingly large resources, sometimes allow for deposit accounts. The Library of Congress does this and so does the Clearinghouse for Federal Scientific and Technical Information as well as other government-owned facilities. The advantages in this sort of financial arrangements do away with the necessity for time-consuming pursuit of price quotations and individual prepayments. Since microforms, especially those in lieu of interlibrary loan, often are quite inexpensive, considerable administrative cost can be saved with deposit accounts.

References

1. Veaner, Allen B. "Developments in Reproduction of Library Materials & Graphic Communication, 1967," *Library Resources and Technical Services*, 12: 205, Spring 1968.
2. Veaner, Allen B. "The Crisis in Micropublication," *Choice*, 5: 448, June 1968.
3. *Ibid.*, pp. 450-452.
4. Veaner, Allen B. "Microreproduction and Micropublication Technical Standards: What They Mean to You, the User," *Choice*, 5: 740, September 1968.

Additional References

Diaz, Albert. "Microreproduction Information Sources," *Library Resources and Technical Services*, 11: 211-14, Spring 1967.
Hays, David G. *A Billion Books for Education in America and the World: A Proposal.* Santa Monica, Calif., Rand Corp., 1968.
Scott Peter. "The Present and Future of Government Documents in Microform," *Library Trends*, 15: 72-86, July 1966.

MICROFORM INFORMATION SOURCES/PUBLICATIONS

by Albert Diaz

Information about publications available in microform can be found in sources that fall into six categories: (1) Combined lists/general (these list publications available from various publishers without regard to subject matter); (2) Combined lists/specialized (these, too, list publications available from various publishers but they are type (dissertations, newspapers) or subject (history, music, law, etc.) oriented; (3) Guides and union lists (guides list individual titles within microform projects or the holdings of a given library or collection and union lists enumerate the microform holdings of a number of libraries; (4) Report literature abstracting services (*Government Reports Abstracts, Research in Education*, etc.); (5) Announcement media (*Microform Clearinghouse Bulletin*, publishers' news-letters); (6) Catalogs. In addition, there are a number of sources that provide guidelines on how to buy micropublications.

Combined lists/general

The first attempt to list microfilms available from many sources was the *Union List of Microfilms* initiated in the spring of 1941 by the Philadelphia Bibliographic Center and Union Library Catalogue. The list was published in 1942 with *Supplements 1-5*, 1943-47, and was cumulated into the *Union List of Microfilms, Revised, Enlarged and Cumulative Edition, 1951*, followed by *Supplements 1949-52* and *1952-55*. There was then a final *Cumulation, 1949-59*, published by Edwards Brothers, Ann Arbor, Michigan, in 1961, which includes more than 52,000 entries representing microfilm accessions reported by 215 libraries in the United States and Canada from July 1, 1949, through July 31, 1959. It excluded newspapers, dissertations, and a number of specialized series such as the Vatican Manuscript Codices and limited itself to materials reproduced on roll microfilm. Although the *Union List* is now primarily of historical interest it is worth consulting when a search in the more current listings fails to turn up the desired title.

The first combined listing of micro-opaques (e.g., Microcard, Micro-print) was the *Union List of Publications in Opaque Microform*, compiled by Eva Maude Tilton and published by Scarecrow Press in 1959. There is a 1961 supplement and a 1964 revised edition. These are essentially listings in dictionary order or entries appearing in publishers' catalogs. Although obviously out of date, *Opaque Microforms* is still of value as it lists individual titles within large projects.

In 1961 Microcard Editions brought out the *Guide to Microforms in Print*, the first combined list of microform publications to include all methods of microreproduction. It is an annual, cumulative list, in alphabetic order, of materials which are available on microfilm, microfiche, and micro-opaques from publishers within the United States. Theses and dissertations are not included. It is not a union list but rather a list of publications offered for sale on a regular basis. This is an important distinction to keep in mind as it means that although non-profit micropublishers are not excluded per se, titles available from university libraries and similar institutions are apt not to be listed unless those titles are actively marketed by the institutions. In addition, the *Guide* concerns itself with titles as offered for sale so that large projects (e.g., all the works cited in Clark's, *Travels in the Old South*) are listed only under the name of the project—titles within projects are not listed unless the publisher markets and sells those titles on an individual basis. The information in the *Guide* is not taken from publishers' catalogs but rather is solicited from the publisher once a year. Publishers not responding are not included.

For each entry in the *Guide* the price is given, the publisher, and the method of microreproduction used. In the 1974 edition there were some 22,000 entries, the output of 108 publishers utilizing thirteen variations of the three basic microforms: roll microfilm, microfiche (including ultra-fiche), and micro-opaques.

The *Guide to Microforms* lists publications alphabetically by main entry. A companion volume, *Subject Guide to Microforms in Print*, appearing annually four to six months after the *Guide*, lists the same publications under broad subject classifications. Subject classifications are assigned by the publishers using a schedule based on that of the Library of Congress. A title is listed under only one classification.

As noted, the *Guide* limits itself to materials available from publishers in the United States. Works issued by foreign publishers are covered in *International Microforms in Print: A Guide to Microforms of Non-United States Micropublishers, 1974/75-* (Weston, Conn.: Microform Review Inc., 1974-)[1], a cumulative, alphabetic arrangement of monographs, journals, newspapers, government publications, and archival materials. As with the *Guide*, entries are accepted as submitted and cross references are mainly left up to the publishers. In the first issue, published in August, 1974, approximately 8100 titles from forty-one publishers are listed. Of the forty-one publishers, twenty-one are from the United Kingdom, nine from continental Europe, seven from Canada, two from Japan, and one each from Australia and Africa.

The most comprehensive listing of microforms is the non-cumulative, *National Register of Microform Masters*, issued in annual volumes by the Library of Congress. In the 1972 edition alone there are some 53,000 entries. The *Register* lists two categories of microforms: (1) Master microforms which is a microform used only to make copies and from which duplicate copies are available at a reasonable price; (2) Master preservation microforms which are master microforms housed in a temperature controlled, fireproof space and owned by a nonprofit institution. The *Register*, therefore, is not a union list of microforms—i.e., it does not list duplicate copies of microforms held by libraries nor does it include any microform that is used by a reader. It records masters that are retained *solely* for the purpose of making other copies.

Included are foreign and domestic books, serials, and foreign doctoral dissertations available from publishers in the United States and abroad. Excluded are technical reports, transcripts, translations, foreign or domestic archival materials, manuscript collections, U.S. doctoral dissertations, and masters' theses.

Monographs and serials are listed in one alphabetic sequence by main entry. A full heading is followed by an abbreviated title, imprint, and collation statements. Location of the microform master is given as are LC card numbers. Volumes do not cumulate previous volumes.

NRMM was first published in September, 1965, followed by another issue in January, 1966, and then by annual cumulations beginning with the 1966 edition. The 1969 edition supercedes and cumulates approximately 14,000 entries for *serials* included in all previous issues, but it contains no monographs. Initially the arrangement was extremely awkward as most titles were entered by LC or NUC card numbers which meant that two searches had to be made, the first to obtain the card number and the second in the *Register*. Beginning with the 1970 edition, titles are listed by main entry. For a number of reasons publication of the *Register* fell behind schedule so that at the beginning of 1974 the latest edition available was the one for 1970. During 1974, volumes for 1971 and 1972, and 1973, were published and it is expected that by 1975 the work will be current.

The *Register*, as are the other current, combined lists, is dependant upon information being supplied to it by holders of the microform masters. Unfortunately, according to a 1969 survey[2], only 165 of the ARL libraries responding were reporting their masters to *NRMM*. The same survey showed that 20 percent had never used the *Register* to search out-of-print titles and only 11 percent checked the *Register* before filming a title. According to a later study (1970/71), Reichmann and Tharpe's, *Bibliographic Control of Microforms* (Westport: Greenwood, 1972) of 174 libraries responding, 105 (60 percent) did not report to the

National Register, 40 reported regularly, 16 promised to begin reporting, and 13 report irregularly. In addition, "Quite a number did not know about the *Register* or did not understand its function; often the difference between the *Register* and the *National Union Catalog* was not clear" (p. 11).

Some important differences between the *Register* and the *Guide to Microforms* and *International Microforms* are as follows: (1) NRMM concerns itself with Microform masters; GM and IM do not; (2) NRMM is not cumulative; GM and IM are; (3) NRMM entries include LC card numbers; GM and IM entries do not; (4) NRMM entries are reviewed by a bibliographer; GM and IM entries are run as received; (5) NRMM contains cross references prepared by bibliographers; GM and IM use cross references supplied by publishers; (6) NRMM lists all microforms that meet the established criteria regardless of source, foreign or domestic, commercial or non-profit; GM limits itself to microform publications sold on a regular basis and thus excludes titles which are not actively marketed; IM lists titles from all sources but most publishers in the 1974-75 edition appear to be commercial; (7) NRMM does not give prices; GM and IM do; (8) NRMM does not list newspapers, archival materials, or manuscripts; GM and IM do; (9) Titles in GM and IM are being offered for sale; duplicate copies of titles in NRMM may or may not be available (e.g., a library may have filmed a copyrighted title for its own use under the fair use doctrine but will not make a duplicate for someone else without permission of the copyright owner).

While *Guide to Microforms, International Microforms,* and the *National Register of Microform Masters*, are the primary, combined lists for microform titles, it should be understood that because of the nature of microreproduction (i.e., duplicate copies can be made from duplicates as well as from masters), the *National Union Catalog* is also a source of information. In the introduction to the 1972 NRMM, libraries are advised that, "Microform copies for use by readers, whether positive or negative, should continue to be reported for listing in the *National Union Catalog.*" Even if a microform listed in NUC cannot be copied due to copyright or other restrictions, the library owning that film should be able to tell an inquirer it obtained the film.

In 1973 a different kind of combined list, *Microform Volume I*, was issued by Updata Publications, 1508 Harvard St., Santa Monica, California 90404. This was followed by *Microform Reference Volume II*. These two volumes list micropublications from various publishers that can be purchased through Updata—i.e., a jobber's catalog. The publisher notes that the entire collections of the publishers represented are not necessarily included and that, "we have reserved the right to eliminate duplications, overpriced titles, and titles that do not adhere to the interests and standards of UPDATA and its customers." Volume II lists 3,500 titles from thirty-five U.S. and foreign micropublishers in alphabetic order by title with subject and author indexes.

Another new approach is the *International File of Microfilm Publica-tions and Equipment*, published in the fall of 1974 by University Micro-films, Ltd., St. John's Road, Tyler's Green, High Wycombe, Bucks HP10 8HR, England. Unlike the other combined lists, this one is issued on microfiche. It contains 11,000 pages of information about micropublica-tions, equipment and services, reproduced on 126 fiche which come in two binders, one for hardware (200 suppliers) and one for publications and information services (120 micropublishers).

Slated for publication in 1975 by Science Associates/International, Inc., 23 East 26th St., N.Y., N.Y. 10010, is *Information Industry Buyers Guide*. This will be a guide to information services in all media, including micro-forms. Its primary value as a microform information source will be in describing services that might not be listed in any of the above combined lists, or which, because of their complexity, cannot be adequately de-scribed in any of the above (e.g., Disclosure, Inc.'s dissemination of SEC corporate reports; Information Handling Services' specifications, stand-ards, and vendor catalog services).

Also in production with a spring 1975 publication date is the *Micro-publishers' Trade List Annual* to be issued by Microform Review Inc. *MTLA* will provide librarians with annual catalogs of approximately 200 micropublishers world wide on 83 microfiche. A printed index is housed in a three ring binder with the fiche.

Combined lists/specialized

The oldest specialized, combined list is *Dissertation Abstracts Interna-tional*, initiated by University Microfilms in 1938 and known as *Microfilm Abstracts* from 1938 to 1951 and as *Dissertation Abstracts* from 1952 to 1969. It lists abstracts, and indexes approximately 35,000 dissertations each year, primarily domestic, available from University Microfilms on microfilm and appears monthly in two separately bound sections: (1) humanities and social sciences; (2) science and engineering. Indices to these dissertations are cumulated in the thirty-seven volume, *Comprehensive Dissertation Index*, 1861-1972, also published by Uni-versity Microfilms. Some 417,000 dissertations, mostly domestic are covered by a keyword title index in thirty-two volumes arranged by sub-ject (forty categories) and a five-volume author index. A detailed review of *CDI* will be found in *RQ*, 14: 61-62 (Fall 1974).

In 1948 another specialized, combined source appeared: *Newspapers on Microfilm*. Now published by the Library of Congress, it has gone through several editions and was recently split into two works, one covering foreign newspapers and one covering U.S. newspapers.

Newspapers in Microform: Foreign, 1948-72, cumulates all previous reports contained in the foreign countries section of earlier editions of

NOM (1948-67), together with reports received through the summer of 1972. The volume lists 8,620 foreign newspaper titles held in 1,935 localities both within the U.S. and abroad. Entries were prepared from reports submitted by 258 domestic and foreign libraries and twelve domestic and twenty-eight foreign, commercial firms.

Newspapers in Microform: United States, 1948-72, cumulates all reports contained in the U.S. section of the various previous editions of *NOM* together with reports received through the summer of 1972. There are a total of 34,289 entries held in 7,457 localities and as the title indicates, microform copies of all types are listed, not just ones on roll microfilm. A review will be found in *Microform Review*, 3: 138-39 (April 1974).

At the printer and due some time in 1975 is the Library of Congress publication, *Manuscripts on Microfilm: a Checklist of the Holdings of the Manuscript Division*. As the name states, this is a checklist of LC's holdings, however, as many of the films originated elsewhere (i.e., LC holds duplicate copies), the book serves as a guide to over 800 microfilmed manuscript collections from many institutions. These collections range from a few letters to extensive collections containing thousands of documents. Entries include: author's name and dates, type of manuscript (papers, records, scrapbooks, etc.), span of years covered, LC shelf number, NUC number, original location of the manuscripts, and number of reels. There are no descriptions, however, if an NUC number is cited further information about the material can be obtained under its entry in the *National Union Catalog of Manuscript Collections*, which itself is a source of information for microfilmed materials as it lists both collections of original papers and microfilmed collections. Each entry is briefly annotated and guides to the collection are cited.

Some other important, specialized lists are:

Hale, Richard W., *Guide to Photocopied Historical Materials in the United States and Canada*. (Ithaca: Published for the American Historical Association by Cornell University Press, 1961.)

Hebrew-Union College. Jewish Institute of Religion. American Jewish Periodical Center, *Jewish Newspapers and Periodicals on Microfilm*. (Cincinnati: Hebrew Union College, 1956.) Supps. 1960-

Hixon, Donald L. *Music in Early America: a Bibliography of Music in Evans*. (Metuchen, N.J.: Scarecrow, 1970.)

Houghton, Stephanie M., Lloyd, David, and Smith, Rita Palmer, *Legal Materials in Microform: a Complete Bibliography*. 2d ed. (Provo: Brigham Young University, 1973) (BYU Legal Research Series #3).

Keller, Michael, "Music Serials in Microform and Reprint Editions," *Notes*, 29: 675-93 (June 1973). Additional guides to music titles available in microform will be found in Arneson, Arne J., "Microformats and the Music Library: A Bibliographic-Use Survey of Recent Trends," *Microform Review*, 4: 25-29 (January 1975).

Lowy, George, *Guide to Russian Reprints and Microforms*. New York: Johnson Associates, 1973.

Ochal, Bethany, "Microforms on Legal Subjects," *Law Library Journal*, 65: 65-88 (February 1972).

South Asian Microform Union List of Citations in South Asia Microform Newsletter, and, South Asian Library and Research Notes. Edited by Joan M. and Henry Ferguson. (Educational Resources Center, University of the State of New York, State Education Dept., 1969.)

Wisconsin. State Historical Society. *Labor Papers on Microfilm: a combined list*. (Madison: Wisconsin State Historical Society, 1965.)

Guides and Union Lists

The term guides is used here to describe works that list or otherwise describe materials found within given microform projects and the term union list is used to describe microform holdings of a number of libraries, whether or not those holdings consist of masters. The former provides a source for individual titles which might not appear in combined lists if they are not sold separately (e.g., a reel of microfilm might be the minimum sales unit and might contain ten titles); the latter are of value in tracking down the original source of a film by contacting the library owning a duplicate copy.

The most detailed source for guides and union lists is, "A Microform Bibliography" which is Appendix 4 of *Bibliographic Control of Microforms* by Felix Reichmann and Josephine M. Tharpe (Westport: Greenwood, 1972). The Appendix is broken down into four sections – Catalogs and Lists, Collections and Series, Manuscripts and Archival Collections, Reference Books – and has a total of 493 entries. Reviews of *Bibliographic Control* will be found in *Microform Review*, 2: 64-65 (January 1973) and *LRTS*, 18: 305-07 (Summer 1974). Also of value is the much shorter list found in, Hall, L.M., "Bibliographic Control of Microforms," *Southeastern Librarian*, 20: 258-66 (Winter 1970).

Selected guidelines and union lists are noted below. Those with dates later than 1971 do not appear in the Reichmann/Tharpe work:

Association of Southeastern Research Libraries. *Major Microform Holdings of ASERL Members, 1965.* (New Orleans: Tulane University, 1965.)

Dodson, Suzanne, "The University of British Columbia Library's Guide to Large Collections in Microform: One Attempt to Minimize a Major Problem," *Microform Review*, 1: 113-17 (April 1972).

Major Microforms in the Five Associated University Libraries: A Reference Guide and Union List. Comp. and ed. by Marcia Jebb. (Syracuse: Five Associated University Libraries, 1973.) Reviewed in *Microform Review*, 3: 232 (July 1974).

New Mexico. University. Library. *Union List of Southwestern Materials on Microfilm in New Mexico Libraries.* (Albuquerque: University of New Mexico, 1957.)

Olevink, Peter. *A Guide to Selected Microform Series and their Indexes.* (Urbana: University of Illinois Graduate School of Library Service, 1973) (Occasional Paper No. 106). Reviewed in *LRTS*, 18: 81-82 (Winter 1974).

Ontario Council of University Libraries. *Union List of Microform Sets in O.C.U.L. Libraries.* Anni Leibl and Jean S. Yolton, eds. (Toronto: Ontario Council of University Librarians, 1971.)

Schubert, Irene and Weaver, Alice, *A Union List of Microform Holdings in Ohio-Assisted Universities.* (Toledo: Reference Dept., University of Toledo Libraries, 1972.) (University of Toledo Tower Series No. 2.) Reviewed in *Microform Review*, 2: 238 (July 1973).

Union List of Selected Microforms in Libraries in the New York Metropolitan Area. Ed. by Eugene P. Sheehy in cooperation with METRO.(New York: Metro, 1973.)

A Union List of Selected Microforms in Washington, D.C. Area Libraries. (Washington: Social Sciences Group. Washington, D.C. Chapter, Special Libraries Association, 1974. (Order from: E. S. Knauff, 2326 19th St. N.W., Washington, D.C. 20009). Identifies microfilm holdings in the social sciences and humanities of thirty-seven cooperating libraries in metropolitan Washington.

Report Literature

The United States government spends millions each year on research and development conducted both by its own employees and by outside

contractors. The results of this research, as well as reports and other docu-
mention submitted to the government as required by various laws, are dis-
seminated in microform by a number of agencies.

NTIS. The National Technical Information Service, 5285 Port Royal Rd.,
Springfield, Va. 22151, of the Dept. of Commerce, is a central source for
the public sale of government-sponsored research, development and engineering reports and other analyses prepared by several hundreds of federal
agencies, their contractors or grantees. Four million documents and microforms are supplied to the public annually. Current summaries of new research reports appear in *Weekly Government Abstracts*, but the main access is the biweekly journal, *Government Reports Abstracts*, which lists
some 60,000 abstracts per year and for which there is a separate *Government Report Index*. In addition, the booklet, *NTIS Information Services*
(July 1974) and successors should be consulted for special projects offered in microform such as, "Pending Civil Tax Cases," "1970 Census,
Population and Housing," "IRS Taxpayer Data by ZIP."

AEC (U.S. Atomic Energy Commission). *Nuclear Science Abstracts*
(Government Printing Office) abstracts and indexes nuclear science literature. It covers scientific and technical reports of the U.S. Atomic Energy
Commission and its contractors, other U.S. government agencies, other
governments, universities, and industrial and research organizations. In
addition, books, conference proceedings, conference papers, patents, and
journal literature on a worldwide basis are abstracted and indexed. Approximately 65,000 abstracts are published each year in two volumes of
twelve issues each. Each issue includes four indexes: subject, personal,
author, corporate author, report number, and subsequently indexes are
cumulated for each volume. AEC reports are available on microfiche
from a number of sources listed in the introduction to the Report Number
Index section of *NSA*. Some non-AEC reports are also available on microfiche; sources are given in the Report Number Index. For details on the
AEC's information and microform activities write: USAEC Technical
Information Center, P.O. Box 62, Oak Ridge, Tennessee 31830.

NASA. (U.S. National Aeronautics and Space Administration).
Scientific and Technical Aerospace Abstracts (Government Printing
Office), abstracts and indexes the results of worldwide research and
development activities in aeronautics, space, and supporting disciplines.
Publications abstracted include scientific and technical reports issued
by NASA and its contractors, other U.S. government agencies, corpora-
tions, universities, and research organizations throughout the world.
Pertinent theses, translations, NASA-owned patents and patent applications
and other separate documents are also abstracted. Each issue has five
indexes: subject, personal, author, corporate source, contract number, and

report/accession number. Cumulative index volumes are published annually and semiannually. Publically available documents are indicated by a symbol and can be purchased on microfiche from NTIS. For details about NASA information and microform services write for the free, The *NASA Scientific and Technical Information System*... *and How to Use It* available from the NASA Scientific and Technical Information Facility, P.O. Box 33, College Park, Md. 20740.

Parallel coverage of scientific and trade journals, books, and conference papers will be found in *International Aerospace Abstracts*, published twice a month by the American Institute of Aeronautics and Astronautics and available from their Technical Information Service, 750 Third Ave., N.Y., N.Y. 10017.

ERIC. The Educational Resources Information Center, a part of the National Institute of Education, Dept. of Health, Education and Welfare, is a system for providing ready access to educational literature. A network of clearinghouses have the responsibility for acquiring, selecting, and processing documents in their area (e.g., career education, disadvantaged, educational management). The documents, themselves, however, are available on microfiche or hard copy print-out from a central source, the ERIC Document Reproduction Service, P.O. 190, Arlington, Va. 22210. Orders are accepted on either an on-demand or subscription basis. Subscribers may order the entire microfiche collection (monthly this amounts to about 950 titles contained on about 1400 fiche) or subsets of the entire collection. Documents are announced in *Research in Education* (Government Printing Office), a monthly abstract journal which concerns itself primarily with the unpublished, limited distribution, or, as it is sometimes called, the "fugitive" type of literature, e.g., technical and research reports, speeches, papers, program descriptions, teacher guides, statistical compilations, curriculum materials, etc. Some 1200 documents are abstracted and indexed (subject, personal, author, institution) in each issue.

SEC (Securities and Exchange Commission). *Disclosure Journal, 1973-* (Disclosure, Inc., 1400 Spring St., Silver Springs, Md. 20910) provides access to a different kind of report—i.e., the approximately 100,000 reports filed with the SEC each year as required by various laws. These reports are available on microfiche from Disclosure, Inc. and are indexed by subject and listed by company name in *Disclosure Journal*.

Announcement Media

The obvious source for announcements of new microform titles is publishers' circulars which can be picked up at conventions or by getting on publishers' mailing lists, and also, publishers' newsletters, e.g., *Microcard*

Bulletin (Microcard Editions), *Serials Bulletin, Source* (University Micro-films), *Micropublisher* (Micro Photo).

There are, in addition, several publications that list new microform titles:

The Microfilm Clearinghouse Bulletin, No. 1, March 19, 1951- , is issued at irregular intervals by the Library of Congress as a supplement to its *LC Information Bulletin.* Initially it listed the more important titles that were submitted to an informal clearinghouse maintained in card file form in the Union Catalog Division, but it now lists primarily projects of LC's Photo-duplication Service from which a microfilm of the back issues of the *Bulletin* is available. In addition, Photoduplication also issues a series of circulars which describe selected titles they have filmed.

Center for Chinese Research Materials, *Newsletter.* The Center was estab-lished in 1968 to acquire, reproduce, and distribute Chinese research materials, particularly with regard to the study of 20th century China. Concentration to date has been on Chinese-language newspapers and journals. Titles are announced in the *Newsletter.* For information write: Center for Chinese Research Materials, Association of Research Libraries, 1527 New Hampshire Ave. N.W., Washington, D.C. 20036.

Foreign Newspaper Microfilm Project, *List of Holdings.* As of 1973, 80 libraries subscribe to this cooperative project which provides subscribers with microfilm copies of 143 foreign newspapers on a current basis. In addition to the current titles, the project has available microfilm copies of another 61 titles that have ceased publication or are no longer available to the project. Newspapers included in the project are listed in the, *List of Holdings*, issued irregularly. The last one as of this writing is dated June 10, 1974. Information about the project may be obtained from: Center for Research Libraries, 5721 Cottage Grove Ave., Chicago, IL. 60637.

Foreign Newspaper and Gazette Report, 1974- , published three times a year by the Library of Congress, gives information on newly microfilmed foreign newspapers, on various foreign newspaper microfilming projects, and on the gazette microfilming project being undertaken jointly by the Library of Congress and the New York Public Library.

The *Bulletin,* 1974- , of the Microfilm Committee of the International Council on Archives (Room 408, National Archives, Washington, D.C. 20408) contains reports on archival microfilming activities.

The *Joint Acquisitions List of Africana* (JALA) (Africana, Northwestern University Library, Evanston, IL. 60201) lists, from time to time, titles added to the Cooperative Africana Microform Project.

Microform Review, 1972- , (P.O. Box 1297, Weston, Conn. 06880) in addition to carrying detailed reviews of micropublications and survey articles (e.g., "A Survey of Africana in Microform") also carries previews of forthcoming micropublications and has a section called, "Clearinghouse on Library Microform Projects," which lists new titles.

Library Resources and Technical Services, carries abstracts of library and information science reports available on microfiche through the ERIC system.

The *Micrographics Newsletter* (formerly, *Microfilm Newsletter*) (P.O. Box 313, Wykagyl Station, New Rochelle, N.Y. 10804) while primarily a "news report for executives who use or market microfilm services and equipment," occasionally carries brief mentions of major microform projects.

News From the Center, published semi-annually, 1967-71, by the Center for the Coordination of Foreign Manuscript Copying, Manuscript Division, Library of Congress, is still of value for information on manuscript microfilming projects.

News Notes of the Canadian Library Association Microfilm Project (151 Sparks St., Ottawa, Ont. K1P 5E3), issued at irregular intervals, lists new titles available from the project, mainly newspapers. Cumulated lists are issued from time to time, the latest being, *Geographical List of CLA Microfilms* (October 1974).

Other journals likely to mention new microform projects include: *Microdoc*[3], *Advanced Technology Libraries*[4], *Microinfo*[5], *ASLIB Proceedings*[6], *Journal of Documentation*[6], *UNESCO Bulletin for Libraries*[7], and *Microfiche Foundation Newsletter*[8].

Catalogs

Catalogs issued by micropublishers, commercial or non-commercial, are of course a primary information source as are promotional leaflets. They are likely to contain titles not yet appearing in any of the combined lists and entries will often include a great deal of bibliographic detail not found elsewhere. The University Microfilms' catalog, *Serials in Microform*, is especially recommended for its length and the comprehensive nature of UM's serial offerings. The 1975 catalog, for example, is 820 pages and lists titles both alphabetically and by subject.

Another catalog of special interest is the *1974-1978 Reference Guide & Comprehensive Catalog of International Serials; originals & reprints*, *microfilms & microfiches, featuring science, technology, medicine, the humanities,* published by Microform International Marketing Corporation and Maxwell Scientific International Inc. (Fairview Park, Elmsford, New York 10532) which when completed will consist of eight volumes. Part 1, published in October, 1974, lists 6,585 items covering only the letter "A", of which microforms constitute about 10 percent. The titles listed are published or handled by MIMC and affiliated firms.

Publishers will gladly send you their catalogs upon request. To find out who's a micropublisher consult the most comprehensive list, *Microform Market Place, and International Directory of Micropublishing, 1974/75- ,* published by Microform Review Inc.[1] The term micropublisher is broadly defined to include any organization that sells information in microform. Organizations that offer reprographic services on request in contrast to marketing microform titles are indicated by an asterisk. In the 1974/75 edition, 372 publishers from throughout the world are listed of which 168 are asterisked. There is a subject index, a geographic index, and an index by personal names, this latter to persons working for micropublishers.

Lists of micropublishers will also be found in the *Guide to Microforms, Subject Guide to Microforms,* Appendix D of Dale Gaddy's, *A Microform Handbook* (National Microfilm Association, 1974)[9] , *International Microforms in Print, Microfilm Source Book* (Microfilm Publishing, 1972-)[10] , and the *National Register of Microform Masters*—the latter is especially good for non-commercial sources.

Libraries wanting as complete a collection of catalogs as possible are advised to consult all the above sources since, for example, *Guide to Microforms* contains a number of publishers not listed in *Microform Market Place.*

Many micropublishers issue an annual, general catalog and a number of specialized catalogs. For a list of catalogs, consult the "Catalogs and Lists" (pp. 60-110) and "Collections and Series" (pp. 112-165) sections of *Bibliographic Control of Microforms* which contain a total of 313 entries. The former consists of catalogs and lists issued by commercial publishers and by libraries, associations, societies, and government agencies. Some merely list microform publications available for sale, but many include valuable annotations and descriptive notes. The latter list microform series, frequently referred to as collections, sets, or projects.

Guidelines

The following do not list micropublications but will be of value to anyone purchasing microforms as they provide guidelines and references on *how* to buy.

Boner, Marian O., "Acquisition of Microforms in Law Libraries," *Law Library Journal*, 63: 66-69 (February 1970).

Darling, Pamela W., "Developing a Preservation Microfilming Program," *Library Journal*, 99: 2803-09 (November 1, 1974).

Gregory, Roma S., "Acquisition of Microforms," *Library Trends*, 18: 373-84 (January 1970).

Criteria for the Procurement and Use of Microforms and Related Equipment by the Libraries of the California State University and Colleges. August 9, 1974. (Available from the Office of the Chancellor, 5670 Wilshire Blvd., Los Angeles, Calif. 90036).

Veaner, Allen B., *The Evaluation of Micropublications*. (Chicago: American Library Association, 1971) (LTP Publication No. 17.)

A last resort is to have the desired material microfilmed for you by the library owning it or by a commercial firm if the library will permit it. For information about photographic services available through libraries consult: Nitecki, Joseph Z., *Directory of Library Reprographic Services*. 5th ed. (Published for the Reproduction of Library Materials Section, RTSD-American Library Association by Microform Review Inc., 1973).[1] Substantially the same names will be found in *Microform Market Place* identified by asterisks. Also of value is the *Directory of Interlibrary Loan Policies and Photocopying Services in Canadian Libraries* (Ottawa: Canadian Library Association, 1973, 88p.).

References

1. Microform Review, Inc. P.O. Box 1297, Weston, Conn. 06880.
2. Schneider, Linda and D.W., "Microfiche Masters, a National Need," *Southeastern Librarian*, 20: 106-07 (Summer 1970).
3. Microdoc, Microfilm Association of Great Britain, 109 Kingsway, London WC 2B 6PJ, England.
4. Advanced Technology Libraries, Knowledge Industry Publications, Box 429, White Plains, N.Y. 10602.
5. Microinfo: micrographics news bulletin, 4 High St., Alton, Hampshire, England.
6. *ASLIB Proceedings, Journal of Documentation*, 3 Belgrave Square, London, SW1X 8PL, England.
7. *UNESCO Bulletin for Libraries*, Place de Fontenoy, Paris 7e, France.
8. *Microfiche Foundation Newsletter*, Microfiche Foundation, Doelenstraat 101, Delft, Netherlands.
9. National Microfilm Association, 8728 Colesville Road, Silver Springs, Md. 20910.
10. Microfilm Publishing, Inc., P.O. Box 313, Wykagyl Station, New Rochelle, N.Y. 10804.

ACQUISITION OF
MICROFORMS AND
MICROFORM EQUIPMENT

1. The libraries will limit the purchase of microform reading equipment to that which is designed primarily to operate between 16X and 24X. For machines providing additional magnification capability, libraries may select an auxiliary magnification in the 42X-48X range to accommodate COM output. Libraries will avoid the acquisition of microform materials produced at a higher reduction ratio than 48X until such time as industry-wide standard reduction ratios are established and acceptable to the Library Directors.
2. The libraries will not purchase large microform sets or collections unless the publisher of such sets will:
    a. *guarantee* in writing that the material is fully indexed;
    b. offer to the purchasing library full bibliographic information for *all separate units* within the microfilmed collection;
    c. guarantee that each reel or cassette pertaining to such collection will have content labels attached to each box or cassette; and
    d. provide bibliographic information that conforms to Anglo-American cataloging rules.
3. The libraries will, where a choice of microform exists, purchase the materials in microfiche and/or 35mm roll film depending upon the content of the material filmed, provided that the microfiche shall not be larger than 4 X 6 inches in size.
4. For silver-gelatin films used for masters and archival types of storage, CSUC libraries will purchase only film conforming to ANSI standard PH.1. 28-1973 for permanent record film on Cellulose Ester base and ANSI standard PH.1.41 for archival record films on polyester bases. For nonarchival films in the working collection, other types of film with a reasonable working life, such as diazo and vesicular films that have been proven not to emit destructive chemicals under normal library storage conditions, are acceptable.

Reprinted from Part II of *Criteria for the Procurement and Use of Microforms and Related Equipment by the Libraries of the California State University and Colleges,* issued by the Office of the Chancellor, California State University and Colleges, 5670 Wilshire Blvd., Los Angeles, Calif. 90036 August 9, 1974, pp. 4-5.

5. Microform materials will not be considered for purchase unless data are provided by the vendor on reduction ratios, image format, and film type.

6. The Library Directors will request funds in the next budget cycle for their institutions to acquire equipment which will quickly and inexpensively duplicate microfiche for the benefit of patrons. This policy is made in recognition of these advantages:
   a. Microfiche resources could be made available to more patrons.
   b. The integrity of the microfiche collection could be better protected and preserved.

7. The libraries will phase out all purchases of roll microfilm which appear on 16mm film and limit purchases of such microfilm materials to those which are available on 35mm film.

8. The libraries will abandon the purchase of micro-opaque cards and microprint except where necessary to complete sets to support academic programs because reliable and inexpensive printers for these materials are not available.

9. The California State University and Colleges will use every opportunity to urge micropublishers who produce micro-opaque materials to make these materials available in microfiche form.

10. Standards for the acquisition of microforms and microform equipment shall be reviewed by the Council of Library Directors at least every third year from the adoption of this policy.

ADDITIONAL READINGS

Boner, Marian, O., "Acquisitions of Microforms in Law Libraries," *Law Library Journal*, 63: 66-69 (February 1970).

Ochal, Bethany J., "Microform Brief," *Law Library Journal*, 68: 33-59.

Sullivan, Robert C., "Microform Developments Related to Acquisitions," *College and Research Libraries*, 34: 16-28 (January 1973).

Veaner, Allen B., "The Crisis in Micropublication," *Choice*, 5: 448-53 (June 1968).

Veaner, Allen B., *The Evaluation of Micropublications*. Chicago: American Library Association, 1971 (LTP Publication No. 17). 59p.

CATALOGING

Introduction

Holmes found in answer to the question, "What problems are experienced in cataloging microforms?" that "the range of answers included the following: There are no problems except markings; the need to use a reading machine slows cataloging; problems in descriptive cataloging result from having to describe sheets, frames and rolls; irregular quality of targets requires added time for verification; cataloging microforms is a 'snake pit' with many unsolved problems; catalogers put microforms on bottom of pile; limited number of personnel experienced with microforms causes delays; there are not enough catalogers to keep up with the work load; catalogers real or imagined problems in working with microforms cause them to put microforms aside, resulting in a constant backlog."[1]

The articles in this chapter were selected to bring out problems and viewpoints rather than to tell readers how to catalog and classify microforms. There is probably no other area of library science in which such diversity exists, nor where the desirable must give way to the practical so often.

Nitecki states one view, "each microform entry should be fully classified and catalogued," but Thomson's survey indicates that, "libraries are not cataloging in full the individual texts in these massive microform collections," referring to collections such as *Short Title Catalogue*, Wright's, *American Fiction, Three Centuries of French Drama*—collections which consist of several thousand titles.

According to the Reichmann and Tharpe study,[2] of 185 libraries responding, 60 percent catalog microforms while 40 percent make many exceptions to the general rules or do not catalog at all. Nine did not catalog, 119 did catalog, 57 did catalog but made exceptions. Close to 60 percent did not classify but rather shelved microforms by sequential numbers.

There is general acceptance of the view that microforms should be cataloged following the rules in the *Anglo-American Cataloging Rules* (1967) and that cataloging not be done for the massive number of reports emanating from ERIC, AEC, NASA, and similar organizations. The disagreement relates to the treatment of collections consisting of hundreds or thousands of titles. As the above quotations indicate, some feel that every microform title should appear in the card catalog with full cataloging information because otherwise patrons may conclude that the library does not own a given title. Another view holds that if an adequate bibliography exists, representation in the card catalog constitutes needless duplication as the bibliography can be marked to show which titles the library holds. This, of course, leaves the problem of how to tell patrons they are to check certain bibliographies.

Those who opt for control through bibliographies may not necessarily feel that individual cataloging is incorrect but rather that it is impractical and that to adhere to such a policy will only result in an unmanageable number of arrears.

Within the bibliography camp there are many alternatives some of which are brought out in Thomson's survey and one of which is described in detail in Elrod's article.

References

1. Holmes, Donald C., *Determination of User Needs and Future Requirements for a Systems Approach to Microform Technology.* July 19, 1969. ERIC ED 029 168, p. 12.

2. Reichmann, Felix, and Tharpe, Josephine, *Bibliographic Control of Microforms.* Westport: Greenwood, 1972.

SIMPLIFIED CLASSIFICATION AND CATALOGING OF MICROFORMS

by Joseph Z. Nitecki

The use of microtexts in libraries indicates a departure from the initial interest in microforms as means for the preservation of records only. Consequent expansion of unclassified microform collections makes them increasingly cumbersome. The importance of microforms as primary material requires full bibliographic description, the variation in their physical format necessitates separate storage facilities, while the arrangement of individual items by broad subjects makes the collection more accessible to the user. This paper describes a method of classifying and cataloging the microform collection in a modern university library.

Nature of Microform Publications

It might be worthwhile, at times, to stress the obvious: the need for cataloging and classifying a library's microform material is self-evident. A microform, by definition, is only a photoreproduction of some records; if the original book is cataloged, its copy should be, too. The content of microform materials does not differ from bookform publications, and hence it ought to be considered an integral part of the library's collection, i.e., each microform entry should be fully classified and cataloged, with author, title, subject and added entries filed in the public catalogs.

The physical limitations imposed by the microform format require special handling of the sensitive film or small size cards; the microform "binding" (e.g., boxes for reels, envelopes for cards, etc.) calls for a different housing arrangement, and the reading technique for microcopies is developed within a special environment (i.e., dim lighting and reading machines). All this points to the expediency of shelving microforms in separate locations; it does not argue away the advantages of a classified collection. The issue of "separateness" applies as much to the special microform collection as to the treatment of special book collections.

Reprinted from *Library Resources and Technical Services*, 13: 79-85 (Winter 1969).

The Argument in Favor of a
Classified Microform Collection

Incomplete cataloging of microforms seriously limits access to the material, while an unclassified microform collection is indeed *de facto* separated from the total library collection.

A brief catalog entry for a microform title is worth as much as a similar entry made for a book form. The need for full bibliographic description of the material is determined not by the physical format of the work, but by its contents. There are different versions of the same work printed, as well as filmed; some of the variations are more significant than the others. But there is no reason, for example, for not having an author card filed under Gerbeir, Sir Balthazar, with the title entry made for "The art of well speaking . . ." and an added subject entry under "Speech," merely because the book is in a microfilm collection only. The original book-form may be out of reach, simply because it was published in 1650, a fact most probably of no significance to the patron interested in its contents.

The argument in favor of classifying a book collection applies equally to the classification of microforms, although the order of reasons given may differ somewhat.

The purpose of classifying, i.e., to provide the most efficient use of the library collection, applies to both cases; but while books are usually closely classified, the microforms seem to be better arranged in a more broadly designated classification system. Since the microforms are usually not displayed on an open shelf, they are better accommodated by a fixed, non-expanding, location. The classification number used here is more the identification code than the subject notation. Yet, grouping of microforms by subject, although of no browsing value, is important to the user, immobilized by his dependence on reading machines. Relatively speaking, a retrieval of microforms on the same subject from drawers closely located to each other, is as convenient a facility as to examine a shelf with books on a similar subject.

The value of the shelflist used as a tool for subject inventory applies equally to book and microform collections. A classified collection makes an evaluation of subject coverage in the library much easier and faster.

In short, any arrangement is always better than chaos; but a classified arrangement similar to that of the rest of the collection is easier to understand and to use.

In the UWM Library, for example,[1] before a re-classification of the microform collection, the reels were shelved in a number of separate groupings, such as, e.g., major newspapers, subarranged by date; other newspapers kept in alphabetical order, but separated from the periodicals;

1. The microform collection at UWM Library has grown rapidly in the last few years; Mr. M Gormley, Director of UWM Libraries, reported in his 1967/68 Annual Report a total of over 38,000 titles and 133,000 bibliographical items in the microform collection.

the monographic microfilms arranged by accession number, and each of the larger microfilm series, such as the *Short Title Catalog*, by its own indexing system. Such a complicated and arbitrary system bewildered the novice, forcing him to learn his way through this unfamiliar maze by a frustrating trial and error method.

Some Variations in Cataloging a Microform Entry

In cataloging microforms, the UWM Library follows the *Anglo-American Cataloging Rules* (1967). The crucial principle in the UWM Library's policy policy is a consideration of each photoreproduction (microfilm, micro-cards or microprint) as a copy of the corresponding work in printed form, i.e., the original work, its facsimile or reprint edition.

If the library has both the original and microform versions of the same work, the microform is treated as an added copy and only a separate shelf-list card is prepared for the microform entry. A note, added on the cards for the book form, ties the two versions together. See examples on page 118.

The collation contains the number of reels or cards, followed by the statement: "On microfilm," "On microcards," or "On microprint." All technical information concerning the microform itself, such as the positive/negative film, its size, number of pages per frame, etc., is omitted. If necessary, these data are added on the box itself.

When a book form edition is added to the collection, with an entry already cataloged as a microform, only a shelflist card for the book form is prepared, with a note referring one entry to the other:

(a) On all cards of the micro-form entry:
   "Also in book form [call number] "

(b) On the shelflist of the book-form entry:
   "Also on microfilm, (MF) [etc.] "

In each case one standard set of cards is filed in the Public Catalogs, and a separate shelflist card is made for each form of the publication. The microforms containing more than one title are classified as sets with separate catalog entries for each title. The films are not cut for cataloging purposes.

(MF)
PN   Educational theatre journal. v. 1-
01   1949-
           [Columbia, Mo.]
           reels. 4 no. a year.

           On microfilm.
           Also in book form, PN3171 .E38.
           Shelf-list card only.
                                    195300   KC

Example 1(a): Shelflist entry for the microfilm added copy.

PN   Educational theatre journal. v. 1-
3171   Oct. 1949-
.E38   [Columbia, Mo., Published by Artcraft Press for the
           American Educational Theatre Association]

               v. in 26 cm.   4 no. a year.
           Also on microfilm, (MF) PN01

               1. Drama in education—Period. I. American Educa-
           tional Theatre Association. II. Title.
           PN3171.E38   371.332505   52-794
           Library of Congress   [2]   195300

Example 1(b): Main entry for the same work in book-form. If the microform version
of a work is the only entry in the library collection, it is cataloged in full, as if it were an
original work, with some minor modifications.

(MF)
CD   "War of 1812 papers" of the Department of State
01   1789–1815. Washington, National Archives, National
ser.M   Archives and Records Service, General Services
588   Administration, 1965. 7 reels. (National Archives
           microfilm publications, no. 588) On micro film.

               1. United States—History—War of 1812. I. Title.

                                    631614.700   DT

Example 2: Main entry for the microfilm version. Library does not have the original
work in book form.

```
(MF)
CD      U. S. National Archives.
01          National archives microfilm publications.
            1947-
            Washington.
            reels.   irregular.

                On microfilm. For the description of the series see:
            U. S. National Archives. List of National Archives
            microfilm publications.
                Each series in the UWM Library collection can
            also be found in the card catalog under its own
            author, title, and subject headings.

            I. Title.                     631614.700      DT
```

Example 3: Main entry card for the series classified as a set, cataloged as monographs.

TABLE 1

CLASSIFICATION SCHEDULE FOR MICROFORMS

	(1)	(2)	(3)	(4)
a	(MF)	(MC)	(MP)	FILM
b	LC CALL NUMBER— LETTERS ONLY			Abbreviated Title
c	ACCESSION NUMBER [Open Entry Serials Start With "o" (Zero)]			Series Number Reel/Card/Etc. Number/Date/Etc.
d	REEL	CARD	BOX	
e	(Number, Date or Letter)			
f	(MF) B 03	(MC) Q 3 Card 2	(MP) H 15 Box A	FILM (STC) Reel 700

Classification Schedule

To separate the microform collection by the type of microform, the class-ification schedule is divided into four main classes: (1) Microfilm (MF); (2) Microcards (MC); (3) Microprints (MP); and (4) Special Collections (FILM).[2]

To combine titles reproduced partly on cards and partly on microfiche (e.g., Newsweek Magazine), the two types of reproductions are classified together as microcards.

The designation "FILM" is provided for temporary classification of long-run sets on microfilms, already in the library collection, reclassifica-tion of which, for reasons of economy, is not contemplated in the near future. Thus, for example, the UWM Library uses the "FILM" classifica-tion for the STC series; but it has classified the American Periodicals Series in (MF).

The call number in the microform classification schedule consists of: (a) location symbol, (b) the letter notation of the LC classification scheme, indicating the general subject of the entry, (c) the accession number, which arranges the microforms within the subject, without disturbing the order of microforms previously classified, (d) the notation, designating the physical "binding" of the microform, (e) consecutive part of the set, based on the original subdivision provided by the publisher of the series (e.g., reel number, date of coverage, or letter designation).

As a rule, all location symbols used in the UWM Library consist of three-letter codes. The two-letter designation of microform location was chosen deliberately to distinguish it from the usual meaning of the "location" symbol. Each microform location code indicates, in addition to the shelving location, also the type of microform, and the corresponding schedule of classification.

The use of brackets in the location symbols differentiates between the usage of letter codes for location symbols and letter class symbols in the LC classification schedule. The bracketing of location symbols became a uniform procedure for all location codes, after the introduction of the three-letter class numbers in the LC's "K" Schedule.

Microforms produced partly on film and partly on cards are classified separately, each part in the corresponding schedule. The subject too general for inclusion in any specific LC schedule are all classified in LC's class "A".

The use of accession numbers within each class eliminates the need for a constant re-shuffling of microforms with each new addition to a drawer. To allow enough space for the regular addition of serials publications, the number "0" (zero) precedes each accession number in the serial entry.

The words "REEL," "CARD," etc., allow for a direct identification of

2. See Table 1.

the physical parts of each set. In special cases, the word "FILM" is followed by a conventional abbreviation for the title of the series, e.g., STC. Thus, in Table 1, the examples given in (f) read as follows:

f(1): The third microfilm serial classified in Philosophy;
f(2): the second card of the third microcard title classified in Science;
f(3): this entry, reproduced in a microprint form, is the fifteenth item added in the Social Sciences class, of which this particular title is placed in Box A;
f(4): this title, in the STC series, is on Reel 700.

Conclusion

The system described in this paper is simple to use and it is easily adaptable to any classification system, since the LC class number can be replaced by any other notation, such as Dewey numbers. The schedule provides for fast and orderly arrangement of physical units of microforms at a low maintenance cost and a considerable saving in servicing the collection.

The arrangement has been in use in the UWM Library since Summer of 1967, proving to be a classification system convenient for the patrons and easily manageable by the library's staff.

AUTHOR AND TITLE ANALYTICS FOR MAJOR MICROFORM SETS

by J. McRee Elrod

It has been stated that "few of the vast micropublication projects which our libraries are called upon to buy are provided with bibliographic controls adequate in quantity and quality."[1] Not only are materials hard to locate, but a hard-copy duplicate may be inadvertently purchased.

At the University of British Columbia (UBC), analytics have been prepared for some sets where commercial cards were not available or were

Reprinted from *Microform Review*, 2: 99-104 (April 1973) by permission of the publisher.
Copyright © 1973 by Microform Review, Inc.

felt to be too expensive. These analytics consist of author and title entries for each item in the set superimposed on a unit card for the set as a whole. Sets for which some analytics have already been prepared by UBC include: *American Fiction* (University Microfilms), *Canadiana in the Toronto Public Library* (NCR Microcard Editions), *English and American drama of the nineteenth century* (Readex), *English Books, 1641-1700* (University Microfilms), *Travels in the Confederate States* (Lost Cause Press), *Travels in the Old South* (Lost Cause Press), and *Pamphlets in the Public Archives of Canada* (Public Archives of Canada).[2]

Analytics for *American Fiction* are, as stated above, author and title of each item in the set on a unit card for the set. At UBC, two copies of each of the cards are filed in the public catalog—one copy under author and one copy under title with the title "highlighted" rather than retyped at the top of the card.[3]

```
          II.2286     Soule, Mrs. Caroline Augusta
                      (White). Wine or water: a tale of
                      New England. . . .
          AMERICAN fiction, 1774-1900.  [Ann Arbor,
          University Microfilms, 1965-
               reels.   35 mm.
          For holdings see Location file.
          Microfilm copy of books listed in
CaBVaU         Wright's American fiction, 1774-1850,
          1851-1875 and 1876-1900.
Author/title anals                     as per its catalogue.
```

The earlier microfiche of *Canadiana in the Toronto Public Library* contained fiche of a card which could be reproduced to create an analytic. Later microfiche have headings which cannot be so used and instead have been typed on unit cards for the set.

Lyon, George Francis.
    The private journal of Captain G.F.
Lyon, of H.M.S. Hecla. 1824.

C356 :
1289
    CANADIANA in the Toronto Public Library;
    early Canadiana selected by members of
    the staff of the Toronto Public Library
    from A Bibliography of Canadiana, by
    Frances M. Staton and Marie Tremaine,
    1934, and first supplement, 1959. Washington, Microcard Editions, 1967-
        sheets. 11 x 15 cm.
    For holdings see Location file.
       Microfiche (negative)
CaBVaU Author and   title anals as per
    Microfiche.

C356
4708 [JEFFERYS, THOMAS] *d.* 1771
    The Conduct of the French, With Regard to Nova Scotia; From its first Settlement to the present Time. In which are exposed the Falsehood and Absurdity of their Arguments made use of to elude the Force of the Treaty of Utrecht, and support their unjust Proceedings. In a Letter to a Member of Parliament. *London: Printed for T. Jefferys, Geographer to His Royal Highness the Prince of Wales, at the Corner of St. Martin's Lane, near Charing Cross. MDCCLIV. (Price One Shilling.)*

    1 p.l., 77, [1] p. 20.8 x 12.7 cm. [1] p. at end contains a list of Jefferys' publications. For a French translation (1755) with notes by G. M. Butel-Dumont, *vide* no.237.
    A ms. note on the fly-leaf wrongly attributes this work to the Sieur de la Grange de Chessieux, who did, however, in 1756 publish a reply to Jefferys' assertions.
                  B.M., D.N.B., Halkett and Laing, L.C., Sabin

     I. Title.

English and American Drama of the Nineteenth Century presented a particularly difficult problem. The set proved unusable when arranged by the headings on the micro-opaque cards, since plays are frequently attributed to actors, editors, or librettists, or are treated as anonymous when authorship is known. The analytics created consist of one title card for each play in the set, plus author information cards for each established author referring patrons to the title cards. The title cards refer patrons to the boxes in which the play originally came, and to the play within the box, by means of a call number, which includes box number and an author number based on the Readex entry. The equivalent of author and title analytics is achieved with many fewer cards than if author/title cards had been prepared for each play.

            Bluebeard re-paired. A worn out
         subject... [18--]

         ENGLISH and American drama of the 19th
E545:   century; American plays, 1831-1900, English
E:10:   plays, 1801-1900. Edited by George
B56   Freedley and Allardyce Nicoll. " New York,
         Readex Microprint Corp. [1965?-
         cards. 23 x 15 cm.
        For holdings sco Location file.
         Micro-opaque.
Title anals as per Its checklist.

```
                    Richards, Alfred Bate,   1820-1876.
E545

           Plays by this author printed in England
           and America during the nineteenth century
           are available in this library in the
           Readex Microprint edition of English and
           American Drama of the Nineteenth Century.
           These plays may be located by consulting
           this card catalogue under the title of the
           desired              play.
           Micro-               opaque.
           Author               information cards.
```

English Books, 1641-1700 analytics are being created by searching the contents of the set against the volumes of *The National Union Catalog, Pre-1956 Imprints* as they are issued. In addition to the author/title analytic, analytics are typed for persons mentioned in the titles of anonymous works.

```
           An essaye upon His Royal Highness the Duke
           of York, his adventure against the Dutch.
           1672.
         ENGLISH books, 1641-1700.  Ann Arbor, Mich.,
           University Microfilms, 1961-
316:            reels.  35 mm.
E3298A      Microfilm copy of books included in
         Wing's Short-title catalogue of ...
         English books printed ... 1641-1700.
```

```
            Delaune, Thomas, d. 1685]
            [Eikōn tou thēriou] Εἰκὼν τοῦ θηρίου,
            or the image. 1684.
            ENGLISH books, 1641-1700. Ann Arbor, Mich.,
            University Microfilms, 1961-
   312:        reels. 35 mm.
   D891      Microfilm copy of books included in
            Wing's Short-title catalogue of ...
            English books printed ... 1641-1700.
```

Analytics created for *Travels in the Confederate States* and *Travels in the Old South*, as for *American Fiction* were based directly on the catalogs of the sets. The micropublishers involved deserve credit for creating usable catalogs.

```
                    Richardson, Albert Deane. The Secret
                    Service. Hartford, Conn., American Pub-
                    lishing Company; Philadelphia, Jones
                    Bros. & Co., 1865. No 39?
             Coulter, Ellis Merton, 1890-        ed.
   C68          Travels in the Confederate States.
             [Louisville, Ky., Lost Cause Press, 1956?-
               cards.  8 x 13 cm.
             for holdings see Location file
             Micro-opaque.
             Contains the items listed in his Travels
             in the Confederate States, a bibliography.
             Author and              title anals as per
   CaBVaU  its catalogue.
```

```
              Smith, Sidney. The settler's new home: or,
              The emigrant's location, being a guide
              to emigrants in the selection of a settle-
              ment, and the preliminary details of the
              voyage . . . London, J. Kendrick, 1849.
          Clark, Thomas Dionysius, 1903-      ed.
 C473         Travels in the Old South.  [Louisville,
          Ky., Lost Cause Press, 1959?-
              cards.  7.5 x 12.5 cm.
          For holdings see Location file.
          Micro-opaque.
              Contains items listed in his Travels in
          the Old South, a bibliography.


 Author/title anals            as per its catalogue.
```

Pamphlets in the Public Archives of Canada are also author and title on a unit card, in this instance retyped from the accompanying list.

```
              Wynn, Charles Watkin Williams, 1775-
              1850.
                  Argument upon the jurisdiction of
              the House of Commons...in cases of
              breach of privilege.  London, 1810.
          Canada.  Archives.
 C354;        Pamphlets in the Public Archives of
 1-951    Canada.  Ottawa, 1968-
                  sheets.  11 x 15 cm.
                  1. Canada - Collections.  2. America -
              Collections.  I. Canada.  Archives./
 CaBVaU   Catalogue of pamphlets in the Public
          Archives of Canada.  II. Title.
          Author-title           anals as per Its
          Catalogue.
```

In all cases—except *English and American Drama of the Nineteenth Century*, for which only one copy of each card is needed—two copies of each card are reproduced as described for *American Fiction*. One copy is filed by author and one by highlighted title. (For *English Books, 1641-1700*, the second copies of cards for anonymous works—both title and added entries—are discarded.)

Consideration is being given to beginning analytics for *Early American Imprints, 1801-1819* (American Antiquarian Society) and Three Centuries of French Drama (Falls City).

References

1. *Advances in Librarianship* 2: 170.
2. All the analytics described here can be ordered for 10 cents per card from Microanalytics, Catalogue Divisions, UBC Library, Vancouver 8, B.C., Canada.
3. "Highlighting" derives from the practice of using a felt-tip marking pen to indicate subject headings on Library of Congress cards as a substitute for typing these headings on the same card.

CATALOGUING OF LARGE WORKS ON MICROFORM IN CANADIAN UNIVERSITY LIBRARIES

by June Thompson

Our library plates are extraordinarily full these days. Solutions to many big problems seem just around the corner with talk of LC's retrospective conversion project, packaged libraries, data banks, etc., filling our professional literature. However in most cases we don't know how far "just around the corner" is, and in the meantime we acquire library materials at an almost fantastic rate. We must service them promptly and we make our individual policies hoping they will prove durable, or at least serve the present well.

Reprinted from the *Canadian Library Journal*, 16: 446-52 (November 1969) by permission of the publisher. Copyright © 1969 by the Canadian Library Association.

EDITOR'S NOTE: This is a report on replies to a questionnaire circulated to other university libraries in December, 1968, by the University of Victoria Library.

One of these problems is how to handle large works on microform such as the *Short Title Catalogue*, the TPL *Bibliography of Canadiana*, Tremaine's *Bibliography of Canadian Imprints*, Wright's *American Fiction, Three Centuries of Drama* (English and American), *Three Centuries of French Drama, Four Centuries of Spanish Drama, German Drama on Microcards, Italian Books Before 1601, Italian Drama on Microfilm*, and one could almost continue *ad infinitum*.

Librarians differ as to how these works should be treated. Some think that every text in these microform collections should be represented in our catalogues as fully as a letterpress edition would be, whether or not there is a good printed bibliography in which library holdings could be indicated. These librarians are hoping that the Library of Congress will come to the rescue or that a collective pressure from librarians will encourage, if not force, microform publishers to issue catalogue cards as part of the cost of the work. Others think that in those cases where a good bibliography exists, representation in card catalogues is needless duplication. Where such a bibliography does not exist they question, at least for the present, the utility of some of these collections, presumably considering servicing individual requests for specific items on interlibrary loan a more realistic approach, usually obtaining copies in microform. This group also cites the tremendous recent impetus in reprint publishing. There are many reprint houses on this continent and in Europe and Asia which are systematically reprinting the texts listed in the big bibliographical works. Many of these specialize in facsimile reproduction.[1]

The professional literature does not clarify the issue. For every article advocating representation in the catalogue—usually by means of cards produced as by-products of computer produced lists or indexes, and only in libraries with narrow subject orientation—one can find another which seems to say the problem is non-existent, or not going to continue to exist, because "it has become feasible to collect, index and disseminate complete libraries of material on selected subjects and to provide the user effectively with an indexed, updated, desktop library."[2]

In order to separate the practical present from the possible future and to learn if a co-operative cataloguing endeavour would meet with enthusiasm, we issued a questionnaire in December 1968. The answers to the two basic questions are tabulated:

Library	What is your present policy?	Would you be interested in a cooperative scheme which would produce full or partial cataloguing for all items on the microform?
University of British Columbia Library	Catalogues as a single large work, with a reference on the card to the printed bibliography. Files *author analytics* if commercially available	Would co-operate fully providing cards meet their specifications. Would require only one card per item.
Simon Fraser University Library	Catalogues as a single large work, with a reference on the card to the printed bibliography.	Would co-operate fully.
University of Alberta (Edmonton) Library	Catalogues these large collections as units, but tries to file a *main entry* for each separate item within them. If cards can be purchased, one main entry is bought. If not, in the cases of microcards, microfiches and microprints, typists type up brief main entry directly from microform. For microfilms, no individual entries are made. Have to rely on printed bibliographies for these.	Could not take on responsibility for contributing copy but would purchase card sets.

Library	What is your present policy?	Would you be interested in a cooperative scheme which would produce full or partial cataloguing for all items on the microform?
University of Saskatchewan (Regina Campus) Library	Catalogues as a single large work, with a reference on the card to the printed bibliography.	Could not take on responsibility for contributing copy but would purchase card sets. Sidney Harland suggested the idea of co-operative cataloguing should be considered either by IPCUR or by COWCUL.
University of Manitoba Library	Catalogues as a single large work, with a reference on the card to the printed bibliography.	"Our present policy was adopted after considerable thought, and we believe it to be valid."
Brandon College Library	Buying only newspaper titles on microform at this time.	Unable to co-operate.
Carleton University Library	Catalogues as a single large work, with a reference on the card to the printed bibliography. "It has been our policy . . . to catalogue them as briefly as possible . . . making use of whatever printed indexes may be available to show the library's holdings."	Not stated.

Library	What is your present policy?	Whuld you be interested in a cooperative scheme which would produce full or partial cataloguing for all items on the microform?
McMaster University Library	Catalogues as a single work, with a reference on the card to the printed bibliography or catalogues and classifies each text separately. Choice depends on index available, homogeneity of collection, etc.	Would co-operate fully. Miss David suggested that the National Library be the central office. She suggested further that the National Library union catalogue provide a list of those already done, as a beginning.
Queen's University Library	Catalogues as a single large work, with a reference on the card to the printed bibliography, annotated to show the library's holdings.	"Policy outlined . . . gives adequate access, and no change is contemplated."
University of Toronto Library	Catalogues as a single large work, with a reference on the card to the printed bibliography.	Could not take on responsibility for contributing copy but would purchase card sets. Robert Blackburn reports: "In our opinion the company or institution responsible for the reproduction of the collection should issue with the reproduction, as part of the cost, a bibliography or list of the items represented in sufficient fullness to be adaptable to the individual needs of each purchaser. We have suggested to the Library of Congress that they give top priority, in their retrospective conversion project, to analytics of the microform series."

Library	What is your present policy?	Would you be interested in a cooperative scheme which would produce full or partial cataloguing for all the items on the microform?
Trent University Library	Catalogues as a single large work, with a reference on the card to the printed bibliography.	Unable to join in a co-operative cataloguing scheme.
University of Waterloo Library	Catalogues as a single large work, with a reference on the card to the printed bibliography.	Would make available cataloguing of individual items already done.
University of Western Ontario Library	Catalogues as a single large work, with reference on the card to the printed bibliography.	Could not take on responsibility for contributing copy but could purchase card sets "if acceptable." Miss Jean Elson suggested hiring a retired cataloguer and providing adequate facilities and staff with access to large libraries, thus making an independent project, which would ensure uniformity. She further suggests the possibility of obtaining a Canada Council grant for the project.
University of Windsor Library	Catalogues as a single large work, with a reference on the card to the printed bibliography. Gives as many subject headings as may be useful to the work as a unit. Intends to file cards supplied by the publisher for Wright's *American Fiction*.	Favourably disposed, but adds that ability to co-operate would "depend upon the manner in which the responsibilities were assigned." Would be able to make available cataloguing of individual items already done.

Library	What is your present policy?	Would you be interested in a cooperative scheme which would produce full or partial cataloguing for all the items on the microform?
Sir George Williams University Library	Catalogues as a single large work, "whenever possible" with a reference on the card to the printed bibliography or index.	Could not take on responsibility for contributing copy. Would not purchase card sets because they would be a "duplication of information which is readily available in great detail in the bibliographies." Michael Hood expressed the opinion that a large part of the material (letterpress editions) is already catalogued.
Mount Allison University Memorial Library	Catalogues as a single large work, with a reference on the card to the printed bibliography.	Could not take on responsibility for contributing copy but could purchase card sets "depending on cost per set."
St. Francis Xavier University Angus L. Macdonald Library	Not stated	Converting collection to LC. Could not co-operate.
Memorial University of Newfoundland Library	Of the type of work in question has only the Pollard and Redgrave, for which they are filing the (main entry) card supplied by University Microfilms.	Could not take on responsibility for contributing copy but could purchase card sets.

The two French-speaking universities, Laval and Montreal, because of the nature of their collections—preponderantly French language—and their cataloguing in French (notes, subject headings, bibliographical terminology) felt they could neither contribute significantly nor receive much benefit from a co-operative endeavour. Daniel Reicher did put forth the interesting suggestion that the British and Americans "should look after their share of the work," i.e., the STC and Wright.

We have not included in the above tabulation the replies of several new university libraries which apparently are not acquiring microforms of the type in question at this time. In all cases they expressed interest in a co-operative scheme but none could co-operate fully.

It will surprise no one, as the survey shows, that libraries are not cataloguing in full the individual texts in these massive microform collections. The number of titles in a single collection can be almost as large as the yearly book intake of some of the reporting libraries. Without exception, libraries are cataloguing these works as a single large unit, with a reference on the card to the printed bibliography where one exists. Several are filing a main entry, or author analytic, or information card in their main catalogues, if it is available commercially. No library mentioned filing of title added entries, though it is expected that for a few works title added entries have been filed. The University of Alberta, Edmonton, which appears to have the most ambitious program, where main entry cards are not available commercially, has typed up directly from the individual card, fiche, or print a brief main entry. They do not attempt to analyse microfilm collections unless, as mentioned, the cards are available commercially.

We need not emphasize the massive undertaking the full cataloguing of all the titles in these collections would be. Even the servicing of commercially available analytics is a large project. The authority work involved requires staff with considerable training, especially since the new rules and the policy of superimposition have interjected complications. The filing and filing revision loads—problems under normal circumstances—burgeon to unwiedly proportions.

The demise of the micro-opaque has been predicted for some time, as well as the limited use of film. There is an increasing trend towards microfiche. At least one firm, Houston Fearless of California, is known to have developed equipment for automatic access to a microfiche store.

This survey, like so many library surveys, raises more questions than it answers. The solution to the problem at hand is not in the hands of librarians alone, but in the cooperation of librarians, scholars, producers of microforms, and government agencies, such as our own National Office of Library Resources.

At the University of Victoria Library we have filed complete card sets—author, title, and subject entries—for the *Three Centuries of English and American Plays*. This cataloguing was done at the University of

Missouri. Some librarians may recall the troublesome conflicts in headings encountered in the filing of these. We have on hand the cards for Evans' *Early American Imprints* (information cards only), Wright's *American Fiction* (full card sets), *Short-Title Catalogue* (full card sets), and *U.S. Documents* series (information cards only). We have acquired recently Angotti's *Source Materials in the Field of Theatre,* the *Clearing House for Sociological Literature* and the *Human Relations Area Files.* Our need to know how other libraries were coping with this inundation prompted our questionnaire.

A consideration of the almost incalculable amount of work involved in articulate representation of these massive works in our card catalogues brings us full circle back to the ubiquitous questions "What are the scope and the function of card catalogues?" and "Which materials are adequately served by traditional cataloguing and which demand indexing?"

Fundamental, then, to the solution of the problem discussed in this article are some definitions—possibly redefinitions—of goals and functions, and a perceptive consideration of the changing nature of the library's stock.

Footnotes

1. Examples of such reprint series are: Johnson Reprint: Canadiana before 1867, Canadiana after 1867; Gregg Press: Americans in fiction; Da Capo Press: The English experience (facsimile reprints of English books printed before 1640); Books for Libraries: Select bibliographies series; Bohn: Antiquarian series, Garrett Press: American short stories series; University Microfilms; Xerox copies of STC texts; Hurtig: Reprints of Canadiana, etc.

2. Williams, B.J.S. Microfilms on informtion retrieval and communications systems. ASLIB *proceedings*, v. 19, no. 7, p. 228.

3. For their report, see *Library resources and technical services*, v. 6, no. 1, Winter 1962, pp. pp. 29-39.

ADDITIONAL READINGS

Brockway, Duncan, "A New Look at the Cataloging of Microfilm," *Library Resources and Technical Services,* 4: 323-330 (Fall 1960).

Dodson, Suzanne, "The University of British Columbia Library's Guide to Large Collections in Microform: One Attempt to Minimize a Major Problem," *Microform Review,* 1: 113-17 (April 1972).

Hale, Richard W., Jr., "Cataloging of Microfilm," *American Archivist,* 22: 11-13 (1969).

ORGANIZATION

Introduction

Microforms have unfortunately been the neglected step-children of libraries consigned to whatever dark corners happen to be available. Holmes in his 1969 study notes, "Approximately one-half of the respondents believed that neither the environment nor the facilities available for the use of microforms were conducive to their proper use. A number of respondents were quite emphatic on this point. . . . It would be fair to say that a majority of respondents . . . believed that work space provided for microform usage by many institutions is very inadequate."[1]

Reichmann and Tharpe in their 1970/71 investigation found that of 168 libraries responding, forty-seven (30 percent) had a professional librarian in charge of their microform collection; two were considering appointing a professional librarian; eighty-nine had clerical help or student assistants in charge; thirty had a clerical staff professionally supervised by other departments. They also found that 40 percent had a caged or vaulted area in the stacks for microforms while 60 percent had a separate room.[2]

The trend today appears to be toward centralization with an area set aside for microforms under the supervision of a librarian with special training. Storage is under heat and humidity controls and ambient light is at normal levels allowing both reading of the microforms and note taking. Access to the microforms is not open. They are checked out as are reserve books.

The papers that follow discuss the major aspects of organizing a microform collection for use: acquisitions, bibliographic control, physical location, centralized or decentralized, administration and staffing, open or closed access, hardware, maintenance and storage.

References

1. Holmes, Donald C., *Determination of User Needs and Future Requirements for a Systems Approach to Microform Technology.* July 19, 1969, ERIC ED 029 168, pp. 6-7.
2. Reichmann, Felix, and Tharpe, Josephine, *Bibliographic Control of Microforms.* Westport, Greenwood, 1972.

DESIGN FOR A
MICROTEXT READING ROOM

by David C. Weber

Since the 1930s every large research library has had a collection of microfilms. In the present decade nearly every major library has acquired a sizable collection of microfilm, microfiche and opaque microsheets. This article is intended to describe design conditions which will create an effective microtext reading-room for these materials.

For the sake of discussion it is assumed that this is a microtext reading-room for a new building, one that is just being planned. A university library would be the typical subject because these libraries have the larger collections of microtexts at present. It seems evident, however, that in the future the young colleges may place major emphasis on microtext collections in their attempt to acquire large collections of documents, and these will be relatively cheap to acquire by virtue of existing microtext publishing projects. Thus, even the very small college may find itself with a large microtext collection and the need to provide adequate reading arrangements for students given assignments which demand use of microtexts.

The first question in planning a microtext reading-room is whether to decentralize the service by placing the materials with or near other materials of the same subject. The arguments in favour of decentralization are entirely based on the convenience of students who may wish to find all material in physics in the science library, or all material on law in the law library. This is a strong argument for decentralization.

The arguments in favour of a centralized location for microtexts are based upon economy of operation, efficiency in library organization and

Reprinted from *UNESCO Bulletin for Libraries,* 20: 303-08 (November/December 1966) by permission of the publisher. Copyright © 1966 by UNESCO.

greater protection for materials. Money invested in the space occupied by microtext reading machines cannot serve other purposes. It is therefore important that the space be used as many hours in the week as possible in order that the cost of the building be reasonable in terms of man-hours of use. There is also the investment in the reading equipment. It is obviously more economical to have the reading machines in one location where a student can find one that is available; whereas, if the machines are spread among several locations in the building or scattered around the campus, the student is likely to try one location for reading equipment and give up if one is not available.

There is also an economy in centralization in terms of the library staff, for microtexts are such small and easily misplaced units that it is advisable for the staff to control their circulation strictly. The machines are also relatively delicate; instructions in machine use and oversight are advisable in order that the microtexts may be protected from damage. Finally, because of the advantages of air-conditioning or air-filtering systems, it is advantageous to assemble the films and the reading equipment in space with the proper controls of ventilation. Unless the entire library building is air-conditioned, this requires bringing the materials into a space so treated.

Still, if the use of the microtexts is heavy enough so that more than one room must be air-conditioned, or more than one full-time staff member is required to service the collection, then the important argument in favour of decentralization can prompt a division of the facilities into two locations. In the long run it seems probable that all major branch libraries will have a sizable microtext collection with adequate staff and adequate facilities. Then the consideration of centralized advantages can be overlooked. At present, however, the microtext reading-room in the typical college or university library should be a single facility placed in a location where staff can give the maximum hours of service.

The next question may be the location of such a room within the library building. This is a rather elusive point because there are many advantages in one or another relationship. The final decision will depend upon the importance of various relationships. Factors which should be considered are the realtionship to the general reference collection, to the photographic laboratory if one exists, to the order department and cataloguing department, to the public catalogue, and to the rare books department and newspaper collection. Some advantage is gained when each of these is close to the microtext reading-room.

For example, the use of bibliographies and indexes makes obvious the advantage of having the microtext reading-room next to the general reference collection. It may be that large microtext collections are indexed through such reference sets as Charles Evans' *American bibliography*, Pollard and Redgrave's *Short-title catalogue of books printed in . . . English . . . 1475-1640*, or the *Monthly catalog of United States*

Government publications, and the library may not be in a position to afford duplication of these sets in a distant microtext reading-room. The photographic laboratory offers the advantage of technical editing for newly received microtexts; it can splice or spool or duplicate new acquisitions and can offer convenient enlargement service for persons wishing to place orders. The advantage in a close relation to the acquisition and cataloguing departments lies in enabling this staff to use the microtext reading machines to authenticate an acquisition or catalogue acquisition. The advantages with respect to the rare book department are that a student wishing to compare a rare book with a copy on microfilm may do so, rare books being loaned rarely for use outside the department except under immediate supervision. The relationship to the newspaper collection is also an important consideration, since, in many libraries, newspapers form the bulk of the microtext collection owing to the problems of storing the originals, given their size and the rapid deterioration of the paper.

Several of these arguments can be invalidated by placing extra microtext reading machines in the order and cataloguing departments or in the rare book department. Extra copies of reference books and a separate card catalogue can make the microtext reading-room bibliographically independent. Specialized staff in the microtext reading-room can handle most simple jobs of film maintenance and cleaning, and more time-consuming technical jobs can be sent some distance to a laboratory. Consequently the questions of relationship are merely for consideration; they should not force a solution which otherwise may be awkward or undesirable.

The next question is whether the reading-room should be placed on the main floor of the building or in the basement or on an upper floor. The relationship to bibliographical tools is an important one and may suggest a place on or near the floor on which the main catalogue and reference books are located. Still, an elevator may minimize the disadvantage of placing the microtext reading-room one or more floors away from this bibliographical center.

Another important aspect to be taken in consideration is the future need for space, for the microtext collection is likely to grow even more rapidly than the others. The microtext reading-room should therefore be located with adjacent space into which it can expand when the need arises and maximum flexibility is desirable. In large American libraries there are examples of efficient microtext reading-rooms located in the basement and others on the top floor or elsewhere in the building; in all cases effective working arrangements can be made, provided desirable relationships are kept in mind in determining and adjusting to the final arrangements.

The decision will usually be taken in favour of a remote location, although, where new libraries rely on microtexts for basic course assignments, a more central location may be distinctly preferable because of anticipated heavy use by great numbers of students.

Different arrangements have been chosen by different libraries. Harvard

University's Widener Library first placed reading equipment near the current newspapers in a stack area adjacent to the current periodical room. In the 1950s a larger space was found on the top floor (where it was adjacent to the university archives). In the present decade it is housed with newspapers and government documents in still larger space in a public stack level beneath the Lamont Library. Other libraries have placed the service next to the newspaper files which account for the major part of the microtexts and are in the greatest use. This is true of the University of Chicago and Stanford University. (Stanford's microtext reading-room is also near the shelves of publications of various government and the Atomic Energy Commission technical reports, materials which are also of first importance in the microtext collection.) Microfilm reading-rooms of the Canadian National Library are next to the newspaper and\periodical reading-room. The University Library of the University of Sheffield has placed the equipment in small rooms adjoining a special postgraduate and academic staff reading-room. Still another solution was found at the McKeldin Library of the University of Maryland where a microtext reading-room was designed near the government document collections and special collections in space up a short flight of stairs from the public catalogue and reference librarians.

Next arises the question of administrative assignment. The choice of department to which the microtext reading-room is responsible may also be a matter of physical proximity. Depending upon staff organization and talents, and spatial relationships, responsibilities for the reading-room could be assigned to the circulation staff, reference staff, photographic laboratory, audio-visual service, rare books and special collections department, or the administrative office. Other possibilities certainly exist. The chief basis for assignment is to place the responsibility where the staff has a strong interest in this material. It need not necessarily be a staff which has the subject education to give reference assistance, since microtext collections are generally universal in subject content and students come to it with a specific reference in hand. A strong interest in this format and its equipment will ensure the requisite attention and service.

When a microtext reading-room is first set up the room is likely to be the part-time responsibility of a staff member whose primary job is in some more traditional aspect of the library. Consequently, responsibility almost surely rests with the department which is located right beside the microtext reading-room and the staff member can conveniently service the collection on a part-time basis. As time goes on the necessity will develop for a full-time attendant in order to handle the expensive equipment and materials and protect the library's investment, as well as to improve its service of this special material.

Once the service is large enough to justify a full-time staff, the responsibility may well be assigned to a department at some distance. For example, a microtext reading-room placed in a basement location may report to a reference department two floors away because of advantages gained by the co-ordination of the work of the microtext attendant with that of the librarians giving special bibliographical assistance to the students. Thus the location and design of the room are not seriously affected by administrative considerations.

The person managing the microtext reading-room should fully understand the fragility of reading machines, the delicacy of film, the importance of guiding students in the use of microtext bibliographies, and materials, and should be able to undertake responsibility for splicing and cleaning the films. If he can also become a specialist in the bibliography of newspapers, government documents or early imprints, this would obviously result in improved service, since these materials commonly account for such a large part of microtext collections.

In deciding upon the precise layout of the microtext reading-room, the following elements and their spatial relationships must be taken into consideration: reading stations, the collection of materials, the catalogue of the collection, the shelves of reference and index books, and the staff service desk. The arrangement will depend upon whether or not students are permitted to select their own materials and to have free access to the reading machines. More often a staff member will fetch the microtext and go with the student to a reading desk to give him brief instruction in use of the machine. In this case the attendant controls shelf access, just as with rare books or manuscripts; and the service desk will be placed between the collection and the reading machines.

Before treating the spatial relationship of these five elements, the particular requirements of each will be described.

Reading desks should be large tables, counters, or specially designed desks. The total area per student must accommodate the machine itself, with space for note taking, the possibility of typing, and a shelf for holding books which may be used in conjunction with a special project. This requires a reading space which is substantially larger than that accorded most students. Since some reading machines will occupy a little more than 1 sq. ft. of the table top while others will approach 4 sq. ft. in size, at the minimum, each reading space should be 2 ft. deep by 4 ft. wide. Far better is provision of a table space 3 ft. deep by 5 ft. in width, and a research library is well advised to make no compromise concerning this larger size. Indeed, for general planning, 40 sq. ft. per reading station should be used.

In libraries which can afford one or more reading-printing machines, the desks for such machines would have to be very close to the staff desk if any control is to be exercised over the number of copies made or if payment for copies is required. Typing can be provided for by having movable typing stands on which portable typewriters may be used, or on which library-owned standard typewriters are available. (Because any vibration of the table will markedly shorten the life of the bulb in the reading machine, no typing should be permitted on the reading table itself.) Each student position should include a local light control and a card holder for instructions on use of the machine. The chairs for microfilm reading should be selected with comfort in mind but should not be reclining chairs since it is preferable to sit close to the machine for the best visibility and for taking hand-written notes or typing.

The collection of microtexts may be housed in several ways. First of all, a distinction should be made between master films and reading films, the former being archival and the latter replaceable copies for student use. The master films should be kept on shelves in a fireproof air-conditioned vault and may be located next to the microfilm laboratory—or even outside the library—rather than near the microtext reading-room. The equipment to house the reading copies must handle both roll form and sheet form. The sheets may be accommodated in card files or file drawers with suitable index tabs. The roll films may be kept either in metal cabinets 42 in. to 48 in. high with shallow drawers or on standard 7½ ft. high book shelves.

It is advantageous to have the most frequently used microtexts in a location closest to the reading desks. Access is quickest to heavily used reels if they are kept in microfilm drawers so that a drawer containing one year or more of a newspaper can be pulled out and the desired roll selected with a single motion. The use of standard shelves is entirely satisfactory protection so long as the room itself has adequate atmospheric controls; and the standard shelves do provide for the greatest economy in shelving. If reels are on book shelves they should be placed in individual microfilm cartons. To shelve more compactly these cartons may in turn be placed in larger boxes for convenience in handling. (Larger boxes which hold six cartons are the most convenient size and weight.)

The card catalogue of a microtext collection will usually be located near the staff service desk. In some libraries, however, the materials may be catalogued only in the main public catalogue so that the student comes to the microtext reading-room with a specific reference and film number in hand. In this case no staff help is given within the room although a shelf list may be available for inventory purposes. Similarly the reference books or bibliographies may be located next to the service desk. It may be useful to have extra copies of the more frequently used dictionaries, atlases, and encyclopaedias available for the use of students working for a considerable length of time in the microtext collections.

The staff service desk needs to be near the entrance, beside any catalogues, and perhaps controlling the shelf area. Light must be ample. The desk needs to be large enough to keep supplies of reels, boxes, paper for the reader-printer, circulation records, etc. The service desk may be a counter, in fact, so that portable machines for loan to professors may be kept in cupboards below. Alternatively a closet would suffice for extra machines and supplies. A telephone is essential for communication with other departments of the library.

With regard to the spatial relationship of all these elements, the general arrangement in the microtext reading-room will depend upon the degree of control which the library wishes to have over its collection and reading machines. One grouping may provide completely free student access to the materials; the students find the microtexts easily obtainable for convenience and speed of use. The other extreme could provide closed access where a staff member obtains each item at the request of the student. This arrangement has obvious advantages for keeping order in files of microfiche and other sheet forms. Or, it is possible to keep a few selected heavily-used titles in space accessible to the students and have other materials controlled by the staff. The choice of the best layout for any one library can be determined only locally. Nevertheless, it is always best to separate the service desk and the collections which need high illumination from the reading stations where subdued lighting is desirable. It should also be possible to arrange the collections so that they are usually closed to students but can be opened at any time.

Some idea of the size of a university microtext facility may be given by outlining Stanford University's provisions for its 11,000 students. The library has, in 1966, about 30,000 microfilm reels, 50,000 microfiche and 250,000 opaque microprint sheets. Because a small portion of the microfilms is desired in the branch libraries for music, education, earth sciences and chemistry, as well as in the Hoover Institution, a reading machine is located in each of these libraries. About 75 percent of the total university microtext collection is housed in an air-conditioned room of 2,400 sq. ft. in the Main Library basement level. There are an attendant's desk, 180 card catalogue drawers, eighteen carrels measuring 5 ft. by 33 in. for reading machines, two carrels measuring 6 ft. by 39 in. for reader-printers, 292 drawers in metal cases for the most-used reels and fiche, 65 sections of bookstacks, and two supply closets.

The engineering specifications for the microtext reading-room should be considered with great care. These will include lighting, electrical outlets, air filter, cooling system, humidity control, and acoustical treatment.

With respect to lighting it is important that provision be made for reducing or adjusting the light intensity around the reading desks while at the same time giving adequate light for the staff and the shelving area. This will require some subdivision of the switching unless adjacent rooms are used, one being allotted to the reading desks and another to the collections. It is useful, as noted above, to have low intensity lights at each reading desk (perhaps 25 watts, each position having a local rheostat) so that the student may adjust it for note-taking or typing as he may wish. Adequate electric outlets must be provided so that each position has at least two to accommodate the machine and also an electric typewriter or other electric appliance. Some reader-printers require ground connexions.

The ventilation design must deal adequately with three problems. The air filtering system is by far the most important owing to the irreparable damage that can be done to machines and microtexts by dust and soot. Cooling is also important in most parts of the world for too much heat will make the film emulsion sticky and thus easily damaged, while too cold a storage condition will make the film stiff. Humidity is the other factor. Extremely dry air will produce film brittleness; high humidity creates favourable conditions for biological attack on the film. Although very strict humidity conditions must be adhered to for master films, the materials for reading use can tolerate greater leeway. Standards should be followed depending upon local conditions and the degree to which the collection must be preserved for future students.

Acoustic control is important because of machine noise. Since students generally prefer individual carrels with privacy for study, the desks may be constructed with a back and sides rising 54 in. from the floor. These dividers provide some sound-conditioning; and acoustic board can be used for extra control as was done at the University of Chicago Library. Acoustic ceilings are especially desirable. Further, in a room which is too quiet interrupted percussive noises create a disturbing effect. Ventilation equipment which makes a low constant background noise consequently gives an impression of greater privacy and quiet for serious study.

Finally, a staff operating manual should be drawn up to ensure a periodic inspection schedule, including cleaning of the film transport mechanism, the glass flats and reading screens, and other essential parts. Some of this work can be done by the library staff, although major work should be undertaken by photographic specialists within the institution or on contract from a commercial firm. However it is accomplished, regular maintenance is important. Libraries are investing many thousands of dollars in building space, microtext reading equipment, and in microtext documents themselves. Students and scholars will be served well only by a library which gives constant attention to the reasonable preservation of such an important library investment.

References

American Library Association. *Microfilm norms*. Chicago, 1966.
American Standards Association. *American standard practice for storage of microfilms*. New York, 1957.
Ballou, Hubbard. *Guide to microreproduction equipment*. 3rd ed. Annapolis, National Microfilm Association, 1965.
Bechanan, H. Gordon. The organization of microforms in the library. *Library trends*. January 1960, p. 391-406.
Eastman Kodak Company. *Storage of microfilms, sheetfilms and prints*. Rochester, 1955. (Pamphlet F-11).
Fussler, Herman H. *Photographic reproduction for libraries; a study of administrative problems*. Chicago, University of Chicago, 1942, chapter 6, section 5.
Metcalf, Keyes D. *Planning academic and research library buildings*. New York, McGraw-Hill. 1965, p. 111-12, 172-3.
Poindron, Paul, ed. *Manuel pratique de reproduction documentaire et de sélection*. Paris. Gauthier-Villars, 1964.
Weber, David C. How to store microfilm cheaply. *Library Journal*, 15 September, 1956, p. 1978-80.

THE MICROTEXT READING ROOM:
A PRACTICAL APPROACH

by Judy Fair

The first of a series of articles is designed to prepare the library and the librarian for creating or renovating a microtext reading room. Aptitudes and attitudes of the person administratively responsible for the room are discussed, and the basic microform acquisition procedures are outlined. A systems approach and careful planning are emphasized.

This series of articles will contain prejudiced, controversial, and perhaps slightly unorthodox ideas. They are meant to be only a starting place, mere guideposts for those who must deal with microtexts face to face, day to day. The library assistant and/or the librarian who must make decisions concerning the microtext reading room operations may find some informative items herein. Administrators may also happen upon a possible solution to a current problem. No matter which position one occupies vis à vis microtexts, certain specific knowledge is necessary. Deciding which titles, which microtext format, which readers, which storage cabinets, which hard copy printers, which indexes, and which chairs to buy for a particular library situation is a complicated responsibility. Discussions with staff members and resultant decisions must cover selection procedures, an appropriate classification scheme, marking and labeling patterns for containers, shelving and storage facilities, equipment service contracts, modernization of lighting, staffing requirements, circulation rules, and user expectations. If the microtext manager is absent, someone has to know how to thread the film into the reading machines, change the bulbs, and find that elusive item for the chairman of the history department or the company's administrative vice president.

Reprinted from *Microform Review*, 1: 199-202 (July 1972); 1: 269-73 (October 1972); 2: 9-13 (January 1973); 2: 168-71 (July 1973); 3: 11-14 (January 1974) by permission of the publisher. Copyright © 1972, 1973, 1974 by Microform Review Inc.

As Alan Meckler has noted elsewhere in this issue, there should be specific training in library schools for microtext librarians, and there should also be official recognition of the job through use of the designation "microtext librarian." Neither of these conditions is likely to be realized at present; however, lack of the former may be supplied by diligent study by the individual. A high-priority undertaking for a librarian newly assigned to microtexts is to become the resident expert on them, overnight if possible. One direct approach to that problem is to read appropriate citations in *Library Literature* along with the publications mentioned in these articles. (Only essential or exceptionally useful sources will be listed herein by the author.) Vital to building one's expertise are: *The Evaluation of Micropublications: A Handbook for Librarians, Guide to Microreproduction Equipment* (5th ed.), *Glossary of Terms for Microphotography and Reproductions Made from Micro-images* (4th ed.), and Bechanan's article in *Library Trends* (January 1960). Other articles may be selected on a random basis; "the ore assay is likely to be very low," but reading such pieces will help to sharpen one's own understanding about the job and its problems.

The microtext manager is the essential bridge between the medium and the user, in as much as the patron cannot browse and therefore does not usually go directly to the microtext, certainly not for first-time use. This communication function is critical to the establishment of a solid and beneficial relationship between users and microtexts. Hence, special expertise—a substantial knowledge of the field—is the essential criterion in the choice of a microtext manager. Librarians sometimes appear to be encouraging microtexts to "wither away" by according them "second-class" treatment. Worse, librarians often transmit to patrons their own negative attitudes toward microtexts. Today such immature attitudes are unrealistic and impractical. A positive approach about microtexts, based not only on enthusiasm but also on learning, is essential. There are far too many uninformed enthusiasts buying and proclaiming the questionable virtues of poor quality microtext projects. To preclude either extreme, negativism or unthinking enthusiasm, one must acquire both knowledge and judgment.

The individual who is to administer the microtext operations should also analyze the existing system and design its replacement; in reality this is not always possible because of staff limitations. In any event, the analysis and design work should, of course, be done by a person with special logical abilities. It will be assumed in these articles that the ideal situation—one person who analyzes, designs, and later administrates the room—prevails. (Other staffing possibilities will be discussed in more detail in a later article.) Ideally the microtext manager would have no other duties, but in today's library that is, in many cases, an unrealistic approach. The microtext manager can, however, be given additional nonprofessional help or be released from some duties in order to concentrate on microtexts. The librarian should be familiar with analytical processes, and some mechanical aptitude is an added virtue. The microtext facilities manager should also be vested with the authority and status needed to participate in the decisions concerning the operations. The position must be recognized as a legitimate one by the entire staff, not as simply a minor, disagreeable, undesirable task. Efficient facilities do not just occur; they require planning and effort by a capable and intelligent person.

Another high-priority task is to analyze the existing local situation regarding microtexts. The challenge may be to plan a new facility or revitalize the old arrangement. One aspect of such an analysis is the condition of equipment. For example, it may be possible to have existing equipment repaired either by the manufacturer or by a qualified local agency. On the other hand, the cost and effort of repairs (and the age of the equipment) might be great enough to warrant it more desirable to purchase new machines.

For precise and useful design of the microtext reading room one *must*, I believe, use a systems approach. Outlining and flow-charting the situation will clarify the problems and suggest possible solutions. The possibility should not be overlooked that the library assistant, if there is one, may have experiences and practical knowledge to contribute. Additional input for one's planning may come from visits to other libraries. Such trips will also point out the variety of planning ideas about microtext reading rooms. One might wish to approach a facility in the guise of a user to discover both good and bad aspects of an operation. If trips are not possible, one should probably avoid sending out questionnaires to already very busy librarians. A close acquaintance in another library might be willing to describe that particular facility, but presumption of that kind on a large-scale basis is unreasonable.

During reading, discussing, and flow-charting, it is most important to place the patron's needs at the center of the deliberations. One very simple test of a library's attitudes toward microtexts and users is the ease with which it is possible to find the microtext reading room. The sense of frustration and active dislike felt by some users for microtexts is undoubtedly contributed to by their lengthy search for the facility. Another common indication of disregard on the library's part is a generally poor-quality facility. The room may be prominently located but sadly neglected because of the low position of microtexts on the library's list of priorities.

It may take days or weeks to arrive at an outline of procedures that is workable and understandable to all affected staff members. Perseverance does carry the reward of a final organization of one's own thoughts. Facts, figures, and sound arguments must be used to convince the administration of the necessity for establishing a good microform reading room, especially when the cost is likely to be high. Explanation and justification of one's position about centralization versus decentralization of the collection, about personnel relationships with other departments, and about use and lending procedures, as well as other decisions, will be necessary. A sound analysis and system or outline provides a strong logical means of presenting one's assessment and evaluation.

The rest of the information to be presented in this series will deal with specific operations. The procedures which must be analyzed in the context of the conditions within a specific library. The first of these procedures, chosen arbitrarily, is acquisitions.

In many libraries today the person responsible for the microtext reading room knows very little about what materials are being ordered. Consequently, questions from users about the library's ownership of a certain title may be answered incorrectly or the unexpected arrival of a large set could cause a real shelving crisis. To avoid such difficulties and to be fully aware of the library's microtext acquisitions, the librarian should be included in the flow of information from the requestor to the Order Department. During the systems analysis phase, the librarian should learn from Order Department staff the procedures for ordering microtexts. Then, consideration should be given to how departmental and/or individual routines might be altered to include the microtext manager in the transfer of information. If possible, several alternatives should be developed in flow-chart format, but they should be kept as simple and as close to effective existing procedures as possible. There is usually no need to propose drastic changes in organizational routines. Probably the end result need be only a 3 × 5 inch "P-slip" typed as a duplicate of the request or a carbon from the purchase order. A file of the slips might be kept as "ordered" and "received" by either the microtext librarian or the Order Department. A useful place for such a file is in the microtext reading room itself, even though the facility manager may have a desk elsewhere in the library. Then, as questions arise about the acquisition or receipt of a microtext or about varying main entries, they can be answered quickly by checking the microtext order file. When a routine has been approved by those affected, a memorandum for general distribution will help to explain the new procedures to the library staff.

Another responsibility that will devolve to the microtext librarian is that of helping library staff and patrons identify or verify requests. Copies of the *Guide to Microforms in Print* and the *Subject Guide to Microforms in Print* should be ordered if they are not already held by the library. Copies of catalogs from the major micropublishers, listed in the beginning pages of the *Guide*, should also be requested. These catalogs can be filed alphabetically in a pamphlet box in order to keep supplemental loose sheets and advance notices from publishers with their major catalogs. A vigorous effort should be made to have the latest editions of these catalogs on hand. Two other valuable acquisitions tools are the *National Register of Microform Masters* and *Newspapers on Microfilm*. A brief discussion of these two Library of Congress publications may be useful in establishing their value. The *Register's* previous arrangement by LC card number made searching a particular title tedious at best. The newest edition (1970) contains about 64,000 serial and monograph entries in one alphabetical arrangement with about 10,000 cross-references. The entry format has been revised to make the listings easier to read. The 1970 edition is free to *National Union Catalog* subscribers and costs nonsubscribers $12.50. The seventh edition of *Newspapers on Microfilm* has also been revised and enlarged to include about 41,000 titles. The arrangement is still by geographic location, but the titles are in strict title listing, not keyword-in-context. Successive entry cataloging, better seen than described to be understood, has been used to provide access to the various titles of any one newspaper, virtually eliminating cross-references. More information about either title can be obtained by writing to: Editor, Catalog Publication Division, Library of Congress, Washington, D.C. 20540.

Some requests will be extremely difficult to identify. L. M. Hall in the *Southeastern Librarian* (Winter 1970) describes a variety of lists to use for both acquisition and later bibliographic control. Every librarian has favorite sources for verification; perhaps it would be possible through a cooperative effort to publish a compilation of such sources published. The Order Department staff of one's own library may have their own special tools and should be consulted about that probability. Batching problem citations to be worked on at the same time is a further step toward efficiency.

The success of efforts to include the microtext manager in the acquisitions process depends to a considerable extent on staff attitudes toward microtexts and their ordering. Previously a requestor may have casually submitted a title to be ordered and then trusted the system to obtain and process it. Performance can be improved by showing that the new procedure is more rapid and efficient. It is important also to indicate that there is no need or desire to remove anyone's decision-making authority.

Occasionally microtext items arrive on the microtext manager's desk with no sign of identification. Some information may be deduced from the title page of the item; sometimes the order has been sent out as a regular monograph order and has missed the special file. If the item has not been ordered or paid for, it is usually best to return it to the manufacturer rather than incur the expense of searching, cataloging, and storing an originally unwanted item.

To summarize, the microtext librarian is the focal point of the organization or reorganization of the microtext reading room. The person chosen should have displayed some previous talent for logical thinking and should begin by outlining the actions necessary to create a good facility. The flow of acquisiton information should be directed through that person as a first practical step in managing the facility and its service. Future chapters will address problems of bibliographic control, equipment, staffing and other subjects.

Literature Cited

Bechanan, H. Gordon. "The Organization of Microforms in the Library." *Library Trends*, 8: 391-406 (January 1960).

Guide to Microforms in Print. (Washington: Microcard Editions, 1962/1963−.)

Hall, L. M. "Bibliographic Control of Microforms." *Southeastern Librarian*, 20: 258-266 (Winter 1970).

National Microfilm Association, *Glossary of Terms for Microphotography and Reproductions Made From Micro-Images.* Edited by Donald M. Avedon, 4th ed., NMA Information Monograph No. 2 (Annapolis: National Microfilm Association, 1966).

National Microfilm Association, *Guide to Microreproduction Equipment.* Edited by Hubbard Ballou, 5th ed., (Annapolis: National Microfilm Association, 1971).

National Register of Microform Masters. (Washington: Library of Congress, 1965−).

Newspapers on Microfilm, compiled by G. S. Schwegmann, Jr. 6th ed. (Washington: Library of Congress, 1967−).

Subject Guide to Microforms in Print. (Washington: Microcard Editions, 1962/1963−.)

Veaner, Allen B., *The Evaluation of Micropublications: A Handbook for Librarians.* LTP Publication No. 17 (Chicago: American Library Association, 1971).

Weber, David C. "Design for A Microtext Reading Room." *Unesco Bulletin for Libraries*, 20: 303-308 (Nov.−Dec. 1966).

Part I dealt with the selection of a microtext manager and with procedural considerations in the acquisition process. Part II continues the discussion about acquisitions, including consideration of format, variation, and reliability of publisher-supplied project information. The Library's search for an adequate system of bibliographic control is examined. Cataloging methods, classification schemes, and hardcopy guides and indexes are discussed as components of bibliographic control.

The microtext manager should educate key members of the acquisition or selection staff regarding microtext formats. Often there is no format decision to make, as the desired material is available only in one format. But the staff should be alert to possible alternatives. If a needed item were available in opaque, or non-transparent positive card format, and the library had no opaque viewing equipment, a considerable sum could be wasted by a careless purchase. When considering transparencies such as film or fiche, one must be aware of the choice of negative or positive polarity. If a Xerox Microprinter is available, and it has been set for positive polarity, one can order positive film or fiche and produce positive hard copy. However, negative film cannot then be copied on the same machine. Other reader-printers simply reverse the polarity, producing positive copy from negative film and vice versa.

In the debate about which polarity is easier to read, one should consider the type of viewers available. In viewers with translucent screens, the light is directed at the screen from behind shining through the film directly into the eyes of the patron; thus the total amount of light reaching a person's eyes will be much less with negative film. Viewers where the light does not shine directly into the eyes of the users but is directed onto a flat surface are good for use with positive film. One should also be aware that negative film seems to mask the existence of lint, dust, or other foreign matter which might be visible and distracting to the patron if the film were positive.

Another consideration is, that in reproducing hard copy from negative microtext, more toner is necessary for production of a good quality copy from the film. Thus the microtext manager has an important responsibility in this seemingly minor, and often casually made decision.

She/He can prepare an easily understood chart or table describing the types of microtext format and the best choices for that library's purchases. A glance at the chart would be sufficient to allow the selection staff to choose the appropriate format. Equipment requirements for these formats can also be included in the chart. Attention to such details can prevent not only a waste of money but also an uncomfortable, frustrating experience for the user.

The problem of material available in one format only, and the format being unreadable on the library's present equipment, has no ready solution. Some day it may be possible to specify a particular format for a title. Until such time, several other alternatives might be considered. When asking that new machines be purchased, be sure to include cost and use data to justify spending a large amount for machines to be used relatively little. It can be pointed out that collections already purchased may be simply ignored and wasted due to lack of equipment. A cooperative arrangement to use a nearby library's or office's machine could be considered, but possible damage may occur to the microtext if transported carelessly or to the machine if used by someone unfamiliar with the mechanism.

In the acquisition of a "package"—a set of microtexts, external guides, and equipment—all components, not just the titles being offered, should be carefully considered. If one part of the package is of poor quality, the value of the project may be considerably decreased. If the index is insufficiently detailed or difficult to use, the patron will not find the information he is looking for or will simply give up the search. If the reading machine is poorly designed or is defective optically or mechanically, the patron will be discouraged from using the resource a second time. However, if the material included in the collection is not within the scope of the library's collection parameters, no librarian should be lured into a purchase by the seeming benefits of equipment or bibliographic aids offered with the material. Enthusiasm for the viewer being offered or interest in an unusual index should not overwhelm the basic selection decision in evaluating substantive content of the project.

In the selection of any material the microtext manager and all selection staff should proceed with Veaner's checklist, pp. 25-28 in hand. "In a more perfect world," answers to those questions should be readily apparent from the publisher's literature describing the project. Unhappily the brochures are generally vague and all too often so are replies to direct questions in letters to the publishers. Sometimes a project or single work is needed badly enough to warrant the purchase of a less than fully satisfactory product. I can only urge that those decisions be made after the most careful consideration of the cost and use factors involved. The potential use of large projects is particularly difficult to assess. Before large sums are invested, the microtext manager should consult with those library patrons who would be interested or who would know of the possible interest of others. If possible, enough correspondence with the publisher should be carried on so that the microtext manager is fully aware of both the values and the weaknesses of any project or publication. There are few regulations or standards for advertising of projects, and the general approach is often to present a "glowing" description while omitting such items as reduction ratio and type or size of film used. There is seldom a "money back guarantee," once you've bought it, it's your problem. One can attempt to negotiate with the publisher for some type of guarantee or at least samples of the product, with varying degrees of success. It is understood that the National Microfilm Association is planning to form a committee to consider standards or guidelines for publishers' brochures. Veaner's checklist could easily serve as the basis for these standards as could the ANSI Standard Z39.13-1971. Advertising of Books. Correspondence with publishers should be straightforward, with questions stated clearly and indicating that purchase may be dependent on satisfactory answers. Most companies appreciate user and prospective user feedback and may even be persuaded toward improvements by suggestions and comments.

Another method of "reviewing" a collection or project is to visit a nearby library which has the set and use and evaluate the set from both the librarian's and the patron's point of view. If such visits are infeasible it may be possible to correspond with a helpful librarian who has worked with the collection. Again Veaner's checklist can be used as a guide to the questions which one should ask.

After the acquisition procedures have been delineated, the microtext manager should study, recommend, or possibly even design the methods of bibliographic control which best suit the users' needs, the physical arrangement of the reading room, and the existing bibliographic practices of the library. A manager's first problem may be the physical location for any or all of the microtexts. He/She will have to consider grouping all parts of the collection in one area to create a centralized facility or locating various subject-related groups of microtexts with books and other materials on the same subject.

Another form of decentralization may occur because of the need to duplicate heavily used materials in a variety of locations. The centralization versus decentralization issue may be relevant only to large library systems. Weber's article has a concise and very useful discussion of the factors involved in this decision. As an ideal, one might strive for as little decentralization or as little duplication as possible, particularly for monetary reasons. However, each decision should also assess reader needs and easy availability to heavily used materials as part of the decision. If some decentralization of the microtext materials is necessary, the acquisition procedures, the bibliographic control methods, and service and staffing arrangements should be carefully planned and coordinated for all units. (The location of the reading room within any given building will be discussed in a later article on the environment for microtexts.)

The microtext manager should then attempt to evaluate possible systems for classification and cataloging of microtexts. This evaluation will necessitate study of alternatives, careful and thorough presentation of these alternatives to fellow staff members, and a sound, logical basis for whichever procedure is chosen. To begin one's analysis, consider the following items as a "checklist."

1) possibility and availability of an assistant or attendant to provide preliminary reference help and location guidance;
2) the variety of contents of the microtexts, e.g. serials, monographs, technical reports, etc.;
3) the variety of formats, e.g. film, fiche, opaques;
4) users' needs in terms of a shelf locator as well as a description of the publication as a microtext to be indicated by the call numbers.

The controversy about a reader's ability, need, or desire to browse is likely to appear soon after one begins this phase of managing microtexts. I would suggest that browsing through books is a very different procedure from "browsing" through microtexts and would urge any manager not to allow discussion of this point to slow down progress toward a decision as to the appropriate scheme. It is obvious that no one classification system is uniquely suited to all libraries, but the microtext manager should be able, with her/his expertise, to present arguments, alternatives, and usable arrangements to reference, cataloging, and administrative staff. She/He should also be able to encourage such groups to arrive at a decision and to proceed with the method chosen without delays. Such action can be achieved on occasion by assisting in the restructuring of the library's procedures as needed to accomplish the cataloging.

The simplest approach to a classification system is to use a format designation and a sequential number, e.g., MICROFICHE 1, 2, 3, etc. The cataloger's energy can then be applied to more complete descriptive and subject cataloging of the item. There are a variety of arguments which are used against this approach, the most popular one being "this is not the way it's been done in the past." There is little virtue in perpetuating a "bad" system even though over half the material has been classified in that system. I would suggest that a "bad" system, one which is unnecessarily complicated in terms of the function it should perform, merely adds to user confusion and frustration, and thus compounds his resistance to microforms.

The provision of analytics for individual titles of large projects has been a major problem. These questions are appropriate in the search for a solution: if the publisher supplies cards, does the cataloging provided match the bibliographic standards of the library? If no cards are provided, or the quality of cataloging is poor, how will the cataloger or the Catalog Department find time and manpower to produce the cards? Even if the cards are acceptable, can the staff and resources be found to file them? Some of the solution may have already been reached during the acquisition process if it was decided to accept a publisher's work either as satisfactory or as a compromise solution. It is an unhappy fact that many libraries, of varying sizes, have accorded a less than immediate priority to the solution of the microtext cataloging problem and have thereby created a backlog of uncataloged, almost inaccessible materials. The low priority status may be due to format differences and unfamiliarity with microtext cataloging, to the probable low usage as compared to items such as reserve or user-requested books, or even to the lower relative cost of the project in microtext as opposed to a reprint edition. There are very real problems of bibliographic control and sound solutions are not reached hastily, but every effort should be made by the microtext manager to expedite the flow of materials through the technical processing stages. Dispatch can be aided by a clear presentation, by the manager, of possible alternatives, their weaknesses and strengths, and the manager's informed judgment as to the best solution for that particular library's situation. The manager should strive to be knowledgeable in all areas of microtext administration and should also strive to pass along this knowledge logically and concisely to both administrative and professional personnel.

A commonly advocated, and occasionally well-used, component of bibliographic control is preparation and publication of a local guide to microtext holdings. The University of Nevada, Reno, and the University of British Columbia, Vancouver, have both produced excellent guides. The guides list information about each set or collection held by the library and also include thorough descriptions of the indexes or other bibliographic aids that are related to each set. The UBC guide is loose leaf so that updated information can be inserted quickly and easily. Until the distant day when a national index to all publications appearing in microtext appears, libraries will need to educate users as to microtext holdings on a library-by-library basis. (See Part I for a discussion of the *National Register of Microform Masters.*) Microtexts should be publicized by a variety of means, and an individual library's guide to its own holdings can form the basis for such publicity. Displays, bibliographies, exhibits, announcements, demonstrations, lectures, even simple signs must be considered as devices for educating the user about microtext resources. Guides should include precise, careful descriptions of indexes or other materials which help to identify individual items within the microtext project. Such guides are time consuming to prepare and may involve coordination of a number of individual efforts to produce a thorough and useful publication. The microtext manager should have the authority to direct production of the guide and to assign responsibility for compilation as necessary. (He/She may, on the other hand, be the only person involved in the creation of such a guide.) As Dodson and Thomson point out, libraries should coordinate their efforts. But I would suggest that a library, no matter what size, would benefit its users by providing a simple listing, for example, of the newspapers available on film at that particular library. In an area where there are many resources, it might be possible for the local chapter of a library association or an ad hoc group to work together on compilations. National efforts at listings continue to be made, especially for newspapers, but numerous patrons may go unserved in the meantime if no local guides are produced.

The Association of Research Libraries' report by Tharpe and Reichmann on bibliographic control of microform publications, to be released late this summer, includes an "extensive" listing of "large microform publications." Libraries might want to use that list or those of UBC or Nevada as foundations or examples for a local list. A computer produced guide might also be considered by some libraries, because of the ease of updating future editions. Another possibility is to annotate a publisher-supplied index or commercially available bibliography with indications of the library's holdings and their locations.

In summary, there are serious considerations involved in the choice of a method of bibliographic control, and the microtext manager should study the possibilities thoroughly in regard to his/her particular situation. The manager should strive to prevent a backlog from developing while bibliographic procedures are being discussed. A guide to the library's microtext holdings should not be overlooked as an additional tool for bibliographic control.

Literature Cited

Association of Research Libraries, "Final Reports of Microform Project Completed," *ARL News-letter,* no. 55, June 1972, p. 2.

Association of Research Libraries, *Interim Report,* Part Two: Determination of an Effective System of Bibliographic Control of Microform Publications by Felix Reichmann and Josephine M. Tharpe, Contract no. OEC-0-8-080786-4612(095.) Washington, D.C., A.R.L., 1970. 90p.

Dodson, Suzanne, "Microforms in the University of British Columbia Library," Vancouver, B.C., 1971. Typewritten.

Dodson, Suzanne, "The University of British Columbia Library's Guide to Large Collections in Microform: One Attempt to Minimize a Major Problem," *Microform Review,* 1: 113-17 (April 1972).

Private communications concerning "Summary of the Meeting of the Special Advisory Group to Task I of the Microform Project," Assoc. of Research Libraries, March 4, 1971.

Rendall, Marian K., *A Guide to Some Research Collections in the University Library,* Kenneth J. Carpenter, ed. Reno, University of Nevada, 1971.

Thomson, June, "Cataloging of Large Works on Microform in Canadian University Libraries,"

Canadian Library Journal, 26: 446-52 (Nov./Dec. 1969).
Veaner, Allen B. *The Evaluation of Micropublications: A Handbook for Librarians.* Chicago: American Library Association, 1971. (LTP Publication No. 17). 59p.
Weber, D.C., "Design for a Microtext Reading Room," *Unesco Bulletin for Libraries,* 20: 303-08. (Nov./Dec. 1966).
Weyrauch, E.E., "Microforms and Their Place in Academic Libraries," Kentucky Library Association *Bulletin,* 35 (Jan. 1971). Pages 17 and 18 are relevant.

Part I dealt with the selection of a microtext manager and with procedural considerations in the acquisitions process. Part II continued the discussion of acquisitions and the choice of a bibliographic control system. Part III considers further aspects of bibliographic control and lists some factors to remember in the choice of a physical location for the microtexts within the building.

1. Distinctive Classification Requirements for Microtexts

A simplified classification scheme for microtexts was recommended in Part II. No matter which classification scheme is chosen, however, there are procedural difficulties and hazards that must be avoided or resolved.

For example, serial and newspaper titles on microfilm must be shelved in a way that will allow constant but predictable expansion. If these titles are shelved strictly by classification number, a large amount of shelving, which might be put to better use in the meantime, will remain empty to ensure future storage space for the title for a given number of years. When that space is finally utilized, another problem arises—that of shifting the entire collection to accommodate further growth. A partial solution to these problems is to shelve serial and newspaper titles in a separate area, with "dummy" blocks inserted on the shelf where those numbers would logically appear to indicate the separate location of those items. Some libraries arrange their newspapers on microfilm alphabetically by title, within the separate area. To give the entire microtext collection a consistency and to provide some capability for unassisted use. It is recommended that newspaper and other serial titles be included in the classification scheme, especially if the sequential system is used.

Size designation does not have the same importance in the call number as the format designation does. Moreover, the question of providing a size designation as an element of the call number or as a location indicator is one that can easily stall any decision about classification. The microtext manager should be alert to this stumbling block.

It is highly desirable to develop and organize a classification scheme to proceed numerically around the room in an explicitly logical pattern. It is unfortunate that many libraries are unable to have their classification systems proceed logically from the top stack floor to the botton or vice versa. Irregular arrangements, caused by uneven growth, failure of construction to keep up with growth, or changing use patterns, all contribute to shelving irregularities. Thus no stack floor designation is assigned as part of the call number. Instead, most libraries rely on charts posted prominently in the stacks, as well as other devices to call the user's attention to the arrangement of the classification scheme. Introducing the shelving arrangement of the microtext reading room to the user is most easily handled by an attendant. For microtexts it is possible and desirable to create self-instructive devices, such as charts and one-page handouts. It is also helpful to have easily readable labels on stacks and cabinets to identify their contents.

The microtext manager can obtain insights into shelving theories and pitfalls from the stack supervisor or circulation librarian. A refresher glance at one's library administration textbook might also provide some useful advice. (The question of the allocation of shelving resources will be discussed in future articles.)

2. Special Classification Problems

When doing retrospective cataloging of microtexts, if at all feasible the entire collection should be classified under one scheme. This may mean delays; however, there are ways of establishing priorities for cataloging. Since with sequential numbering any two subjects may sit next to each other on the shelf; hence potential use or need may determine which material is classified first.

There are reasons why retrospective classification in a completely consistent manner is not always possible. Often a large number of microtexts will have been classified in a previously chosen scheme. In that case, the recommended approach is that already commonly used by libraries changing from Dewey to LC for book classification. After a specified date, all materials are classified under the currently adopted scheme with few exceptions, and shelved in a separate area. Usually extensive efforts are made to inform patrons of the change and new shelving arrangements. The microtext user will also need extra encouragement and direction to find the number given to him/her.

Some libraries neglect to indicate on cards in the public catalog that the publications in question are in the microtext reading room. Confusion caused by this practice can be simply remedied by stamping an appropriate designation on the main-entry card.

The microtext manager must be ready to explain alternatives for a classification scheme to technical processing personnel. Samples showing alternative formats and illustrating how particular difficulties (series, serials, differences in size) can be handled are good aids in discussions with technical processing librarians, some of whom may not be familiar with the peculiarities of microforms. It is often difficult to visualize a classification system in the abstract; part of the manager's responsibility is to present the alternatives in as concrete a way as possible.

3. Indexes and Catalogs

Hard-copy indexes should be duplicated for branch libraries and reference and rare-book departments if budgets permit. The microtext manager should orient library staff about microtext resources, including a thorough review of the indexes. Most bibliographic aids will seemingly be nonstandard compared to book and periodical indexes; a micropublisher does not always use indexing criteria that a librarian would choose. Appropriate library staff should be carefully instructed in the use of those indexes. (Such orientation lectures or demonstrations also give the manager a chance to "practice" the presentation before a friendly audience of colleagues before speaking to other groups. Suggestions for improving demonstrations may be solicited from the practice audience. However, the microtext manager should be thoroughly familiar with the material before presenting it to any group.)

An important additional bibliographic aid is a card file in the microtext reading facility. A main-entry card catalog, a title-entry catalog, as well as a shelflist, should be located with the microtexts, especially if the reading room is any distance from the regular card catalog. The patron who is sent back and forth by the system is not likely to be an enthusiastic user.

4. Receiving and Processing Routines

Having settled on a *simple*, workable classification scheme, the microtext manager should next establish and document routines to be followed upon receipt of an order of microtext and/or an invoice. Even in small libraries, an established routine is needed to prevent confusion, ensure payment, and provide easy assimilation of the item into the collection. If the microtext manager receives the microtext directly from the postman or mail room, she/he should be alert to forward the material to the appropriate person for clearing the payment and receipt records. The microtext must then be routed for cataloging and marking.

A brief statement about marking is appropriate at this point. "Marking" and "labeling" are used here to refer to the process of stamping the box or envelope with the library property stamp and putting the call number in a convenient and prominent location on the box or envelope. Because of the increasing usage of eye-readable headings on both film and fiche, the necessity of physically marking the fiche or film with the call number is a questionable use of labor and materials.

As personnel changes occur, it is difficult to keep new people informed about all the peculiarities of a system. A new employee may be puzzled by an assignment to mark microfilm containers unless there is an established written procedure. From time to time, the microtext manager should inspect the flow of microtexts through the procedures to avoid a variety of minor but annoying and possibly cumulative problems.

An important factor in any routine is flexibility, which allows exceptions to be processed with dispatch. The manager should carefully outline all the combinations of both normal and exceptional circumstances while designing the processing system. For example, it should be remembered that microform issues of serials and newspapers ought to be recorded in the "serials record" with their hard-copy counterparts as well as being marked before being sent to the microtext reading room. In addition, some libraries may want to have a second check-in record at the actual shelving location. This second check-in is useful in large libraries where it is possible to misplace items the size of one box of microfilm. As another example, unpacking, inventorying, and marking a large shipment of 400 reels may need to be done somewhere other than the order or catalog department. A simplified flowchart of receipt and subsequent procedures might look something like the chart on page 161.

A flowchart aids the manager in analyzing specific steps involved in processing the microtext. The minutiae of the receiving, recording, labeling, marking, and shelving processes should be carefully detailed and explained by the manager to appropriate members of the staff. Solutions to processing procedures may often be found by using an existing procedure established for processing hard-copy material, perhaps with slight modification. Certainly it is not always necessary to create new routines just to accommodate a different terminology. New procedures should be developed as necessary to handle the functional differences of microtexts.

5. Location of Microtext
Reading Room or Facility

As a first criterion, the area or rooms should be *centrally* located. Since some newer reading machines do not need significantly reduced light levels in which to operate, there is no longer any need to place the reading room in the basement or attic corner of the building. Part of the users' resistance to microtexts stems from the usually unattractive and often depressing ambience of the reading room. Sometimes patrons cannot even *find* the facility. In an existing building, the manager should make a conscientious and considerable effort to study the building plans and the current space usage in order to make constructive and persuasive suggestions for a change in location. If the manager succeeds in bringing the

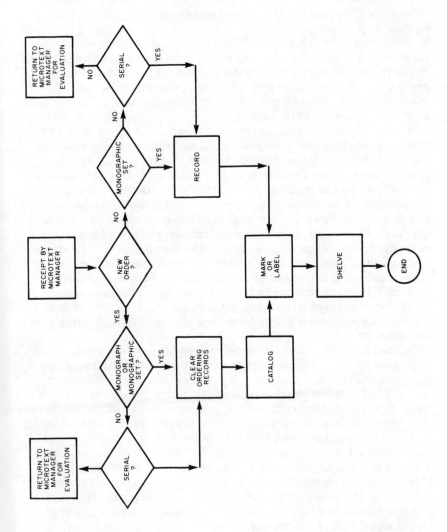

facility "up out of the basement," some effort should be spent at this point on publicity about the microtext resources and their availability. Posters, announcements, and brightly colored directional signs can be used to highlight such a move and pique potential users' curiosity at the same time. Even if the location of the room remains the same, new, prominent signs are highly desirable.

Of course it is not always possible to have a central location or sometimes even new signs. In such cases, the manager must make sure that staff members, particularly those in reference positions, are fully aware of the microtext resources and are kept up to date on new acquisitions. In short, deliberate effort should be made to direct library patrons' attention to the microtext resources and facilities.

If the collection occupies one or more rooms, every effort should be made to have a full-time attendant specifically assigned to supervise the room and the users. If the microtexts occupy a section of a very large general reading room, someone already on duty might be given the responsibility to watch for and assist potential users. In either case, the attendant may indeed be the microtext manager; in these days of budget cuts and overburdened staffs, I do not mean to suggest needless staff increases. On the other hand, administrators must consider the cost of nonuse of expensive resources and careless use of expensive equipment. The attendant might easily be a student or retired community member's whose salary would need not be as high as a professional librarian's. Individuals who enjoy helping people and who understand simple machines are ideal for the position. Rapport between the manager and the attendant is essential, and the manager should provide careful and thorough training for the attendant.

In small facilities, it may be satisfactory simply to have an area within a larger reading room defined for microtexts rather than have one or two rooms set aside for this purpose. It may be desirable to delimit the area as well as to call attention to it. The noise of opening and closing microfilm cabinets or of the manager instructing patrons in the use of the machines may necessitate using book stacks or some type of sound absorbing divider to set off the microtext area from the general reading or studying areas.

Reference librarians or attendants on duty in the room should be well schooled in the instruction of users and in the use of the machines; even though none of these staff members is in charge of the microtexts, each should be able to assist a patron. The microtext manager should be ready to suggest a variety of staffing patterns that might be used to ensure continued supervision of the microtext area.

6. Planning A Microtext Reading Facility

Most often the microtext manager will inherit a microtext reading room.

For the fortunate few who can plan a new facility, there are several points to consider: (1) location of the room, (2) future expansion of the facility as the collection and its use increase, and (3) electrical outlets, air conditioning and heating ducts, light fixtures, and other physical necessities of the collection. Those managers attempting to remodel or work within an existing space should consider how well the space within the facility is used, whether there are simple changes that can be made easily to increase effective use of the space, and what more complex changes are possible. In either case, the microtext manager must plan with attention to detail. A careful consideration of all the physical characteristics of the room and of all the use patterns of the area is an effective procedure. Traffic flow, location of equipment, tables, cabinets, shelves, windows, light switches, doors, and electrical outlets are only some of the factors that must be taken into account. Moving representational squares (as pieces of furniture) around on a scaled floor plan is a graphic method of determining possible combinations and arrangements within the area or rooms.

In summary, the microtext manager should understand the problems that may be encountered in choosing a method of bibliographic control, plan carefully the routines to be used upon receipt of the microtexts, and check these procedures from time to time. Considerable attention should then be given to the location, possible renovation, and staffing of the microtext reading room. Future articles will deal with equipment and general ambience of the room and with staffing and service considerations.

Literature Cited

Scott, C. F. "Microforms Reading Room at the University of London Library." *MICRODOC* 6 (1967): 65-67.
Weber, D. C. "Design for a Microtext Reading Room." *Unesco Bulletin for Libraries* 20 (November-December 1966): 303-308.

Part I dealt with the selection of a microform manager and with procedural considerations in the acquisitions process. Part II continued the discussion of acquisitions and the choice of a bibliographic control system. Part III considered further aspects of bibliographic control and cited factors in the choice of a physical location for microforms within the building. Part IV focuses on the environment and the equipment within the microform reading room.[1]

Importance of Technical Considerations

In an investigation of the environmental requirements for microforms, the microform manager will become aware of the importance of careful attention to numerous details related to microfrom technology. For example, he will learn that the microform reading room, or at least the area where film is stored, should ideally be kept at a temperature of not more than 70° F and a relative humidity of between 40 and 60 percent. Prolonged exposure to relative humidity above 60 percent may damage or destroy the gelatin of the film by facilitating the growth of fungus, which could eventually cause the emulsion to become tacky and the film base to buckle.[2] It may be very difficult and expensive to achieve these conditions within the limitations of the existing microform reading room, but every effort should be made to explore remedies that would bring the environment as close to ideal as possible. (Kodak Pamphlet P-108, *Storage and Preservation of Microfilms,* available free from Eastman Kodak, Rochester, New York, provides guidelines for storage conditions.)

The microform manager may feel uneasy about many details if he does not have an appropriate technical background, but proper care and storage is one fo the most important responsibilities of the manager. To learn something about microfilm technology in a relatively painless manner, he should refer to one or more of the following sources:

The Evaluation of Micropublications by Allen B. Veaner (ALA, 1971), Part I;

Fiche and Reel by E. Stevens Rice (Xerox University Microfilms, rev. ed., 1972);

Introduction to Micrographics by Don M. Avedon (National Microfilm Association, 1973);

The Invisible Medium: The State of the Art of Microform and a Guide to the Literature by Frances G. Spigai (ERIC, 1973);

Records Management Handbook, Microform Retrieval Equipment Guide (U.S. National Archives and Records Service, 1970).

Despite the duplication of information among the five, the manager may find one explanation more understandable than another. Continuing reference to the material will help relieve any uneasy feelings. *(The Microfilm Technology Primer on Scholarly Journals* by Franklin D. Crawford, published by Princeton Microfilm Corporation, 1969, is not recommended.)

The differences in composition, use, and storage among silver halide, diazo, and vesicular film types are of particular importance. Veaner's *Evaluation* (pp. 12-17) has a lucid, understandable description of the image-producing mechanism for each of them. Use and storage conditions vary; for example, it is recommended that some vesicular film be stored in plastic boxes. Kalvar recommends that its vesicular film not be interfiled with other film types. The archival properties of both diazo and vesicular film have not yet been established by recognized standards organizations.

For a carefully thought-out checklist and recommendations for details of the reading room environment, the microform manager should refer to

Determination of the Environmental Conditions Required in a Library for the Effective Utilization of Microforms by Donald C. Holmes (ARL, 1970) ED 046 403. His report incorporates guidance relative to the general conditions in the microform reading areas, a design for a general-purpose microform study carrel, a brief look at the supporting functions (technical processing), and storage and handling conditions. (He also lists valuable suggestions for teaching the use of microforms and related equipment.) Requirements for lighting, painting of ceiling and walls, acoustical treatment, air treatment, temperature, space, and security are discussed concisely. Weber's article also has a discussion of general environmental requirements. Holmes' explanations of the reasons for these specifications should be noted carefully by the microform manager before he attempts to correct inadequacies in the local situation. Corrective measures will involve some expense, and the manager should be prepared to explain the need for them. Administrators may be unaware of the technical considerations involved in dealing with microforms, and the manager's knowledge, if properly communicated, can help develop better understanding of these matters.

Weber's article also contains a helpful description of the reading tables, chairs, service desk, and the spatial relationships of the furniture. Following are additional problems: insufficient electrical outlets to operate the readers at peak efficiency; writing space for both left-handed and right-handed users, overly darkened and thus uninviting location, (although most of today's readers do not require greatly subdued lighting); lack of attention to the cleanliness and orderly condition of the reading area.[3] The microform manager may wish to list particular environmental conditions and plan to evaluate fulfillment of them at periodic intervals.

Storage Devices and Equipment

The standard storage device for microfilm reels, microfiche, and microopaque cards is the steel filing cabinet. The Microforms and Equipment section of the March 1972 issue of *Library Technology Reports* presents an extensive survey of cabinets, giving manufacturer and model number, price, dimensions, number of drawers, storage capacity for 16mm roll film, 35 mm roll film, 3 X 5 fiche, and 4 X 6 fiche, and additional comments. The microform manager will find this report, like others from the Library Technology Program (LTP), a valuable resource for information about equipment. An alternative method for storing film, at greatly reduced cost and with some sacrifice in protection, is the use of cardboard containers on metal shelving. (See Weber for details.) Such containers, holding six boxes of 35mm roll film each, may be placed on standard shelving and may be stacked two high on a shelf. There will also be some inconvenience of access with this method. Holmes favors metal cabinets; both he and

Forrest Carhart, Jr. (former director of LTP), emphasize that whatever containers are used, they should be chosen carefully to avoid those which, through physical or chemical decomposition, might be damaging to the film. Some libraries use card catalog cabinets for storing fiche and cards, although these cabinets provide less adequate storage than the steel filing drawer variety. "Carousel" storage arrangements are a recent development, emphasizing convenience and rapid access. The microform manager will also need to know the arguments for and against cartridges and cassettes as film holders. *Library Technology Reports,* May 1972, presents a thorough and lucid discussion of the issues by Dr. Francis F. Spreitzer. However, with today's budgetary restrictions, many libraries may not be in a position to consider these containers. The Spigai report (pp. 17-18) discusses both containers and storage equipment.

Equipment Evaluation

The microform manager will be called upon to evaluate the readers owned and possible candidates for purchase. To begin an evaluation, the manager should consult the following sources for informative lists of characteristics to look for and questions to ask: the Holmes report, the National Archives handbook, the Spigai report which details the LTP's list, Sherman's article in *Computerworld*, Supplement, p. 2, October 25, 1972, Weyrauch's list in Kentucky Library Association *Bulletin*, January 1971, and Massey's list in the *Virginia Librarian*, vol. 17:4, 1970. The next step is to consult Ballou's *Guide to Microreproduction Equipment* (NMA, 1971) and the 1972 supplement.

The evaluation should also include "hands-on" experience. Often it is possible to arrange a demonstration in the library. If one is in a place somewhat removed from metropolitan areas and salesmen seem reluctant to pursue a possible sale, try to obtain a machine on a trial basis. The institution's purchasing department should negotiate details of the trial period to avoid misunderstanding about intent to purchase. Evaluate the needs of the users carefully and consider future collection development plans in order to determine how many and what type of reader to buy. Be sure to consider special features and accessories in an evaluation; occasionally, by spending a small additional sum, the library may be able to provide greater convenience or extra service to the user. In the case of interchangeable lenses, however, the manager must also consider the additional security and care required. Determine the dimensions of the machine being considered; make sure the tables or carrels for supporting or housing the equipment provide adequate space both for the base of the machine and any air space necessary to the proper functioning of the machinery. Check service arrangements and guarantees carefully. Some companies sell both reconditioned used machines and discounted new machines, and their products should not be overlooked. Similar procedures should be used to evaluate reader-printers. It is particularly important, although expensive—$200 to $1,000 per year—to have a regular service arrangement which includes both preventive maintenance and emergency servicing for reader-printers.

Equipment Service and Maintenance

The microform manager should obtain an extra copy of the operating instructions and service manual, if available, when new machines are purchased. One copy should be included in the procedures manual for the reading room and one should be kept near each machine. The microform manager should clearly understand routine maintenance procedures (servicing details are usually included in the literature provided with the machine). All staff members working with the microform machines should be instructed in their proper operation and care. Daily routines for cleaning glass flats, dusting the equipment, checking the lamps, and other maintenance chores should be established. However, the microform manager should make additional checks of the equipment every day as a preventative measure. Materials required for the care of the machine, tools, extra lamps, etc., should be stored nearby in a secure area.

In summary, the microform manager must achieve a level of technical understanding about both microforms and reading machines. Valuable resources and equipment may be damaged severely or totally ruined if he is not aware of their specific environmental and handling requirements. Sources giving highly detailed information about those requirements have been cited. The purchase of a reading machine should be preceded by a careful evaluation of the library's needs and "hands-on" trials and comparisons. Thorough and orderly maintenance of expensive machines is an additional concern of the microform manager.

The *Library Technology Reports* of the LTP of the American Library Association have been mentioned several times earlier. These reports can provide the microform manager with detailed information about the characteristics of the equipment he administers. Equipment selection and policy considerations are discussed, and a wealth of material about the machines is included. Similar reports from Great Britain's National Reprographic Centre for documentation contain technical evaluations and detailed illustrations of the machines. For interesting reading about the library community's wrestlings with the problems of microforms and related machines, see the Council on Library Resources, Inc., *Annual Report*, particularly for 1960.

References

1. The word microform is now used instead of microtext in the title and throughout the article. Several readers have pointed out that microform is the standard generic term for any form containing microimages; microtext refers generally to micro-opaques. Adherence to a standardized terminology is important for clarity and understanding, thus the change.
2. Appendix A to the American National Standards Institute Standard, Ph5.4-1970, "Storage of Processed Silver Gelatin Microfilm," This standard is available for $3.25 from ANSI, Inc., 1430 Broadway, New York, N.Y. 10018.
3. Mr. Leedom Kettell, Xerox University Microfilms, in private correspondence.

Literature Cited

Avedon, Don M. *Introduction to Micrographics.* Silver Spring, Md.: National Microfilm Association, 1973. 27p.

Carhart, Forrest, Jr. Speech presented at the Annual Conference of the American Library Association, Chicago, June 1972.

Holmes, Donald C. *Determination of the Environmental Conditions Required for the Effective Utilization of Microforms.* Washington, D.C.: Association of Research Libraries, 1970. 44p. (ED 046 403.)

Massey, Don W. "The Aching Eye: The Use of Microforms and Viewers by Scholars and Researchers." *Virginia Librarian,* 17:4 (Winter 1970): 23.

National Microfilm Association. *Guide to Microreproduction Equipment,* 5th ed. Edited by Hubbard Ballou (Annapolis, Md.: National Microfilm Association (1973). 793p.; 1972 *Supplement,* 160p.

Rice, E. Stevens. *Fiche and Reel,* rev. ed. Ann Arbor, Mich.: Xerox University Microfilms, 1972. 22p.

Scott, C. F. "Microform Reading Room at the University of London Library." *MICRODOC* 6 (1967): 65-67.

Sherman, Alonzo J. "How to Pick the Best Reader." *Computer World,* supplement (October 25, 1972): 2.

Spigai, Frances G. *The Invisible Medium: The State of the Art of Microform and a Guide to the Literature.* Stanford, Calif.: ERIC Clearinghouse on Media and Technology, 1973. 31p.

United States. General Services Administration. National Archives and Records Service. Office of Records Management, *Records Management Handbook: Microform Retrieval Equipment Guide.* Washington, D.C.: Office of Records Management, 1970. 69p.

Veaner, Allen B. *The Evaluation of Micropublications: A Handbook for Librarians,* LTP publication, no. 17. Chicago: American Library Association, 1971. 59p.

Weber, D. C. "Design for a Microtext Reading Room." *Unesco Bulletin for Libraries* 20 (November-December 1966): 303-308.

Weyrauch, E. E. "Microforms and Their Place in Academic Libraries." *Kentucky Library Association Bulletin* 35 (January 1971): 23-24.

Part I dealt with the selection of a microform manager and with procedural considerations in the acquisitions process. Part II continued the discussion of acquisitions and the choice of a bibliographic control system. Part III considered further aspects of bibliographic control and cited factors in the choice of a physical location for microforms within the building. Part IV focused on the environment and the equipment within the microform reading room. Part V will include suggestions for staffing, the preparation of and operations manual, circulation procedures, and statistical record keeping.

Staffing Considerations

If the microform reading area is part of a larger room, staff members already present or on duty there can be assigned responsibility for helping patrons use the microforms. If the reading area is a separate room, a special attendant will be required to provide service as well as security control while the room is open. Obviously, user assistance is the most important function of the staff. There are also routine duties that must be performed, and those responsibilities should be included in staff job descriptions. For example, to maintain integrity of the files (avoid filing errors), it is generally desirable to have users return material to a central point and to have reshelving done only by trained staff members. Shelvers could be part of the regular shelving staff of the library; if there is a specific attendant for the microform area, however, that person could be responsible for the reshelving. Another example is equipment maintenance, which is a crucial, daily operation and should be the responsibility of a specific individual. A third example is the task of assisting users with auxiliary bibliographic tools, indexes, and abstracts. While duties of this type could be given to various staff members, the best and most appropriate method of providing both satisfactory user assistance and proper equipment maintenance is to assign these responsibilities to one individual.

Another concern will be to schedule and provide service during as many hours as possible and/or practical. In some libraries, patrons have indicated their preference for early morning, late evening, or weekend hours. Special staffing arrangements may have to be considered to provide access at such times. Libraries with a limited personnel budget might consider closing the room at less popular times instead of attempting to increase the hours of service. It is particularly important to provide reference assistance and instruction in the use of the equipment during all hours the facility is open.

The library may be fortunate enough to have personnel positions for both a professional librarian as the microform manager and a qualified nonprofessional assistant as the reading-room attendant. That situation would be ideal, but often it is unrealistic and unattainable. If it is not possible to appoint a professional librarian as microform manager, a thoroughly trained, interested, and highly motivated assistant may provide quality service and also be capable of assuming many of the manager's functions, particularly if given additional part-time support. Other staffing patterns, such as the division of responsibilities among staff members or assignment of a number of student assistants for limited service, may be solutions, depending on the individual library's personnel resources. A most important consideration is that the staff be courteous, knowledgeable, and, if possible, enthusiastic persons who will attempt to provide every patron with a pleasant and positive experience using microform.

Reading room attendants should be carefully and thoroughly trained.

If the microform manager reading-room attendant combination is effected by the library, the attendant should be able to perform all the necessary operations and services of the microform facility in the absence of the manager. An additional aspect of this training is encouraging personnel to take pride in understanding and using the equipment properly and in helping the patrons. To provide that service to the user, the assistant should be given in-depth instruction in the use of reference books and bibliographic guides to the collections. If there is no manager, reference librarians may be designated as instructors for the reading room assistants.

The Staff or Operations Manual

To provide guidance for personnel and to promote effective operation of the microform reading room, the manager should compile a manual covering the day-to-day routines. It should provide detailed instructions, with examples, for recording holdings, ordering supplies, marking and shelving, dusting and cleaning the machines, reshelving, and statistics keeping. Circulation policies and procedures, general library policies, and directions for overall supervision of the reading room should also be included. Equipment operation and maintenance booklets can be placed in a separate notebook as the basis of a preventative-maintenance (PM) plan or routine. The PM notebook could also specify how often various tasks need to be performed. A manager who is unsure about machine maintenance should ask the vendor for both a demonstration and written instructions on the routine.[1] The manager should attempt to understand the procedures as thoroughly as possible; preventive maintenance—especially proper, frequent cleaning—is the key to better functioning and longer lasting equipment (it also prolongs the useful life of the microforms). A third notebook could contain descriptive reminders of the important reference and bibliographic tools to be used for patron assistance. When more than one person is involved in the operation of the microform reading room, one of the most important aspects of the manual is the indication of who is responsible for making particular decisions and who is responsible for specific operations. Although it is time-consuming to prepare, a fully detailed manual can serve as the basis for staff training, the source of answers to daily or routine questions, and the authority for decisions that must be made in the absence of the manager.

The microform manager may also wish to prepare a manual of instructions for evaluating both micropublishing projects and reading equipment. The basis for this manual would be the procedures outlined in Allen B. Veaner's handbook, *The Evaluation of Micropublications* (ALA, 1971). These procedures may require considerable effort by the manager, but the library must take steps to insure that these comparatively expensive products are of high quality. (A small equipment investment on the order of $250-500 is required to carry out evaluation procedures efficiently and without risk of damage to the materials.—See *The Evaluation of Micropublications*, p. 32.) Returning faulty products is frustrating and annoying, but there cannot be blind acceptance of poor workmanship if the library is going to have any return on its investment. Furthermore, faulty products will not disappear from the market until the producers realize that libraries are not going to accept them. To evaluate equipment, use the procedures discussed in various *Library Technology Reports*. (The Council on Library Resources, Inc., is developing a book-microfiche package designed to allow the layman to evaluate microfiche readers and reader-printers.) As the library's microforms expert, the manager should continue to sharpen and refine her/his judgment with these tools.

Statistics

To assess the size of a library's total collection, it is often desirable to count each piece of microform. Equally often it may be necessary for the manager, because of inadequate past records, to insure the accuracy of such a number by taking inventory. Once this task has been performed, however, the manager or assistant can then add new acquisitions to a running total. (Library administrators may also want a separate yearly total.) Packing slips frequently note the number of reels, fiche, cards, etc., and provide a convenient means of obtaining necessary infromation. If proper instructions have been given and an easily understood and usable record-keeping form has been designed, staff should not have difficulties adding daily acquisition figures. Determining the number of titles or volumes within a set of microforms, however, is more difficult. Sometimes publishers' information about that number is not reliable, so the microform manager may have to check each reel or fiche to ascertain the desired count.

The number of users per day is an important figure for administrative purposes and may be easily obtained by a simple counting device like a turnstile (if feasible) or by an attendant's count of people entering the room. Other settings may require an hourly check of equipment usage to estimate total use of the facilities. Counting the type and noting the contents of items left on reshelving tables may be used as an indication of what parts of the collection are being used.

Development of detailed information about users may necessitate the use of a sign-in register, the actual questioning of individuals, or the provision of a form to be filled out before receiving the materials. Before implementing any of those practices, the manager should consider that they are very likely to discourage, frustrate, annoy, and thus drive away first-time microform users. If comprehensive information must be obtained for a special reason, such as an administrative survey, the manager should make every effort to explain the reason to the users and to provide a data-gathering form that is convenient to use.

Just as estimates of the book space remaining in the stacks are needed, similar measurements should be taken within the microform reading room. Square feet of floor space, linear feet of shelving, and drawer and cabinet capacities—both the total amount in the room and the amount currently in use—will need to be measured. These figures may be used to estimate the future space requirements for the collection and are often valuable in planning new facilities.

Circulation of Microforms and Equipment

Traditionally, microforms have not been circulated because of their fragile nature and the relative lack of availability of portable reading machines. However, there are benefits to be gained from the lending of microforms, mainly in increased acceptance of the medium and of appreciation of extended library service. The patron, expecting to encounter an unfamiliar object in restrictive circumstances, is pleasantly surprised and positively influenced by discovering that microforms can be checked out "just like books." That microforms are delicate should be impressed upon the borrower but not in a threatening or discouraging manner. The loan period may be shorter than that for books to allow closer control of the materials. If the library decides to circulate reading machines, they should be good quality, sturdy units. To reinforce the positive experience mentioned above, the equipment should be carefully maintained. Operating instructions should be given verbally to the borrower and supplemented with a descriptive handout repeating the directions. Accurate records of the items loaned and of the borrower's identification should be kept to insure return or, if necessary, replacement of materials.

Publicity

Publicizing microforms has received little attention in the literature. There are a number of ways to publicize the resources of the microform collection. A regularly scheduled tour, complete with "hands-on" experience for as many participants as possible, may be instituted and the schedule reported in the community, company, or school newspaper. During the tour, the manager should be sure to demonstrate all the types of equipment and indicate and identify staff who may be asked for help during future visits to the facility. Handouts describing the services, the collections, and general information (such as the hours of access) can be distributed. Time for questions and answers should be scheduled as part of the tour.

The microform manager should consider issuing brief descriptive handouts on the institution's microform resources. Materials might be grouped by subject, with careful statements of content and dates covered; the handout should include bibliographic guides that aid in use of the collections. Lists of resources by type of publication—such as current newspapers or periodicals—are also helpful. As the manager becomes familiar with the collection, other possibilities will become apparent.

Gordon Bechanan, suggests that offering extra services, such as cleaning, splicing, winding, sale of reels and boxes, etc., for personal films may also be a way to attract people to the reading area. Utmost care should be taken so that these extra services are not offered at the expense of the library's primary functions.

As a last look at the microform reading room, the following suggestion may offer a useful approach to developing a workable, usable facility: think, or walk, through the path the user must follow to obtain and use a microform. A path clearly marked by clear signs and helpful people will make the new user enthusiastic and comfortable with microforms. As an example, labeling each machine as to the type of microform which can be read at that machine is a simple but helpful step; it seems obvious, yet few reading rooms have such signs.

The Microform Committee

If the library is large enough or has an extensive microform collection, a microform committee might be chaired by the manager and used to discuss and/or decide general policies about the acquisitions, cataloging, or circulation of microforms. This body could also consider more specific matters, such as surveys of users or reading room arrangement, as necessary. Sometimes the committee plays a valuable role in that, by establishing policy within the committee, personal confrontations are avoided. The committee may not agree with the manager on all points and should not be viewed as a "rubber-stamp" body.

Summary

These five articles have attempted to highlight at least the important aspects of the operation of the microform reading room. In these days of funding difficulties, more attention needs to be focused on strenthening this service area. Administrators especially should devote some of their already limited time to consideration of these resources and their management. One of the most efficient ways to accomplish this is to appoint a microform manager who can become a specialist in the care and handling of microforms and the administration of the microform reading room.

Microform resources and equipment in libraries are too expensive and too valuable to be treated in an off-hand manner.

References

1. Mr. Leedom Kettell, Xerox University Microfilms, in private correspondence.
2. Bechanan, H. Gordon, "The Organization of Microforms in the Library," LIBRARY TRENDS, 8: 391-406 (January 1960).

Literature Cited

Veaner, Allen B. *The Evaluation of Micropublications: A Handbook for Librarians*, LTP publication, no. 17. Chicago: American Library Association, 1971. 59p.

EXCERPTS FROM *DETERMINATION OF THE ENVIRONMENTAL CONDITIONS REQUIRED IN A LIBRARY FOR THE EFFECTIVE UTILIZATION OF MICROFORMS*

by Donald C. Holmes

General Microform Reading Area

The use of microforms requires the same environmental conditions, except for lighting, as are found in a well designed library area. The microform reading room should have facilities designed for the protection of the microforms and the comfort of the user.

In arranging the furniture and equipment, it is desirable to place the staff desk near both the room entrance and the catalog. This enables a staff member on duty to aid users and to exercise whatever supervision or control may be necessary. Generally speaking, the area in which the microform use copies are stored should be set apart (not necessarily by partitions)

Reprinted from part IV, "Findings" and part V, "Teaching the Use of Microforms and Related Equipment" of Donald C. Holmes, *Determination of the Environmental Conditions Required in a Library for the Effective Utilization of Microforms. Interim Report.* November, 1970. (ERIC ED 046 403), pp. 7-24.

from the area in which the microforms will be used. One advantage in such a separation is more efficient use of floor space, and, in addition, the arrangements for lighting can be made more flexible and convenient. Obviously, the staff member's desk and the bibliographer's desk must each be in a well lighted area, yet so arranged that the light will not disturb the users of the microform readers.

Lighting

General lighting in the microform reading area should be of low intensity. The light measured by meter at the work surface should be 15 to 20 footcandles and should be indirect, reflected light. The level of light should be adequate for moving about, but should be of lower intensity than that required for reading or other desk work. If possible, the general lighting intensity should be adjustable by employing a commercially available dimming device. If the reading room is large, it is desirable to control separate sections of the room's general lighting intensity in accordance with the desires of individuals working in particular areas of the room.

If it is necessary to use a room with windows for the microform reading room, curtains or shades should be provided to control entering daylight, which is highly variable and can often interfere with the reading machine screen image. To guard against this, reader screens should be turned away from the windows a full 180°.

Ceiling and Walls

The ceiling and walls of the reading room should be treated with materials to prevent undesired light reflections from interfering with the reading machine screen image. Glossy paints should not be used. A diffuse, reflective, white material is recommended on the ceiling since it is to serve as a component of the indirect lighting system for the room.

Acoustical Treatment

Acoustical treatment of the reading room should be provided to reduce noise created by reading machines, typewriters, and required conversation of patrons and staff. Many available materials for wall and ceiling acoustical treatment have appropriate light reflection characteristics and can serve dual roles. Further, noise reduction can be gained by covering the floors with a good grade of institutional carpeting.

Air Treatment

The room must be air conditioned and have proper air filtration, humidity and temperature. The air must be constantly filtered to eliminate extraneous matter harmful to microforms, such as dust and industrial gases. Humidity must be maintained at a level which will keep the film flexible but which will not encourage the growth of molds. To be avoided is a condition so dry that static electricity will be generated, thereby attracting dust particles to the film as it is used.

Temperature

Temperature control for greater than normal reading room capacity will be required. Taken into account must be the body heat of the maximum number of persons who may use the room and the considerable heat given off by projection lamps, motors and auxiliary desk lamps. Temperature should be kept below 80° F for the comfort of the users. Recommended relative humidity levels are between 40% and 60%.

Space Requirements

The area needed by users of microforms will vary in accordance with the nature of their work. One using microforms continuously will need more work space than another who consults a film for a few minutes only. Reader stations arranged back-to-back, to take advantage of common electrical outlets as well as common aisles, will usually save floor space. A minimum work space of roughly 40 square feet per user should be provided for furniture, equipment and aisle space. Table height must be coordinated with the chair provided. Reader-printers require more space than simple reading machines to provide access for paper loading and other servicing.

Electrical outlets properly placed and in sufficient number must be provided and, of course, sufficient electrical power must be available.

Security

Microforms used in reading facilities are, or certainly should be, service copies only; i.e., like books they are relatively expendable. While the investment in microforms at times may seem very high, it is generally true that book for book, volume for volume, the unit cost of a microform edition of older materials (ignoring the question of unavailability of hard copy) may be lower than for a paper edition. This is mentioned to place in perspective the value of the microform as compared to books or other generally available materials in the library collections; and, further, to put forth the idea that protection for microforms need not be carried to an extreme. Security measures need not differ greatly from those imposed for regular book material. For certain microforms, however, such as sheet microforms which might be easily carried off without authorization, a charge or other record of use might be warranted. Only the library staff should refile microforms.

Microform Workroom

Essential to the efficient operation of a microform reading room is an adjoining work station at which microforms can be inspected, identified, cleaned and, if required, repaired. Periodic spot inspection of the collections, inspection of microforms used outside of the control of the library, occasional splicing or resplicing of broken film, and film cleaning are the major tasks to be performed at the work station. The inspection of microforms prior to their acceptance and cataloging by the library may also be carried out at the station.

Reading machines are required for close inspection. A quick, general inspection of roll film and microfiche can be accomplished, however, using a light box and magnifying lens. Essential equipment for the work station would be a light box, a pair of film rewinds mounted on a table, a film splicing machine, a magnifying lens and film cleaning equipment.

Over the years, the Library of Congress Photoduplication Service developed by "trial and change" a functional film inspection and splicing desk. More than twenty of these desks are now in use and they have proved to be convenient as well as an efficient aid for the technicians who work with them. It would seem that such a desk or desks could serve many of the requirements of the microform work station.

Thermal butt weld splices are used exclusively by the Library of Congress Photoduplication Service, and, therefore, the desk is equipped with a hinged plate to which the butt weld splicers are attached. For splicing, the machine is pulled forward to accept the film held between the rewinds. For light box inspection and other tasks performed at the desk, the splicers are pushed to the back on a hinged plate with the read part disappearing below the table top. Other features of the desk are: a built-in light box; a limited storage space for reels in work process; an eye shielded light for desk top illumination; a pair of film rewinds; and drawers to house supplies and personal items belonging to the technicians.

Film cleaning also may be done at the desk. Roll microfilms and microfiches may be satisfactorily cleaned with the non-toxic solvent, Freon TF, and lint proof cloths, high quality chamois or fine, chemically produced sponges. Carbon tetrachloride should not be used in the cleaning process because of its toxicity.

The Central Microform Library
(Non-circulating)

The non-circulating central library concept has been particularly successful for special libraries using microfiche. In lieu of making material available for use on the premises, diazo or vesicular copies (fiche-to-fiche) are made of desired titles, from intermediate copies, in response to requests of researchers, teachers and others entitled to the service. Typically, the researcher, or his secretary, places the order and carries it away in a single transaction, since copying can be accomplished in a few minutes. Requests can also be made by telephone and the fiches delivered by messenger or even mailed. This service is often free of charge to the user in industrial libraries where costs are absorbed in overhead. In academic institutions, a nominal fee would probably be required.

Fiche-to-fiche duplicating equipment and staff to operate it are required in such a library. Microform reading machines, both portable and non-portable, are usually furnished for permanent assignment or for loan by the library

A prerequisite to the assignment or loan of a microform reading machine is an indoctrination in the proper use and care of the machine.

Additional Microform Reading Areas

If microforms are dispersed within a library or among a number of libraries according to subject, the additional microform reading facilities should conform as much as possible to the conditions set forth above for a general microform reading room.

Microform Carrel*

The survey conducted during the interim study, *Determination of User Needs and Future Requirements for a Systems Approach to Microform Technology*, revealed that library users believed presently available microform reading machines were inadequate for prolonged use. One of the reasons frequently cited for this belief was that the height and angle of reading machine screens were fixed. The fixed position required the reader to be in a disciplined posture which had to be maintained with little or no

---

*EDITOR'S NOTE: Carrels similar to the ones proposed here have been custom made for the Bobst Library at New York University and a manufacturer of library furniture plans to offer them as a standard item in the near future.

variation for the duration of use. Not only do individuals vary in height and bulk, but human muscles and nerves demand, for comfort, occasional changes in posture. It was recommended that a microform reader carrel be designed that would easily permit a change in the height and angle of the reading machine screen in order to accommodate the comfort requirements of the individual user. Other desired features of the carrel were adequately illuminated auxiliary work space for note-taking, and shelving for a limited number of reference books.

Specifications for the carrel are as follows:

1. Carrel dimensions:
   height: 60 in.
   width (ID):   60 in.
   depth (ID):   54 in. (Pull-out shelves extended)
2. Height of work space table and normal height of reading machine stage: 29 in. above floor.
3. Width of work space table: 28 in.
4. Depth of work space table: 32 in.
5. Adjustable shelves to be placed above rear of work space table.
6. 2 in. clear space to be provided on side and at read of reading machine stage.
7. 27 in. turntable to be centered within the designated area (30 in. × 30 in.) for reading machine stage.
8. Stage to move 4 in. above and 4 in. below normal position, with stop positions at any place within the 8 in. travel.
9. Turntable to revolve on pivot, 30° maximum, with provision to lock at any position.
10. Turntable to tilt from horizontal position 6° upward from front or back, with stop positions any place within its travel.

Supporting Functions

Cataloging

The key to the successful integration of microforms in a library collection is probably the treatment to which they are subjected by library staff in making them available in the reading rooms. The priority assigned to technical processing of microforms—accessioning, cataloging, shelflisting, etc.— can either establish a new research tool in a library or can bury the information beyond the ability of user and reference librarian alike to locate it. Processing of microforms should enjoy equal priority with microforms, i.e., hard copy. Otherwise, technical services personnel are allowed to make arbitrary judgments on which format takes precedence over content. By such logic, a novel by Spillane in eye-legible print is more important than

the Dead Sea Scrolls in microform. Yet failure to assign priority in processing in accordance with content rather than eye-legibility of print per-
sists and probably is the most serious road-block impeding full and free
use of micropublications.

While on the subject of equal treatment, it is appropriate to remark that
the environment in which catalogers of microforms work should be at
least as comfortable and convenient as that provided the users of the end
product. This environment should include ready access to acceptable
microform reading machines, adequate training in their use and provision
of all facilities mentioned in connection with microform reading areas.

Inspection

A prerequisite for effective processing of microforms is proper inspection.
Microforms should be inspected as soon as possible after receipt for both
technical and bibliographic equality.Technical inspection should verify that
the microform is on a safety base carrier, that all images are properly
aligned, and that they are fully legible, clear, sharp and evenly lighted.
Scratches, abrasions, dust and dirt impair the life of microforms, as well as
reading equipment; their presence should be detected and ameliorative
measures taken.

Microfilm should be wound on reels in length of no more than 100 feet
and should be provided with at least 18 in. of leader and 18 in. of trialer.
Splices are a potential source of trouble in reading machines and should
not be present when microfilms are delivered by the publisher or producer.
The existence of splices made with cellophane, pressure-sensitive tape
should be cause for immediate rejection of the film.

The reels of film should be received in boxes that allow easy access to
the reels and are made of material free of chemicals harmful to the film.
Outside dimensions of the boxes should not exceed 4 in. X 4 in. X 1-9/16
in. for 35mm film. Each box should bear a label on one end, giving as
much of the bibliographic information taken from the enclosed microtext
as possible, without crowding the label. If the reel is part of a set, the
label should also indicate the reel number and a full citation of the bibliographic contents of the particular reel (inclusive dates, volumes, etc.),
criteria for bibliographic arrangement, and targets.

Material which requires more than one roll of film should be divided on
a systematic and bibliographically acceptable basis. Serials should be
divided so that each reel contains the issues for an entire volume or volumes. Newspapers should be divided on a regular calendar basis. All sections of newspaper files should be recorded on the film. Numbered or lettered sections should appear in numerical or alphabetical order, followed
by unnumbered sections.

Appropriate targets should appear at the beginning and end of each reel of film and as necessary throughout the film. The first frame on a reel of film should contain the one word, "START," and the last frame the word, "END." The height of the letters measured on the film of these and subsequent targets referred to should have a minimum height of 2mm (0.8 in.). Following the "START" target and preceding the "END" target, there should be bibliographic targets identifying the work.

For newspapers, the target should provide at least the country and city of publication, the title, and the inclusive dates filmed. For monographs, the author, title, edition (if other than the first), place of publication, publisher and date of publication should be provided; for serials, the title, place of publication, inclusive volumes and dates recorded. For manuscripts, a general description of the material should be given. If the material covered by the bibliographic target extends over more than one reel, a secondary bibliographic target indicating the contents of the particular reel should appear immediately following the primary bibliographic target. Bibliographic data should be established in conformity with the *Anglo-American Cataloging Rules* and *Rules for Descriptive Cataloging in the Library of Congress* and supplements thereof.

The name of the organizaiton or institution responsible for the actual filming and the year of the filming should be provided in a preliminary target. With microfilms of newspapers and serials, there should appear a list of missing issues filmed on a separate frame or frames immediately after the bibliographic target and, if used, the secondary bibliographic target. If the file is fragmentary, a list of issues filmed may appear.

An indication of the reduction ratio should be provided on one of the preliminary targets by inclusion of a metric rule fifteen centimeters long.

Microfilm of newspapers whould include a target indicating the month of publication preceding the issues of each respective month. When several volumes of a serial have been filmed, a target indicating each volume (or year, or year and volume, as appropriate) should appear before the issues for that volume or year.

Faults in the original (i.e., mutilated or illegible pages) should be shown by targets indicating that the faults were not errors in filming.

Reproduction from Microforms

Until recent years, the reproduction of library materials, either from bound volumes or from microform, was performed by commercial service companies or by the relatively few libraries equipped with photoduplication laboratories. Hard copies (eye-legible copies) were produced from microforms in a darkroom, using photographic projection equipment, materials and wet processing. Such procedures often required more time than the library patron could tolerate for his "walk away with" reference needs. Manufacturers have responded to this problem by designing reader-printers which combine the functions of microform reading machines and automated darkroom processing facilities into a single housing or box for operations in a normally lighted room. Most reader-printers have fixed enlargement ratios and some difficulties are encountered when the reduction ratio of the microform is not compatible with them. Reader-printer viewing screen sizes and the dimensions of the prints produced by the machines may also contribute to these difficulties.

As with microforms reading machines, a variety of reading screen sizes are available. The reading screen size of a reader-printer often parallels the dimensions of the prints which it produces. For this reason, the size of the reader-printer screen chosen for library use is more important than the screen size of a microform reading machine. By manipulating a microform to cause sections of its image to appear on the microform reading machine screen, it is possible, although not convenient, to view an entire image even though the screen is too small to accommodate it all at one time. If the dimensions of the viewing screen of a reader-printer and the hard copy that the machine produces are too small to record the entire microform image at hand, neither manipulaiton of the microform nor adjustment of the machine can produce a satisfactory reproduction.

A number of processes are employed by various reader-printers for making hard copy from microforms. Some reader-printers deliver prints that contain chemicals that may damage neighboring library materials with which they may be interfiled. Some deliver damp prints that curl in the process of drying. Some provide prints with white backgrounds and black letters when positive microforms are used; however, most require negative microforms to accomplish this. Some produce prints with poor blacks that lack contrast with their backgrounds and are difficult to read. Many require critically accurate exposures that cause wastage with trials to produce fully satisfactory reproductions. Some use papers that in time change background colors from white to shades of yellow or brown. Some require specially made paper, with metal sandwiched between its two outer layers, which is stiff to handle and cracks when folded.

It is recommended that before purchasing a reader-printer for library use, the machine be acquired on loan or by rental purchase agreement to learn if it will satisfactorily perform the desired functions using the microforms at hand.

Maintenance

There can be no doubt that poor care and maintenance of microform reading equipment has a very adverse effect on the user. Unsatisfactory condition of equipment speaks louder than words that microforms are not high priority library resources, but rather something to be tolerated, a mere substitute for a hard copy version of the "real document."

Neglect is the most eloquent unspoken indication that a person holds an object in low esteem, whether it be a house, a lawn, an automobile or a beard that is allowed to degenerate. Unless the librarian has sufficient regard for the use of microforms he is likely to give little or no attention to the upkeep of equipment which is an indispensible auxiliary to the use of microforms. A negative or positive attitude toward microforms on the part of the librarian will in this wordless manner be quickly communicated to the potential user. Any microform program must entail, for these reasons as well as more obvious ones, routine, but genuinely attentive, maintenance effort for the reading equipment. This should include a daily check, and a daily or weekly cleaning, as well as a regular preventive maintenance routine. Additionally, the timely repair of defective equipment should be provided.

Teaching the Use of Microforms and Related Equipment

General

Acceptance of microforms by library patrons is dependent to a large degree upon the attitude of the library staff toward the medium. For this reason it is essential that the library staff, particularly the chief librarian, thoroughly understand microforms, their use, and the operation of the related equipment. Only then can users be persuaded that microforms have real utility and are a medium with which a person with no special aptitudes can work. If, however, the head of the library is negatively disposed toward the micro-format, or if he is ignorant of its virtues and the mechanics of its use, it is almost certain that his viewpoint will be transmitted to at least a portion of the staff and thence to users. Moreover, because of the many other demands upon the library's space, money and personnel for functions which he understands much better, the librarian is less likely to establish or support an effective microform activity, especially since it is not an inexpensive undertaking. Education, then, must begin at home—with the chief librarian and his senior staff. Somehow they must be convinced that microforms are a modern form of publishing which would otherwise be hard pressed to build and expand their information resources to the level commensurate with the academic programs.

Staff Training

In training the staff, operation of microform equipment should be given emphasis equal to that given the intellectual aspects of administering the collection. Much of the dissatisfaction with microforms, felt by librarian and user alike, is caused by the frustration and embarrassment resulting from inability to competently operate reading machines. The librarian, finding himself inept as he attempts to assist or instruct a user, often reacts by developing a dislike for the source of his embarrassment and, in consequence, tries to avoid contact with it. By his reaction, he also tends to prejudice the user against microforms and associated equipment, frequently in an overt fashion. The user, encountering similar difficulties, readily accepts the negative attitude.

Few persons not in the business of selling microforms or reading machines would claim that such equipment especially that used with roll film, is easy to operate. Most first-time users will have at least some difficulty with roll film readers and many will make a complete botch of it, even to the point of damaging the film. Quite a number of individuals will be so repelled by the initial difficulties that they will not make another attempt except when forced to do so. Nevertheless, years of experience with novice-users' encounters with microform machines have demonstrated to custodians of microform reading rooms that careful explanation of the operation of the devices, coupled with a modicum of practice and study of printed instructions, will enable almost anyone to do a satisfactory job of using them. Therefore, it is important to carefully and patiently explain the details of operating microform reading machines and to provide detailed printed instructions for the user to refer to when on his own. It is also highly desirable for a staff member always to be available who would be able and happy to assist when difficulties arise.

Training the staff to operate reading equipment should not, in the main, be left to sales representatives, although it can be quite helpful to use whatever training services they provide to develop an understanding on which to base an instructional program. The man who sells the machine is ordinarily the best person to ask first. He should also be able to provide instruction manuals.

User Training

Training for the user should include oral instruction, demonstration and provision of a user's manual. Initial instruction can be provided to groups of new users, but during the first time a person actually loads, operates, and unloads the equipment he should be given personal assistance to see that he has gotten "the hang of it." This applies particularly to microform readers and to all reader-printers. If training classes are held for groups of potential users, it would be well to supply a training film. Among other things, it should illustrate the special characteristics peculiar to microforms (such as images requiring 90° rotation, positive and negative images, etc.), using samples from either sections cut from defective film or a specially prepared film.

Instruction should include explanations of how to use equipment to the best advantage, as well as techniques for circumventing or lessening the effect of limitations of microforms. For example, small text can often be made more readable by using a lens of greater magnification than that required to produce an image equal to the size of the original; or eye-legible reader-printer copies of tables or graphs can be made, to be referred to when reading the associated text in microform.

The importance of user attitude to the success of a library microform program can hardly be over-emphasized. Librarians should imbue a positive viewpoint toward the medium as a source of information, and minimize any incidental factors which may tend to produce anxiety or excessive caution in the user. The importance of feeling comfortable and familiar with the minor technicalities of the machines has been stressed. Also important is to underplay the danger of damaging the film or the equipment. While it is true that microfilm is in some ways a more fragile medium than most books and that reading machines and film can be relatively easily damaged by misuse, this consideration must be subordinated to the objective of encouraging the freest possible use of microform materials. Users should be encouraged to report damaged film or equipment without concern that they will be required to pay for the damage. Such reporting can be made a part of a general scheme whereby the user is invited to comment on any aspect of the total system which is deficient, whether it be film damage, poorly processed microforms, missing pages, unsatisfactory environmental conditions in the reading area, bibliographic deficiencies, incorrect shelving, or any other unsatisfactory circumstance he experiences. Wherever this technique can be made to operate, it offers an excellent means of keeping tabs on a number of factors related to the adequacy of the installation. Toward this end, it is worth considering a very simple form, copies of which can be kept near each reading machine and on which the user can note any difficulty or deficiency he encounters.

Manuals

Operating manuals should be as clear and concise as possible. They should be illustrated to the maximum degree practical. In particular, illustrative diagrams should be included for threading microfilm reading machines (header position for microfiche reading machines). Any other function likely to cause difficulty or to result in damage to the media or equipment should be carefully explained and illustrated. Instructions should include a trouble-shooting section to enable the user as often as possible to clear the fault without assistance. However, each situation which suggests a condition from which damage might result if the user attempts to correct it should be clearly marked as one for which assistance should be sought.

Generally, the user's manual should not explain procedures which the user should not perform, for example, replacement of lamps in readers and adding developer to a reader-printer. At the same time, it is desirable to include a limited amount of information concerning cleaning of the equipment. If there is a doubt as to whether manuals provided by equipment manufacturers are satisfactory, a worthwhile procedure is to try them for a while. If they are not, it is usually best to produce a new manual rather than add to the existing one.

THE ROLE OF MICROFORMS IN THE SMALL COLLEGE LIBRARY

by Kathleen M. Heim

A rule of thumb concerning microforms in the small college library: *modest budgets may dictate modest collections, but they need place no restraint on the effective utilization of an available resource.*

In major research institutions, microform acquisitions and facilities may be geared to potential as well as current needs, and microform programs may be as broadly conceived as the projects which scholarship and research might envision. In the small college library, however, microforms represent an investment whose justification lies at least as much in the actual use they attract as in the collection they enhance.

But this is what is so exasperating about the presence of microforms in the small college library: they are not sufficiently used or appreciated on their own merits. The small college library cannot hope to emulate the great research libraries, where $15,000 for a microfiche edition of the United States congressional hearings from 1869 to 1934 is entirely appropriate. Such collections utterly eclipse anything the small library might be capable of acquiring. Nevertheless, it is not on the basis of an in-depth research collection that the presence of microforms is grounded at the small college library.

Besides the necessarily sorry comparison with the great research institutions, several factors seem to inhibit the use of microforms in the small

Reprinted from *Microform Review*, 3: 254-59 (October 1974) by permission of the publisher. Copyright © 1974 by Microform Review Inc.

college library: patrons do not like microforms, librarians regard overseeing the hardware as a nuisance, and the libraries have failed to integrate
the microform resources into the educational programs by which they
serve the college. None of these factors is beyond adjustment: each of
these inhibitors of microform use will yield to recognition of the need for
a microform program per se in the small college and to the will to take the
measures necessary to insure a vigorous program. It is simply a matter of
determining to take microforms seriously as an educational resource requiring its own special cultivation in the small college environment.

What follows is a number of practical recommendations grounded in
the experience of one small college library that chose to maximize the use
of its microform capability, in spite of its limited collection and without
expanding its investment. The guiding assumption was and remains that
exposure to microforms is vital to scholars and research scholarship at all
levels, for the undergraduate no less than for the professional.

The keystone of an enterprising microform program is on designated
microform manager, whose responsibilities run the gamut of promotion,
maintenance, and patron education—the kind of role that only a small library staff member might assume. The entire success of a microform program will hinge on the enthusiasm and technical abilities of the microform
manager.

Ideally, this charge should go to the reference librarian. (Though it is
tempting to delegate the running of the microform room to the audiovisual
staff or media specialist because of the hardware involved, it is more in
keeping with the type of information stored on the microforms that the
reference librarian handle them. Content, in this case, not the carrier,
should dictate responsibility.) Upon accepting the task, the microform
manager must convince himself that his new duties have a significance that
transcends simple maintenance of the collection and care for the machines.
He must also be an A-1 salesperson as he extols his wares and develops a
solid patronage. His program ought to include the following: creation of a
pleasant microform reading room environment; maintenance of records
for hardware and software; a handbook of microform use; a "star" in the
collection; bibliographic control of the software and housing of pertinent
bibliographic apparatus in the microform room; library instruction in the
use of microforms; cooperative programs concerning microforms at the local level; and continuing self-study.

The Microform Reading Room Environment

This is the essential counter to user distaste for microforms, a distaste that
must be accepted and understood. As noted in the review of micropublications appearing in the 1971 volume of *Advances in Librarianship*, "The
microfilm industry and micropublication in particular are finally beginning

to admit what many librarians and users have long known: people don't like microforms; they prefer hard copies."[2] In light of this preference, it makes sense to design a context for microform use that complements as far as possible the context provided for hard copy use.

One central consideration is regard for the privacy of the user. A recent study of seating preference in a college reserve room found that students tended to locate themselves in order to avoid others.[3] Why suppose—as cramped microform facilities in so many small libraries seem to—that because an individual is doing reading that requires a machine, he will happily forego habits that otherwise cause him to retreat to quiet corners? Clearly, microforms should be accessible in a context that will afford users the same comforts and privacy they seek when reading hard copy.

If the library is fortunate enough to have an entire room designated as a microform area, a number of things can be done for user comfort. Adequate space for books and note taking can be made available at each machine. A wall chart with samples of the various microform formats owned by the library can help to demystify the microform. Machines can be labeled according to the format that they read. (Users new to the microform room will often try to insert microfilm into a microfiche reader. Though the proper procedures may seem elementary to the librarian familiar with microforms, the user's ability to frustrate himself when confronting "the machine" cannot be overestimated. Help him!) Even something as simple as color coding labels on microform storage cabinets by format can add to the warmth and efficiency of the room. Remember, users *are* reluctant to use microforms; any psychological support the librarian supplies will contribute significantly to their acceptance of microform use.

Maintenance of Records for
Hardware and Software

Just as patrons shirk engaging the hardware, so librarians tend to regard the maintenance of these machines as distasteful. There is little reason for them not to do so. Robert F. Asleson, president of University Microfilms, noted in a 1972 article in *Library Resources and Technical Services*, "We realize that we in the microform industry have not done the job we should have done in providing you with the equipment, providing the systems, and making it fun and easy to work with microforms."[4] This leaves the maintenance of the equipment and the creation of retrieval systems up to the resourcefulness of the librarian, no less than the task of encouraging users to handle the hardware in the first place. But this, too, can be accomplished once the problem is met on its own terms.

Hardware repair is unavoidable and it is expensive. A library budget that must provide for continual repair of microform hardware is liable to have its microform allotment cut. One way that the librarian can circumvent frequent external maintenance of microform machines is by keeping histories of each machine. If a microform reader's handle refuses to turn when a certain kind of film is loaded, record this in the machine's history. This will prevent the next person given care of the room from needlessly calling for repairmen. Along with the service history of each machine should be noted the types of lamps it uses, their cost, where to obtain them, the machine's serial number, whereabouts of operator's manuals, names of sales and service representatives, and any particular idiosyncrasies of that particular machine. These records should be readily available to anyone who is ever responsible for the library.

Fifteen minutes spent at the beginning of each week checking machines, polishing lenses, and cleaning viewing screens will also help to alert the microform manager to the use made of each machine and its operating condition. Most microform readers are relatively simple machines that need little more than a screwdriver for minor adjustments. Operator's manuals will generally give the limits to which troubleshooting should extend and after which a repairman should be called.

The software needs records, too. Circumstances surrounding each major purchase should be noted. One is sure to find odd items in the collection which seem barely usable because their acquisition is shrouded in the past history of the library. The most common example of this is material supportive of a particular faculty member's doctoral dissertation.

Data which explains the reason for each purchase may help in creating an awareness of its presence and use long after the faculty member who initiated the purchase has left the institution.

A Handbook of Microform Use

This needs to be but a simple production. The best way to insure its validity for potential users is to sit before each machine, diagram its parts, and note each step needed to get the microform on the machine and available in soft display. Be sure to note whether the machine provides image rotation. It is very disheartening for the microform manager who thought he has provided adequate instruction on machine use to come upon a patron contorted into an agonizing position as he attempts to read a microfilm display upside down.

Include in the handbook a chart of the room. Number each station and provide an explanation (see Figure 1). In a small library, there may often be times when the room is unattended and those on duty may not be conversant with microforms. Attempt to answer all possible questions in the handbook without overwhelming the user.

Give handbooks to all staff members. Be sure student workers are capable of using microforms—they can be of much help to patrons if the microform manager is not available. Make the handbooks convenient and evident to users.

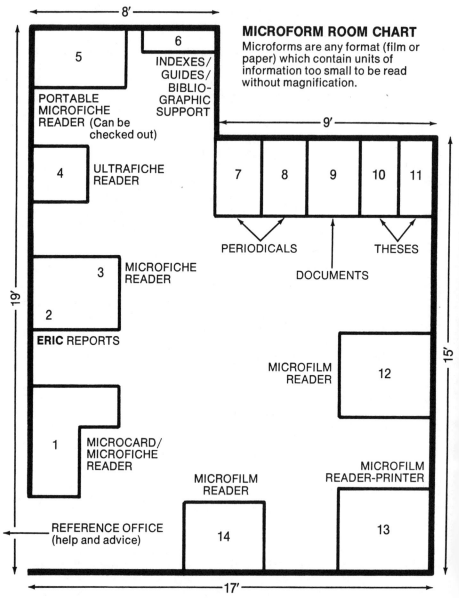

MICROFORM ROOM CHART

Microforms are any format (film or paper) which contain units of information too small to be read without magnification.

There are a number of different kinds of microforms in this room. Each requires a different sort of reader. Explanations coded to the chart above are found on pages 3-10 of this Handbook.

(From **HANDBOOK TO MICROFORM USE,** Rosary College, River Forest, Ill.)

FIGURE 1

Microfiche
2   **Hoccleve, Thomas,** 1370?-1450?
        Hoccleve's works ... Ed. by Frederick J. Furnivall ...
        London, Pub. for the Early English text society by K. Paul,
        Trench, Trübner & co., limited [etc.] 1892-1925.

        3 v. 1 illus., facsims. 22½ cm. (*Half-title:* ... Early English text
        society. Extra series, no. 61, 72, 73) 14 sheets. 3 x 5 in.

        CONTENTS.—I. The minor poems in the Phillipps ms. 8151 (Chelten-
        ham) and the Durham ms. III. 9. 1892.—II. The minor poems in the
        Ashburnham ms., addit. 133. (Now in the possession of the editor.)
        Edited by Sir Israel Gollancz. 1925.—III. The regement of princes,
        A. D. 1411-12, from the Harleian ms. 4866, and fourteen of Hoccleve's
        minor poems from the Egerton ms. 615. 1897.

        I. Furnivall, Frederick James, 1825-1910, ed. II. Gollancz, Sir
        Israel, 1864-1930, ed. [III. Title]

        PR1119.E5   no. 61, 72, 73   12—18035
        Library of Congress   [59r25j1]

MICROCARD

429   **Morris, Robert,** 1818-1888.
            Life in the Triangle, or, Freemasonry at the present
            time. By Rob. Morris ... Louisville, Printed by J. F.
            Brennan & co., 1854.
            284 p. 12°.

Samples of card
catalog entries
for microforms.

            1. Freemasons—Fiction. I. Title

                                                    9-17367†

            Library of Congress   HS435.M87

MICROFILM.
83
        German foreign ministry: miscellaneous docu-
        ments, 1920-1945. Washington, National
        Archives of the U.S. [n.d.]

        microfilm. 4 reels.

        1. Germany - Foreign relations, 20th century.

FIGURE 2

A "Star" in the Collection

If the library has nothing in microform but newspapers and backruns of periodicals, the collection can be made more attractive by the purchase of at least one relatively unique title in microform. This is not in emulation of the large research libraries but is to demonstrate to users the type of research possibilities microforms represent. Thomas Jefferson's papers can be purchased for slightly over $100 in microform, and such an item will give the microform manager a concrete example of the sort of archival and research material that are available to even isolated researchers because of microform technology.

This purchase should be made in accordance with the needs of the individual college and possibly in connection with a tenured faculty member's major interest on the theory that that will be a major point of investigation for students for some time to come.

Bibliographic Aids

All microforms should be fully cataloged in the main card catalog—something that can be done more easily in the small college than in the research library. In place of call numbers, a directive to the microform room indicating format and accession number should be noted (Figure 2).

It is obviously more convenient for users if the *New York Times Index* is in the same room as the microfilmed newspapers themselves. Any materials that are held in microform but indexed in hard copy should be contiguous. This may involve a rather substantial amount of hard copy in the microform room because ERIC indexes, bibliographies of specially owned collections, the *Union List of Microforms*, and *Guide to Microforms in Print* as well as micropublishers' catalogs should all be housed in the microform area.

In addition, literature about hardware and the technological advances of microforms can be gathered in this area. Various government publications and periodicals devoted to microforms might also be housed here. The reasons are threefold: ease of consultation for the user; ease of consultation for the microform manager; and the psychological support created for the user by the sight of hard copy in a room filled with cabinets and machines.

Instruction in the Use of Microforms

Where library instruction is fully integrated into college course work, the reference librarian encounters and counsels students at every step of their academic progress. It is at this point that the small liberal arts college can surpass the university in initiating and fostering the use and understanding of microforms. It can prove quite stimulating to all aspects of library instruction—even advanced bibliography courses—in the microform room. A reader-printer and fiche reader can create student interest because they represent an advanced technology that permeates the more prosaic and conventional areas of library instruction. By instilling students early on with a respect for the availability of information *regardless of the carrier,* students will be encouraged to explore the possibilities of microforms. Nevertheless, it will take some direct proselytizing to create a sense in students that microforms are no more anomalous a means of information storage than a tape cassette or codex book. It is certainly the small college reference department's responsibility to insure that the graduates of the institution are conversant with microforms.

Cooperative Programs

A modest pooling of microform resources at a local level can expand the base from which the small college librarian operates. Once convinced of the need to create a greater awareness of microforms, the microform manager might encourage other libraries in similar circumstances to join in a consortium in support of a local union list of microform resources.

To do this, questionnaires should be distributed to each school in order to discover what hardware and software each school owns. It is likely that this query will reveal that nearly all in the consortium have at least one strange and wonderful item on microform. In our case, we owned part of the Lyle Wright American fiction collection, another library had the *Chicago Tribune* published during the Civil War, and another had the *London Times.*

By pooling the knowledge of combined resources and making this known to each other through a union list, all of the small colleges involved greatly increased their microform potential. If cooperating libraries will allow direct borrowing of microforms, a student from one college is able to circulate material to be read at another college or public library more convenient to him. The opportunity to circulate microforms to students from other institutions in the consortium, as well as to one's own, is another factor which creates a receptive mood to the microform format on the part of users. Experience shows no more reason to expect losses or damage to circulating microform than to hard copy.

Continuing Self-Study

Both questionnaires periodically distributed to users of the microform room and direct personal interviews can monitor user satisfaction with the microform facilities and program. A study taken at the outset of such a program could reveal special desiderata, such as more space for books and note taking, a reader more comfortable to use, or an area reserved for the consultation of indexes. Such self-study can also create a sense of the importance of microforms for the entire library staff. And one should not overlook the fact that completed surveys indicating the need for more extensive facilities are impressive documentation at budget meetings.

Conclusion

The above ideas can be consolidated under the enthusiastic auspices of a microform manager into a workable microform program for even the small private school of modest means. Though the small college library cannot hope to imitate the research collection of a large university library, it can create a viable, well-used collection by a marshalling of available resources. Microforms do have a role in the small college; they provide students with a sense of scholarship at large and the means of availing themselves of resources at hand.

References

1. The impetus for this article came from a *Micrographics Seminar for Librarians* sponsored by the National Microfilm Association held March 9 and 10, 1973.

2. Allen B. Veaner, "Micropublication," in *Advances in Librarianship*, ed. Melvin J. Voigt (New York: Seminar Press, 1971), p. 181. Although Veaner goes on to explain the merits of microforms, "lightness of weight, compactness, portability, variable image size (if proper viewing equipment is available), cheapness and ease of duplication, speedy up-dating of computer-based information, massive storage capacity, preservation and dissemination of rare or fragile originals, ready availability of hard copy as needed, ease of replacement, and economy," these mertis are hardly the considerations that function in a small college library's decision to commit itself to a vigorous microform program. Rather, the small college must develop a rationale based in the educative realm rather than the technical.

3. Diane Fishman and Ruth Walitt, "Seating and Area Preferences in a College Reserve Room," *College and Research Libraries* 33 (July 1972): 284.

4. Robert F. Asleson, "Microforms: Where Do They Fit?" *Library Resources and Technical Services* 15 (Winter): 61.

ADDITIONAL READINGS

Bechanan, H. Gordon, "The Organization of Microforms in the Library," *Library Trends*, 8: 391-406 (January 1960).

"Deliberations," [Discussion by conference participants on the library use of microforms] in *Microform Utilization: the Academic Library Environment, Report of Conference Held at Denver, Colorado, 7-9 December 1970*. Denver: University of Denver, 1971, pp. 169-213. (Also ERIC ED 048 071).

Holmes, Donald C., *Determination of User Needs and Future Requirements for a Systems Approach to Microform Technology*. July 19, 1969, ERIC ED 029 168.

Schwarz, Philip J., "Instruction in the Use of Microform Equipment," *Wisconsin Library Bulletin*, 67: 341-3. (September 1971).

HARDWARE

Introduction

Ideally a microform reader for libraries should enlarge material back to its original size and should reproduce an entire page on the reader's screen. The goal is compatibility between the microform and the reading machine and this is accomplished by developing and adhering to standards. Standards, however, require control over the size of the material to be filmed. This control is relatively simple in a closed system where the dimensions of a technical report or a parts list page can be determined in advance of filming. This is not the case, however, with library materials whose normal range is from octavo to newspaper size.

Thus a reader which has an 8½ × 11" screen and magnifies 24X will reproduce an entire page at full size of anything whose dimensions are 8½ × 11 or less and which was filmed at a 24X reduction. This would include most books and such magazines as *Time* or *Atlantic Monthly*, but not *Life, Saturday Evening Post*, or a newspaper—the text would be enlarged to full size but only a portion of the page would appear on the screen. If the reading machine has interchangeable lens it would be possible to get the entire page on the screen by using a lens of lower magnification but then the text would be enlarged to less than its original size. In the case of 10 point or 12 point type this might not be a problem, but another difficulty with library materials is that a page may contain several type sizes some of which (a 6 point footnote, for example) may require full enlargement to be legible.

Manufacturers can and do make machines which meet existing standards. It is to their advantage to do so. But, these machines for the reasons noted above, may not meet the needs of libraries.

Another problem unique to libraries is that they retain materials indefinitely and cannot afford to replace old microforms which may now be non-standard. This is not the case in a closed system as such systems are almost always based on a cost effective analysis so that, for example, Sears could discard a 16mm cartridge system in use for their parts catalogs for many years when they found that an ultrafiche system would be more economical. In addition, in a closed system, information becomes obsolete quickly so that replacement is necessary whether it be with the same microform at a different reduction ratio or with a new microform.

Libraries, on the other hand, cannot throw out old microforms and replace them with new formats. Thus libraries which, for example, purchased microfiche made to the now obsolete COSATI standard which called for an 18X reduction need machines that enlarge 18 times—but they also need machines for currently issued fiche made to the NMA standard which calls for a 24X reduction. And a machine for microfilm. And a machine for opaques. And a machine for ultrafiche. Etc.

Another factor to bear in mind is the size of the library market which for an equipment manufacturer is small. Most closed systems require hundreds or thousands of machines and this is the market that influences most manufacturers.

Among the complaints voiced most often by librarians about reading machines are: (1) Need for many different models to accommodate the various sizes and formats; (2) lack of uniform sharpness on the screen; (3) lack of uniform brightness on the screen (hot spot in the middle); (4) need to refocus after moving from one page to another; (5) darkened room required—insufficient screen light for use in normally lit rooms; (6) configuration of machines requires user to remain more or less in one position; (7) manufacturers' disinclination to put clear cut operating instructions on the machine; (8) lack of image rotation; (9) image much less satisfactory than that of original document; (10) magnification should be slightly higher than reduction; (11) mechanical requirements such as threading, inserting, and positioning microforms need to be eliminated.

In the articles that follow the emphasis is on how to evaluate readers and reader-printers.

WHY DON'T THEY MAKE MICROFORM MACHINES FOR LIBRARIES?

by Roger C. Miller

Introduction

As a library professor with responsibilities for a large microform collection, I cannot find a viewer or viewer/printer that meets all of my requirements for library use. I am particularly concerned about the student or patron in a public library who encounters a viewer for the first time. Perhaps if I ask a number of questions, engineers will answer them when they design machines in the future. Librarians should ask similar questions before they purchase a new model.

How many models have operational instructions or diagrams permanently placed on the front of the machine for quick orientation? You may find a machine with a paper label placed on it as an afterthought. The more common sight is a hand-drawn diagram or embossed tape mounted by the library staff which is easily mutilated or removed by students. Directions that are stamped on the machine or on a metal plate securely fastened to a front panel would be an improvement.

Why aren't the controls clearly designed and permanently marked? It is difficult to identify the controls on some machines. Focus and scanning controls in particular are difficult to distinguish. Control identification has improved on some motorized and microfiche viewers in recent years.

A problem common to both motorized and manual open reel microfilm is that the take-up reel with the reversed film is returned to the shelf if the user fails to rewind the film. One can avoid this problem by placing a cotter pin through the take-up spindle so that the reel cannot be removed. Cartridge supply reels which do not allow the end of the film to leave the cartridge have been introduced. It is expensive, however, to convert a large open-reel collection. If future volumes are obtained in cartridge

Reprinted from *Microform Review*, 2: 91-92 (April 1973) by permission of the publisher.
Copyright © 1973 by Microform Review Inc.

form, it will be necessary to purchase special machines or converters for present equipment.

How many handles, knobs, and other parts are missing from viewers? Since engineers don't always design machines for unknowledgeable operators or for long periods of operation, parts disappear or break when controls are pulled, pushed, twisted, and turned in the wrong directions. Some parts disappear because it is characteristic of human nature to turn, loosen, or remove parts of a machine while spending long hours with it.

Why have machines been designed for quick retrieval of information without instructions? Because they have been designed primarily for the office and industry. In these situations everyone has his own viewer or a few people can be thoroughly instructed in the use of them. In a university library, hundreds or even thousands of students use viewers for the first time every semester. Often the only orientation, if any at all, is given to an entire class. To make the situation worse, only a small percentage of people in a library will ask for help or report an out-of-order viewer, so it is important to design easy-to-use, sturdy, trouble-free machines.

Why aren't manufacturers' catalogs and manuals useful? Many somewhat gratuitously describe the machine as "perfect for the office environment." But how many manuals give full instructions for properly cleaning the machines? How many manuals are revised and updated as the company becomes aware of problems reported by librarians who purchase their equipment? How many clearly describe preventive maintenance procedures?

Do manufacturers ever conduct comprehensive machine surveys or circulate questionnaires? Where do they field test machines? I know of tests in business and government offices. I know of tests in large universities where large microform collections are a relatively small part of the total collection. Students in large universities often avoid microforms. Why not field test machines in a small college or emerging university where a large portion of the collection is on microforms? In libraries of this type, microforms cannot be ignored. Students and faculty have experience on which to judge new machines.

There are many questions almost too obvious to mention; however, some manufacturers cannot answer them satisfactorily. Does the machine load and unload easily? Before purchasing a machine, try to operate it yourself without instructions from anyone, particularly the salesman. Many students will do just that when it is in your library! Does the roll microfilm reader scratch the film? (Librarians should occasionally check heavily used titles for scratches.) Does the equipment-especially motorized viewers and cooling fans—make too much noise when in operation? Noise may not be a factor with one or two machines. But it could be bothersome with ten or more machines. Is the size and cost out of proportion? Funds and space saved with the purchase of microforms can be taken by the cost and size of the machines.

The most important factor to consider before the purchase of any machine is the service contract. Is a serviceman available for repairs within a day? Does the contract state that you will receive preventive maintenance two to four times a year? Some machines require more maintenance than others. Will parts be replaced free of cost? If you do not have maintenance personnel on the staff or cannot get a company service man to your library within a reasonable length of time, do not purchase the machine!

There are indeed many advantages to microforms, but at this time the hardware is a barrier between the student and the information. Until machines that require little supervision and less maintenance are designed, microforms will not be fully accepted by librarians.

READER EVALUATIONS

by Robert A. Morgan

The reason I was selected to give this luncheon talk is because of the work we recently completed for the Library Technology Program in which we evaluated a group of viewers with a particular eye to their suitability for use in libraries. We were selected to do this because we have an extensive background in optical instruments and don't have any products competitive with these viewers; we could be intimately conversant with the technology involved and still able to evaluate this work impartially.

When we first became interested I thought it would be easy to develop some straightforward criteria by which to evaluate this equipment and could measure the selected viewers but I found it is a lot harder than you think it would be to evaluate a viewer. The first thing we found out is that there is a contest going on between micropublishers to see how many shaped and sizes and reduction ratios they can come up with. This, of course, introduces a problem. There is a problem also from the manufacturers point of view, for the people whose viewers we were evaluating; I think it is good to get other viewpoints here. Most of you are librarians and you can agree with each other how awful this situation is and that better viewers should exist, but it might be interesting to see a little of

Reprinted from *Microform Utilization; the Academic Library Environment. Report of Conference Held at Denver, Colorado, 7-9 December 1970.* Denver: University of Denver, 1971, pp. 216-224. (Also, ERIC ED 048 071).

the other side, what a manufacturer might be looking at.

Confronted with this wide variety of forms he is going to look for some kind of design that will have a wide market so he needs a substantial amount of versatility. Try to imagine yourself as a manufacturer about to introduce a new product. The first thing you think of is the Edsel. You don't want your product to be an Edsel. You are going to be putting a lot of money out to introduce this product. Even a very simple product like a microform viewer represents a very substantial investment. You couldn't do it, except under unusual conditions, for less than $100,000. Probably it would cost $300,000. This goes into engineering design, and tooling, and manufacturing startup costs, and sales promotion. It is a very costly business to launch a product. Think of what this means in these terms; as a conservative estimate you are going to spend $100,000 to do this, and you have to make some money back. If it turns out well you can make 5% on your sales. Internal revenue will let you keep ½ of that so you make 2½%. If you put $100,000 into the development, you have to sell $4 million in viewers just to get back what it took to get started. That's a lot of viewers. You have to look for something with quite wide applicability. You might have some idealism and think you will make the best viewer in the world. You see what other people are doing that sells and you think at least you will get your share of the market. This is why the readers that you see on the market tend to cluster around sameness, as it does in many products. It's like a distribution curve with some very good at one end and some very bad at the other end and most of the viewers are sort of in the middle. You might wish this were not true, but it is a point of view that does exist, so it tends to explain in some measure why you get what you do get.

The LTP report of May 1970 that we prepared covers the 10 viewers we evaluated. There will be another report in a few months on another group of viewers we are working with now. It just came to my attention that there is a report by Sherman of Saginaw, Michigan that may have interesting information of this nature. In evaluating the viewers we used some elaborate instrumentation that would not be available to you, but I want to talk about the things we did in ways that might suggest things you could do in evaluating your readers. There are two things you have to consider (1) what the reader is for, and (2) how it will perform: what it does and how well it does it. In considering what it is for, there are two aspects to this, (1) what microforms you want to use it for, and (2) what environment you will use it in. The environment consists of ambient conditions and the personnel that will use it. As for the microforms, we have been distressed by the proliferation of them. If you try to select a viewer that will cover all of them you will do it at the expense of other advantages so you might give consideration to having several kinds of viewers. You might not have your equipment like a fleet of cars that are alike but rather have some for different, specific purposes. You might get the best performance-to-cost ratio if you do this. If you get a viewer that satisfies 90% of the users most of the time and some people have to go elsewhere part of the time for the other 10% of their material, that may be a good buy; if you try to get equipment for all-inclusive coverage you may pay quite a lot for that. You have to consider what microforms you will be using and whether positive or negative, and so on.

For the environment, the illumination of the screen is very important and you probably don't want to make users go into a dark closet to use the readers because it is hard to take notes there and the contrast is disagreeable. If you have a bright reader in a surrounding that is very tiring on your eyes. It is like working on a dark desk and having a light paper in the middle of the desk. The pupils of your eyes don't know whether to enlarge or contrast. They don't know what to do. You may notice it is more restful to work on a light-colored desk. The same thing is true here. You would like to have a reader that you can use in a quite light environment. As far as the personnel who will be using the readers are concerned, if you are selecting for one person you have more freedom than if you are selecting for public use. For public use you have to have something with clear and simple instructions. One person can learn to use a complicated machine, but you don't want to have to spend a lot of time teaching and re-teaching all the users. These matters of the environment are important matters. Mr. Wheeler mentioned this yesterday, that the same viewer may perform well in one situation and be very poor in another situation. You can't just take somebody's word as to whether or not one is good and one is bad. You have to consider carefully the use environment. The physical situation is important and also the kind of users.

How well a viewer performs becomes largely a matter of image quality and the convenience of the controls. The image quality can be evaluated by considering the sharpness of the image, the quality of illumination, and the contrast. The sharpness of image is difficult to define. One way is in lines per millimeter of resolution. Another approach is in terms of modulation transfer function. Neither of these is 100% right. They don't have one-to-one correspondence. Modulation transfer function is difficult to describe and to measure except in a laboratory with special equipment. It tends to show the gradual deterioration of image quality as the material that you read gets finer and finer. Lines per millimeter also tends to do this but you can sometimes have poor value in lines per millimeter and have very readable images on the screen. You are better off to compare viewers than to compare numbers. Even if your numbers are very scientifically prepared, comparing numbers is not as good as comparing images on the screen because you get the whole environment when you compare images. If you are forced to have a numerical measure then you have to use it, but this number is a subjective thing and two different people get different numerical answers.

Another matter that is important is quality of illumination, whether or not it is even. The sufficiency is not too great a problem; often it can be improved by reader position such as not having the viewer face an uncovered window or not having it directly under a light. You can find within a room some positions that are better than others for viewers. What is very important is the evenness of the illumination. If you see a bright spot in the center and dim corners, that is a very tiring situation. It is like working with a light paper on a dark desk. Your eye works differently under different circumstances. This may be a coincidence, but people used to use dark wooden desks more than they do now and they had lower levels of illumination than they do now. In that low level of illumination the dark desk may have caused the iris of the eye to open up so one could see better what was on the paper. Now, in typical office situations, you have bright lighting; if you have a dark desk it opens the iris and it is open too wide to look at a white paper. This is like a viewer; you want it in a fairly bright room, to have a bright screen, to have a lot of contrast, and you want even illumination. Sometimes the illumination of a screen is so uneven that if you move your head to one side then one side of the image will almost be extinguished. It is very tiring to have to keep your head in one position for a long period of time. You can make measurements of illumination with a meter or you can just make comparisons of the viewer. It is easier in this case to take numerical measurements and compare them but you still should compare the viewers.

The viewer with a "hot spot" or bright spot in the center is a very tiring one to look at. This is often a problem in a viewer with a short optical path (which is usually to say a small viewer). You could have a small viewer with a folded optical path of mirrors in which case you probably would have better evenness of illumination. Anybody who is a photographer will understand this readily because when you have a wide angle lens on your camera you tend to have underexposure in the corners; the same condition prevails here plus some other things. The short optical path is equivalent to your wide angle lens in the camera and you don't get good corner illumination. Something you should look for in this connection is quartz iodide lamps. These are very good lamps but, typically, they don't have a fixed relationship between the filament and the socket. If you have just put one in the socket where the last one came out, in exchanging a burned-out lamp, you may not have the filament in exactly the same position. A viewer like this should have some provision for focusing this lamp. You should be able to move it around a little bit and you should be able to view the screen while you move it around because you don't want to have the situation like you have with a TV set: when you move the controls around you can't see the screen and if you are far enough away to view the screen you can't reach the controls. For the viewer, you would want to see the screen while making this lamp adjustment because, outside of a laboratory, the only way you can get the adjustment done correctly is by looking at the screen to see when you have even and bright illumination. You also, in all cases, should use the lamp recommended by the manufacturer and be sure it is down firm in the socket because just a little displacement of that filament can destroy the image quality and evenness of the illumination; you might think the viewer is very bad when it just needs to have the filament adjusted correctly.

Several people have mentioned ambient lighting and the difficulty of using a viewer in bright situations. One thing you can do is simply reverse the screen. That diffusive coating on the screen is usually on the inside to protect the screen and it ought to be on the outside for the convenience of the user. It is true that it will eventually wear out and get scratched, but you are really trying to satisfy the user rather than to protect the screen; so if you turn it on the outside the user will be much less sensitive to reflections from lights. These screens are quite durable. You can get them scratched and they won't degrade the image too badly. Material in spray cans is available that will freshen a screen that has been damaged. People take much too good care of the screens instead of the people using the viewers.

About contrast, this is apt to be more trouble with positive than with negative film because there is more light getting inside the viewer. Lack of contrast arises when extraneous light gets up on the screen from being reflected around inside the viewer. Then, it washes out the contrast between the light and dark areas. Unless you make careful measurements you can't tell whether it has good contrast or not. You just see a degradation of image quality. Again, I would advise comparing viewers because when you compare the composite image on the screen you don't care what reason it is that makes the image bad, you just care about the composite image.

Curvature of field is another thing. An image does not come to focus on a flat plane. Most often it comes to focus on a spherical surface. The screen is a flat plane so you have to find some good focus about halfway between good in the center and good in the corners. When you are checking resolution you shouldn't just look at the center of the screen because that's where the lens image is best; look also in the corners. It is hard to read on a viewer that you have to keep focusing when you go from the top to the center and then on to the bottom. This will occur when you have excessive curvature of field. That's a viewer to reject because you can't correct that problem. You don't get very good pictures with a wide angle lens and this situation is like that. It is hard to design such a lens that is well corrected. This speaks in favor of a large viewer with a long optical path which usually means a large box. You would like to have a small viewer but this is one of the trade-offs you have to make. This doesn't mean that a large viewer is necessarily going to have a good image, but it is easier.

Another distortion you may have is something also recognizable by camera people and that is a pin cushion distortion or barrel distortion. That occurs if you project a square image and it comes up on a screen as a pin cushion shape or where the sides bulge the other way. This is not necessarily bad for image quality in terms of reading and if you don't notice it just by looking at it that may be all right, but there might be some cases where a user that you are serving would want to make measurements from a graph that is being projected and then you would want to give thought to this distortion. You can just hold a ruler to the lines and see if they are straight and up to the left hand margin and see if that is straight. There is also a keystone distortion and this is not a defect of a lens; it results when a mirror is out of position. This could be an ordinary defect that would suggest condemning a viewer that otherwise was good. A screw could shake loose in shipment and a mirror could get out of adjustment and the image would come up to the screen with a keystone shape. If this happens you cannot get good focus all over the screen, so if you cannot get good focus this may be the reason. A mirror can be put back in place.

Another thing that affects image quality is how flat the film is held. If the film is not perfectly flat between plates there is a good chance that some part of the film won't come to focus on the screen. This is a very sensitive thing; one-thousandth of an inch out of position can be recognized as a degradation of performance on the screen; a good quality image is that sensitive to the position of the film. This is a problem with cassettes. Some cassettes won't hold the film very flat. If the film is not flat, you will lose good imagery by the curvature of the film. This is a highly magnified problem when it reaches the screen.

There are some other things that could show up, but all of them affect image quality if they are important. If they don't affect image quality then they aren't important. The best comparison is image quality. The best test is "try it before you buy it." Don't pick it out of a catalog. Test it out in the real situation.

There is another kind of viewer that will be finding its way into the library environment soon. This is the viewer associated with its own film in some sort of self-contained system. This may add to the proliferation of microforms but it probably will be acceptable because the film and viewer come as a package so you don't have to worry so much about it. Representatives of this type are Microform Data Systems, NCR with their photocromic system, Image Enterprises, Library Resources, and a new device my company has just introduced. Probably Image System's Card Systems should be included in this. Various reduction ratios are being used: 200X, 150X, 100X, 70X, 42X, 24X.

I have had some reservations about describing equipment that my company is putting out because I didn't want to interject a commercial note, but in view of the interest in this subject I will describe it. We have a storage and retrieval device. It is helpful to put such a thing in an economical context because you can imagine better where it might fit. Depending upon configuration, it is from $5,000 to $8,000. This device is a box a little smaller than an office desk and has two films in it. There is a main data base on 105mm film and an up-date film on 16mm film. The main data base is laid out in fiche format just like you were making microfiche except it isn't cut—it is left in a roll. Every image space on it is assigned an address which has 3 coordinates, a fiche number, a column number and a row number. In many situations you get information on film that tends to become obsolete and here and there a frame is out of date. That's why we have the up-date film so you can generate, very inexpensively, just those images that have become obsolete on the main data base. Beside each image on the up-date 16mm film we have a machine-readable code that designates the address that is being replaced by this image. It has a fiche number and column and row taken from the main film. You enter the system by keyboard or by computer. If you enter the keyboard you key in a 7-digit number. Then both of these films are searched simultaneously. If the material that you have requested is on the up-date film that frame comes up to the screen, but if that number is passed on the up-date film is signified there is no such up-date frame and the main data base is valid so that comes up to the screen. On the 105mm film we have about 100,000 pages. An alternate way of using this is to consider those situations where you don't know the address to which you want to go. In that case you may wish to converse with the computer to help with the identification problem and over a phone line the computer will direct the user to display on the screen the image that will be an answer to the inquiry.

This equipment is a sort of descendent of the Intrex work and that described by Mr. Pemberton for the New York Times. I guess a lot of other things are going on in this same area. If it seems like a lot of money that MIT has been spending in working out Intrex, you can see there is a very useful fallout from that because this system we have been using was developed by Roger Summit at Lockheed with a great deal of influence from Intrex. Such projects have continuing side benefits not immediately apparent. We have demonstrated our machine; the computer was at Lockheed in Palo Alto and we were in Houston. We had on film abstracts of OE documents. The computer was programmed by Lockheed to know a lot about these documents and can identify them and locate them on the film. A user could sit at the teletype and ask the computer questions and get down to a number of abstracts he wanted to see. The computer then would send the addresses for these and they would come to the screen sequentially. Lockheed's program is called DIALOG and you don't have to know a lot about the articles to get what you want. These kinds of systems we have felt were just around the corner for libraries and I think we have just turned that corner.

DESIRABLE CHARACTERISTICS FOR READERS AND READER-PRINTERS

by Donald C. Holmes

Characteristics considered desirable for a microform reader are listed be-low in Section A, and for a microform reader-printer in Section B. It is thought that a reader-printer should incorporate all of the characteristics deemed desirable for a reader. Hence, these are not repeated. Only characteristics pertaining to the print capability appear in Section B.

Certain assumptions were made in preparing these design characteristics. It was assumed that a combination roll film and sheet microform reader (or a combination roll film and sheet reader-printer) would complicate construction problems and would be likely to cause the user difficulty when changing accessories for use of either rolls or sheets. Roll film readers should accommodate 35mm and 16mm microfilm, and micro-fiche readers should accommodate sheets up to 5 in. X 8 in. Further, it was assumed the readers or reader-printers would be a "permanent" fixture in a reading room (either on tables or as part of carrels) as opposed to their being portable for circulation. Finally, it was assumed they would be used to read materials for a long period of time as opposed to their being used as scanning devices only.

A. Readers

1. DIMENSIONS

The size and weight of the reader will depend largely on the ability of the manufacturer to integrate in a compact fashion the design char-acteristics listed below. It would be inappropriate to specify a particular size and weight.

Reprinted from Appendix D of Donald C. Holmes, *Determination of the Environmental Conditions Required in a Library for the Effective Utilization of Microforms. Interim Report.* November, 1970. (ERIC ED 046 403), pp. 33-37.

2. SCREEN
   a. *Size*
   Screen size should be at least 11 in. wide by 14 in. high. For reading newspaper on microfilm, it is desirable to have a screen at least 15½ in. wide to accommodate a 1:1 blowback of a newspaper.
   b. *Angle*
   The reading angle on the screen should be variable to prevent fatigue caused by reading in a fixed position.
   c. *Height*
   Screen height above the table should be variable to enable reading ease for tall and short users.
   d. *Illumination*
   The screen should be evenly illuminated from the corners to the center.
   e. *Brightness*
   Brightness should be adjustable to accommodate:
   1) Reading positive and negative microforms
   2) Various degrees of ambient lighting.
   f. *Surface*
   Screen surface should be non-glare to suppress reflections from the surrounding area.
3. IMAGE QUALITY
   a. *Type of Projection*
   There should be internal projection to allow for use under conditions of ordinary lighting.
   b. *Resolution*
   The image should appear with sufficient definition as to compare favorably with the original from which the microform was produced. (The Library Technology Program's microform reader test program specifies resolution of 5.01/mm at the center and 4.01/mm at the edges and corners as good performance.)
   c. *Focus*
   The focus of the image should be constant and should not be affected by vibrations caused by normal machine use or changes in filmgate temperatures.
   d. *Distortion*
   The image should appear bright, clear and sharp and refocusing should not be required to read any portion of it.
4. MAGNIFICATION
   The reader should provide a range of magnifications from 15X to 24X. A single lens system, providing variable magnification and automatic focusing, is preferable to a series of interchangeable lenses which require careful storage, installation and maintenance.

5. IMAGE ROTATION
   Image rotation of 360° should be provided.
6. FILM TRANSPORT ASSEMBLY
   The glass flats which hold the film in place must be separable and
   easily removed for cleaning. The glass flats should automatically
   separate when the film advance knob is rotated and it should be impossible to advance the film if the flats are closed.
7. FILM ADVANCEMENT
   It should be possible to advance and reverse the film at two speeds—
   at a rapid speed and a slower speed. If the film drive is motorized, it
   should be variable between high and low speed.
8. CONTROLS
   All controls, e.g., film advancement, focusing, scanning, etc., should
   be easily accessible from a seated position. All controls should be
   clearly labelled.
   a. *Focusing*
      The focusing device should operate smoothly and easily and should
      move the image to either side of the "in-focus" position with a
      single turn of the hand. It should be securely mounted so that no
      lateral shifting of the image occurs during focusing.
   b. *Scanning*
      A scanning device should be provided for both horizontal and
      vertical positioning.
   c. *Magnifying*
      A variable magnification knob should be provided to allow the user
      to determine (with a zoom lens or an autofocus lens and screen)
      the most legible size of the image.
9. HEATING, COOLING, NOISE
   The filmgate temperature must be within the acceptable limits
   specified in ANSI Standard Methods of Testing Printing and Projection Equipment, Z38.7.5 and Microfilm Reader Standards, PH5.1. A
   cooling system should be provided if required to meet these specifications and if provided its operation should be silent.
10. ELECTRICAL POWER REQUIREMENTS
    The reader should be operated on standard 120 volts, 60 cycles.
11. SAFETY FACTORS
    All surfaces, corners, and edges of the reader should be free from
    burrs and roughness to prevent damage to film or hands. The reader
    should have a stable base to prevent its being knocked over. There
    should be no hazardous electrical current leakage.
12. MAINTENANCE
    All accessories should be attached to the machine. Parts should be
    easy to attach and accessible for cleaning and repair. The projection
    lamp should be of a type readily available from commercial sources
    and easy to change. Glass flats, mirror, screen, and lenses should be

easy to clean.

13. OPERATION

Operation should be simple and clearly illustrated. A diagram for threading reels should be provided at each reading station. Simple, well illustrated, attractive instructions should also be provided.

B. Reader-Printer

1. PROCESS

Ideally, the printing process should yield positive hard copy from both negative and positive micro-transparencies at the flick of a switch. Recent announcements from a manufacturer of microform reader-printers indicate that machines capable of producing positive prints from both positive and negative prints are forthcoming. In the meanwhile, although some reader-printers employing an Electrofac process are capable of producing positive prints from negative and positive film, one must select either a negative-positive machine, which produces positive prints from negative microtransparencies, or a positive-positive machine, which produces positive prints from positive microtransparencies. Mr. Hawken's discussions of processes in the Library Technology Program's publications, *Enlarged Prints from Library Microforms* and *Copying Methods Manual* are most useful.

2. QUALITIES OF THE HARD COPY
   a. Sharp, clear, legible.
   b. Non-curling.
   c. Non-smearing.
   d. Non-fading.
   e. Capable of being marked with pen, pencil, felt-tip, typewriter.
   f. Permanent paper and image.
   g. Available in two sizes—8½ in. × 11 in. and 11 in. × 14 in. to allow compatibility with existing filing systems.

3. CONTROLS
   a. Print button should be easily accessible from a seated position.
   b. Multiple copy feature would be desirable.
   c. It should be possible to install a coin meter.
   d. Finished hard copy should be accessible from a seated position.

4. SPEED OF PRINT PROCESS
   Print processing should be completed within 30 to 45 seconds.

5. PRINT AREA
   There should be marks on or beside the screen to indicate the exact dimensions of the image that will be produced in hard copy.

6. WASTE
   Exposure control should be automatic and sufficiently accurate that

trial exposures are not required. Wastage normally should not exceed 5%.

7. QUIET OPERATION
   The reader-printer should have a quiet operation, making it suitable for use in an open reading area.

8. MAINTENANCE
   If a process involving the use of solutions is employed, the solution trays should be easily accessible for filling and easily removable for cleaning with the least possible hazard of spillage. The rollers should also be readily accessible for daily cleaning. Loading the paper supply should be an easy operation.

EXCERPTS FROM *MICROFORM RETRIEVAL GUIDE*

GENERAL FACTORS IN EQUIPMENT SELECTION

Many of the functional and operational considerations which affect equipment selection pertain to all readers and reader printers regardless of the type of microform. These factors are considered below.

Electrical Systems

Power. The standard current in the United States is 115-volt 60-cycle. All U.S.-made readers and reader printers operate on this current. In many European and South American countries, 220-volt 50-cycle current is standard. Some manufacturers have models available which can easily be adapted to foreign and other special power service. Several portable readers can be battery operated or adapted to automotive or aircraft electrical systems.

Lamps. Standard projection bulbs are used in many reference units. Many manufacturers now use more expensive, specially designed lamps which

Reprinted from *Microform Retrieval Guide*. Washington: General Services Administration, 1970. (Federal Stock No. 7610-181-7579), pp. 12-35.

maintain approximately the same light output during the life of the lamp. Bulb or lamp failure is the most frequent maintenance item in readers and reader printers. It is well to keep a spare on hand. The life of a lamp depends on both the lamp type and the electrical system in the unit. To determine the number of lamps needed per year, estimate the number of hours each reader will be in use during the year and divide by the rated lamp life. It is generally good practice to allow the lamp to cool before moving portable readers. Projection lamps run hot, and a burned out lamp should be allowed to cool before attempting to replace it.

Cooling. Because projection lamps generate both light and heat, the projection system and film plane must be cooled to protect the film. Larger readers usually have a motor-driven blower to do this. The design of smaller units is such that convection cooling is often sufficient. The film is also protected by heat-absorbing glass elements in the projection condenser system. Regardless of the cooling system, no external part of the reader normally touched by the user with the exception of hot air vents, should be more than warm to the touch.

Screen

In most microdocument systems it is desirable to have the reader screen present an entire page of information at or near the original size. Half page or partial page images on a screen can be useful and are acceptable with some types of document systems, such as newspapers and engineering drawings. However, in making a decision about a reader or reader printer, the purchaser should be aware of the following facts regarding reduction, enlargement, original document size, and reader screen size:

1. The original sheet sizes of common documents in inches are:

Federal Government letters	8 W×10½ H
Federal Government legal documents	8 W×13 H
Commercial letters	8½ W×11 H
Commercial legal documents	8½ W×14 H
Computer printout, two sizes	14 W×11 H
	8½ W×11 H
International (ISO), A-4 size	210×297 mm.
	(8¼ W×11¾ H)

Engineering
drawings   A size 8½ W×11 H
                           11 W×8½ H
                           B size 17 W×11 H
                           C size 22 W×17 H
                           D size 34 W×22 H
                           E size 44 W×34 H

2. The reader screen must be equal in size to the original document if it is necessary to present the entire document page at the original size. However, most documents have unused margins, and a screen slightly smaller than the original document may adequately display the information area of a document page at original size.
3. A smaller screen will also display a full page of text when the reader enlarges the image to less than original size. For example, an 8½- × 11-inch document, originally reduced 24×, can be accommodated on a 7¼- × 9½-inch screen when enlarged 20×. The characters in the text and illustrations will be proportionately smaller also.
4. A letter-size image that must be rotated 90 degrees to be right reading will require a screen 11 inches wide as well as some form of image rotation. Such images often contain tabulated data and charts or graphs.

Color. Screens can be of a neutral color, when lighted, or have a slight tint. The tinted screens are used by some manufacturers to reduce potential eye strain. Images photographed in color will show better color fidelity when projected on a neutral screen.

Type. Most readers and reader printers project images from the rear onto a translucent screen. These screens often have a matte surface on one side and a shiny surface on the other. The matte surface facing out will reduce glare and ambient reflections. The shiny surface facing out will give an apparent increase in image sharpness. A reflecting screen is an opaque one on which the images are projected for viewing.

Physical Features

Readers and reader printers are available in a variety of forms to suit the environment in which they will be used, the user's need, the system, and the cost. The basic forms are:

1. *Lap readers.* Designed for portability and personal use, they are available at present only as microfiche readers.
2. *Portable readers.* These are readers which either fold into a case similar to a portable typewriter case or are compact and portable. They are available for 16-mm. film, aperture cards, and microfiche, and are

generally used on an intermittent basis.
3. *Desk readers and reader printers.* These are usually intended for more continuous use and are placed on a desk, table, or stand.
4. *Free-standing units.* These self-contained readers and reader printers have integral bases and are designed to stand alone.

Many manufacturers offer a list of accessories as well, such as floor stands, combination stands and microform storage units, adaptors for other types of microfilm, and other capabilities. The number of operating features, controls, and accessories on any unit is directly related to its cost. As a minimum, nearly every reader has an on-off switch and a control for focusing. And all reader printers have some means for controlling print time.

Human Factors Interface

A reader or reader printer should be comfortable to use. The controls should be located where they are easily accessible while the user is in the normal viewing position. The film loading operation should be simple and readily understandable after the first explanation and demonstration. The control of the film movement should be smooth, allowing for rapid movement to specific document areas and for fine adjustments to center pages on the screen. The unit should stay in focus moving from one page to the next. Any large-scale film movement should necessitate no more than a minimal focus adjustment. When indexing systems are part of the unit, they should be simple to comprehend and use. Human factors are largely subjective. They can be evaluated only by testing the equipment under actual operating conditions.

Optical Systems

Manufacturers specify readers and reader printers by image magnification (24X means the image is magnified 24 times). Most units have fixed magnifications that cannot easily be changed in the field, even though the purchaser may select one from a choice of magnifications at the time of ordering. Nevertheless, the purchaser will find many units available with magnifications changeable in the field. These are generally one of three types: units with lens systems that are interchangeable by removing one lens from the holder and dropping in another; dual magnification units, with magnification changed by means of a lever of mechanism; or systems that provide continuously variable magnification over a specified range using zoom lenses or mechanically varied optical paths. Variation in magnification is important to the user who will receive microforms from more than one source at very different image reductions. In this case, interchangeable lenses or continuously variable magnification can be considered. For the user who will need reference to images of documents over a broad size range, such as newspapers and smaller publications, continuously variable systems or dual magnification units should be considered.

Image Rotation. When the microforms used contain images which are not right reading in the normal orientation of the microform in the reader, some type of image rotation is needed. In the tables in chapters III-VI, the following notations are used:

1. *None.* The user must turn his head to view the screen image when it is not right reading or, in the case of microfiche and aperture cards, the microform must be removed from the machine, turned 90 degrees, and reinserted. One 16-mm. roll film reader can be used upright or turned on its side for reading.
2. *Optical rotation.* Images are rotated by a lever or knob that rotates a prism in the optical system.
3. *Mechanical rotation.* Rotation is accomplished by turning the film transport 90 degrees.

When image rotation is a factor, either of the last two methods can be quite satisfactory in a given case. The choice is mainly one of user preference.

Maintenance

In general, the quality of the image displayed or the paper copy provided is directly related to the cleanliness of the optical system and the printing mechanism. Microfilm's worst enemy is dust. Dust on reader screens, mirrors, and other optical elements decreases light and illumination levels, sometimes significantly. Dust particles on the film or film holding mechanism damage the film and, when enlarged 20 to 40 times, may look like confetti on the screen and impair readability.

Preventive maintenance will make a considerable difference in the long-term usability of the equipment. Use of a dust cover when the equipment is not in use is recommended. Following the manufacturer's recommendations, cleaning of the screen, lens, internal mirrors, and condenser elements should be done on a routine basis. As noted earlier, lamps should be replaced as burned out or when the lamp envelope has darkened, decreasing light output. (Take care not to touch the old lamp when it is still hot.) A spare lamp should be available. Most units provide easy access to the lamp. Some have a clip inside for storage of an extra lamp.

Glass flats or optical flats of plastic are often used to hold the film flat in the optical system. They should be easily removed for cleaning or should be easily accessible and cleaned in place. On reader printers, loading of the paper and imaging chemicals and removal or cleaning of the printing mechanism should be easy and convenient.

Major maintenance problems should, of course, be referred to qualified maintenance personnel.

Warranties and Service

Manufacturers' warranties and maintenance service vary considerably. Most will warrant their hardware against defective parts for periods of time ranging from 30 days to 1 year. The warranty does not normally include lamps. Some manufacturers include labor costs during the warranty period, and some do not. Some manufacturers have service contracts available after the initial warranty period. Rental equipment frequently includes maintenance service by the supplier. Some smaller manufacturers may request the return of the hardware to the factory for service if they do not have locally available service engineers.

In general, the simpler the device the less the purchaser need be concerned with length of warranty or availability of local service. Once the simplest microfiche reader has been received and installed in good repair, there is little to go wrong. If defective parts are discovered, replacements can often be obtained from the factory and installed by the user. Conversely, for reader printers and the more mechanized readers, length of warranty and the availability locally of trained service personnel and service contracts should be discussed prior to equipment selection or purchase.

CONVENTIONAL ROLL MICROFILM READERS AND READER PRINTERS

The two most commonly used roll microfilms are 16-mm. and 35-mm. A typical reel contains up to 100 feet of standard base film or 200 feet of the new thin films. Roll film on reels can be used in some readers and reader printers having motorized drives, but most commonly rolls are used in machines that are manually operated. Accordingly, this section covers only units which are not motorized. Roll film stored and handled on conventional reels normally has only minimal indexing aids, such as flash cards or sequential frame numbers. In this category are:

1. Universal Readers which accept both 16-mm. and 35-mm. roll film. Many of these units can also be adapted to accept microfiche and film jackets as well.
2. Readers for 16-mm. roll microfilm.

In addition, this section covers reader printers which will accept 35-mm. or 16-mm. roll microfilm or both.

Physical and Operational Characteristics

A conventional roll microfilm reader normally is a simple device consisting of:

A hand-cranked film transport mechanism.

An optical projection and enlarging system.

Controls: on-off, focus.

Translucent screen. (One widely used reader projects the image on an opaque reflecting screen.)

Housing.

In addition, the reader printers have:

Paper transport and printing mechanism.

Special printing controls.

The user normally performs the following functions in order to display an image on a reader:

Turn switch on.

Place reel on reader, thread film through film gate, and attach to take up reel.

Focus.

Wind to desired image.

To produce a print on a reader printer:

Set print timer to proper exposure.

Press print button.

Very little maintenance is needed for these units. The reader should be dusted at least once a week. The most critical parts are the film transport mechanism and the film gate. Glass flats at the film gate should be cleaned with glass cleaner. Manufacturer's instructions for cleaning and maintenance of the printing mechanism of reader printers should be followed carefully.

Special Factors in Equipment Selection

Conventional roll microfilm readers or reader printers employing either 16-mm. or 35-mm. film are typically used for newspapers, books, periodicals and other library reference materials. 16-mm. units are generally used for correspondence files, personnel files, security storage files, and business records for which there is a lower incidence of reference.

Film Transport. Roll film is manually transported in one of two ways on units of this equipment class. In the simplest case, identified in the equipment tables as "reel crank," a hand crank is attached to the spindles on which the film reels are mounted. In many units, film is driven forward or reversed through a mechanical linkage from the film spindles to a reversible crank. Though more costly, this method is more convenient.

A few of the units in this category can be adapted to or accept cartridges or magazines. Since many of the conventional roll film machines are intended for library use, their design enables them to accept microfiche, jackets, and aperture cards as well. In most of these units the unit microforms are positioned manually.

Film Gate. For optimum sharpness of the screen image, the film must be held flat in the film plane. Two types of film gates are used for this purpose; they are:

1. *Open throat.* The film rides in open air. Such units normally use edge guiding or other methods to keep the film in the focal plane.
2. *Glass flats.* The film is held in the focal plane between two pieces of optically flat glass.

While the latter method will often provide the sharper image, the glass flats must be kept clean to minimize film damage. To further protect the film, these glass flats can be:

1. *Floating.* The flats pivot on a central axis so that they rotate with the film as it moves.
2. *Manual open* (and close). The flats must be separated manually each time the film is transported.
3. *Auto open* (and close). The flats open automatically when the film is moved.

Obviously each mechanization of a function contributes to cost and the purchaser can best weigh the above factors by his own experience.

MOTORIZED ROLL FILM READERS AND READER PRINTERS

The majority of mechanized readers and reader printers use 16-mm. microfilm in containers called magazines, cartridges, or cassettes. Most of these units are designed to use one or more image-locating techniques. At least one unit used 16-mm. film with 8-mm. images in a duo (double row) sequence. These readers and reader printers vary greatly in their degree of sophistication and price. The degree of sophistication is related to the unit's retrieval capabilities.

In this category are:

1. A limited number of portable readers.

2. A number of desk model readers and reader printers.

3. One or more free-standing readers and reader printers.

Physical and Operational Characteristics

A standard 100-foot length of 16-mm. microfilm can accommodate 2,000 to 3,000 letter-size images. Thin base film can be put into a cartridge, thus doubling its capacity in pages. However, the user should be aware that thin base films do not work equally well in all reader and reader printer models, and many models require modification for thin base films.

The most widely used motorized readers consist of:

A screen, either neutral in color or tinted blue or green.

A slot or holder to accommodate the magazine or spindle for the supply reel.

A film transport mechanism that either automatically threads the film through the machine and rewinds it into the magazine or transports manually threaded film.

An optical projection and enlarging system.

Controls: on-off, focus, and slow and fast motor drive for transporting film.

On the manually controlled retrieval systems either an odometer indicator or an index scale along the screen. On automated retrieval systems, pushbutton control keyboards and logic circuitry for image location.

A housing.

In addition, a reader printer has:

A paper transport and printing mechanism.

Additional controls for printing.

In order to display an image on the most widely used units, the user normally performs the following functions:

Turn switch on.

Insert cartridge.

Press lever or turn motor control knob to forward.

In manually controlled units, move film via control lever or knob to image location as indicated by the odometer or index strip on the screen. On automated units, press control buttons on panel for predetermined page location.

Focus.

To produce a print on a reader printer:

Set timer or exposure control.

Press print button.

The maintenance considerations discussed earlier pertain to this class of equipment as well. Because of the generally higher level of use of the motorized units however, it is even more important to perform preventive maintenance on the film gate and printing mechanism.

SPECIAL FACTORS IN EQUIPMENT SELECTION

Applications for the equipment in this class are those systems involving high levels of reference to COM-generated roll film, listings and directories, catalogs and parts lists, indexes, maintenance literature, military and other specifications, and account status reports.

Film Transport. The units in this class, with one exception, are designed either to handle roll film, cartridges, and magazines with manual threading or to automatically feed or transport film using the cartridge, magazine, or cassette for which the unit was designed. One unit will automatically feed film from standard reels and can be adapted to unit microforms.

Film transport is controlled in one of three ways:

1. Using a lever similar to a light switch in which motion of the lever to the right makes the film go forward; and to the left, rewind.

2. Using a knob or dial which is turned clockwise for forward transport and counterclockwise for rewind.

3. Using a keyboard to step forward a predetermined number of images or to a predetermined image number.

In addition, some units provide a manual control to assist in fine image positioning on the screen.

Since the method used to control film transport in the more automated units is often directly linked to the image finding method used on the film, the latter factor becomes a key one in equipment selection of the more automated type.

Film Gate. The methods described earlier for holding the film flat in the focal plane pertain here. In addition, a method identified in the equipment tables as "platen" is used. The platen is a floating-top glass flat in a holder that rides on edges designed to provide controlled glass-to-glass separation. In this method, care must be taken to be certain that the platen is the one designed for film of the thickness transported.

MICROFICHE AND MICROFILM JACKET
READERS AND READER PRINTERS

This section describes only microfiche readers and reader printers in the 15X to approximately 40X magnification range. Most of the hardware operates in the range designated for the COSATI format, 18X to 20X; or in the NMA format at 22X to 26X. Readers and reader printers designed for microfiche can be used as well for microfilm jackets; therefore, all equipment in this class has been given the single designation, "microfiche."

Microfiche readers and reader printers are available in lap, portable, desk, and free-standing units.

Most microfiche readers display the image at approximately original size. An increasing number of microfiche readers have some means of determining or indicating the row and column index coordinates of the image being projected on the screen. Thus, these readers and reader printers also have limited retrieval capabilities as well.

Physical and Operational Characteristics

The microfiche reader is the simplest type of microfilm reader in current use. Accordingly, it is generally less expensive than a comparable roll film reader. Most microfiche readers are intended for desk use. Most of them consist of:

A screen, either neutral color or tinted blue or green.

Glass flats and a method to transport the microfiche from frame to frame.

An optical projection and enlarging system.

Controls: on-off, focus.

Index grid or frame locator.

A housing.

In addition, a reader printer has:

A paper transport and printing mechanism.

Additional controls for printing.

The user normally performs the following functions in order to display an image:

Turn switch on.

Open glass flats. (In some readers these open automatically when they are extended to a full forward position. Other units may require the flats to be opened manually.)

Insert microfiche (Readers differ. In some units, the microfiche must be inserted bottom edge first and right side up in order to project the image right reading on the screen. Another reader may require the microfiche to be inserted in a different position.)

Move film carrier to desired image as determined by index coordinates or by experiment.

Focus.

To produce a print on most reader printers:

Set print timer to proper exposure.

Actuate print mechanism.

Special Factors in Equipment Selection

Microfiche and jacket reference units are widely used for technical, research, and management reports; personnel and other "people" files; parts and industrial catalogs; maintenance literature; library reference documents; and COM-generated microfiche.

Film Carrier. Any film carrier will accommodate its stated maximum sheet size and anything smaller. Normally, it is easiest to use a film carrier with microfiche or jackets of the same size. Smaller-size microfiche may be difficult to orient properly in larger film holders.

Practically all microfiche units use glass flats in the film carrier to hold the microform flat, protect it, and assist in image positioning. Some glass flats are removable for cleaning; if not, it should be possible to clean them in place easily.

In many units the glass flats are opened manually by raising the top flat to insert the microfiche. In others the flats open automatically, usually when the carrier is moved to the full forward position. Either method is quite convenient, and the choice is one of personal preference.

Image Location. With the microfiche in the carrier, image position or location can be indicated in several ways; they include:

X and Y coordinates. As the fiche is moved, X (column) and Y (row) coordinates related to the microfiche grid format are indicated on dials or scales by letter and number designators.

Grids. Location is indicated by a pointer on a grid located in front of the user and in the plane of the film carrier. Depending on the machine and the magnification, many manufacturers offer grids for COSATI, NMA, and special microfiche formats.

Film Transport. Motion of the film carrier to position images is provided in several ways:

Manual. The film stage (in the absence of a carrier, the microfiche itself) is moved by hand in both the X and Y directions.

Dials. The film carrier is moved by turning dials similar in appearance to the channel selector on a TV set.

Joystick. The film stage is moved with a joystick or push-pull-rotate shaft.

Pointer. Manual movement of the carrier is accomplished by holding the pointer which indicates location on the grid.

Automatic. Motion is other than direct manual control, such as push-buttons for X and Y coordinates on the microfiche.

With respect to film transport and image location, almost any combination of the above capabilities can be quite convenient. Hence the absence of some control of carrier motion and image location is almost totally unacceptable.

MICROFORM INFORMATION
SOURCES/HARDWARE

by Albert Diaz

Sources of information on hardware fall into three categories: (1) Evaluations of specific equipment; (2) Specifications about equipment without evaluations; (3) Guidelines on how to purchase equipment and what to look for.

Evaluations

Perhaps the best source for information and evaluation of equipment is the "Microform and Equipment Reports" section of *Library Technology Reports*, a subscription service offered by the American Library Association which provides libraries with periodic reports, based on tests, on practically anything they are likely to buy including microform hardware. All machines are given an impartial evaluation from the library viewpoint so that the subscriber receives not only specifications but a critique as well and one that is based on library needs.

Among the reports published by LTP are: *Microform Readers for Libraries* (May 1971); *The Selection of a Micro-opaque Reader* (Sept. 1966); *The Selection of a Microfiche Reader* (Sept. 1966); *A Survey of Microform Readers* (Jan. 1972).

A specialized but useful work is Albert H. Leisinger, Jr's., *User Evaluations of Microfiche Readers for Archival Materials.* 1973. ERIC ED 077 542; also, *Microform Review*, 2: 177-209 (July 1973).

Specifications

The major source for microform hardware specifications is the *Guide to Micrographic Equipment*, edited by Hubbard Ballou. It is published by the National Microfilm Association[1] and is now in its sixth edition (1975). The current edition is in three, hardbound volumes: *I. Production Equipment* (304 pp.); *II. User Equipment* (160 pp.); *III. COM Recorders* (40 pp.);

which contain specifications, prices, and a picture of each micrographic device. Volumes may be purchased individually and a loose leaf version with standard three-hole punching is available.

Another work to be published in 1975 which is now being prepared is, *A Guide to Microfiche Equipment Available in Europe*, compiled by the Microfiche Foundation.[2]

Also of value from the National Microfilm Association are *National Micro News*, the NMA's monthly newsletter, the *Proceedings*, in which are published papers given at the annual convention, the *Journal of Micrographics*, a bi-monthly, and the free, annual, *Buyer's Guide to Microfilm Equipment, Products and Services*. The serial publications carry information about new equipment and the *Buyer's Guide* provides, among other things, a detailed listing of equipment producers from whom descriptive leaflets can be obtained by writing.

Specifications will also be found in:

U.S. National Archives and Records Service. Office of Records Management, *Microform Retrieval Equipment Guide*. (Washington: GPO, 1970; also ERIC, ED 051 865.)

The above has also been issued as: McKay, Mark, ed. *A Guide to Microforms and Microform Retrieval Equipment*. (Washington: Applied Library Resources, 1972; also ERIC, ED 059 750.)

Gordon, Ronald F., *Microfiche Viewing Equipment Guide*. 3rd ed. (Alexandria: Defense Documentation Center, 1973) (NTIS, AD 767 500).

Gordon, Ronald F. *16mm Microfilm Viewing Equipment Guide*. (Alexandria: Defense Documentation Center, 1973) (NTIS, AD 718 000).

International File of Microfilm Publications. (University Microfilms, Ltd., 1974).[3] Consists of 126 fiche containing 11,000 pages containing information from 200 hardware suppliers and 120 micropublishers.

Another source, and one that is often overlooked, is magazines having to do with data processing, records management, or business systems, many of which are distributed free of charge on a controlled circulation basis. Some of these are: *Administrative Management*,[4] *Business Graphics*,[5] *Data Management*,[6] *IMC Journal*,[7] *Information and Records Management*[7] *Infosystems*,[8] *Microfilm Techniques*,[7] *Records Management Quarterly*,[9] and *Reprographics Quarterly*.[10]

These magazines run surveys on readers and reader-printers from time to time which usually include specifications on new equipment but not evaluations. Issues immediately before and after NMA's annual convention (April or May) often feature new equipment. *Infosystems*, for example, once a year on the eve of the NMA show gives attention to the role of microfilm in information management. The April 1974, issue contains a work-chart directory of 184 readers and reader-printers from thirty-nine companies and a directory of thirty COM recorders available from sixteen suppliers.

It must be emphasized that microreproduction is a rapidly growing and rapidly changing field and that therefore the latest information is to be obtained from manufacturers' circulars and through consultation with their representatives.

Guidelines

Two articles that review reading equipment problems from the librarian's point of view are:

Tate, George F., *Microform Readers—the Librarians Dilemma*. (Provo: Graduate Department of Library Information Science, Brigham Young University, 1972). (ERIC, ED 071 728). Reviewed in, *Microform Review*, 2: 312-13 (October 1973) and in, *College and Research Libraries*, 34: 294 (September 1973).

Miller, Roger C., "Why Don't They Make Microform Machines for Libraries?", *Microform Review*, 2: 91-92 (April 1973).

Useful guidelines will be found in, *Criteria for the Procurement and Use of Microforms and Related Equipment by the Libraries of the California State University and Colleges*, pp. 1-4 issued by the Office of the Chancellor, 5670 Wilshire Blvd., Los Angeles, Calif. 90036, August 9, 1974.

Another valuable work is, *How to Select a Reader or Reader-Printer*, a twenty page, illustrated consumer guide published by the National Microfilm Association.[1]

Articles that tell you how to evaluate reading machines rather than evaluating specific ones include:

Barrett, J., "The Evaluation of Microfilm Readers," *Journal of Micrographics*, 6: 51-63 (November 1972).

Morgan, Robert A., "Reader Evaluations," in, *Microform Utilization: The Academic Library Environment. Report of Conference Held at Denver, Colorado, 7-9 December, 1970.* (Denver: University of Denver, 1971), pp. 216-24. Also, ERIC, ED 048 701.

Sherman, Alonzo J., "How to Select a Microform Reader or Reader-Printer," *Information and Records Management*, 6: 62-66 (April 1972).

Additional references will be found in, "Microform Reading Devices: A Selective Chronological Bibliography," *Microform Review*, 3: 134-36 (April 1974).

References

1. National Microfilm Association, 8728 Colesville Road, Silver Springs, Md. 20910.
2. *Microfiche Foundation Newsletter*, Microfiche Foundation, Doelenstraat 101, Delft, Netherlands.
3. University Microfilms, Ltd., St. John's Road, Tyler's Green, High Wycombe, Bucks HP10 8HR, England.
4. *Administrative Management*, 51 Madison Ave., N.Y., N.Y. 10010.
5. *Business Graphics*, 7373 N. Lincoln Ave., Chicago, IL. 60646.
6. *Data Management*, 505 Busse Highway, Park Ridge, IL. 60068.
7. *IMC Journal, Information and Records Management, Microfilm Techniques*, 250 Fulton Ave., Hempstead, N.Y. 11550.
8. *Infosystems*, Hitchcock Publishing Co., Hitchcock Building, Wheaton, IL. 60187.
9. *Records Management Quarterly*, 24 N. Wabash Ave., Chicago, IL. 60602.
10. *Reprographics Quarterly*, c/o NRCd, Hatfield Polytechnic, Endymion Road, Annexe, Hatfield, Herts, aL10, 8AU, England.

HUMAN FACTORS

Prepared by
Office of the Chancellor
California State University and Colleges

1. GENERAL:

   a. In this document, the term reader also refers to a reader-printer, and the term microform includes microfilm, microfiche, and micro-opaque.

Reprinted from Part I of *Criteria for the Procurement and Use of Microforms and Related Equipment by the Libraries of the California State University and Colleges*, issued by the Office of the Chancellor, California State University and Colleges, 5670 Wilshire Blvd., Los Angeles, Calif. 90036, August 9, 1974, pp. 1-4.

  b. The reader should be sturdily constructed and capable of with-
     standing hard usage. Controls, especially gears, should be made of
     high-quality materials.
  c. The reader should operate on standard 110-120 volts AC, 60 cycles.
     The electric connection of the reader should fit a standard outlet.
  d. A portable reader should be lightweight and trimly designed, with
     a carrying handle securely fastened to the machine. Durability is a
     particularly important consideration in a portable reader.
  e. When in use, the reader should create a minimum of noise from the
     operation of motors and fans.
  f. All reader lenses should be coated.
2. INSTRUCTIONS:
  a. Instructions should be simple, with nontechnical diagrams explain-
     ing loading, unloading, and operation.
  b. Instructions shall be printed on each reader or on a plate attached
     to the reader. Information indicating the proper orientation of the
     microform to the reader is helpful and should be required.
3. LOADING AND UNLOADING:
  a. The process of inserting and removing microforms should be
     simple to accomplish and easily understandable after the initial
     instruction.
  b. Loading shall be external to the reader and the reader so designed
     that all loading apparatus is free of obstructions to the hands.
     Ideally, the user should be able to load and unload the reader while
     seated. Take-up reels shall be affixed to the reader by a mechani-
     cal locking device which can be removed for maintenance.
  c. Inserting and unloading the microform must be possible without
     scratching or damaging it.
4. CONTROLS:
  a. All controls shall be clearly visible, labeled, and readily accessible
     from an operator's normal viewing position.
  b. The user should be able to manipulate the controls without sig-
     nificantly changing his position at the reader.
        The controls should require a minimum of effort—physical and
     mental—to operate. They should advance and reverse the micro-
     form smoothly and evenly. Motorized controls should have no less
     than two speeds, a fast forward and a scanning speed. The clutch
     or brake device on readers with motorized controls shall be guaran-
     teed to operate in such a way that is does not damage film under
     normal operating conditions. All machines shall have manual con-
     trols for positioning the film, including the ability to rotate images
     through 180° in both directions.
  c. There should be mechanical control of carrier motion and image
     location. Direct manipulation of the microform is not acceptable.
  d. For fiche readers, the ability to indicate row and column coordi-

nates of the images projected on the screen is highly desirable.
5. SCREEN:
   a. The screen shall be made of unbreakable or shatterproof material. It shall be resistant to scratching, and the coating shall resist cracking or peeling. The screen shall be accessible for cleaning and shall have a nonglare and, except for opaque screens, nonreflective surface. Screens shall not be excessively directional.
   b. A lightly tinted screen is desirable to minimize eyestrain, although it is recognized that the tint may interfere with the fidelity of color film. Green is the preferred color tone of the screen, although gray is acceptable. Adjustment of room illumination can compensate for unsatisfactory screen tint.
   c. The screen shall be large enough to permit the display of the full width of a page of text of a book or periodical.
   d. The screen shall be in the normal sight line of the average-sized operator when he is seated before it and shall permit the operator to adopt a natural reading position.
   e. The best screen angle and distance between the viewer and the screen will vary among users. Ideally, the screen angle should be adjustable to allow for individual differences. A screen angle of 75° to 80° is recommended. Perpendicular screens are not acceptable.
6. IMAGE:
   a. For ease in viewing, the projected image shall be at least the approximate size of the original. The quality of the projected image should compare favorably with the original document. Image resolution for small screen readers (not exceeding 12 inches in any direction) shall be at least 3.6 lines/mm in the screen corners and for large readers not less than 3.2 lines/mm in the corners measured using NBS.1010 microcopying test charts.
   b. The image shall be legible under all likely ambient lighting conditions.
   c. The image shall remain in focus while the film is in slow motion or stationary following a change in frames.
7. LUMINANCE:
   a. A reader designed for ambient light of 275 ± 10 lux (30 ± 1 ft. candles) shall have a minimum screen brightness of 109 candelas/sq. meter (32 ft. lamberts) at the center of the screen, a fall off at the corners for small-screen readers (screens not exceeding 12 inches in any direction) of not more than 75%, and a fall off at the corners of large-screen readers of not more than 90%, as measured by the American National Standard Method for Measuring the Screen Luminance of Microform Readers with Translucent Screens, PH5. 10-1969.
   b. Ideally, the illumination should be adjustable to permit a user to

dim or brighten it in order to adjust for ambient lighting or individual preference.

8. ADAPTABILITY:
   a. Quality shall not be sacrificed for the sake of versatility.
   b. A reader should accept several sizes of a given type of microform:
      — Microfilm: 16 and 35mm
      — Microfiche: 3 X 5 and 4 X 6 inches
      — Micro-opaque: 3 X 5 and 6 X 9 inches.
   c. Variable magnification is desirable. The method for changing from one magnification to another shall be simple and provide for the security of the lenses.

9. MAINTENANCE;
   a. The design of the exterior of a reader is an important factor in keeping it clean. A machine with multiple surfaces will catch and hold dust, which in turn can damage the machine and the microform. Therefore, readers shall be easy to clean, maintain, and repair. Simple instructions and diagrams explaining the construction, cleaning, and repair, plus recommendations for maintenance, shall accompany each reader.
   b. Maintenance and repair service of microform equipment shall be *guaranteed* by the manufacturer.
   c. Lenses and all glass surfaces shall be easily accessible for dusting with a camel's hair brush.
   d. The lamp shall be readily accessible to maintenance personnel for changing, simple to replace, fit readily into its socket, and have a long life expectancy. *Proprietary systems of illumination shall be avoided.*
   e. For reader-printers, standard maintenance operations (such as changing paper, replenishing chemicals, and removing and cleaning the printing mechanisms) shall be simple to perform.
   f. Coin receptacles on coin-operated reader-printers shall remain secure when machines are opened to replenish paper supplies and to accomplish other maintenance work.

10. SAFETY:
    a. The machine shall conform to all UL (Underwriters Laboratory) and other safety requirements, such as the following:
       — The reader shall be stable on its base.
       — No external part of the reader shall exceed 125°F (52° Celsius) during machine operation. Temperature of the film gate shall not exceed 167°F (75° Celsius) during machine operation.
       — All surfaces, corners, and edges shall be free of burrs and rough spots.

11. ENVIRONMENT:
    a. The ideal environment for reading microforms in a library is a carrel for each reader with individual light control and a facility

for both vertical and horizontal positioning of the machine. The reader should be mounted on a surface no higher than 26 inches.

b. Prospective purchasers of microform readers should consider how much surface area the reader occupies on the table or desk, since there should be enough work space at each machine to accommodate books and the taking of notes. A pull-out shelf can add to available space.

c. Ambient light control is required. Ideally, room lights should have a dimmer control. Dim light is best for viewing, since a blackened room can contribute to eyestrain, while a fully lit room can interfere with the contrast on the screen. Direct window light should be avoided.

d. Reading room areas should be adequately ventilated for safety and comfort.

ADDITIONAL READINGS

Ballou, Hubbard, W., ed. *Guide to Micrographic Equipment.* Vol. I, *Production Equipment* (304p); Vol. II, *User Equipment* (160p); Vol. III, *COM Recorders* (40p). Silver Springs, Md.: New York, 1975.

Barret, J., "The Evaluation of Microfilm Readers," *Journal of Micrographics,* 6: 51-63 (November 1972).

Holmes, Donald C., *Determination of User Needs and Future Requirements for a Systems Approach to Microform Technology.* July 19, 1969. (ERIC ED 029 168).

How to Select a Reader or Reader-Printer. Silver Springs, Md.: National Microfilm Association, 1974. 24p.

Leisinger, Jr., Albert H., "User Evaluations of Microfilm Readers for Archival and Manuscript Materials," *Microform Review,* 2: 177-209 (July 1973).

Library Technology Reports. Chicago: American Library Association.

"Microform Reading Devices: A Selective Chronological Bibliography," *Microform Review,* 3: 134-36 (April 1974).

Schwarz, P.J., "Instruction in the Use of Microform Equipment," *Wisconsin Library Bulletin,* 67: 341-3 (September 1971).

Sherman, Alonzo J., "How to Select a Microform Reader or Reader-Printer," *Information and Records Management,* 6: 62-66 (April 1972).

Tate, George F., *Microform Readers—the Librarian's Dilemma.* Provo: Brigham Young University, Graduate Department of Library and Information Science, August 1972. ERIC ED 071 728. 35p.

Weber, David, C., "Specifications for a Superior Microtext Reading Machine," *American Documentation,* 16: 246-47 (1965).

STORAGE

Introduction

Adequate storage of microforms is a subject that librarians have to a large degree ignored in the past. As with microform readers, any free space was considered satisfactory.

With air conditioning now viewed more as a necessity than a luxury, one of film's major enemies, high temperature, is vanishing.

Low temperature, however, is not enough. Microforms represent a considerable investment to most libraries, one that should last as long as books printed on the best papers, but care must be exercised in the handling and storage of all microforms. The papers in this chapter cover what and what not to do.

STORAGE AND PRESERVATION
OF MICROFILM

INTRODUCTION

Photographic film has become an important documentary material over the past twenty-five years, and the use of film for this purpose is growing rapidly. The increasing quantity and value of microfilm records used in financial institutions, libraries, government offices, and industrial firms have focused attention on the care of such records to make certain that they last as long as possible.

In general, the care needed for storing photographic records is little more than that for storing written paper records, although there are some requirements peculiar to the storage of photographic film.

The permanence of photographic records depends on the chemical stability of the film, how the film is processed, and the conditions under which the processed film records are stored. The stability of the film layers is determined in manufacture and processing, while storage is controlled by the user. This pamphlet discusses the composition and properties of film as they relate to film permanence and it describes the essential requirements of good processing and storage practices.

DEFINITIONS

It will be helpful in understanding storage requirements if the composition and structure of microfilm are described, and definitions of commonly used terms are given.

Base or Support—A flexible or rigid plastic material which is coated with a thin, light-sensitive, image-forming layer. The thickness of the base varies with different film types; it is generally 0.0025 to 0.008 inch.
Emulsion—The image-forming layer. For unprocessed black-and-white

This is a reprint of the Eastman Kodak pamphlet, *Storage and Preservation of Microfilm* (Kodak Pamphlet P-108). Copies are available from the Business Systems Markets Division, Eastmak Kodak Co., Rochester, N.Y. 14650.

silver films, it is composed primarily of minute silver halide crystals suspended in gelatin. Exposure to light in a camera or printer causes no visible effect, but there is an invisible change which produces a "latent image." To obtain a visible, usable image, the exposed material must be chemically developed, fixed, and washed.

Acetate Film—A general term used to describe all films having supports made of cellulose acetate, cellulose triacetate, cellulose acetate propionate, or cellulose acetate butyrate.

Nitrate Film—A photographic film with a base consisting primarily of cellulose nitrate. Nitrate-base films decompose with age and are not suitable for permanent records. The manufacture of nitrate film by Eastman Kodak Company in the United States of America was discontinued in in 1951, but older nitrate motion-picture films are often found in storage. It is not always possible to determine by visual examination if a film has a nitrate base. However, neither Kodak nor Recordak films in any width made specifically for microfilming nor Eastman 16mm motion-picture films were ever made on nitrate base.

Polyester Film—A photographic film having a polyester base. This type of base manufactured by Eastman Kodak Company is called Kodak Estar base. It is exceptionally tough and strong and has excellent dimensional stability. Microfilm emulsions on Estar base are currently supplied for many purposes.

Safety Film—Any photographic film that meets the requirements of ANSI PH1.25—1965[1] or its latest revision. All safety films (both acetate and polyester) manufactured by Eastman Kodak Company meet these requirements. This means that they are difficult to ignite, are slow-burning, and are low in nitrate nitrogen content. Safety film base is chemically very stable and, if properly stored, is believed to last as long as the best rag papers.

Archival-Record Film—Any photographic film that meets the requirements of ANSI PH1.28—1969[2] and ANSI PH1.41—1971,[13] or their latest revisions. Only safety film can qualify as archival-record film. To comply with ANSI Specifications, archival-record films must have a gelatin-silver halide emulsion developed to a black-and-white image. Images formed by dyes—such as diazo or color—or other means are not approved as archival-record films. The film must also meet certain processing requirements.

RECORD CLASSIFICATION

On the basis of required retention, photographic records can be classified broadly into those for commercial purposes and those for archival purposes.

Commercial Records—Those processed and stored to provide reasonable permanence. They include those photographic records made for general business purposes. Such a period may require a span of 10 years.

Archival Records—Those processed and stored to provide maximum permanence, perhaps for hundreds of years. Any irreplaceable pictures or records that are likely to be of lasting interest should be included in this category. Historical records on microfilm are an example. All microfilms processed by Kodak Microfilm Processing Laboratories meet the archival standards established by the American National Standards Institute, Inc. [2]

STORAGE HAZARDS AND PROTECTION

There are a number of hazards to the satisfactory storage of photographic film that apply to records intended for either commercial or archival storage. In fact, it is not always possible to predict the desired life of records at the time they are made.

While films of either commercial or archival interest are subject to the same hazards, the storage protection provided for them will differ in degree because of a number of factors. These include the cost of providing storage facilities, desired record life, frequency of record use, value of the records, etc.

Fire Protection—All Kodak microfilms are approved by Underwriters' Laboratories, Inc., as slow-burning films. Even though photographic records will burn considerably slower than paper, the same precautions against damage by fire should be taken for them as for paper records of comparable value.

Depending on the importance of the records, fire protection provided can vary from the full protection described below for valuable records to that provided by ordinary office storage.

Storage Vaults—The highest degree of protection for a large number of records is afforded by a fireproof storage vault or record room. It should be located and constructed in accordance with the local building code, Fire Underwriters Regulations, and the requirements of the National Fire Protection Association[3] for a valuable-record room, except that an approved, controlled air-conditioning unit should be installed. While NFPA discourages the air conditioning of such an installation, the fire hazard introduced by openings for air-conditioning ducts can be overcome by the use of Underwriters'-approved, automatic, fire-control dampers. These can be installed in the ducts in accordance with recommendations of NFPA. Sufficient insulation should be provided in the vault to permit satisfactory temperature control at all seasons of the year and to prevent moisture condensation from forming on the walls.

Cabinets and Safes—For smaller quantities of records, a fire-resistant cabinet or safe of the type approved by National Board of Fire Underwriters[3] will provide considerable protection. Such a safe should protect records against a severe fire for at least four hours.

Many fire-resistant safes and cabinets use a type of insulation that, when heated, releases moisture and thus fills the interior of the safe with steam during a fire. This can cause melting or stripping of the film emulsion layer, and loss of the image. For protection, films stored in such a safe should be placed in moisturetight cans, as described later.

Fire-resistant safes are also available with an inner chamber sealed against moisture. These are classified by Underwriters' Laboratories, Inc., as Class 150 Record Containers. Film damage caused by steam is not a problem with these safes.

The question is sometimes raised as to whether microfilm stored in drawers or cabinets designed to resist fire for several hours might, in case of a fire, generate enough pressure to damage or explode the cabinet. There is no danger of an explosion from the storage of either Estar-base or acetate-base safety film under these conditions. There are in acetate film base small amounts of organic materials, as well as moisture, which will expand under heat and, under some conditions, might generate *slight* pressure. However, such intense heat would be required on the outside of the fire-resistant cabinet that the cabinet would be seriously damaged from the fire before appreciable pressure developed.

Effects of High Temperatures—In addition to complete loss by fire, damage to film records can also occur if they are exposed to very high temperatures. Excessive heat causes film to buckle because of shrinkage at the edges. When severe, this distortion affects the ease with which the information can be taken from microfilms, either by projection (for reading) or by printing onto another film.

Tests indicate that microfilms on acetate base that have been conditioned at a relative humidity of 50 percent or lower will withstand 250 F for 24 hours without significant loss in readability or printability. At 300 F, severe distortion may occur in a few hours.

Films that have been conditioned at a relative humidity higher than 50 percent may show objectionable distortion in somewhat shorter times or at lower temperatures. Higher humidities, however, are undesirable for other reasons, as explained in another section.

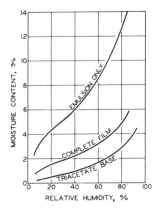

These curves show the relationship between relative humidity and the moisture content of a typical positive emulsion, tri-acetate film base, and a complete negative film at equilibrium at various relative humidities at 70 F.

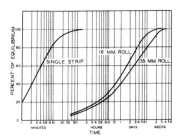

Rate of conditioning a typical positive safety film from 20 per-cent to 50 percent relative humidity at 70 F.

Water Protection—Film records should be protected from possible water damage, such as from leaks, fire-sprinkler discharge, and flooding. If possible, storage facilities should be located above basement levels. Storage cabinets should be raised so that the lowest shelf or drawer is at least 6 inches off the floor and should be so constructed that water cannot splash through ventilating louvers onto the records. Drains provided should have adequate capacity to keep water from a sprinkler discharge from reaching a depth of 3 inches.

If the record-storage area should become flooded, prompt steps should be taken to reclaim any records that were immersed. Allowing these records to dry even partially will cause the layers to stick together. If there are no local facilities for rewashing and drying the films immediately, the films should be placed in a water-filled container and sent to a laboratory where they can be washed and dried properly.

Effects of High and Low Relative Humidities—The choice of humidity level depends more upon how film records are used than upon their classification as commercial or archival records. Keeping record use in mind, the best relative humidity for storage is the lowest that can be achieved practically and controlled reliably.

High Humidity—Storage in moist air such as that frequently found in basement rooms, and storage humidities above 50 percent should be avoided; relative humidities of 35 percent or less are best for minimizing the possibility of growth of microscopic blemishes. A definite upper limit on relative humidity is established at 60 percent for protection against fungus.

Low Humidity—At low humidities, problems of brittleness or static might arise if the films are to be handled frequently. However, in the case of inactive films (regardless of their intended permanence), the increased protection that low humidity gives against microscopic blemishes might be desirable.

Very low humidities have, in the past, caused film to be brittle. However, film of current manufacture has not been found to exhibit brittleness or breaking tendencies under normal handling, even at relative humidities as low as 15 to 20 percent. Old film that is found to be brittle at low humidity should be reconditioned to a higher humidity before use. One day's storage is usually sufficient for conditioning a dry 16mm roll halfway to a higher ambient relative humidity; to bring it to full equilibrium requires about a week. In each case, both sides of the roll should be exposed to the air.

Low humidity affects the curl of film, causing a slight contraction of the emulsion layer and resulting in a slight curl toward that side. This is generally believed to be an advantage because the concave emulsion surface is better protected against abrasion. However, excessive curl may cause difficulty in focusing some microfilm readers. This can be avoided by conditioning the film to a relative humidity of 30 to 50 percent before use.

Film handled at very low humidities may also develop a static charge as it passes through a reader or rewinder. This static charge will attract dust particles that can damage the emulsion by chemical action or physical abrasion. Therefore, it is important that any film-handling area be kept clean. If film is kept in a dry storage area, but is used in an office area of a higher humidity, static problems will be kept at a minimum.

Humidity Control

*Air Conditioning—*Properly controlled air conditioning of the storage area is recommended for the optimum long-time preservation of archival film. The air should be filtered to remove dust, cleansed of gaseous contaminants if necessary, and controlled to the desired relative humidity and temperature. Inactive film should be conditioned to this environment and then placed in corrosion-resistant metal cans sealed with a good-quality, rubber-base, pressure-sensitive tape. Film that is used frequently might be kept in unsealed metal cans in the conditioned storage vault.

Where air conditioning is not practical and high humidities are likely to be present, the humidity of the storage area can be lowered by electrical refrigeration-type dehumidifiers. These are readily available and inexpensive. The storage space should first be vapor-sealed by covering the walls with asphalt or aluminum paint, or, better, paper-laminated aluminum foil or other water-vapor barriers. A humidistat set at the desired level of humidity should be used to control the dehumidifier. The humidity level should be checked frequently with a reliable hygrometer, such as a sling psychrometer.

Dehumidifiers using crystals of calcium chloride or other desiccants *should not* be used. They create a danger of fine dust particles getting on the film and causing abrasion when the film is used. Also, when some chemical-desiccant particles are trapped in rolls of microfilm, they may form bleached spots.

If the use of an electric dehumidifier, is not practical, inactive films can be protected from high humidities and contaminants by first drying the film and then sealing it in metal cans. It is easy to dry a small collection of films by keeping it for two or three weeks in a desiccator with a suitable quantity of activated silica gel, and then transferring it quickly to cans and sealing them immediately with good-quality, rubber-base, pressure-sensitive tape. Larger collections may require the temporary use of a dry-conditioned cabinet or room to permit conditioning of the film in a reasonable time.

*Humidification—*Humidification is not necessary or desirable unless the prevailing relative humidity is under 15 percent for long periods of time and unless the film is used frequently and physical troubles are encountered. Neither water trays nor saturated chemical solutions should be used for humidification of storage cabinets because of the more serious danger of over-humidification. Even humidification controlled by instrumentation is risky unless "fail-safe" devices are installed.

Fungus Growth—When photographic films are stored for any length of time in an atmosphere having a relative humidity above 60 percent, there is a tendency for fungus (often called "mold" or "mildew") to grow on either the emulsion surface or the back of the film or on the film reel. The higher the relative humidity, the greater the chance of fungus attack and the more abundant its growth (fungus spores are found in the air everywhere, and they will germinate and grow under favorable conditions). The only real protection against fungus growth is to make certain that the conditions are unfavorable for its growth.

If fungus growth has progressed far enough, it will cause serious and permanent damage to the film. This takes the form of distortion of the emulsion and eventually causes chemical breakdown so that the gelatin becomes sticky and readily soluble in water. Water or water solutions *should not* be used for the removal of fungus growth because either may lead to disintegration of the image. The film should be cleaned by wiping it with soft plush or cotton moistened with an approved film-cleaning liquid. This procedure is described in detail in a separate pamphlet.[4]

Microscopic Blemishes—Some processed negative microfilms in storage for two to twenty years have developed microscopically small colored spots or blemishes. These spots were first discovered in 1961. The fogged leader at the outside of the roll is most frequently affected by the blemishes, which are generally red or yellow in color and are smaller in size than the image characters (for example, a typewritten letter reduced 20X) on the microfilm. On occasion, these spots progress further into the roll and appear in image areas. A more detailed description of the blemishes and of the techniques used in inspecting microfilm is given in *National Bureau of Standards Handbook 96.*[5]

The spots are believed to be caused by local oxidation of image silver, resulting in the formation of minute deposits of colored colloidal silver.[6,7] Possible oxidizing agents entering from outside the roll of microfilm are aerial oxygen, whose action on the film is strongly accelerated by moisture, and atmospheric contaminants, such as peroxides, ozone, sulfur dioxides, hydrogen sulfide, and nitrogen oxides, all occurring in industrial atmospheres.

The conditions under which microfilm is stored have been found to play an important role in the development of these blemishes. Storage in cool, dry air that is free of oxidizing gases or vapors is an effective means for arresting their formation and growth. Storage in sealed metal cans is a sound preventive measure, if this is practical and consistent with the humidity requirements.

The use of a very small quantity of potassium iodide in the fixing bath (0.2 gram per liter) has also been found to provide a good degree of protection against these blemishes. If proper storage conditions are maintained, this processing modification, used by Eastman Kodak Company for processing since May, 1964, is an effective preventive against blemish formation.

A protective gold processing treatment provides the highest degree of protection against microscopic blemishes and may be applied either as a part of the processing procedure or as a post-processing treatment.[15,16]

Chemical Contamination—Air contaminants may add an oxidizing or reducing effect to the atmosphere. This, in turn, may cause deterioration of film base and a gradual fading of the photographic image as well as the formation of the microscopic blemishes mentioned above. Typical examples of such contaminants are paint fumes, hydrogen sulfide, sulfur dioxide, and similar gases. If an area is to be painted, any films stored there should be removed beforehand and should not be returned to the area for a two-week period. The removal of contaminating gases from the air requires special consideration.[8]

Contaminants can come from illuminating gas, coal gas, and certain chemical plants; they are present in harmful concentration in most industrial and urban areas. For this reason, an archival storage vault should be located as far as possible from such areas. When a contaminated atmosphere cannot be avoided, steps should be taken either to eliminate the fumes by air conditioning the storage area or to protect the film from contact with the atmosphere by sealing it in metal cans.

In addition to atmospheric contaminants, care should be taken about other materials kept or used in the storage area. It has already been mentioned that nitrate-base films should never be used for permanent-record films. Furthermore, such films should *never* be stored with safety-film records (either in the same room, or if the rooms are connected by ventilating ducts in the same building) because gases given off by decomposing nitrate film will damage or destroy the image on safety-film records.

The use of rubber bands around rolls of film is also to be avoided since any residual sulfur used in rubber vulcanization promotes the growth of microscopic blemishes. Adhesive tapes, tape splices, bleached papers, and printing inks may have the same undesirable effect.

Theft Protection—Safes provide good protection against the theft of valuable records. Where such records are large in number, it might require using vaults of burglarproof construction. Theft of important records involves a double peril—that of classified films falling into unauthorized hands and the complete loss of valuable information. Protection against the latter can, of course, be provided by storing duplicate records in another location.

PROCESSING FOR PERMANENCE

Processing is one of the most important factors affecting the potential permanence of photographic records. The removal of residual processing chemicals, the exclusion of dirt contamination, and uniform drying are factors normally controlled by proper processing.

Fixing Baths—In the fixing step, the undeveloped silver halide crystals in the emulsion are converted to soluble silver compounds which can be washed away with water. The chemicals most commonly used for fixing are sodium or ammonium thiosulfate (commonly called "hypo"). The fixing bath may also contain other chemicals to maintain a desirable pH, provide hardening, stabilize the solution, protect the image from microscopic blemishes, etc.

If hypo or silver salts are retained by the film, they can breakdown, especially under poor storage conditions, to produce a yellow stain and fading of light lines. The effect of residual silver compounds is mentioned in ANSI PH4.12—1954[9], ANSI PH1.28—1969, and PH1.41—1971. A method of testing for residual silver compounds is given in the latter two standards.

In general, a hardening fixer is desirable if there is any danger of abrasion for example, by rollers contacting the wet emulsion, or when drying capacity is limited. For maximum washing efficiency, a nonhardening fixer, or a hardening fixer plus a washing aid, should be used.

As noted previously, the resistance of microfilm to the formation of microscopic blemishes is increased when trace amounts of potassium iodide are added to the fixing bath. A concentration of 0.2 gram per liter is recommended.

Time of Fixation and Replenishment—To make sure that there is enough time for the fixing reaction to be completed, specific recommendations for each type of film should be followed. A good rule of thumb is that the fixing time should be at least twice the time it takes to clear the milky appearance from the emulsion. Prolonged fixing should be avoided since, in time, the hypo will start to dissolve the silver image.

The formation of soluble silver thiosulfate salts, which wash out easily, is promoted by keeping a high ratio of hypo to silver in the bath. This is accomplished by frequent replacement or by proper replenishment of the fixing bath.

To provide complete fixing, it is a good plan to use two baths, treating the film in the first bath until the emulsion has cleared and then transferring it to the second bath for an equal time. The first bath does most of the work and the second bath converts the last traces of undeveloped silver to soluble silver compounds. When the first bath approaches exhaustion, it is discarded and the second bath is put in its place. A fresh fixer is then prepared and used for the second bath. In this way, the second fixer bath is kept fresh and active.

It is advisable, wherever possible, to recover silver from the fixer. In addition to the economic benefits, removing silver from the fixer increases efficiency of the fixer, permits better washing, and provides ecological benefits. [17,18]

Washing—Adequate washing is essential to the permanence of microfilm. After all of the undeveloped silver halide has been converted, the emulsion is still saturated with the chemicals of the fixing bath and some dissolved silver compounds. If these were not removed by washing, they would slowly decompose and attack the image, causing discoloration and fading. This effect is accelerated greatly by high humidity and temperature. Also, the smaller the grain size of the image, the greater is this reaction. Since most microfilms are composed of very fine grains, they are very sensitive to this effect.

For good washing a rapid flow of fresh water should be used. To improve washing, counter-current systems and spray systems are possibilities in processing-machine construction. Washing efficiency decreases rapidly with decreased temperature and is very low at temperatures below 15.5 C (60 F). High wash-water temperatures produce the most efficient washing, but emulsion reticulation can result if the wash-water temperature is too high or if it is not kept close to that of the other processing solutions. In some cases, extremely soft water can also cause reticulation.

Washing Aids—Using a washing aid, such as Kodak Hypo Clearing Agent, greatly increases both the rate and thoroughness of hypo removal during the washing step. This treatment is especially recommended when an acid hardening fixer has been used.

After fixing, the film is first rinsed to remove the major portion of hypo; next the film is treated in Kodak Hypo Clearing Agent Bath; then it is given a final wash.

NOTE: The use of special hypo eliminators, such as Kodak Hypo Eliminator HE-1, is not recommended for microfilm because these eliminators contain oxidizing agents that can contribute to the formation of emulsion blisters and microscopic blemishes.

Residual Hypo Test—The accepted criterion for adequate washing is the Methylene Blue Method described in ANSI PH4.8—1971.[10] This standard also describes the Silver Densitometric method, which has been suggested as a simpler "go" or "no go" procedure. (See "A Technical Note—New Residual Thiosulfate Test Methods," by M. L. Schreiber, *The Journal of Micrographics*, Vol. 5, No. 1 (Sept-Oct, 1971), p. 53.) By either of these methods, a clear area of the film is tested. These new methods allow residual hypo tests to be run up to two weeks after processing. An even simpler, but less sensitive, method is the use of the Kodak Hypo Estimator in conjunction with Kodak Hypo Test Solution HT-2. This test gives an indication of residual hypo, but it should not be used as a measurement for meeting the requirements of the ANSI specification.

Squeegee—The use of an adequate squeegee as the film leaves the water-wash and enters the drying section is very important. Otherwise, residual water droplets will dry to form visible surface defects. In wound-up rolls, these spots may provide places where microscopic blemishes can form.

Drying—Drying should be uniform. The drying air should be filtered so that airborne particles of dirt or potentially harmful chemical dusts often present in processing laboratories will not become imbedded in the emulsion while it is tacky.

Commercial or archival films that are to become a part of an active file system should not be over-dried. (Film that is too dry will not only tend to be brittle but will also be prone to static electricity so that it will pick up dust easily.) At the same time, it should be dry enough so that, when it is stored, there will not be an excessive amount of moisture that could promote defects. A good aim point is 35 percent relative humidity at 70 F. Inactive archival films will need further drying in order to meet the aim point recommended in the table on page 249.

Gold Treatment—When maximum permanence is desired, microfilm should be gold-treated either as part of the processing or in a post-processing treatment before storage. The protection this treatment gives against oxidation is the most effective means for preventing the formation of microscopic blemishes. [6,7]

Lacquering—Extensively used microfilm records are often damaged by abrasion and scratching. Thus, for some active files, lacquering is economically justified. Under rough handling, of course, the lacquer coating itself may become abraded; but if so, it can be removed and a new coating applied. The film can thus be completely rejuvenated, provided that the scratches have not reached the film emulsion.

A second advantage of a lacquer coating is that it offers some protection from fungus growth if the film is stored improperly. Fungus growth will start on the lacquer surface before attacking the emulsion layer. If discovered in time, the lacquer can be removed and the film will be undamaged. A lacquer coating will also keep adjacent film layers of microfilm records from sticking together when subjected to very high humidities.

SPECIAL STORAGE AND HAZARDS

Underground Storage—Most large industrial organizations and government agencies have developed methods for safeguarding vital records in the event of a war or a natural catastrophe. Many have begun keeping their vital records in underground repositories located many miles from large metropolitan areas. When microfilm is kept underground in caves, mines,

tunnels, subbasements, or similar locations, special care should be taken
to make certain that there is adequate control of the relative humidity.
Film should not be stored where the relative humidity exceeds the
limits recommended for commercial or archival storage. If humidity cannot be controlled satisfactorily, the film must first be dried (as described
earlier on page 240) and then placed in a moistureproof container. The
film must also be protected, as in other types of storage, against airborne
dirt or chemical contamination.

Frequently in underground situations, proper film-storage conditions,can
be achieved by simply heating the cool, moist air that is present. For example, conditions in a typical mine may be 50 F and 90 percent relative
humidity; by heating the storage area to 72 F, the relative humidity is
reduced to 40 percent. Where it is not practical to lower the relative humidity adequately by this means, supplementary dehumidification may
be required.

Effects of Nuclear Explosions—The protection of vital microfilm records
against the effects of nuclear explosions is mostly a matter of providing
sufficient blast and fire protection. Processed microfilm is essentially
unaffected by radiation even of the intensity encountered in the vicinity
of a nuclear explosion. Best protection from blast and fire is afforded by
removing security files from potential target areas. Storage in underground
vaults, with duplicate copies in different locations, provides the greatest
security.

Time-Capsule Storage—Microfilms to be placed in time capsules or sealed
in the cornerstones of buildings require special preparation. The film
should be processed according to ANSI PH1.28—1969 or ANSI PH1.41—
1971 and then dried to a very low relative humidity (5 percent is recommended) prior to packaging. The loading of the dried film should also be
done under the same conditions of low relative humidity. If a conditioning room is not available, the film can be dried over activated silica gel.
A quantity of not less than 5 ounces of gel per 100 feet of 16mm film is
suggested. The coiled film should be kept above the silica gel in a desiccator for at least two weeks.
    During desiccation, the film should be in the form intended for final
storage (wound on itself or a glass rod, not on a conventional core or reel)
because its brittleness and the possibility of rapid reabsorption of moisture
make it inadvisable to rewind the film after desiccation. When removed
from the desiccator, the film should be transferred immediately to the
capsule and sealed tightly.
    The capsule should be a stainless steel cylinder which can be sealed
tightly with a screw-on gasketed cover. When there is more than one roll
of film, it is a good idea to separate them by a stainless steel disk of the

same inside diameter as that of the capsule. Usually, cores, reels, or wrapping of any kind are not included so that only the film itself is put into the capsule.

HANDLING AND FILING FILM RECORDS

Well-planned filing systems and the proper handling of film records are important in the storage of records. The custodian should set up safeguards against loss or misplacement of valuable records and also make sure that the methods of filing and handling do not add unnecessary wear to the records. Where films are used frequently, duplicates should be made for this purpose and the originals retained in storage.

Continual handling of film, even under favorable conditions, causes some wear; but wear will be accelerated greatly by certain factors which can be controlled. Scratching can occur if the film is dirty or the equipment is poorly maintained or wrongly used; "cinching," which also causes scratches, occurs when the film is allowed to slide, layer on layer (for example, when the end of a loose roll of film is pulled); tearing and fingerprinting occur if the equipment and handling methods are not suitably chosen for the work.

Dirt can be removed from film by wiping it with a lintless fabric pad moistened with Kodak Film Cleaner. The cleaning operations should be carried out in an atmosphere of about 50 percent relative humidity to minimize the possibility that the film will become electrostatically charged and attract dust particles. Cleanliness of the work space is essential to success in these operations. Static discharge devices are available for use when handling film which has been in dry storage. Alternatively, the film can be conditioned to a higher relative humidity before cleaning and then reconditioned to the original low relative humidity. Other suggestions for improving handling operations can be found in *Storage and Care of EASTMAN and KODAK Motion Picture Films.*[11]

INSPECTION

The potential life of photographic records depends largely on atmospheric conditions—temperature, humidity, cleanliness—and the manner in which the film is used. If storage conditions are kept within the limits suggested in the table on page 249, inspection of an adequate number of properly selected lot samples should be made at two-year intervals.

While archival film should definitely be kept under the recommended storage conditions, film records of commercial value may have more leeway in terms of storage humidity and temperature. Where humidity is not controlled closely, film should be inspected more frequently than at two-year intervals. Depending on the extent and duration by which temperature and humidity exceed the recommended ranges, the intervals between inspections should not initially exceed six months and then, if no deterioration is noted, can be extended but not to exceed one year. This inspection schedule is recommended by American National Standards Institute, Inc. (See ANSI PH5.4—1970).

Sometimes film inspection is considered to be too laborious and costly and is neglected for many years, occasionally with unfortunate results. Perhaps it is not always possible to open every film can or to rewind every roll at the recommended frequency. Rather than omit inspection entirely, a few rolls should be selected at random from the film collection each month for examination. This will provide some protection at a relatively small cost. If there is indication that film records are not keeping properly, storage conditions should be improved and other protective treatments given the film. Also, copies should be made of films that show signs of deterioration.

SUMMARY OF REQUIREMENTS FOR STORAGE AND PRESERVATION OF MICROFILM RECORDS

Storage Facilities—The selection of type of storage vault, safe, cabinet, or area must be based on the value of the film records and their intended storage life. In general, separate metal cans for individual rolls are recommended. These should be stored in metal cabinets which have adjustable shelves or drawers and louvers or openings in the walls to allow free circulation of conditioned air through the cabinet. Cabinets should be spaced in the room so as to eliminate any stagnant air pockets or localized areas where temperature and humidity may reach higher levels than the general condition.

Although the same storage principles apply to commercial and to archival records, much greater care must be taken to obtain maximum protection for archival records; makeshift or temporary arrangements should not be considered.

	Commercial Records	Archival Records
Film	Safety film that meets all requirements of ANSI PH1.25—1965	Safety film that meets all requirements of ANSI PH1.28—1969 plus ANSI PH1.25—1965 and ANSI PH1.41—1971
Residual Hypo*	Not above 3 micrograms per square centimeter	Not above 0.7 microgram per square centimeter†
Residual Silver Salts	—	Negative test required
Storage Atmosphere Temperature‡	Preferably 70—75 F; Maximum of 90F	Maximum of 70 F
Relative Humidity	Preferably 30—35% Maximum of 60%	Inactive Files: 15—20% Active Files: 30—40%
Air Conditioning	Not necessary unless film records are subjected to frequent or sustained high humidity§	Essential
Air Purification	Normal cleanliness	Cleanse of airborne gases, dirt particles, and other contaminants

*Expressed as sodium thiosulfate ion.

†This level is low enough to cause no visible impairment of the image after moist incubation as specified in ANSI PH4.12—1954. It is also safe for those records where even slight staining is unacceptable, and has a considerable safety factor where legibility is the prime consideration.

‡If the storage temperature is sufficiently low, or if the air where the film is to be handled is quite moist, the film must be left in its closed container until it warms up to approximate room temperature. Otherwise, condensation of moisture will occur on the cold film surfaces.

§Dehumidification may be necessary even though automatic air conditioning is not practical.

REFERENCES AND BIBLIOGRAPHY

1. "American National Standard Specifications for Safety Photographic Film," PH1.25—1965.

2. "American National Standard Specification for Photographic Films for Archival Records, Silver-Gelatin Type, on Cellulose Estar Base," PH1.28—1969.

3. "Protection of Records," NFPA 232—1967, National Fire Protection Association, 60 Batterymarch Street, Boston, Massachusetts 02110.

4. "Prevention and Removal of Fungus on Processed Films," Pamphlet No. AE-22, Eastman Kodak Company, Rochester, New York 14650.

5. "Inspection of Processed Photographic Record Films for Aging Blemishes," C. S. McCamy, *National Bureau of Standards Handbook 96*, January 24, 1964.

6. "Microscopic Spots—A Progress Report," D. G. Wiest and R. W. Henn, *National Micro-News*, *70*, 249—257 (June, 1964).

7. "Microscopic Spots in Processed Microfilm—Their Nature and Prevention," D. G. Wiest and R. W. Henn, *Photographic Science and Engineering*, 7 (5), 253—261 (1963). "Microscopic Spots in Processed Microfilm: The Effect of Iodide," R. W. Henn, D. G. Wiest, and Bernadette D. Mack, *Photographic Science and Engineering*, 9 (3), 167—173 (1965).

8. "Air Conditioning for Protection," G. K. Saurwein (Harvard University Rare Book Library), *Heating, Piping and Air Conditioning*, 13: 311, May (1941).

9. "American National Standard Specification for Methods for Indicating the Stability of the Images of Processed Black-and-White Films, Plates, and Papers," PH4.12—1954.

10. "American National Standard Test Method for Determining the Thiosulfate Content of Processed Black-and-White Photographic Film and Plates," PH4.8—1971.

11. "Storage and Care of Eastman and Kodak Motion Picture Films," Kodak Pamphlet No. II 19*.

12. "American National Standard Practice for Storage of Processed Silver-Gelatin Microfilm," PH5.4—1970.

13. "American National Standard Specifications for Photographic Film for Archival Records, Silver-Gelatin Type, on Polyester Base," PH1.41—1971.

14. "American National Standard Methylene Blue Method for Measuring Thiosulfate and Silver Densitometric Method for Measuring Residual Chemicals in Films, Plates, and Papers," PH4.8—1971.

15. "Gold Treatment of Microfilm with the Recordak Prostar Processor," Eastman Kodak Company, Kodak Pamphlet P-176.

16. "A Gold Protective Treatment for Microfilm," Eastman Kodak Company, Kodak Publication P-177.

17. "Silver Recovery with the Kodak Chemical Recovery Cartridge," Eastman Kodak Company, Kodak Publication J-9.

18. "Recovering Silver From Photographic Materials," Eastman Kodak Company, Kodak Publication J-10.

*This article is an extraction from the Kodak Data Book, "Basic Production Techniques for Motion Pictures," (P-18), available from your photographic dealer. If he does not have this publication in stock, he can order it for you, or you can send your order and remittance to Eastman Kodak Company, Rochester, New York 14650.

All ANSI Specifications are obtainable from American National Standards Institute, Inc., 1430 Broadway, New York, New York 10018.

STORAGE AND HANDLING

by Donald C. Holmes

Microfilms, like books, need suitable storage and care in handling. Properly processed stored silver emulsion films will remain in good condition as long as the best papers. To attain this long life both books and films need optimum storage conditions. For microfilms, these conditions are described in the latest American National Standards Institute's Standard Ph5.4, "Storage of Processed Silver Gelatin Microfilm."

This standard cautions against using any materials near the film which will deteriorate and give off peroxides or other oxidizing agents. It is emphasized that the use of paper and rubber products are to be avoided and that only non-deteriorating plastics or inert materials should be used for container coatings.

Temperature and Humidity

Temperature and humidity limits are also specified by the standard, and their effects are discussed. It is established that low relative humidity and temperature lessen the possibility of degradation of the film.

However, the standard also indicates that maintaining these conditions constantly is also important, since cycling the film in both high and low temperatures and humidities, if not carefully controlled, may cause physical and chemical changes. Therefore, the lowest convenient constant temperature and relative humidity below the values stated will provide the best storage conditions.

Where silver films must be available for regular use, it is not feasible to adhere fully to the American National Standards Institute's standard. The life of the film can be adversely affected by careless handling, exposure to contaminated atmospheres, high relative humidity and temperature. Tests

Reprinted from part IV, "Findings" of Donald C. Holmes, *Determination of the Environmental Conditions Required in a Library for the Effective Utilization of Microforms. Interim Report,* November, 1970. ERIC ED 046 403, pp. 19-22.

indicate that, ideally, silver film can safely be used for extended periods in a temperature of 80°F or less and humidity of 60% or less. However, normal temperatures and relative humidities for human comfort will probably prove satisfactory for use of microforms without damage.

While the ANSI standard does not include diazo or vesicular film, most of it applies equally well to them. Tests have indicated that diazo film will fade if exposed for long periods to ultraviolet light. With normal use and if filed in library filing cabinets, it is known to remain substantially unchanged for over 20 years. Its total life could be much longer. Vesicular film, if not properly processed, can deteriorate when exposed to high temperatures. When stored at temperatures below 80°F and a relative humidity of 60% or lower, its life appears to be very long.

Storage Equipment and Facilities

The storage standard previously referred to details the care needed in the selection of storage supplies, equipment and facilities. An article in the *International Micrographic Congress Journal*, (Second Quarter, 1969), and the accompanying bibliography of original source material, provide much additional information. In addition to temperature, humidity and air purity conditions, other important factors should be considered.

1. Microfilm, either for use or archival storage, should be well protected from physical or chemical damage by placing it in containers which are free of acid, sulphur and peroxide. Corrosive metals should not be used.
2. Specially designed filing facilities, such as upright drawer files, are available for 35mm and 16mm film boxes, aperture cards, various sizes of microfiches and jackets. Shelving is also available for microfilm containers.
3. Some years ago it was a common practice to put a humidity stabilizing solution in the bottom portion of filing cabinets in which microfilm was stored. This practice has been almost completely abandoned and is not recommended.
4. The storage facilities should be constructed with either a metal, well covered by inert paint, or with stainless steel or aluminum.
5. Films should be stored high enough above ground to avoid flood damage.
6. Interfiling of vesicular and silver film for archival storage is not recommended. While no interaction has been observed between diazo and silver film, some authorities advise against it. Interfiling of use copies is acceptable. A study on this latter subject appears in the *1958 Proceedings of the National Microfilm Association*.

7. When it is not possible to store valuable films in a fire-proof vault, a fire rating of at least one hour should be required for storage cabinets.
8. Unless sheltered from water, film should not be stored in an area where fire sprinklers are installed. In fires, internally generated steam accounts for a substantial part of the damage.
9. Tightly packed films are less affected by either fire or humidity than loosely packed films.
10. Uric acid from hands and skin deteriorates silver film, and care should be exercised to handle the film only at its edges.

Storage of Master, Intermediate and Use Copies

The term, "master copy," is susceptible to a number of definitions, but it usually means the camera negative. If it is not available, the master copy is the nearest generation to the camera negative. In either case, this film is normally treated with great care, stored in archival storage conditions described in American National Standards Institute Standard, Ph5.4, "Storage of Processed Silver Gelatin Microfilm," and brought out for use only when absolutely necessary.

Most libraries do not possess master microform copies and for this reason details of archival storage are not provided in this report. (The standard referred to does provide complete details and may be obtained from the American National Standards Institute, Inc., 1430 Broadway, New York, N.Y. 10018.)

An "intermediate copy" is often called a "sub-master" and is a direct copy from the master. It is made for the purpose of making additional contact copies so as to protect the master from wear and possible damage resulting from too frequent removal from and return to archival storage conditions. The intermediate is often stored in favorable but accessible facilities.

A "use copy" is usually made from an intermediate or a master and is intended to be used in a working file. While comfortable working temperatures and humidities are generally satisfactory, ideal storage conditions should not be over 70°F for extended periods and the relative humidity should not exceed 60%. High temperatures and particularly high humidity encourage fungus growth, blemishes, cause layers of film to stick together, and also speed chemical reactions and deterioration if films have not been properly processed.

Microform use copies may be shelved in a variety of ways. The most satisfactory method employs specially constructed slide-drawer metal cabinets. These cabinets are designed specifically to accommodate reels of microfilm or sheet microforms. Their use minimizes incidents of misfiling and loss of microforms, protects them from dust and dirt, and efficiently utilizes floor space. The cabinets are approximately the height of the familiar office file cabinets but some are constructed so they may be double or triple stacked where ceiling height permits. Although multiple stacking reduces required floor space, such a practice diminishes convenient access to the higher drawers and is not recommended for active microform files.

A method frequently employed for shelving microfilm reels in libraries is to place them in their labeled container boxes on regular stack shelves. Open-stack shelving makes use of readily available space, but space utilization is not efficient, dust protection is not offered, and losses occur when boxes are pushed out of sight to the rear of the shelf.

Where "in-house production facilities" exist, shallow depth shelves have been inexpensively fabricated of wood or sheet metal to house limited collections of reel microfilms around the walls of the microform reading room. Some libraries have had such shelves installed on the walls of book stack areas. While this type of storage is not as desirable as storage in cabinets specifically designed for the purpose, the cost is small by comparison and, in any event, it is preferable to use standard stack shelves because it saves space and reduces incidence of loss.

With the exception of the ink printed micro-opaque cards manufactured by the Readex Co., which are furnished in labeled, dust protective boxes, sheet microforms are generally stored in slide-drawer cabinets to maintain their orderly arrangement and to protect them from dust and loss. The boxes supplied by the Readex Co. have dimensions that resemble an average book and are conveniently housed on stock shelves. Photographic type micro-opaques that are not laminated have a strong tendency to curl and must be stored in cabinet drawers or boxes under constant pressure to maintain them in a flat condition for use. Rigid blocks of substances not harmful to the cards, with a minimum thickness of ½ in. cut to the size of the cards and inserted as separators at intervals of 25 to 50 cards, are almost a necessity to maintain a full file drawer of nonlaminated cards in a non-curl condition.

A recent development for microform storage is the cartridge carrousel filing system for both roll and sheet microforms. Single tiered, desk-top units, movable at finger touch, to seven tiered, motor driven units up to 9 feet in diameter, are available. A single tiered, desk-top unit is said to house 5,000 microfiches in special cartridges, while a tier of the large diameter carrousel is said to house more than 125,000 microfiches. Such equipment is not inexpensive, but its cost might be justified by need for compact storage of high use material requiring rapid access.

RECOMMENDATIONS FOR
THE STORAGE OF PERMANENT
RECORD MICROFILM

In order to realize the potential for long-time storage of this microfilm, it is essential that the facility for film storage be kept within a specific temperature and humidity range. Extremes of temperature and humidity can damage microfilm. American National Standard PH5.4-1970 includes the following requirement for archival storage: The relative humidity should not exceed 40%, the temperature should not exceed 70° Fahrenheit, and the rapid cycling of humidity or temperature should be avoided. High temperatures and high humidity normally encourage fungus to attack film emulsions as well as causing other chemical deterioration problems. Extremely low relative humidity, below 15% or 20% for instance, for extended periods of time can result in extreme film brittleness. Such film should be conditioned to higher humidity before use.

The microfilm you have just acquired has been carefully processed and packaged to meet all American National Standards Institute specifications for permanent record microfilm. As custodian of this valuable microfilm record compliance with these requirements coupled with the careful use in well maintained and regularly cleaned microfilm reading equipment will ensure the maximum useful life of the film.

Photoduplication Service
The Library of Congress
Washington, DC 20540
May 1974

This is a reprint of a statement prepared by the Photoduplication Service, Library of Congress, Washington, D.C., May, 1974.

ADDITIONAL READINGS

"Directory of Microfilm Housing Equipment," *Information and Records Management*, 6: 32-36 (May 1972).

Eaton, George T., "Preservation, Deterioration, Restoration of Photographic Images," *Library Quarterly*, 40: 85-98 (January 1970).

McCamy, C. S., and Pope, C. I., "Redox Blemishes—Their Cause and Prevention," *Journal of Micrographics*, 3: 165-170 (Summer 1970).

McCamy, C. S., et al., "A Survey of Blemishes on Processed Microfilm," *Journal of Research of the National Bureau of Standards*, 73A: 79-99 (January-February 1969).

Microfilm Storage Cabinets: A Survey. Chicago: Library Technology Project, American Library Association, March, 1972. 26p.

Nelson, Carl E., "A Status Report on Micro-Blemishes," *IMC Journal*, 7: 17-21, 26 (Second Quarter, 1969).

Oliva, John J., "Microfilm Cartridge Systems at the Prince George's Community College," *Journal of Micrographics*, 6: 89-92 (November/December 1972).

BIBLIOGRAPHIC CONTROL

INTRODUCTION

Three basic problems are involved in the bibliographic control of microforms. One is internal (bibliographic information included on the microform itself). The second is external—that is, bibliographic coverage of the entire universe of micropublishing in order to determine whether a given title is available in microform and from whom. The third is what Simonton[1] calls "bibliothecal"—the bibliographic coverage within a library of the microforms it owns a task made difficult by micropublishing projects whereby hundreds or thousands of titles cited in a bibliography or related to a given subject are made available in microform.

Internal bibliographic control is not the problem today that it was fifteen to twenty years ago when there were no guidelines. Now there are numerous guidelines, standards, and specifications, some of which are included in the "Specifications" chapter of this book, and micropublishers, for the most part adhere to them, although as late as 1967 Veaner noted, "the performance of many micropublishers has been far from satisfactory. Films have been sold without leaders or trailers, with unlabeled boxes. . . . Every conceivable technical and bibliographic fault has been present in all but a few micropublications."[2]

The current state-of-the-art as regards external controls is discussed in the "Microform Information Sources/Publications" piece in the "Acquisitions" chapter of this book and the bibliothecal problem is touched upon in the introduction to the "Cataloging" chapter.

The papers in this chapter deal primarily with the external and bibliothecal problems. Included are Simonton's report on the study he conducted in the early sixties under a grant from the Council on Library Resources and the results of a similar study conducted over a decade later by Reichmann and Tharpe. Also included is the introduction to an issue of the *National Register of Microform Masters*, a work which was a direct result of Simonton's recommendations. Commentary on the *Register* will be found in "Microform Information Sources/Publications" in the "Acquisitions" chapter of this book.

References

1. Simonton, Wesley, "Bibliographical Control of Microforms," *Library Resources and Technical Services*, 6: 29-40 (Winter 1962).
2. Veaner, Allen B., "Developments in Reproduction of Library Materials and Graphic Communications, 1967," *Library Resources and Technical Services*, 12: 203-14, 467.

THE BIBLIOGRAPHICAL
CONTROL OF MICROFORMS

by Wesley Simonton

Preface

The purpose of the present study, as stated in an early draft of the request for funds to the Council on Library Resources, has been "to develop with the cooperation of scholars, librarians, and the producers of microforms a comprehensive mechanism for bringing scholarly material in microform under bibliographic control. The specific and immediate project proposed is a study in consultation with a number of interested groups of the problems to be solved before such a mechanism can be evolved, and the preparation of a report identifying these problems and proposing tentative solutions."

It should be noted that this study is concerned only with the problems of the bibliographical control of materials which have been reproduced in microform. It is not concerned with such topics as the physical aspects of the various media and their reading devices, with evaluation of any of the large micropublishing projects, with consideration of what sort of material should be reproduced in microformat, or of the most appropriate medium of microreproduction for particular bibliographical forms (i.e., newspapers, periodicals, monographs, etc.). Further, attention has been

Reprinted from *Library Resources and Technical Services*, 6: 29-40 (Winter 1962).

devoted exclusively to those microforms which, so far as can be determined, are destined to be retained permanently in libraries or other comparable institutions.

The study has been carried out under the auspices of the Association of Research Libraries, with the advice and help of an advisory committee consisting of Herman Fussler, Director of Libraries, University of Chicago; Stanley Pargellis, Librarian, Newberry Library; and George A. Schwegmann, Jr., Chief, Union Catalog Division, Library of Congress. Data and opinion have been gathered through visits and correspondence with individuals and interested corporate groups: (1) librarians, in public, academic and special libraries; (2) representatives of scholarly and professional associations, including the American Association of Law Libraries, the American Council of Learned Societies, the American Historical Association, the American Library Association, the American Theological Library Association, the Association of Research Libraries, the Modern Language Association of America, the National Microfilm Association, the Society of American Archivists, and the Special Libraries Association; (3) commercial producers of microforms, most notably the Microcard Corporation, the Microcard Foundation, the Readex Microprint Corporation, and University Microfilms; (4) bibliographical agencies which have been or may be involved in the bibliography of microforms, such as the Philadelphia Bibliographical Center and Union Library Catalogue, the National Union Catalog, the H. W. Wilson Company, and the R. R. Bowker Company.

The importance of the topic and the desire of all parties to achieve solutions of the many problems involved have been reflected in the courtesies extended to the author on every hand. Without exception, the welcome has been cordial and the data requested have been provided completely and promptly.

Introduction

The problems involved in the bibliographical control of microforms grow out of three general considerations. *First*, microreproduction has become a medium of publication as well as a method of making copies. So far as libraries are concerned, at least, the problems derive not so much from the use of microreproduction to provide a single copy on demand as from the fact that books, serials, newspapers, and other types of materials are now being produced either originally and solely in microform or as simultaneous or later versions of a paper-copy original. Further, material published in microform presumably can be kept in print indefinitely. Beyond this, assuming sufficient demand or a sufficiently important demand, works which are no longer "in print" can be brought back into print, or, for that matter, corpora of manuscript material heretofore available only in single geographical locations can be put "in print" for wide distribution.

Second, the life of a microform copy in many instances will be longer than the life of its paper counterpart. *Third*, the rapid development of the technology of microreproduction has made it relatively easy to make a microscopy of virtually any textual material.

In attempting to answer the questions and problems arising from these developments, the present report proceeds on the assumption that for bibliographical purposes the intellectual content of a microform is more important than its physical format. It follows, then, that microforms should be listed and cataloged according to the same methods and the same criteria as those employed in successful attempts at bibliographical control of the traditional carriers of knowledge, insofar as possible. This is true of all microforms, whether they represent copies of previously-extant materials or materials first made available through the medium of microreproduction. The problems and methods of the bibliographical control of microforms are inextricably bound up with the problems and methods of bibliographical control in general.

For purposes of this report, three facets of the bibliographical control of microforms have been identified:

1. "internal bibliographical control of microforms," that is, the control provided by the bibliographic information included on the microform itself

2. "bibliothecal bibliographical control of microforms," that is, the measures employed in individual libraries to organize and catalog microforms

3. "external bibliographical control of microforms," that is, the control provided by bibliographies, lists, and other records of microforms.

Internal Bibliographical Control of Microforms

The necessity for adequate internal bibliographical controls for microreproductions, in the form of bibliographical identifications and targets placed at the beginning of the microreproduction, has long been recognized, and little more can be done here than to add to the exhortations of the past. The main reason for the lack of effective internal bibliographical controls has been the preparation of microreproductions by persons uninterested in or unaware of the information which should be included on the microcopy. The present study and other developments in this area, hopefully, have made most of the parties concerned more aware than before of the problem. The most important current development is the revision of the ALA *Guide to Microfilming Practices*, by the special Library Standards for Microfilm Committee of ALA, under the chairmanship of Peter Scott. This document, when completed, should provide a detailed guide for the preparation of scholarly microfilm and, by extension, of other microforms.

Because of the imminence of publication of the revised *Guide*, no attempt will be made in the present report to present detailed recommendations concerning the introductory information which should be placed on microforms. However, the following twelve items may be specified, of which the first five should always be given, the others only as necessary or appropriate: (1) macroscopic legend (a brief bibliographic citation, legible with the naked eye); (2) full bibliographic citation, prepared according to standard ALA and LC rules; (3) date and agency of filming, plus distributing agency, if different; (4) reduction ratio; (5) intended location of master negative; (6) contents or gaps; (7) location of original material (in the case of rare books or other items which have been subjected at some time to a full bibliographical description); (8) an introduction to the material, containing background information concerning it, ideally prepared according to instructions such as those in *The Preparation of Records for Publication on Microfilm* of the National Archives (this ordinarily only for manuscript materials); (9) reference to a separate index or description of the material, published or unpublished; (10) any necessary statements concerning restriction on use of the reproduced material, literary rights, provenance, etc.; (11) the form of the microform (microfilm, microfiche, Microcard, etc.); and (12) image placement. (The last two items need be included only in those instances where it may be feasible or desirable to reproduce a copy of the introductory information to serve as a form reporting the existence of the microform to a central agency for bibliographical purposes, as discussed subsequently in this report.)

Bibliothecal Bibliographical Control of Microforms

In the area of bibliothecal bibliographical control of microforms, that is, measures employed in individual libraries to organize and catalog microforms, three broad problem areas may be discerned: (1) to what extent are microforms to be cataloged; (2) how are they to be described as physical objects; and (3) how are they to be arranged.

Extent of cataloging of microforms. The economics of acquiring and cataloging library materials have been significantly changed by the advent of microforms as a major factor in library holdings. The relatively low cost and ease of acquiring individual titles and large bodies of materials have given new depth to the old problem of how thoroughly library collections should be cataloged. By and large, librarians have hitherto attempted to provide at least a main entry for each of the bibliographically-independent works (books, periodicals, etc.) in their collections, leaving unrecorded the bibliographically-dependent works (chapters in books, articles in periodicals, etc.). Now that it is possible for any library to secure microform copies of all of the titles listed in Evan's *American Bibliography*, the question arises—are the microform copies to be considered bibliographically independent, like their paper copy counterparts, or bibliographically dependent, in the sense that they may be identified by reference to the Evans bibliography?

With full recognition of the magnitude of the problem, it still must be asserted that decisions concerning the need for cataloging and the depth of cataloging should be based on the importance of the content of library materials (and, to a lesser degree, on the ease with which they may be located if they are not cataloged) rather than on their physical format. It is therefore essential that every effort be made to develop cooperative or centralized analytic cataloging for multiple-title micropublishing projects, of the sort provided by the University of Michigan Library for STC films. Even with a limited number of subscribers, this project has been successful and self-supporting over the years, at a cost to participating libraries of only 50 cents per title. Most microform publishers are willing to expedite such projects if librarians are willing to undertake them. The logical agency to pursue these activities is the Subcommittee on Micropublishing Projects of the Committee on Resources of ALA.*

Physical Description of Microforms. With regard to the physical description of microforms in library catalogs, two basic problems may be identified: first, how to relate the microform to the original work of which it is a copy and second, how much information concerning the physical form of the microform is necessary or desirable on the catalog card. In considering the first of these problems, it is convenient to identify two theories of the cataloging of microforms, which may be termed the "facsimile theory" and the "edition theory." The facsimile theory may be said to be primarily concerned with the intellectual content of the work, in that it considers all microforms to be reproductions of previously existing works, whether these works have been "published" or not, and is not concerned with whether the microform represents publication or is intended merely as a single copy. In describing the microform, it attempts first to describe the original, and then to add to this description the pertinent items for identifying the microform. The edition theory, on the other hand, is more concerned with the physical object. It draws a distinction between those microforms which may be called "editions," in the sense that several or many copies are produced, which are widely available, and those microforms which represent single copies. Further, in describing the microform, greater prominence is given to the physical format of the microform than that of the original of which it is a copy. The present Library of Congress *Rules for Descriptive Cataloging* at times follow the facsimile theory and at times the edition theory.

*EDITOR'S NOTE: This is now the Micropublishing Projects Committee, Resources Section, Resources and Technical Services Division, ALA.

The examples on pp. 39-40 illustrate the differences between current LC practice in the descriptive cataloging of microforms and the practices to be employed if the facsimile theory were to be adopted in all cases. On the basis of these examples, several observations may be made. *First*, under the facsimile theory, any bibliographical entity once described need not be described again, except to add a brief note if some new physical form has been used. (Hopefully, this practice could be extended even to manuscript collections. Cards prepared for the National Union Catalog of Manuscript Collections might provide the basis for the description of microcopies of such collections.) *Second*, if desired, it would be possible for a library which had microfilmed an item from its previously-cataloged collection to limit the change on the catalog card to the call number. *Third*, the facsimile theory relegates to the last position on the catalog card information concerning the physical features of the item in hand. (This should not create problems in library catalogs, where the call number includes indication of the physical format of the item, but conceivably it could present problems in the bibliographical listing of microforms.) *Fourth*, the facsimile theory makes possible the wider use of LC cards in cataloging microreproductions, since the card for the original may be easily used, with the addition of a note concerning the microform. *Fifth*, the edition theory gives greater prominence to the facts of publication of the microform. *Sixth*, the edition theory results in separating copies in a bibliography or a catalog which is based on date, such as the *National Union Catalog*.

It is recommended that in the course of the present revision of Section 10 of the Rules for Descriptive Cataloging at the Library of Congress, serious consideration be given to an attempt to apply the facsimile theory in all details of the cataloging of microforms and that research libraries of the country follow this principle, so that uniformity of microform cataloging practices will be at least as great as that of book cataloging practices.

In considering the information regarding the physical aspects of the microform which may be presented on the catalog card, it is possible to identify the following eleven items which should be considered for inclusion in any description of a microform: (1) the form of the microcopy, i.e., microtransparency, micro-opaque, reel or sheet form, etc.; (2) the number of pieces, if more than one; (3) whether the item is positive or negative; (4) width (of reel microfilm) or size (of items in sheet or card form); (5) location of the original paper copy (at least for rare or unusual items); (6) date and agent of filming; (7) location of master negative (if item in hand is a copy thereof); (8) reduction ratio; (9) image placement; (10) length (i.e., feet of film); and (11) density.

The decision as to how many of these items should be recorded on the catalog card must depend upon the purpose of that card. Strictly speaking, none of these items needs to be given in order to list or service the microform in the library, and if the microform has been properly made, most of these items will be recorded on the microform. If none of these items were included on the catalog card, it would be possible to use the same card to represent a microfilm prepared to replace a discarded cataloged book as that used for the book itself, by changing only the call number. However, if the catalog card prepared locally is intended to serve as the record or as the basis for the record of the item in a union catalog or union list (as discussed later in this report), obviously certain of these items need to be included. The present *Rules for Descriptive Cataloging* call for inclusion of the first seven items in this list, either directly in the rules or by example. *It is recommended that the Rules be rewritten so as to make explicit rather than implicit the inclusion on the catalog card of the first seven items in the list above.*

Methods of Arranging Microforms. With regard to methods of arranging microforms in libraries, no single method will be recommended in this report, since this is primarily a policy question subject to varying decisions in different libraries, with many factors external to this report necessary of consideration. However, the major choices are presented below, for guidance in making the decision.

Leaving aside those works which are essentially self-cataloging or self-indexing, such as U.S. government documents on Microprint, arranged in *Monthly Catalog* listing order, or the reproduction of titles from Evans arranged according to Evans number, the librarian may choose from among several degrees of subject arrangement of his microforms, depending upon the importance he attaches to classification. At least five degrees of subject classification of microforms may be distinguished: (1) no classification whatever, the microforms being arranged in accession or alphabetical order; (2) a broad classification based on the bibliographical form of the original work (book, serial, newspaper, manuscript, etc.); (3) representation in the classified shelf list, combined with accession order filing; (4) a broad subject classification, as for example the degree represented by the letter classes of the LC classification, supplemented by a running accession number within each class; and (5) complete classification including shelving of microforms in classified order.

In deciding among these alternatives, it must be recognized that, as of the moment at least, browsing among microforms is not widely practiced. At the same time, however, if one is convinced that microforms should be treated as much like codex books as possible on the theory that both forms are designed to carry information, it is possible to make a stronger case for the subject classification of microforms, at least in a library which classifies its books by subject, than has traditionally appeared in the literature on the subject. It should also be kept in mind that while to date most library collections of microforms have been centralized, it is quite likely that eventually departmental or divisional libraries organized on a subject basis will be considered quite incomplete if they are limited to codex materials. A microform collection arranged at least in broad subject classes will permit the identification of materials on a subject basis much more readily than one arranged in accession order.

External Bibliographical Control of Microforms

The basic bibliographical needs of the scholar and the librarian may be expressed as (1) a record of published materials, (2) a record of available materials and, (3) a record of locations of materials. The structure of the "external" bibliographical control of microforms must take account of these needs, without ignoring the basic consideration that microreproductions of previously extant works constitute copies rather than editions and should therefore be listed and recorded in that same way and in the same place as the originals, insofar as possible.

Record of Published Materials. To make our records of published materials as complete as possible, it is desirable that any microform which represents original publication, such as *Wildlife Disease* and Hanley's *Index to Rimes in American and English Poetry*, be listed in the bibliography appropriate for the particular bibliographical form involved. Thus, *Wildlife Disease* should be listed in *New Serial Titles*, and Hanley's *Index* should be listed in *Publishers' Weekly* and *Cumulative Book Index*.

It is recommended that the Association of Research Libraries make vigorous representation to the publishers of such works and the compilers of the appropriate bibliographies that such titles be included in our basic bibliographical records.

Record of Available Materials. A record of materials available in microform is needed by the librarian and the scholar in order to avoid duplication of filming and to make known what is available for reproduction of copies. To date, this need has been met in part by the *Union List of Microfilms* and by *Newspapers on Microfilm*, both of which locate master negative copies. However, the record has been incomplete, in that many libraries and other agencies have not reported to the compilers of these lists and the lists have not included materials issued in micro-opaque form for which a master negative exists.

It is therefore recommended that a new bibliographical record be established, devoted to listing those titles for which a master negative* exists. Broad recommendations concerning the scope, form, and other major details of this record are presented below. As the record is compiled, further discussion of these points by all interested parties will doubtless be necessary.

---

*The term "master negative" is used here to designate a film which is used only for making prints. A "master," or "file," negative should never be used for ordinary reading or reference.

Scope. The goal should be to list all negatives which are retained as "file" or "master" negatives, including (1) negatives prepared for the making of micro-opaques, (2) works filmed abroad, (3) items whose use is restricted, in the sense that positive copies may not be made, and (4) titles already listed in other printed bibliographies, both of originals and of microforms, such as the *STC*, the *Microfilm Catalogue, Basic Baptist Historical Materials, Dissertation Abstracts*, the forthcoming *Guide to Photocopied Historical Materials*, etc.

With regard to the types of materials which should be considered for listing, it is possible to define three broad categories:

1. Materials which should definitely be included
   a. serials
   b. newspapers
   c. separately published monographs—books, pamphlets, etc.
   d. manuscripts (single works)
   e. manuscript collections
2. Materials which it is impossible or undesirable to include
   a. government documents (at least those included in large scale projects such as those of Readex Microprint)
   b. subject-oriented collections, such as chemical patents and projects like those of the Petroleum Research Corporation
   c. unitized records such as the Human Relations Area File
   d. technical report literature
3. Borderline materials
   a. dissertations
   b. copies of card catalogs and other unpublished indexes
   c. materials of genealogical interest (vital records, court records, etc.)
   d. public records, including archival collections

Form. *It is recommended that the record be maintained or published in sections, reflecting the bibliographical form of the original.* This would have the two-fold advantage of simplifying the description of the items and facilitating the use of the record, by relating it to the general pattern of bibliography. The question of possible publication of part or all of the record is discussed below.

Information included for titles recorded. In addition to the bibliographic citation, prepared according to standard procedures, and indication of location of the copy filmed in the case of rare or unusual materials, certain technical information concerning the negative should be included, in order to identify the auspices and circumstances of filming and to indicate what kind of a copy can be made from the negative. These items include: (1) reduction ratio, (2) image placement, (3) width of film, (4) indication whether positive or negative, (5) date and agent of filming, (6) intended location of the master negative, (7) length of film, and (8) format (for sheet film).

Method of compilation. The first step in the preparation of the record of master negatives is the assembling at a central agency of copies of many existing bibliographies, some of them printed and some in card form, some from public agencies, some from private or commercial agencies. The logical agency to undertake the work is the Microfilm Clearing House of the Library of Congress, with the assistance, possibly, of the Manuscripts Division and of the National Union Catalog of Manuscript Collections of the Library of Congress. After the existing records have been brought together in the central agency, it is essential that all subsequent filming be reported to the agency. Widespread publicity will be necessary to secure the cooperation of all interested parties, both institutional and commercial. Standard report forms will need to be worked out, similar to those presently used for reporting to the Microfilm Clearing House, but it is only realistic to assume that many agencies will find it desirable, perhaps mandatory, to report in their own individual way, including the use of copies of catalog cards. A large amount of editorial work at the central agency cannot be avoided.

As reports are assembled and received at the central agency, the possibility of publishing part or all of the record should be investigated in greater detail than has been possible in the preparation of this report. In view of the magnitude of the record, experimentation with machine methods of preparation will perhaps be necessary. *It is recommended that the order of priority of publication of the various sections of the record be as follows:*

1. newspapers (probably in the form of new editions of *Newspapers on Microfilm*)
2. serials
3. separately published monographs, including perhaps dissertations and films of unpublished indexes
4. manuscript collections, including perhaps public records, archival collections, and genealogical materials
5. manuscripts (single works)

Location of copies of microforms. The third basic bibliographical need is a record of location of usable copies. On the assumption that a microform copy should be treated bibliographically as much like its original as possible and that a microform copy may be just as usable as a paper copy, it is recommended that microform copies be listed in the same union catalogs and union lists as are appropriate for their originals, insofar as possible. Thus, a microcopy of a book published in 1860 should be recorded in the

National Union Catalog; a microcopy of a book published in 1960 should be listed in the *National Union Catalog*; a microcopy of a periodical should be listed in *New Serial Titles* or the *Union List of Serials*; a microcopy of the Adams papers should be recorded in the National Union Catalog of Manuscript Collections.

It is therefore recommended that libraries and other comparable institutions report their holdings of usable copies of microforms to the National Union Catalog at the Library of Congress, according to the same criteria as those employed for the reporting of copies of the original. (Ideally, books should be reported to the National Union Catalog, serials to *New Serial Titles*, and manuscript collections to the National Union Catalog of Manuscript Collections. The recommendation of a single recipient for all reports is made with a view to simplification of the reporting procedure, in the hope of securing wider participation.) The impact of the additional load on the appropriate catalogs and bibliographies may force reconsideration of the present criteria for listing locations in these records, but to exclude copies *per se* is clearly illogical.

Summary and Recommendations

On the assumptions that the problems and methods of the bibliographical control of microforms cannot be divorced from the problems and methods of bibliographical control in general, and that microforms should be listed and cataloged in the same places and in the same manner as their originals whenever possible, specific recommendations have been made in this report as follows:

1. Efforts should be made to ensure that microforms which represent original publications should be listed in bibliographies of printed materials as appropriate.

2. Details of a proposed new bibliographical record of master negatives have been presented. The purpose of the record would be to indicate what materials have been filmed, in order to avoid duplication of filming, and to make known what materials are available for reproduction of copies.

3. Library copies of microforms should be listed in the same union catalogs and union lists as are appropriate for their originals, insofar as possible. Libraries and other comparable institutions should therefore report their holdings of microforms to the National Union Catalog, at the Library of Congress, according to the same criteria as those employed for the reporting of copies of the original materials.

4. Bibliographical and technical information which should be specified at the beginning of any microform have been identified. Publicizing of this information should be effected through the approval and wide dissemination of the revised ALA *Guide to Microfilming Practices*, as soon as it is available.

5. Efforts to provide separately issued catalog cards for titles included in large scale micropublishing projects should be encouraged.

6. In the physical description of microforms, an attempt should be made always to describe first the original work, supplementing this description with a description of the microform. It is recommended that the Library of Congress apply this principle in its revision of the microforms section of its *Rules for Descriptive Cataloging.* Recommendations are also made concerning the extent of description of microforms as physical objects.

PRESENT LC PRACTICE

Frarey, Carlyle James
  Subject heading revision by the Library of Congress, 1941-1950. Rochester, N. Y., University of Rochester Press for the Association of College and Reference Libraries, 1954.
    3 cards. 7½ x 12½ cm. (ACRL microcard series, no. 15)

  Microprint copy of typescript. Collation of the original: iii, 97 1. diagrs., tables. 29 cm.
    Thesis (M.S.)—Columbia University
    Bibliography: leaves 94-97.

The Medical examiner. v. 1-7, Jan. 3. 1838-Dec. 26, 1844; new ser., v. 1-12 (no. 1-144), Jan. 1845-Dec. 1856. Philadelphia, Lindsay & Blakiston.
    10 reels, (American periodical series. 1800-1850. 428-437)

  Microfilm copy (positive) by University Microfilms, Ann Arbor, Mich. Collation of the original as determined from the film: 19 v. illus.
    Frequency varies.
    Title varies: 1843, The Medical examiner and retrospect of the medical sciences.—1844-53, The Medical examiner and record of medical science.
    United with the Louisville review to form the North American medico-chirurgical review.

Lang, William Bailey
  Views with ground plans of the high-

FACSIMILE THEORY

Frarey, Carlyle James
  Subject heading revision by the Library of Congress, 1941-1950. [n.p.] 1951.
    iii, 97 1. diagrs., tables. 29 cm.

    Thesis (M.S.)—Columbia University.
    Bibliography: leaves 94-97.
    Microprint copy. Rochester, N. Y., University of Rochester Press for the Association of College and Reference Libraries, 1954. 3 cards. 7½ x 12½ cm. ACRL microcard series, no. 15.

The Medical examiner. v. 1-7, Jan. 3. 1838-Dec. 26, 1844; new ser., v. 1-12 (no. 1-144), Jan. 1845-Dec. 1856. Philadelphia, Lindsay & Blakiston.
    19 v. illus.

    Frequency varies.
    Title varies: 1843, The Medical examiner and retrospect of the medical sciences.—1844-53, The Medical examiner and record of medical science.
    United with the Louisville review to form the North American medico-chirurgical review.
    Microfilm copy (positive) by University Microfilms, Ann Arbor, Mich. 10 reels. American periodical series. 1800-1850. 428-437.

Lang, William Bailey
  Views with ground plans of the high-

land cottages at Roxbury (near Boston) designed and erected by Wm. Bailey Lang. Boston, Printed by L. H. Bridgham and H. E. Felch, 1845. (American culture series, 31:10)

Microfilm copy (positive) made in 1956 by University Microfilms, Ann Arbor, Mich.
    Collation of the original: [10] 1. 9 plates (incl. 3 plans)

Menzel, Johanna Margarete, 1930-
    German-Japanese relations during the Second World War. Chicago [Dept. of Photoduplication, University of Chicago Library] 1957.
    Microfilm copy (positive) of typescript.
    Collation of the original: 539 1. illus. Thesis—University of Chicago. Includes bibliography.

land cottages at Roxbury (near Boston) designed and erected by Wm. Bailey Lang. Boston, Printed by L. H. Bridgham and H. E. Felch, 1845.
    [10] 1.9 plates (incl. 3 plans)

Microfilm copy (positive) made in 1956 by University Microfilms, Ann Arbor, Mich. American culture series 31:10.

Menzel, Johanna Margarete, 1930-
    German-Japanese relations during the Second World War. Chicago, 1957. 539 1. illus.
    Thesis—University of Chicago Includes bibliography.
    Microfilm copy (positive) of typescript, made in 1957 by Dept. of Photoduplication, University of Chicago Library.

SOME PROBLEMS OF MICROFORM UTILIZATION IN LARGE UNIVERSITY COLLECTIONS

by C. Edward Carroll

University library administrators have rather successfully devised methods for handling conventional library materials such as books and journals. Some have even assumed responsibility for nonprint materials and have moved toward the multimedia instructional materials approach which is becoming prevalent in community colleges and the better liberal arts schools. Yet few university library administrators have solved the many problems which arise when significant portions of their collections come to them in that unconventional format which is commonly known as microforms or microtexts.

Reprinted from *Microform Review*, 1: 19-24 (January 1972) by permission of the publisher. Copyright © 1974 by Microform Review Inc.

The decision to include nonbook materials, such as films, tapes, slides, and phonodiscs, is often a conscious one and is usually preceded by long-range planning. Additionally, the university librarian has on his staff, or can easily employ, librarians who are especially trained to cope with the problems of administering such nonbook materials. Library schools are consciously equipping their graduates to appreciate and operate within the multimedia instructional environment.

Building a collection of microfilms, on the other hand, is not always the result of a deliberate decision on the part of the librarian. True, a decision may be made to substitute microfilmed newspapers for hard copy in order to conserve space, and he may be accustomed to purchasing dissertations on microfilm. Usually, however, the decision to purchase microforms is forced upon the librarian because the desired material is not available in conventional (macroprint) format. He thus makes an incremental decision and before long he finds that he has accumulated a considerable store of valuable collections, each presenting peculiar problems of cataloging, storage, preservation, retrieval, and dissemination. Since library schools in the past have not concerned themselves with preparing persons to administer microtext collections, the librarian usually does not have a staff member who is knowledgeable in such matters. The result is that someone "who is not afraid of machines" is assigned responsibility for the burgeoning mass of materials.

The true extent of such collections in academic libraries is not accurately known. Only recently have library statistics been expanded to take account of microforms. In 1966, the American Library Association published *Library Statistics: A Handbook of Concepts, Definitions, and Terminology*, which sets forth procedures for reporting microform holdings, indicating that microtexts are not to be included in volume counts reported by librarians. Following this agreed-upon standard, the annual Higher Education General Information Survey, required by HEW, now requests separate statistics for "rolls of microfilm" and "number of physical items of all [other] forms of microforms." The Association of Research Libraries, in its annual academic library statistics questionnaire, asks for similar information, although it continues for some unknown reason to distinguish between microcards and microprint sheets, even though both are opaque microtext forms. In its final statistical compilation, ARL unfortunately lumps *all* microform units together instead of maintaining the "microfilm" and "others" categories as suggested by *Library Statistics* and requested by HEW.

Despite the clear instructions in the statistics handbook and the annual requests of HEW and ARL, thirty-two of the seventy-six ARL libraries did not report their microform holdings as asked for in 1969-1970. ARL is continuing its effort to obtain accurate counts for all research libraries so that the full extent of such holdings can be known. Yet some libraries continue to accession microforms and to include them in their volume count. This practice presents an inaccurate picture of the "size" of their libraries, even though such reporting may present a truer picture of the bibliographical depth of their collections. Be that as it may, the reported statistics of microform holdings in academic research libraries alone is truly impressive. As of June 30, 1970, seventy-four members of the ARL reported a combined total of 34,410,400 microform units. [1] Among libraries in the United States, Syracuse University reported 1,187,763 units, making it the largest microform collection. The University of Missouri at Columbia reported 893,464 units, making it the second largest collection in the United States.

Obviously, collections of such size and complexity present peculiar problems of administration and utilization. It is the purpose of this article to comment on some of these problems and to suggest ways in which these extensive and valuable intellectual resources can be more effectively utilized.

Perhaps one should begin with a definition of microforms or microtexts. The one given by Klaus W. Otten in a recent article is admirably concise. The term *microform*, he says, "refers to all records of human-readable documents which require, for reading or viewing, magnification devices." [2] The generic term *microform*, however, tends to gloss over the many media, sizes, reduction ratios, and formats which it encompasses. Microforms come as roll film (35mm and 16mm, positive and negative, on open reels and in cartridges); as microfiche (4 × 6, 3 × 5, and at various reduction ratios); aperture cards (sometimes keypunched for machine manipulation); opaque microcards (3 × 5 and 6 × 9). Each of these many sizes and formats requires not only customized storage facilities but, more important, different reading or viewing devices.

Herein lies the most obvious and expensive problem for the library director—providing physical access to the collection. A decision to purchase any microform collection carries with it a commitment to purchase one or more appropriate reading devices. And if the library is to serve its patrons without discriminating against the microform user, it must also provide a means of making a hard copy printout from the microtext for later reference. This necessitates the purchase of a printer. Although reader-printers are now quite common for filmed materials (microfilm and microfiche), printers that will make hard copy from opaque microtexts are less common. One model is available and should be purchased by every library which has holdings in opaque microtexts.

The purchase, operation, and maintenance of readers and reader-printers, which are required to make microforms readily accessible to patrons, put considerable strain on library budgets already overtaxed by rising costs of conventional library materials. Very real savings in storage space and in per-volume cost of microtexts must be balanced against the very real additional costs of providing machines, personnel, and specially designed reading areas—all of which are necessary if the microform collection is to have its optimum impact on the research efforts of the institution. To boast of large collections of inaccessible materials in a university library (whether they are in micro- or macrotext) reveals an all-too-common type of academic snobbishness.

Microform readers and reader-printers occupy considerable floor space, and for various reasons cannot usually be placed in areas used by readers of macrotexts. Even the improved carrel-type microfilm readers require rooms with subdued lighting, and microcard readers require more extensive light control. Reader-printers are usually placed in a rigidly supervised area, since the cost of printout macrotext copies is usually borne by the library patron. Also, the operation and maintenance of reader-printers require trained personnel. As more rugged coin-operated microprinters are marketed, it will probably become as common for students to make their own copies from microforms as it is now for them to make their own photocopies from books. Increased sophistication in the use of various microform reading devices, which librarians are observing among entering college students, will also help to reduce the need for constant manning of microform collections.

But, at present, the most obvious problem facing the library director is to make microform collections physically accessible by providing adequate machines and comfortable reading areas.

A more subtle problem which must be overcome in many academic communities is the unspoken assumption that microforms are, at best, only substitutes for the real thing. One purchases microforms only if the desired item is out of print. Even the, the used-book market must be ransacked before the acquisitions librarian turns reluctantly to an easily available and much less expensive microform. Parenthetically, one must observe that reprint dealers are growing fat on the prejudices of the academicians. Most professors, including librarians, will stoutly affirm the superiority of the reprint over a microform, even if the latter costs 90 percent less.

Because of this negative attitude, which relegates microforms to second-class citizenship among library materials, the library director finds little support or encouragement when he attempts to build a consistent, viable collection. Nor does the acquisition of microforms meet with enthusiastic response from library staff members. They usually view microforms as a never-ending mass of easily acquired materials to be cataloged and referenced without any increase in personnel. Part of their discouragement may stem from the commonly held belief that a microform is but a book in miniature and, perforce, must be treated exactly like a book. The fact that microforms usually are acquired as collections, and that access to collections requires a different approach from access to individual books, seems not to have occurred to most librarians. Unless each item is fully cataloged and the set of cards properly filed, librarians tend to think that it is not really a part of the library's holdings. Yet it is patently infeasible to individually catalog the thousands of items which make up many micro-publishing projects. Even if full sets of cards for each item were made available by the micro-publisher, Doctor Felix Reichmann questions the wisdom of cluttering up the public card catalog with references to the individual items in those massive collections. [3] What is needed is a more imaginative approach to bibliographical control for microforms than has yet been devised. More on that later. The point here is that, lacking such control and sharing the prejudices of the teaching faculty, librarians have not given microforms a fair chance. Overcoming these prejudices of faculty and colleagues is the second major problem which the university library director faces in administering his microform collection.

This attitude among scholars of considering microforms something less than the real thing has led to the use of microforms mainly for the republication of older, out-of-print, or bulky materials. It has also resulted in leaving the decision of what should be republished up to microform entrepreneurs who tend to create, ex post facto, a market for their products rather than producing what the community of scholars really needs. As librarians and scholars come to accept microforms as legitimate, and begin to systematically define their needs, they may find that micropublishing has a vital role to play in presenting new materials.

Fortunately, attitudes are changing. The greater technological sophistication of younger scholars and college students and the success of some recent micropublishing projects indicate that the message is more important than the medium. Researchers are learning that large masses of material can be scanned or referenced more efficiently with modern reading devices. Very few present-day library users would request bound copies of the *New York Times*.

Materials from the Educational Resources Information Centers have convinced educators that basic research need not remain on library shelves. Current research reports are quickly and economically placed in the hands of practitioners through microfiche. In some places, notably the University of Missouri, computer searches of the ERIC data base speed the identification and retrieval of relevant documents. The success of ERIC and the *New York Times* leads one to suspect that Otten is correct in predicting that microforms will become the major medium for "new information" in reference and research libraries.[4]

One reason for the growing popularity of microfiche for presenting new material is the ease with which constantly evolving or changing data bases can be revised or added to. An example of this use of microfiche to update a data base is the Micrographic Catalog Retrieval System now in use in scores of libraries. Each week, as new catalog cards are produced by the Library of Congress, they are microfiched and rushed to subscribers. Not only does the weekly cumulated update eliminate the time-consuming filing of proof slips, it also gets the needed cataloging data to the libraries much earlier than it is received by those who depend on proof slips or the printed National Union Catalog.

Another problem facing the library administrator, but one over which he has very little control, is that created by the lack of standardization in the production of microforms and microform equipment. The almost endless variations in types, sizes, and reduction ratios used in producing microforms create many problems: the purchase of a multitude of reading devices and printing machines, an increase in maintenance costs, discouragement for users, and complications in staff training. Hopefully, some standards will emerge from the plethora now on the market, but the spectacle of the two leading ultramicrofiche publishers not being able to agree on the size of microfiche or the reduction ratio is not at all encouraging. The recent conference on microform utilization held in Denver recognized the importance of standards, but also took note of the practical problems of arriving at them in a free enterprise system. The participants advocated "a family of standards general enough to permit innovative development but firm enough to prevent incompatibility with presently used equipment." [5]

This lack of standards among microforms, resulting as it does in a variety of forms and a diversity of machines, places a burden upon the library director who must provide adequately trained staff to assist patrons, if the collections are to receive maximum intelligent use. Since all disciplines utilize microforms, the person in charge must not only be trained in the use of various formats and machines; he must, like every effective reference librarian, have an acquaintance with the subject matter with which he is working. Thus, while it is generally true that the most efficient method of housing and referencing microforms is to centralize them in one location, such centralization may effectively discourage their use. Ideally, microforms in a particular discipline should be housed adjacent to hard copy materials in that same discipline. Since this would require an economically infeasible duplication of reading and printing devices (one discipline may have materials in many types of microforms), some judicious centralization is required. However, it is obvious that microtexts which relate to materials housed in a branch library must be housed in that branch and referenced by the subject specialist assigned there.

Some centralization of microform holdings also is mandated by the reluctance of some librarians to deal with nonconventional materials. It is sometimes easier to develop positive attitudes in nonspecialists than it is to alter the mental set of some librarians. Their distaste for microforms is often communicated to patrons, creating barriers to wide use of the materials.

The most heavily used microforms are those located near related macrotext materials and referenced by librarians who have positive attitudes toward them. Centralization or decentralization thus becomes a function of the size of the microform collection as well as the administrative organization of the university library and the attitudes of the librarians. In a medium-sized library, housed in one central building, the patrons are perhaps best served by centralizing all microforms and their indexes in one well-lighted room under the supervision of a general reference librarian, and providing an adjacent room with light control for housing the various reading machines.

In a large library arranged according to broad disciplines, or having branch libraries serving professional schools, the patron is usually best served by some decentralization of the microform collections.

The major unresolved problem in handling large microform collections is that of bibliographic control. Bibliographic control simply means the ability to tell the library patron whether your library has a particular item on a particular subject. That problem has been rather satisfactorily solved for the user who is inquiring about books and periodicals in conventional format. The catalog, with its author, title, and subject cards, and the various periodical indexes, are familiar to most library patrons.

Yet, in its microform collections, the library may have literally thousands of books, periodicals, newspapers, and reports which are not listed in the card catalog nor indexed in any of the periodical guides. This extensive collection constitutes a "hidden library" of resources to which the library's users are denied access. As indicated earlier, this writer does not suggest that a card should be placed in the public catalog for every item on microform; but there is a pressing need for the library to provide some form of bibliographic control for every single item in its collections. It is just as vital to provide bibliographic access to microform materials through adequate reading and printout devices.

Two suggestions have been made for solving this problem. Many librarians contend that micropublishers must assume responsibility for providing bibliographic guides to the microfilm projects which they market. They recommend that librarians refuse to purchase materials which do not include such guides as a part of the package. [6]

Yet it is unfair to blame the publishers for not supplying the necessary bibliographic apparatus since the profession has not yet clearly defined what type of apparatus is needed. The traditional demand has been for full card cataloging, and those micropublishing projects which have met with the most positive response from librarians have been those which provided card sets. Yet, most catalogers find such cards unusable without extensive revision, and it is indeed questionable if a library should provide either the card catalog space or the personnel needed to revise and file such cards.

Teachers of cataloging in our library schools need to pioneer in new methods of bibliographic control for microforms just as Dewey and Poole devised new methods of bibliographic control for books and periodicals. Only after librarians have defined their bibliographic needs in this area can they castigate micropublishers for not meeting those needs.

It has also been suggested that a National Microfilm Agency be formed to promote quality control and encourage acceptable bibliographic practices. It would seem appropriate that such an agency might sponsor a comprehensive index to micropublishing, providing detailed analytics to all microform collections. Such a tool could serve the local library as a guide to its collections much as the various periodical indexes serve as guides to the library's periodical holdings.

Until these basic problems of physical access, changing attitudes, standardization, and bibliographical control are solved, academic libraries will continue to amass great collections of rich research materials which will remain largely unused—microform mausoleums—imposing but seldom visited.

References

1. Association of Research Libraries. Academic Library Statistics, 1969-70.
2. Otten, Klaus W. "A Hypothesis: Microform will become major medium for new information in reference libraries," *Journal of Micrographics* 4: 266 (July 1971).
3. Speech by Dr. Reichmann at the Midwinter Meeting of ARL, Los Angeles, January 1970.
4. Otten, Klaus W. *op. cit.* p. 266.
5. *Conference on Microform Utilization: the Academic Library Environment*, Denver, Colorado, December 7-9, 1970 (University of Denver, 1971), pp. 193-94.
6. *Ibid.*, p. 211.

THE UNIVERSITY OF BRITISH COLUMBIA LIBRARY'S GUIDE TO LARGE COLLECTIONS IN MICROFORM: ONE ATTEMPT TO MINIMIZE A MAJOR PROBLEM

by Suzanne Dodson

The problem of the bibliographic control of large collections in microform is a perplexing one. The number of large collections has increased tremendously over the past few years, as anyone working in the area knows only too well. I recall someone remarking recently that anyone with a camera and something to film needed little else to become a micropublisher. And indeed, as one views (somewhat uneasily in my case) the rapid

Reprinted from *Microform Review*, 1: 113-17 (April 1972) by permission of the publisher. Copyright © 1972 by Microform Review Inc.

proliferation of publications in microform, one cannot help wondering just how valid some of the publishing ventures really are.

Micropublications fall into two categories; individual items, and collections. By individual items I mean separate bibliographic entities like *The New York Times*[1] or a microform edition of Andrew Garrett's *Fische der Südsee*.[2] These publications are easily dealt with by both library and library patron alike. Bibliographic control presents no special difficulties. It is far easier for a library to catalog and to shelve *The New York Times* on microfilm than it would be to house the printed version. The patron's access to the newspaper on microfilm is simple and convenient. He is more likely to find the page he wants in the microfilm version than if he uses a bound set in a library plagued by the average run of "page-removers." His access to the microfilm through the main card catalog is no different than it would be if the newspaper were in printed form. An additional benefit is that often the price of the microform version is considerably below that of the printed one. *Fische der Südsee*, for example, may be purchased for approximately $10 on microfiche.[3] The reprint is priced at around $100.[4] The only real difference is that the medium necessitates the use of equipment. This is barely noticeable, if the reading equipment is well designed and maintained. Poor equipment or good equipment in disrepair creates a very definite difference between using microforms and using printed publications, but this is a situation which I will not consider at this time.

The problem of bibliographic control becomes really serious when one encounters large collections in microform. With the purchase of one set a library can add thousands of titles to its collection. In some instances catalog cards can be purchased from the publisher for titles in the set, but these cards are often limited to author entries only. In other instances there are no catalog cards and a library must catalog each item in the set. A good example of this latter type of collection is University Microfilms' *Early English Books, (STC II)*,[5] based on Wing's bibliography, *Short-title Catalogue of Books Printed in England, Scotland, Ireland, Wales and British America, and of English Books Printed in Other Countries, 1641-1700*.[6] This microfilm project, which consists so far of about 400 reels of film, is slated to take sixty-eight years to produce. It has been in production for the past ten years, which means that University Microfilms still has fifty-eight years of filming upon which to reflect. (One cannot but be impressed with their optimism!) However, the results of their labors produce something less than unalloyed pleasure for their customers. They state that catalog cards are available for this set, which seems very nice until one reads the explanatory footnote. "Catalog cards for the series are available from Library of Congress, Washington, D.C., U.S.A. Must be ordered by individual title."[7] In other words, forget it. A library would have to search and order individually catalog cards for each of the thousands of titles in this set, and this is just not economically feasible.

The example used above is not an isolated one. As I mentioned previously, many of these sets contain literally thousands of separate bibliographical entities, and if catalog cards are not provided with the set, it is the rare library which can afford to do the cataloging. This means that unless the library does catalog the set there may be only one basic entry in the card catalog to represent thousands of books. It also means that the library staff must go to great lengths to attempt to ensure that the patrons are aware of the large microform collections. It often happens that people using the main card catalog assume that if they do not find the item they want listed there, then the library does not have it. And, unhappily, too many people stop searching at this point, so that even if the library's reference staff is completely knowledgeable about the microform collection, they are frequently never given a chance to direct the potential user to it. When catalog cards *are* provided, the task of incorporating them into the card catalog can prove to be a herculean one beyond the all-too-mortal capabilities of the library in terms of both space and time. In 1968 the University of Victoria circulated a questionnaire to other university libraries asking about their microform cataloging policies and a report on the results states: "It will surprise no one, as the survey shows, that libraries are not cataloging in full the individual texts in these massive microform collections. The number of titles in a single collection can be almost as large as the yearly book intake of some of the reporting libraries. Without exception, libraries are cataloging these works as a single unit, with a reference on the card to the printed bibliography where one exists. Several are filing a main entry, or author analytic, or information card in their main catalogs, if it is available commercially. No library mentioned filing of title added entries, though it is expected that for a few works title added entries have been filed."[8]

Dr. Felix Reichmann of Cornell remarked, during a meeting of the Association of Research Libraries in January 1971, that "the major problem in bibliographic control of microforms centers on the control of large microform series, involving hundreds and even thousands of titles. Traditional cataloging practice calls for the preparation of full analytics for these sets. Now all of us are aware of the difficulties presented to technical services departments by the need to analyze large series. Often there is not enough staff to accomplish the task and libraries will content themselves with a series entry only. When staff and time are available, full analytics exacerbate the problem of file size, assuming there are enough filers to put the cards into the catalog. In spite of my predilection for full cataloging for every title owned by a library, I must admit this practice cannot continue. Keep in mind that several micropublishing projects already underway involve thousands of titles each. Even when catalog cards are supplied for each title by the publisher, there often is not the staff to file these cards and, even if there were, the available catalog space may not accommodate them. This situation is bound to get worse, in view of the growth

of the micrographic industry. You will note, of course, that I am not even
touching upon the cataloging problems caused by individual libraries
adapting catalog cards in order to be internally consistent. Further, we all
know that the cataloging copy supplied by some microform publishers
is often incomplete and inaccurate."[9]

Allen Veaner, in discussing the bibliographic control of microforms,
says, "I think that if we don't [provide better bibliographic control],
pretty soon the people charged with the purchase of major microform
projects are just going to start thinking twice about whether they should
pour a lot of good money (which you know is very hard to get these days)
into very expensive projects which are in danger of remaining buried away,
inaccessible to the prime clientele of the institution. Something has to be
done, whether it turns out to be book-form catalogs, computer printouts,
individual catalog cards, or whatever. The publishers must take responsibility for providing the bibliographical tools for the end use of . . . [the]
product, just as the publishers in conventional print take responsibility
for putting title pages in books."[10] (Catalogers may not always take too
sanguine a view of the way in which the latter responsibility is discharged!)

Librarians may feel that the micropublishers have neglected the problem
of bibliographic control in their haste to produce even larger collections,
but the micropublishers are not ready to assume all responsibility for the
dilemma. "The question of Library of Congress cards comes up again and
again," states Larry Block of Bell and Howell. "Should they be included
with a collection, should they be a part of the collection automatically?
Should there be a separate charge for them so they can be purchased
either separately or with the collection? Will they be used in the future
in the same manner as at present, or will libraries eventually use computer
indexing so that Library of Congress cards will not be needed? As I see it,
the setting of standards by mutual agreement will be a good thing, and I
think I can speak for micropublishers that it will be definitely welcome;
I do feel that this kind of direction hasn't really come in a particularly
strong way from the libraries themselves. We have heard complaints, we
have read articles, but conferences are still going on among librarians regarding the use of microforms and what microforms should contain, and
these meetings do not include micropublishers. That seems a one-sided
kind of discussion that won't really yield particularly good results; libraries have a responsibility. I think, in return for the satisfaction that they
want to get from the micropublishing industry, to let us in on the total
problem."[11]

In our library we have regarded the large collections in microform as a
mixed blessing. Thinking positively, microforms have enabled us to conserve precious space and to obtain materials which would otherwise be
inaccessible. Thinking negatively, we have problems. Five years ago I
found myself custodian of a rapidly expanding collection of microforms
and, as I quickly came to realize, an equally expanding headache. (Our

collection numbers over 1,250,000 "pieces" of microform, if one considers one reel of microfilm, one microfiche, etc. as one piece.) We had invested a considerable sum in some marvellous collections but few users knew we had them. One hardly likes to see valuable material lying unused and neglected by the library's patrons. Worse still, because we did not know what we had, we were duplicating material by buying, in printed form and often at considerable expense, books which we already had in microform. It was difficult to remember that many of the items listed in out-of-print and reprint catalogs were in the library, in microform, parts of large collections which had not received adequate cataloging for each item in the set. Wherever possible we have, of course, attempted to buy catalog cards for our collections from the publishers. We have also tried to catalog as much of the material for which cards are not available as we could, but our problems have been experienced by every other library.

In an effort to alert our staff, both reference and acquisitions personnel, to the material we had, I began to develop a guide to large collections in microform for the University of British Columbia (UBC).[12] This guide was begun strictly as a reference aid to our own collection, but in 1970 I discovered that Dr. Felix Reichmann and Miss Josephine Tharpe, both of Cornell University, were working on a related project as part of a study done by the Association of Research Libraries for the United States Office of Education.[13] Dr. Reichmann, Miss Tharpe, and I hope to combine our efforts to produce a guide which will help to provide libraries everywhere with assistance in maintaining a more effective system of bibliographic control of their microform collections. The guide which may appear as the result of our collaboration is still in the most preliminary stage. In the interim however, a bibliography of about five hundred microform series will be published as part of the study done by the Association of Research Libraries.

The guide which I discuss below is the one originally designed for the University of British Columbia Library. It is by no means complete, but to date it describes thirty-eight collections. Since I began the project a number of libraries have shown an interest in the guide and I have been happy to be able to provide them with copies. (There are now copies as far afield as Ottawa and New York.) I hope in return to receive comments and suggestions from the recipients of the guide so that I can improve its content and format. Since my guide is now in use outside our own library I have tried increasingly to include information which is generally useful as well as information specific to our own situation.

Basically the guide is a looseleaf arrangement, with each entry separate, filed by title. I have attempted to include information about each set which I feel would be useful not only to libraries having the sets in their collections but also to those libraries which might be contemplating purchase, or to those which, while never likely to have the set in their collections, might well wish to know about the set in order to borrow items through interlibrary loan. The information I have listed includes price, publisher, format, arrangement, bibliographies, guides, etc., and content. I realize that some information (prices and addresses, for example) will change, but each entry is dated and a looseleaf format would provide the means for updating and for adding new entries.

All the information included in the guide is available elsewhere, but often from many different sources. Frequently, valuable aids to the use of a particular set are hidden in publishers' catalogs or brochures. Hopefully, the guide will eliminate the need to dig through a lot of miscellaneous material.

Although primarily concerned with providing a means of access to these large collections, the UBC guide includes additional information of a general nature. There is a section which describes the various types of microform; microfilm, microfiche, microcard, etc. (In any future guide I would note the advantages and disadvantages of each type.) I have also listed briefly those bibliographic aids which we find particularly useful as guides to microforms in general; titles like *Guide to Microforms in Print*.[14]

I believe the addition of a world list of the major publishers of materials in microform would be of value. I would include their addresses and a brief description of the subject areas which they are likely to cover. *The Microfilm Newsletter* has published a *Guide to Micropublishers* but it lists only commercial publishers in the United States.[15]

All this does not offer the solution to the problem of bibliographic control of microforms but it is an attempt to alleviate the problem in those areas where it is most acute. And even as an attempt it is by no means unique. Mrs. June Thomson says, "Many libraries feel that the only immediate solution is in the publishing of printed and constantly updated guides to their microform collections and, through publicity programs, educating both librarians and library users as to the wealth of material they have on microform."[16] Another report states "Individual libraries spend a lot of time in trying to develop guides to their own collections."[17] Two recent examples of this type of publication are the *Union List of Microform Sets in O.C.U.L. Libraries*, published by the Ontario Council of University Librarians,[18] and the University of Nevada's *A Guide to Some Research Collections in the University Library*.[19]

This unnecessary duplication of effort is sad; an archaic solution to the problems presented by one of the newest forms of information in our libraries. At the very least, let us make a start by joining forces and consolidating the information we have.

References

1. *The New York Times* (New York, 1851-   ). (On microfilm.)
2. Garrett, Andrew, *Andrew Garrett's Fische der Südsee*, beschrieben und redigiert von Albert C.L.G. Günther (Hamburg, L. Friederichsen & Co., 1873-1910).

3. Microcard Editions, *Catalog 11; Titles Available on Microfiche and Other Microforms 1970-71* (Washington, D.C., 1970), p. 20.

4. *Books in Print 1970; an Author-Title-Series Index to the Publishers' Trade List Annual.* Vol. 1, *Authors* (New York, R. R. Bowker c. 1970), p. 769.

5. *Early English Books 1641-1700. (STC II)* (Ann Arbor, University Microfilms, 1961-   ). (On microfilm.)

6. Wing, Donald Goddard, *Short-title Catalogue of Books Printed in England, Scotland, Ireland, Wales and British America, and of English Books Printed in Other Countries, 1641-1700* (New York, Index Society, 1945-1951).

7. University Microfilms, *Series Programs of University Microfilms, a Xerox Company* (Ann Arbor, University Microfilms, July 1970). (Brochure.)

8. Thomson, June, "Cataloguing of Large Works on Microform in Canadian University Libraries," *Canadian Library Journal, XXVI* (November-December 1969), p. 450.

9. Association of Research Libraries, Minutes of the 77th Meeting, Los Angeles, California, January 17, 1971. p. 9. (Typewritten.)

10. Veaner, Allen B., "Bibliographic Controls," *Microform Utilization: The Academic Library Environment.* Report, Conference, Denver, Colorado, December 7-9, 1970, (Denver, Colo., University of Denver, 1971), p. 70.

11. Block, Larry, "Fiche Collections," *Microform Utilization: The Academic Library Environment.* Report, Conference, Denver, Colorado, December 7-9, 1970, (Denver, Colo., University of Denver, 1971), p. 83.

12. Dodson, Suzanne, "Microforms in the University of British Columbia Library," (Vancouver, B. C., 1971). (Typewritten.)

13. Association of Research Libraries, *Interim Report.* Contract Number: OEC-O-8-080786-4612(095) (Washington, D.C., Association of Research Libraries, 1970).

14. *Guide to Microforms in Print* (Washington, D.C., Microcard Editions, 1961-   ).

15. *The Microfilm Newsletter; A Monthly Report for Business Executives Who Use or Market Microfilm Services and Equipment,* II, No. 12 (August 1971), p. 7.

16. Thomson, June, "Cataloguing of Large Works on Microform in Canadian University Libraries," p. 451.

17. *Microform Utilization: The Academic Library Environment,* p. 206.

18. Ontario Council of University Librarians, *Union List of Microform Sets in O.C.U.L. Libraries.* Anni Leibl and Jean S. Yolton, eds. (Toronto, Ontario Council of University Librarians, 1971.)

19. Rendall, Marian K., *A Guide to Some Research Collections in the University Library,* Kenneth J. Carpenter, ed., (Reno, University of Nevada, 1971).

FOREWORD TO THE
NATIONAL REGISTER OF MICROFORM MASTERS, 1973

The *National Register of Microform Masters* is a catalog of master microforms which have been produced for the sole purpose of preserving printed material on film. By definition, a master microform can be used to produce other copies of the work; however, copyright law or local regulations may forbid the production or purchase of copies in some cases. No film is listed here which, to the knowledge of the editors, is available for patrons or clients of an institutuion to use as a reading copy.

The *National Register of Microform Masters* is designed to serve several purposes. Because it lists those works for which master microforms already exist, it can be used to avoid the useless and expensive rephotographing of materials, and by making known to prospective purchasers the ownership of master microforms, it provides essential information on the thousands of microforms that are not restricted by law or custom. The *Register* constitutes a reference and research tool for perishable works that have been given a new existence in microform.

Scope

The *National Register of Microform Masters* is concerned only with master microforms, that is, those that are retained solely for the purpose of making other copies. Usually these masters are negatives, but under unusual circumstances a positive may serve as a master microform.

The *Register* reports master microforms of foreign and domestic books, pamphlets, serials, and foreign doctoral dissertations but excludes technical reports, typescript translations, foreign or domestic archival manuscript collections, U.S. doctoral dissertations, and masters' theses. Newspapers are listed in a separate publication, *Newspapers in Microform,* and archival materials and manuscript collections are reported in the *National Union Catalog of Manuscript Collections.* Both of these publications also

Reprinted from the *National Register of Microform Masters, 1973.* Washington: Library of Congress, 1974, p. v-viii.

list microform copies (usually positives) that may be used by readers. Microform copies of monographs that are for readers' use should continue to be reported to the *National Union Catalog*.

Frequency

The *Register* is issued each year. Each edition presents new reports and does not supersede any previous issues.

History

Particularly after the Second World War, the proliferation of microform copies of every type of printed material created problems of bibliographical control of this material, and libraries responded in a variety of ways. As early as 1942 the Philadelphia Bibliographical Center and Union Library Catalog published the first edition of *Union List of Microfilms,* which reported monographs, serials, and dissertations held on microfilm by U.S. libraries. The Library of Congress and the Association of Research Libraries published the first edition of *Newspapers on Microfilm* in 1948, and a number of special lists of archival materials, manuscripts, dissertations, and special collections on microfilm appeared during the early 1950s.

In 1961 the Philadelphia Bibliographical Center discontinued the publication of its *Union List of Microfilms,* and at the urging of the American Historical Association, the Association of Research Libraries commissioned Wesley Simonton of the University of Minnesota Library School to make recommendations for a national program of bibliographical control of microforms. Simonton urged that "a new bibliographical record should be established to list those titles for which a master negative exists." The primary purpose of such a record would be to forestall the "duplication of costly master negatives," because it was anticipated that producers of microforms would uselessly photograph works of every kind unless there were a central data source which could tell them what had already been filmed. Since the Library of Congress already published the *National Union Catalog* and had established a Microfilming Clearing House in 1949 to report on microfilming projects, it seemed to be the logical place to receive and publish such information. With financial support from the Council on Library Resources, the first issue of the *National Register of Microform Masters* appeared in September 1965, and after publication of a small issue in January 1966, the catalog was continued as an annual publication.

Microform Standards

Librarians were also concerned about a number of preservation problems. Film supposedly had a much longer life expectancy than paper, but it had been shown that inferior film deteriorated rather rapidly, especially if it was stored under unfavorable conditions. Furthermore, commercial producers of microforms came and went, and the supposedly indefinite preservation of rare materials could as easily be thwarted by the owner's decision to go out of business as by the deterioration of the film. Librarians were dismayed by the prospect that unique materials might be saved from oblivion by microfilming only to have the film itself destroyed or lost.

From the beginning, therefore, the *National Register of Microform Masters* attempted to identify "those microform masters that meet the requirements for . . . preservation [of our intellectual heritage]." Since it was impossible to visit the shop and storage facility of each microform producer, a rather arbitrary distinction was made between commercial producers and nonprofit institutions. It was assumed that the large university and public libraries which engaged in microfilming would use the best materials and would store their products under the best conditions so that their films would not perish. It was evident too that these nonprofit institutions would not go out of existence except under the most extreme circumstances. Every issue of the *Register* has therefore given prominence to the following statement:

Two categories are listed in the *Register:*
1. Master microform:
   a. A microform used only to make copies and
   b. from which single copies are available at any time and for a reasonable price.
2. Master preservation microform:
   a. A master microform that is housed in a temperature-controlled, fireproof space and
   b. owned by a nonprofit institution.
Microform masters listed in this publication must meet the specification of the American National Standards Association [and its successor, the American National Standards Institute, Inc., 1430 Broadway, New York, N.Y. 10018] in regard to film quality and permanence and should, if possible, meet the requirements for completeness, collation, image placement, reduction ratio, target, etc., as set down in the current specifications for microfilming published by the Library of Congress.

Some commercial producers of microforms actually have outstanding production and storage facilities which are superior to those of some nonprofit institutions with only limited resources. The commercial products remain classed in the first category and are denied the designation of "preservation microform" simply because the editors of this catalog are not able to establish criteria for production or to examine the physical plants of individual commercial firms. The reader should be aware that many unstarred items in this list are of the highest quality and would merit identification as preservation masters if the list could reflect an objective evaluation of each producer.

The stipulation in Category 1 that "single copies are [to be] available at any time and for a reasonable price" must be understood to include the reservation "if no copyright is infringed." Many items that have been filmed are of such age that copyright is not involved. But in the case of recent publications, especially in periodical literature, there may be many instances where court litigation would arise. Prospective purchasers of microforms may possibly be confronted by legal restrictions of some kind as the copyright questions evolves in the courts.

Arrangement

Early editions of the *Register* were arranged by Library of Congress catalog card number and National Union Catalog number; the few items which had neither identification were arranged in a separate alphabetical sequence by main entry. Experience showed, however, that users either did not know what the number was or how to find it on a catalog card, or considered that identifying the number was too laborious. Beginning with the 1970 volume, therefore, all items have been listed in one alphabetical sequence by main entry, and reports published between 1965 and 1969 are being reissued in the new format in the current volumes.

The original plan for the *Register* envisioned separate publications for serials, monographs, and manuscripts. *Newspapers on Microfilm* had been in existence for some years, *Dissertation Abstracts* had been well established by a commercial firm, and it seemed logical to extend the distinction of materials by form. The *National Union Catalog of Manuscript Collections* began publication in 1962, reporting both original materials and microfilms of materials not available in any other form. The 1965 issue of the *National Register of Microform Masters* contained only monographs; the 1969 edition contained only serials. The 1966-68 volumes contained both, but in separate sequences. Eventually the large gray area where serials and monographs meet suggested the futility of segregating the two, from the standpoint of both editors and users, and since 1970 both have been arranged together in one alphabetical sequence after the manner of the *National Union Catalog.*

Entries

Most entries in this bibliography can be found in the *National Union Catalog,* and as a consequence full bibliographic information is not duplicated here. Whether the work is in the *National Union Catalog* or not, the information provided here must be sufficient to correctly identify each work. Reports therefore consist of the complete main entry as established in the *National Union Catalog* or a main entry established according to Library of Congress practice, together with a condensed title and imprint and collation statement. Appropriate cross-references are provided whenever there is the possibility of an alternate entry. If a Library of Congress printed card is available for the work, the card number is given in the lower right-hand corner of the entry. Such cards, of course, usually refer to the original printed edition.

The location of the microform master or masters is reported in the lower left-hand corner of the entry by the combination of a symbol and an abbreviation. The symbol, consisting of capital letters with or without lowercase letters, identifies the owner of the master microform; the abbreviation, appearing as one or more lowercase letters, reports the form and character of the microform. Thus DLC m* means that the Library of Congress holds a negative master preservation microfilm. A list of symbols and abbreviations follows this introduction. In some instances series notes such as (Evans 44883) or (American culture series, 85: 8) appear after the abbreviation as an aid in ordering film from producers who list their materials by these series numbers.

Reporting

If the *Register* is to fulfill its purpose, especially its primary purpose of preventing the useless duplication of microforms, it is most important that both commercial and nonprofit institutions report their holdings of master microforms. These reports should be directed to: Library of Congress, National Register of Microform Masters, Catalog Publication Division, Washington, D.C. 20540. Microform copies, whether negative or positive, that are for use by readers should be reported to: Library of Congress, National Union Catalog, Catalog Publication Division, Washington, D.C.. 20540

Inquiries

The *National Register of Microform Masters* is compiled and edited by the Catalog Publication Division; questions and suggestions of an editorial nature should be directed to that division at the address cited above. Correspondence regarding subscriptions and other business matters should be addressed to the Card Division, Library of Congress, Washington, D.C. 20541.

William J. Welsh
Director, Processing Department

CONCLUSIONS AND RECOMMENDATIONS

by Felix Reichmann and
Josephine M. Tharpe

Technology and its products are not a panacea, the computer does not solve all library problems, reading cannot be equated with information retrieval, and microimages will not render printed books superfluous. However, the librarian must be familiar with the computer and automation and must use machines whenever warranted; information retrieval is a significant part of library work and microforms a substantial segment of libraries' holdings.

The descriptive cataloging of microforms should follow established rules. It should be practically identical with the cataloging of the original except for notes identifying the item as a microimage. Notes designating type of microimage and number of reels or fiche are generally deemed essential.

Maurice Tauber suggested in 1940 that "cataloging of films is both desirable and necessary, classification is neither."[18] Classification of other microforms is also unnecessary, as is use of the first two letters of Library of Congress classification to split up the microform collection among departments of a library. Selection for a departmental library does not fully match library classification. Moreover, long and bitter experience has proved how dangerous it is to shortcut basic rules of processing.

Libraries cannot cope with the burden of analyzing the many large series on microform they have acquired; moreover, the size of public catalogs is increasing much too rapidly. Therefore, a national, machine-readable index of microform publications that can be broken down into a multiplicity and variety of indexes tailored to the particular needs of a given library should be established.

Libraries should be protected against inferior reproduction methods. As Allen Veaner pointed out in 1967, "the performance of many micropublishers has been far from satisfactory. Films have been sold without leaders

Reprinted from Felix Reichmann and Josephine M. Tharpe, *Bibliographic Control of Microforms.* Westport: Greenwood, 1972, pp. 31-33, by permission of the Association of Research Libraries. Copyright © 1972 by the Association of Research Libraries.

or trailers, with unlabelled boxes; inadequately processed films have been offered; excessive reduction has been used by some stingy producers to save a few pennies worth of film. Every conceivable technical and bibliographic fault has been present in all but a few micropublications."[19] He later concluded, in his standard book on micropublications, "Individual libraries can accomplish only a small portion of the immense task of inspecting and evaluating . . . all micropublications. There is therefore a need for the establishment of a national testing and certifying agency for micropublications . . . as recommended to A.R.L."[20]

Excellent norms for controlling production have been worked out by the Copy Methods Section of the American Library Association. They have to be enforced, and every attempt should be made to reach an international agreement. Copyright legislation should be broadened to give some protection to bona fide publishers of microforms. International consistency should be sought so that microforms will be listed in national bibliographies. National microform centers must be established if bibliographic control of all microforms on a worldwide basis is to be achieved.

Specific recommendations:

1. The Library of Congress should give high priority to the processing of microforms. It should consider the inclusion of microforms and analytics for them in the MARC project.

2. Professional journals should publish papers that stress the importance of assigning adequate manpower to the processing and servicing of microforms.

3. A detailed cost and feasibility study of a machine-readable index for analytics of series in microform should be made. The national index should be capable of providing a complete index for all the series any given library possesses.

4. Every effort should be made to support the *National Register of Microform Masters*. The Library of Congress should engage in a major publicity campaign through papers in professional journals and speeches at professional meetings to explain the objectives, scope, and uses of the *National Register*. The Library of Congress should identify departments and individuals in American libraries responsible for reporting to the *National Register* and should maintain systematic contact with them.

5. A national microform agency should be established to set standards for both production and bibliographic control of microform publications. It should evaluate all forthcoming microform publications and promote the proper processing and servicing of microform collections. It should provide an up-to-date international microform bibliography and directory of microform publishers.

6. Establishment of national centers to set and enforce norms for the production and bibliographic control of microforms should be encouraged. Efforts to establish identical norms and coordination between centers all over the world should be promoted.

7. Copyright legislation should be modified to include protection of the product of bona fide publishers of microforms. Parallel legislation in all countries should be sought so that microforms may be included in national bibliographies.

8. Norms for the production and bibliographic control of microforms should be enforced.

9. Every effort should be made to have identical norms established all over the world.

Notes

18. Maurice F. Tauber, "Cataloging and Classifying Microfilms," *Journal of Documentary Reproduction* 3 (1940): 10-25.

19. Allen B. Veaner, "Developments in Reproduction of Library Materials and Graphic Communications, 1967," *Library Resources and Technical Services* 12 (1968): 203-14, 467.

20. Allen B. Veaner, *The Evaluation of Micropublications; A Handbook for Librarians*, an LTP Publication No. 17 (Chicago: Library Technology Program, American Library Association, 1971).

ADDITIONAL READINGS

Applebaum, Edmond L., "Implications of the *National Register of Microform Masters* as Part of a National Preservation Program," *Library Resources and Technical Services*, 9: 489-93 (Fall 1965).

Diaz, Albert, "Microform Information Sources/Publications." (See the "Acquisitions" chapter of this book.)

Hall, L. M., "Bibliographical Control of Microforms," *Southeastern Librarian*, 20: 258-66 (Winter 1970).

Reichmann, Felix, and Tharpe, Josephine M., *Bibliographic Control of Microforms*. Westport: Greenwood, 1972.

Schneider, Linda and D. W., "Microfilm Masters, A National Need," *Southeastern Librarian*, 20: 106-08 (Summer 1970).

Schwegmann, George, "The Bibliographical Control of Microforms," *Library Journal*, 8: 380-90 (January 1960).

Veaner, Allen B., "Bibliographical Control," part II of "Micropublishing," *Advances in Librarianship*, 2: 169-73 (1971).

Veaner, Allen B., "The Crisis in Micropublication," *Choice*, 5: 448-53 (June 1968).

Veaner, Allen B., *The Evaluation of Micropublications*. Chicago: American Library Association, 1971 (LTP Publication No. 17).

APPLICATIONS

INTRODUCTION

Two of the five applications in this chapter describe various aspects of retrospective microfilming—that is, the reprinting in microform of previously published material.

The ERIC piece, however, describes a use of microforms that began several decades ago when Xerox University Microfilms started placing doctoral dissertations on microfilm and which came into prominence in the 60's when the Atomic Energy Commission and the National Aeronautics and Space Administration began putting technical reports on microfiche.

The problem faced by these agencies was one of a great many reports for which the demand was highly limited. In the past such reports had been duplicated in small quantities and distributed on request until the supply was exhausted.

Microfilm had been considered and rejected because the length of the reports was such that only a few feet of film was required per report. This meant several reports on one reel or maintaining thousands of small segments of film in canisters. Either approach presented major problems when it came to making duplicate copies.

Microfiche solved the problem as most reports could be reproduced on one or two fiche and these could be easily duplicated, thus allowing for an on-demand system whereby a report is reproduced on fiche but no inventory is made. The master fiche (or a duplicate "working" master) is then stored. Whenever an order is received the master is retrieved and a duplicate made. With the advent of rapid reader-printers, a further step was possible—producing enlarged copy from the master microfiche. Since the masters can be stored indefinitely at minimal cost all titles placed in the system become permanently available—none need ever go out of print as the cost of making a duplicate, micro or enlarged, from a master placed in the system yesterday is the same as from one made from a master ten years old.

DEVELOPING A
NATIONAL FOREIGN NEWSPAPER
MICROFILMING PROGRAM

by John Y. Cole

In recent years, American research libraries have devoted an increasing amount of attention to the acquisition and microfilming of foreign newspapers. In addition to the Association of Research Libraries (ARL) Foreign Newspaper Microfilm Project, large-scale microfilming programs have developed at the Library of Congress and several other research institutions. In 1972, in accordance with the recommendations of the ARL Foreign Newspaper Microfilm Committee, the Library of Congress expanded its foreign newspaper activities and assumed responsibility for coordinating a national foreign newspaper microfilming program. The author reviews cooperative endeavors in foreign newspaper microfilming from 1938 to the present and discusses the current efforts of the Library of Congress toward the development of a national program.

Since World War II, the microfilming of foreign newspapers has been a subject of growing importance to American research libraries. Increased interest in international affairs and new area studies programs have made access to a comprehensive selection of foreign newspapers a necessity for scholars and government officials alike. Taking advantage of the convenience and permanency of newspapers in microfilm format and recognizing the cost-saving benefits of joint endeavors, research libraries have attempted to meet this need through a variety of cooperative foreign newspaper microfilming projects. The most successful single enterprise has been the Foreign Newspaper Microfilm Project sponsored by the Association of Research Libraries (ARL) since 1956. The project is administered for the ARL by the Center for Research Libraries in Chicago. By 1968, however, the number of foreign newspaper titles and separate microfilming projects had proliferated so rapidly that the ARL Foreign Newspaper Microfilm Committee, which oversees the ARL project, began seeking an expanded national approach to the problem. After a research study, the committee

Reprinted from *Library Resources and Technical Services*, 18: 5-17 (Winter 1974).

recommended a coordinated national effort to insure efficient and comprehensive coverage of foreign newspapers among research libraries. In accordance with the committee's recommendations, in 1972 the Library of Congress (LC) expanded its foreign newspaper activities and assumed responsibility for coordinating a national foreign newspaper microfilming program. The purpose of this article is twofold: (1) to outline the cooperative efforts in foreign newspaper microfilming between 1938 and the present that prepared the way for developing a national program, and (2) to describe the current efforts of the Library of Congress, and particularly those of the newly established office of coordinator of foreign newspaper microfilming, toward making that program a reality.

Foreign Newspaper Microfilming, 1938-1968

The first major cooperative project was established in 1938 when Harvard University received a grant from the Rockefeller Foundation for the "reproduction on microfilm of current files of foreign newspapers." Thirty-seven important titles were selected for microfilming and positive microfilm copies were offered to other libraries on a subscription basis. The price, which included the full cost of the positive microfilm and a pro rata share of the negative, depended on the number of subscribers. The newspapers filmed at Harvard were included in the earliest listing of newspapers being microfilmed in the United States, the "Preliminary Checklist of Newspapers on Microfilm" by George A. Schwegmann, chief of the Union Catalog Division of the Library of Congress.[1] The Harvard project proceeded satisfactorily during the World War II years, but it was recognized by all as only a limited step in meeting the needs of research libraries.

The total problem of "research materials on microfilm" was faced in a 20 December 1946 letter from Librarian of Congress Luther Evans to Paul North Rice, ARL executive secretary. Evans' suggestion for a nationally coordinated and cooperative plan for the "microfilming of extensive runs of library materials" had a great impact on newspaper microfilming. Among other proposals, Evans urged the establishment of a microfilming information clearinghouse; he also asked that an ARL committee be formed to assume responsibility for the "planning, distribution, publicity, standards, and pooling" of library resources for microfilming. As a result of Evans' letter and subsequent discussions, the ARL Committee on Microfilming Cooperation was formed.[2]

The committee, under the chairmanship of Vernon Tate of Massachusetts Institute of Technology, decided to limit its activities to newspapers "since the need appeared most urgent in this field." Attention was devoted immediately to the drafting of bibliographic and technical standards for microfilming, the establishment of an information center, and the compilation of a union list of newspapers already microfilmed. The Union

Catalog Division of the Library of Congress assumed responsibility for preparing the union list, which was published in 1948 as *Newspapers on Microfilm: A Union Check List*.[3] At the request of the committee, on 5 July 1949 the Library of Congress established a Microfilming Clearing House to serve as a central source of information about "extensive microfilming projects involving newspapers, serials, and manuscript collections either contemplated, underway, or completed at various institutions."

The committee concentrated on the preservation of nationally known domestic newspapers because it believed that, at least for the present, foreign newspapers received enough attention "through the efforts of Mr. Keyes Metcalf of Harvard University, the Pan American Union, and individual libraries." This focus on American newspapers was shared by the Cooperative Microfilm Projects Committee of the American Library Association (ALA), which included several librarians who also served on the ARL committee. The 1953 publication *Selected List of United States Newspapers Recommended for Preservation by the ALA Committee on Cooperative Microfilm Projects*, like *Newspapers on Microfilm*, was edited by the Union Catalog Division.[4] The preface to the *Selected List* contains a "Statement of Principles to Guide Large Scale Acquisition and Preservation of Library Materials on Microfilm," which is still of value. The preface urged that

> libraries concentrate funds for filming in copying original materials instead of investing cooperatively in positive film copies of materials for which negatives have already been made.

This was to be a guiding principle in the formulation of the ARL Foreign Newspaper Microfilm Project three years later. The second edition of *Newspapers on Microfilm* was issued as a companion volume to the *Selected List*.

After the publication of the *Selected List,* the interest of large research libraries began to shift back to the problem of foreign newspaper coverage. One reason was that the relatively new position of the United States as a world power required detailed knowledge of areas of the world that previously had been little known to Americans. The new emphasis also reflected a growing consensus that domestic newspapers could be left to local and state libraries which "should be responsible for building up files from their own geographic areas." Moreover, by virtue of their relative scarcity, foreign newspapers offered better opportunities for cooperative acquisition and microfilming activities.

In 1952 the Library of Congress, on behalf of the ARL Committee on National Needs, gathered holdings information about foreign newspapers from 120 American libraries for inclusion in a union list which would "serve as the basis for the planning of a cooperative acquisitions program in the field of current foreign newspapers." In the preface to the publication that resulted, *Postwar Foreign Newspapers,* the wish was expressed

that the list will focus the attention of librarians on the need for an adequate
national coverage of the foreign press, that it will stimulate a cooperative program
which will ensure such coverage, and that it will form the basis for a planned microfilming program which will best utilize the national resources available for this
purpose.[5]

The listing excluded Latin American newspapers because they were reported in the Pan American Union's *Union List of Latin American Newspapers in the United States,* also published in 1953.[6]

At the same time, possible changes in the Harvard foreign newspaper
project were being discussed. Interest in the Harvard project was increasing, as demonstrated by the acquisition of its microfilm by more than
forty institutions in 1953-54. Early in 1953 the program's administrators
began considering ways to make it "more economical to subscribers." One
possibility, discussed at length at an ARL meeting of 1 February 1953,
was the reshaping of the program into one in which subscribers contributed to a single fund to be used for the microfilming of a wider range of
newspapers than hitherto filmed; positive microfilm would be available for
free loan to subscribers but normally would not be furnished to institutions for retention. The idea of this type of a cooperative project met with
favor, and the possibility of using the successful Harvard experience as the
foundation for a new, national microfilming program was considered seriously. Two possible locations for such a national project were considered:
the Center for Research Libraries, then the Mid-West Interlibrary Center
(MILC), and the Library of Congress. However, Librarian of Congress
Evans felt that, because the Library of Congress was already the center of
many activities, it would be preferable to locate the project elsewhere.
Moreover, it was pointed out that the MILC had already developed a small-
scale cooperative pool of foreign and domestic newspapers, subscribing to
a number of titles from Harvard and acquiring additional ones from other
sources.

In 1954 ARL created a committee, chaired by Herman H. Fussler of the
University of Chicago, to explore and develop a national plan for cooperative library access to current foreign newspapers. Discussion centered on
the concept approved by the committee in earlier meetings, namely, "initiating a national pool of current foreign newspapers in microfilm form to
be available by loan to subscribing institutions." The plan devised by the
committee and approved by ARL provided for the acquisition of approximately 100 current foreign newspapers on microfilm beginning in January
of 1956. The newly formed ARL Foreign Newspaper Microfilm Project
would be administered for ARL by MILC, which seemed "to be the best
situated in the United States to make fast nation-wide loans and handle
the other necessary arrangements of the project." By paying an annual
subscription fee ranging from $150 to $500, participating institutions
could borrow positive microfilm of any title held by the project, which

would film some titles and purchase others from outside sources. Furthermore, positive film of titles microfilmed by the project would be available to the subscribers at cost. This form of cooperative arrangement, in the opinion of the committee, was advantageous for several reasons: it enabled libraries to avoid the high cost of individually microfilming needed titles, while giving those libraries access to a wider range of foreign newspapers; it permitted the microfilming of a greater number of titles, particularly from areas of the world "of unusual interest"; and finally, it utilized previous experience by recognizing that "many titles, while of clear strategic importance, were likely to be subjected to long periods of little or no use." A new ARL standing committee, the Foreign Newspaper Microfilm Committee, was established to administer the project, which began in January 1956 with forty-six institutions subscribing and a first year budget of $14,000.[7]

Many institutions helped the project's start. The Harvard program was absorbed, and the Harvard University library transferred a working capital fund from its original Rockefeller Foundation grant. Harvard also contributed approximately 640,000 feet of negative microfilm for the titles it had been filming since 1938, making positive prints available to subscribers at cost. The MILC newspaper pool was also integrated into the project. The Pan American Union donated 818 reels of negatives of Latin American newspapers for varying periods between 1938 and 1950. The 100 titles originally selected for acquisition were picked by a national committee of librarians, which in turn worked from the extensive list, *Current Foreign Newspapers Recommended for Cooperative Microfilming*, prepared by area specialists at the Library of Congress.[8] From the original 100 titles, the project grew with the result that by 1959 its fifty-four subscribers had access to 146 newspapers published in ninety countries.

It had become apparent, however, that 146 titles were not adequate to meet the needs of scholarship and research. New microfilming programs at other United States research institutions, particularly the Library of Congress, the Hoover Institution, the New York Public Library, and the University of Florida, attempted to meet these needs, as did several commercial micropublishers. The largest microfilming program for current foreign newspapers developed at the Library of Congress. In 1957 the library announced the availability of thirty-one vernacular titles in Oriental languages. The African Studies Association and the library began a cooperative microfilming project for fifteen current African newspapers in 1960. The next year Congress authorized the establishment, under Public Law 480, of a Library of Congress office in New Delhi, a development that soon made possible a large-scale microfilming program for current Indian newspapers. Finally, in 1963 the library announced that it had undertaken a comprehensive program to microfilm approximately 500 current foreign newspapers in lieu of binding. The library was careful to microfilm "in substantially all instances" only newspapers not available on microfilm from the ARL project or from other sources.

As area studies programs expanded, the interest of research libraries in foreign newspapers grew accordingly. Nor was interest confined to current newspapers. While the ARL project was limited to current titles, many other institutions began microfilming retrospective files of foreign newspapers. Once again, the most active program was at the Library of Congress. For example, as early as 1953 the library, with aid from the Rockefeller Foundation, produced *Russian, Ukrainian, and Belorussian Newspapers, 1917-1953; A Union List*, a publication intended to stimulate interest in the preservation of Russian newspapers through cooperative retrospective microfilming.[9] The Photoduplication Service soon undertook such a project for seven important Russian titles. The fourth edition of *Newspapers on Microfilm*, published in 1961, contained entries for 2,580 foreign newspapers published in 106 countries; the sixth edition in 1967 contained entries for 4,640 newspapers from 136 countries.

In 1968 the ARL Foreign Newspaper Microfilm Committee, chaired by John G. Lorenz of the Library of Congress, recognized this widespread interest in foreign newspapers as well as the rapid growth of seperate acquisition and microfilming programs when it expanded its scope beyond that of overseeing the ARL project to include the development of a truly national foreign newspaper microfilming program. The proposed undertaking was to include a minimum of 2,000 foreign newspaper titles and would utilize the resources of the ARL project, the Library of Congress, and other interested research institutions. In 1969, through a grant from the Council on Library Resources, the committee sponsored a feasibility study that resulted in a series of recommendations concerning the development of such a national program. The study, conducted by Norman J. Shaffer, now assistant chief for bibliographic services of the Photoduplication Service of the Library of Congress, was completed in 1970.

The Shaffer Report[10]

The object of the feasibility study was threefold: (1) to determine the breadth of coverage of foreign newspapers required to serve the needs of the scholarly community; (2) to identify institutions wishing to participate in a national foreign newspaper program by microfilming or having commercial firms microfilm newspapers for their collections; and (3) to make recommendations concerning the functions and organization of a proposed coordinating office for a national foreign newspaper microfilming program.

Adequacy of foreign newspaper coverage was gauged through examining the holdings reports accumulated at LC for the next edition of *Newspapers on Microfilm*, tabulating the results of a questionnaire sent to all members of ARL, and discussions with area and language specialists at LC. Although over 800 new foreign newspaper titles had been reported to

Newspapers on Microfilm since the publication of the 1967 edition, Shaffer found general agreement that even wider coverage, especially for Africa and Asia, was needed. For example, he discovered that more than a dozen United Nations members were not represented by a newspaper file on microfilm anywhere in the United States. As a first step in remedying this situation, he recommended the expansion of the number of titles made available through the ARL project. An appendix to the report listed 749 titles, representing 132 countries, specifically recommended by subject specialists for microfilming. The survey also identified forty-three research institutions in the United States with "a real and often enthusiastic interest" in a national microfilming program.

Shaffer found a definite need for the creation of a national coordinating office "to facilitate institutional cooperative filming or acquisitions and to facilitate accessibility through interlibrary loan and other means." He recommended that this office include among its major functions (1) coordinating the selection and microfilming of foreign newspapers, with priority given to current titles; (2) soliciting information from and about commercial sources of microfilm, both in the United States and abroad, to include keeping those sources aware of American scholarly needs and microfilming programs sponsored by research institutions; (3) serving as a central reference point for information about the acquisition and microfilming of foreign newspapers; and (4) publishing a newsletter that would feature announcements, "intention to microfilm" statements, and other information concerning foreign newspapers. The report also recommended the division of *Newspapers on Microfilm* into two separate publications, one listing domestic titles, the other foreign. The Library of Congress was suggested as the site for the new coordinating office because of its large foreign newspaper microfilming program, the location of *Newspapers on Microfilm* and its extensive files at the library, the staff of knowledgeable foreign area specialists, the institution's widespread network of overseas offices and contacts, and because the library already was performing similar national services.

Coordinating a National Program

As previously mentioned, the Shaffer report, endorsed by the ARL Foreign Newspaper Microfilm Committee, led directly to the expansion of LC's foreign newspaper activities; included was the establishment in 1972 of the position of coordinator of foreign newspaper microfilming, a post presently held by the author. The Shaffer report also clearly indicated why a centralized, national approach to foreign newspaper microfilming is necessary: the multiplicity of microfilming programs, combined with increased interest in acquiring foreign newspapers, frequently results in confusion among research libraries and inefficiencies in the production, distribution, and utilization of foreign newspapers on microfilm. There are six large-scale foreign newspaper microfilming programs sponsored by the research community: the ARL project and programs supported by the Library of Congress, the Hoover Institution, Cornell University, the University of Florida, and the University of California at Berkeley. While duplication of microfilming efforts among these major programs appears to be minimal, it is a problem among other libraries which microfilm titles on a more limited scale. In addition, there exist approximately a dozen commercial producers of foreign newspapers on microfilm in the United States and nearly thirty foreign producers and distributors.

Certain steps can be taken immediately to reduce duplication. The Library of Congress, with the cooperation of other institutions, recently has made progress in furnishing updated holdings data about foreign newspapers on microfilm and current information about microfilming programs and technical standards in newspaper microfilming. After careful study, both the ARL project and the Library of Congress have increased the number of current titles being microfilmed. Other steps, however, can only be taken more slowly, particularly those that concern relations between research institutions and commercial micropublishers, the microfilming of long retrospective files of important titles, and the general improvement of researcher access to foreign newspapers on microfilm. Aside from the shortage of funds available for microfilming projects, the major problems in foreign newspaper microfilming appear to have resulted from a lack of current and accurate information and a lack of coordination among various acquisitions and microfilming endeavors. The efficient utilization of foreign newspapers on microfilm as a national research resource does not require a major revision or redistribution of existing programs. What is needed is more effective coordination, increased communication, and, above all, a sense of direction. The Library of Congress is committed to the development of an efficient and comprehensive national microfilming program. Recent efforts along these lines are detailed in the remainder of this paper.

Bibliographic Control. Since 1948 *Newspapers on Microfilm* has been the basic research tool for microfilmed newspapers. Including both bibliographic data and holdings information for each title, it serves, in effect, as a national bibliography of newspapers, and as such it is the key element in the development of a national microfilming program.

Because the necessary bibliographic apparatus has not yet been developed in many areas of the world, foreign newspapers present a more difficult bibliographic problem than newspapers published in the United States. Moreover, while there is less over-all demand for information about foreign newspapers, that demand is usually of a different and more specialized nature. These considerations and the recommendations of the Shaffer report persuaded the Library of Congress to separate *Newspapers on Microfilm* into two volumes, one for newspapers published in the United States, the other for foreign titles. The new format provides the library with greater flexibility in issuing supplements or later editions, and enables the purchaser to select the volume or volumes suited to his needs. The title has been changed to *Newspapers in Microform*, recognizing the increased use of microfiche and micro-opaque techniques in the microphotographic reproduction of newspapers. The volume *Newspapers in Microform: United States, 1948-1972* contains information about 34,289 titles as reported by 843 libraries and 48 commercial firms, and the volume *Newspapers in Microform: Foreign Countries, 1948-1972* contains information about 8,620 foreign newspaper titles as reported by 524 libraries and 40 commercial firms. [11,12] (Holdings reports for newspapers in microform should be addressed to: Library of Congress, Catalog Publication Division, Editor, *Newspapers in Microform*, Washington, DC 20540. Printed form cards and postage-free, preaddressed labels are available upon request.)

The Need for Current Information. In addition to the expansion and more frequent updating of *Newspapers in Microform*, the library, through the office of coordinator of foreign newspaper microfilming, has begun publishing *Foreign Newspaper Report*.[13] This newsletter, issued three times a year, provides research institutions and commercial publishers with current information about various foreign newspaper acquisition and microfilming programs, announcements of newly available titles and cooperative microfilming projects, information about technical standards in newspaper microfilming, and other news concerning foreign newspapers (e.g., newspapers that have changed titles or ceased publication). It also carries "intention to microfilm" statements. The *Report* is now distributed to more than 800 libraries, research institutions, area studies associations, and commercial micropublishers throughout the world.

Foreign Newspaper Report is a crucial part of the clearinghouse function of the office of foreign newspaper microfilming coordinator. The office also provides information and advice about specific titles or microfilming projects and related matters. (Correspondence should be directed to: Library of Congress, Reference Department, Coordinator, Foreign Newspaper Microfilming, Washington, DC 20540.)

Technical and Archival Standards. As the number of research institutions and commercial firms producing newspapers on microfilm increases, the need for enforcement of uniform, high-quality technical standards becomes even more important than before. The office of foreign newspaper microfilming coordinator takes an active interest in standards, particularly in encouraging compliance with specifications considered acceptable by the research community; information about technical standards is available from the office. In addition, in 1972 the library published *Specifications for the Microfilming of Newspapers in the Library of Congress*.[14] This publication has eight major sections: preparation of the files, technical guide, filming procedures, processing the exposed film, inspection of the film, intermediate copies, reference use copies (which includes the criteria employed in evaluating microfilms being considered for addition to the library's collections), and storage. It also includes a glossary of thirty-one terms and a selected list of references.

Commercial Publishers. Many librarians are reluctant to purchase microfilm from commercial micropublishers. There are two principal reasons for this hesitation: (1) the technical quality of the microfilm may not be satisfactory, and (2) librarians prefer to encourage microfilming by a library or research institution. Since 1970 the problem has become more severe as several commercial firms, particularly the Microfilming Corporation of America (MCA), have been obtaining exclusive microfilming and distribution rights to foreign newspapers previously microfilmed by research institutions. Further complications recently have arisen as MCA, after announcing the availability of certain titles, has decided not to microfilm them, and the institutions previously microfilming them have, after delays of from one to three years, resumed the filming. This kind of unfortunate situation is of prime interest to the office of foreign newspaper microfilming coordinator. One obvious need is for better communication between research institutions and commercial micropublishers, a need now being met at least in part by *Foreign Newspaper Report.* Libraries must be kept up-to-date on the offerings and the activities of commercial micropublishers, who in turn should be kept informed about the scholarly needs of the research community and the cooperative efforts already taking place among research libraries to satisfy those needs.

Extending Current Coverage. Using the data gathered during the Shaffer study as a base, the coordinating office is maintaining a detailed list of foreign newspapers recommended for microfilming by area specialists and a list of important titles apparently not now in the collections of research libraries. The number of current foreign newspapers being microfilmed has been increased substantially during the past two years, however, and most of the newly added titles are from Africa and Asia.

As agreed in a special vote of the membership in 1972, the ARL project is adding approximately 20 titles to its holdings. The new titles were selected by the coordinator of foreign newspaper microfilming and the ARL project staff and approved by the Foreign Newspaper Microfilm Committee in January 1973. This addition brings the total number of important current foreign newspapers available to ARL project subscribers on loan to 195. Subscribers may also purchase positive microfilm of titles filmed by the project at cost; nonsubscribers may buy the same titles for cost plus one-third of the cost of the negative. There are now eighty institutions subscribing to the ARL project. (Membership information may be obtained from: Foreign Newspaper Microfilm Project, The Center for Research Libraries, 5721 Cottage Grove Ave., Chicago, IL 60637.)

The Library of Congress receives and permanently retains 950 current foreign newspapers on microfilm. Approximately 65 percent of these titles are microfilmed at the library; the remainder are acquired from other research institutions and commercial sources. The library does not microfilm any titles microfilmed by the ARL project. The current foreign newspapers in the library's collections are listed in *Newspapers Currently Received in the Library of Congress*.[15] Positive microfilm copies of most of the titles filmed by the library may also be purchased (information is available from: Library of Congress, Photoduplication Service Dept. C, Washington, DC 20540).

Expansion of Retrospective Coverage. Thus far, the greatest emphasis in foreign newspaper microfilming has been on getting microfilming of current titles underway. Retrospective files, however, cannot be ignored, and eventually a coordinated effort in the microfilming of early files of foreign newspapers must be part of the national program. Furthermore, the deteriorating condition of many early newspaper files now in the possession of research libraries and newspaper publishers lends some urgency to this gigantic undertaking. Currently, the Library of Congress supports the largest retrospective preservation-microfilming program for foreign titles; the ARL project also plans to begin acquiring and microfilming earlier runs of titles that it makes available. Many foreign newspaper publishers sell microfilm copies of earlier issues of their newspapers and additional microfilming of retrospective files takes place at several universities that have strong area studies programs. Finally, additional titles are being acquired or microfilmed for area studies consortia such as the Cooperative Africana Microform Project, the South Asia Microform Project, and the Southeast Asia Microform Project. Information concerning titles filmed by these projects will be carried in *Foreign Newspaper Report*.

A need also exists for additional union lists of retrospective foreign newspaper holdings. Compilations such as *Latin American Newspapers in United States Libraries: A Union List* not only are valuable bibliographic and reference tools but they also provide a means of locating files to be microfilmed.[16]

Improved Access and the Sharing of Resources. Efficient reader access to a greater number of foreign newspapers is, of course, a major goal of the national foreign newspaper microfilming program. To a considerable degree, improved access depends on factors previously mentioned, such an enhanced bibliographic control, widespread dissemination of current information about microfilming activities, achievement of suitable technical quality in microfilming, and the expansion of both current and retrospective coverage. In addition, a compilation of directioned, such as enhanced bibliographic control, widespread dissemination and that project is being pursued as time permits. A more important consideration relates to interlibrary loan, a principal means of access to these items. Loan policies for newspapers on microfilm are not uniform among research libraries, and information about these policies frequently is not widely known. This is especially true for foreign libraries and research institutions. Information is also needed on the use of foreign newspapers.

Increased sharing of foreign newspapers on microfilm must be a fundamental goal of the national program. As recognized in the deliberations during the 1950s that led to the establishment of the ARL project, the most efficient means of making a greater number of titles available is to concentrate resources on the microfilming of titles never before filmed, rather than on producing duplicate positive copies for a number of institutions. A few positive copies, shared as needed through interlibrary loan or a similar system, is, of course, the ideal. To be sure, many libraries, not content with the knowledge that they have access to newspapers on microfilm, prefer to purchase positive copies for their collections. While questionable, the desire to purchase is also understandable. The efficient sharing of newspapers on microfilm is not possible without improvements in the bibliographic apparatus that will make the identification and location of individual titles relatively easy, or without more convenient physical access to those titles. However, while the principle of local self-sufficiency in foreign newspaper microfilm collections can never be eliminated wholly, much can be done to minimize it. In this sense, foreign newspapers on microfilm present research libraries with a unique opportunity for nationally planned resource development.

References

1. George A. Schwegmann, "Preliminary Checklist of Newspapers on Microfilm," *Journal of Documentary Reproduction* 4: 122-34 (June 1941).

2. Association of Research Libraries, *Minutes of the Meeting* 11th-76th (June 1938-May 1971) constitute the major source for the historical sections of this article.

3. U.S. Library of Congress, *Newspapers on Microfilm* [1st] ed.–(Washington, D.C.: Library of Congress, 1948-   ).

4. U.S. Library of Congress. Union Catalog Division, *Selected List of United States Newspapers Recommended for Preservation by the ALA Committee on Cooperative Microfilm Projects* (Washington, D.C.: Library of Congress, 1953), 92p.

5. U.S. Library of Congress, Serial Division, *Postwar Foreign Newspapers: A Union List* (Washington, D.C.: Library of Congress, 1953). p. i.

6. Arthur Eric Grapp, comp., *Union List of Latin American Newspapers in Libraries in the United States* (Pan American Union. Columbus Memorial Library, Bibliographic Series, no. 39 [Washington D.C.: Dept. of Cultural Affairs, Pan American Union 1953]), 235p.

7. Herman H. Fussler, "A New Pattern for Library Cooperation," *Library Journal* 81: 126-33 (15 Jan. 1956) provides a full description of the origins of the ARL Foreign Newspaper Microfilm Project.

8. Association of Research Libraries. Committee on Cooperative Access to Newspapers and Other Serials, *Current Foreign Newspapers Recommended for Cooperative Microfilming: A Preliminary List* (Washington, D.C.: Library of Congress, 1954), 63p.

9. U.S. Library of Congress. Slavic and Central European Division, *Russian, Ukrainian, and Belorussian Newspapers, 1917-1953; A Union List*, compiled by Paul L. Horecky (Washington, D.C.: 1953), 218p. An expansion of a working paper issued by the division in 1952 under title: *Preliminary Checklist of Russian, Ukrainian, and Belorussian Newspapers Published since January 1, 1917, within the Present Boundaries of the U.S.S.R. and Preserved in United States Libraries.*

10. Norman J. Shaffer, "Study to Develop Recommendations for a National Foreign Newspaper Microfilm Program," 244p. Presented at 30 June 1970 meeting of Foreign Newspaper Microfilm

Committee, Association of Research Libraries. Summary in U.S. Library of Congress, *Foreign Newspaper Report* (1973) 1: 3-5.

11. U.S. Library of Congress. Catalog Publication Division, *Newspaper in Microform: United States, 1948-1972* (Washington, D.C.: Library of Congress, 1973), 1056p. Available for $30 from: Card Division, Library of Congress, Navy Yard Annex, Washington, DC 20541.

12. U.S. Library of Congress. Catalog Publication Division, *Newspapers in Microform: Foreign Countries, 1948-1972* (Washington, D.C.: Library of Congress, 1973), 269p. Available for $10 from: Card Division, Library of Congress, Navy Yard Annex, Washington, DC 20541.

13. U.S. Library of Congress. *Foreign Newspaper Report, 1973-* (Washington, D.C.). Copies are available to research institutions and libraries at no charge from: Library of Congress, Central Services Division, Washington, DC 20540. With 1974, no. 1 the title changed to *Foreign Newspaper and Gazette Report.*

14. U.S. Library of Congress. Photoduplication Service, *Specifications for the Microfilming of Newspapers in the Library of Congress* (Washington, D.C.: Library of Congress, 1972), 17p. 1964 edition by S. R. Salmon published under title: *Specifications for Library of Congress Microfilming.* 1972 edition (LC 1.6/4: N47) available for $.30 from: Superintendent of Documents, U.S. Government Printing Office, Washington, DC 20402.

15. U.S. Library of Congress. Serial Division, *Newspapers Currently Received & Permanently Retained in the Library of Congress, 1968-* (Washington, DC: for sale by the Supt. of Docs., U.S. Govt. Print. Off.) Supersedes the division's *Newspapers Currently Received,* last issued in 1950. 1972 volume (LC 6.7: 972) available for $.35 from: Superintendent of Documents, U.S. Government Printing Office, Washington, DC 20402.

16. *Latin American Newspapers in United States Libraries; A Union List,* compiled in the Serial Division, Library of Congress, by Steven M. Charno (Conference on Latin American History, Publication, no. 2 [Austin: Published for the Conference on Latin American History by the Univ. of Texas Pr., 1969]), 619p.

ERIC/EDUCATIONAL RESOURCES INFORMATION CENTER

ERIC, a part of the National Institute of Education, stands for Educational Resources Information Center. ERIC was originally conceived in the U.S. Office of Education in the mid-1960s as a system for providing ready access to educational literature. At the time ERIC was first discussed, the literature was uncontrolled. Research reports, submitted to OE by their contractors and grantees, received an initial scattered distribution and then disappeared. Reports from other sources generally remained equally inaccessible. ERIC was intended to correct this chaotic situation and to provide a foundation for subsequent information analysis activities and attempts to spread the use of current developments.

Because of the decentralized nature of American education, education's

Excerpted from various leaflets issued by ERIC, National Institute of Education, Washington, D.C.

many specializations, and the existence of numerous professional organizations, ERIC's designers opted for a network of organizations rather than a single monolithic information center located in Washington. ERIC was conceived, therefore, as a network of "clearinghouses" located across the country in "host" organizations that were already naturally strong in the field of education in which they would operate.

Contracts with clearinghouses originally gave them responsibility for acquiring and selecting all documents in their area and for "processing" these documents. "Processing" includes the familiar surrogation activities of cataloging, indexing, and abstracting. This scheme has worked out very well. Virtually all observers of ERIC have concluded over time that the network of clearinghouses does a better job of ferreting out the current literature of education than one single information center in Washington could ever do. With their specialized subject expertise, clearinghouse staff are well qualified to manage ERIC document selection functions. Decentralization has paid off as well for information analysis and user service activities However, decentralization was not the complete answer. In order order to generate products that included the output of all network components, information gathered by the clearinghouses had to be assembled at one central place. ERIC's final design, therefore, included decentralized clearinghouse operations integrated around a central computerized facility which serves as a switching center for the network. The data recorded by each of the clearinghouses is sent to the facility to form a central data base from which publications and indexes are produced. Bibliographic control of this data is achieved principally by the monthly abstract journal, *Research in Education*, and distribution of duplicate copies on microfiche and hard copy print-out through the ERIC Document Reproduction Service.

Similar arrangements are used to supply the public with copies of reports added to the system. A basic decision for ERIC was to make documents available from a central source instead of just informing users that a given document existed. It was, therefore, necessary to provide a document reproduction service where any non-copyrighted document announced could be obtained. (When permission is obtained, copyrighted materials are also reproduced.) In other words, ERIC was developed as a complete document announcement and retrieval service.

Both of these centralized services had entrepreneurial aspects. The Government obviously could not afford to subsidize every user's document needs. The document reproduction effort had to become self-supporting or it would become too expensive within Federal budgets. Therefore, users had to pay for reports they wanted. In the same way, dissemination of the data base is not subsidized by the taxpayer; persons wanting ERIC magnetic tapes are required to meet order processing, tape, and duplication costs. The Federal Government limits its investment in both areas by generating a fundamental data base and then permitting the private sector to market it at prices as advantageous to the public as possible.

In support of this strategy, and also because central facility operations depended on use of advanced technologies (computerized photocomposition and microreprographic technology), these functions were located in the commercial sector.

ERIC, therefore, emerges as a network with four levels. The first or Governmental level is represented by NIE and Central ERIC (the funder, policy setter, and monitor). The second or non-profit level is made up of 16 Clearinghouses located at universities or professional societies. The third or commercial level consists of the centralized facilities for managing the data base, putting out published products, making microfiche, and reproducing documents. Fourth and last are the users who receive the benefits of these activities.

Research in Education (RIE), available from the Superintendent of Documents, is a monthly abstract journal made up of resumes of education-related documents, and indexes to these resumes. RIE covers the broad field of education in all its aspects, announcing timely report literature and recently completed research results to make possible the early identification and acquisition of documents of interest to the educational community.

The resume section displays announcements of documents which have been cataloged, identified by an accession number (e.g., ED-123456), and indexed by subject terms from the ERIC *Thesaurus*; an abstract of about 200 words is also included for each of the approximately 1,200 documents in each issue. There is an indication in each resume of the availability of the document itself. In most instances, the document will be available from the ERIC Document Reproduction Service (EDRS), in microfiche (MF) and/or Hard Copy (HC). Where listed as "not available from EDRS," the alternative source from which it can be obtained is given.

The index sections provide subject, personal author, and institution (source) name access to the resumes; the indexes are also issued in semi-annual and annual cumulations, the latter superseding all prior indexes for that year.

Research in Education is the principal mechanism the ERIC network uses to achieve bibliographic control over the diverse documents found in the field of education, and to announce them. It concerns itself primarily with the unpublished, limited distribution, or, as it is sometimes called, the "fugitive" type of literature, e.g., technical and research reports, speeches and "papers presented at," program descriptions, teacher guides, statistical compilations, curriculum materials, etc. (Journal literature is in turn covered by *Current Index to Journals in Education* (CIJE), a companion publication to RIE).

The documents announced in RIE are collected by the various ERIC Clearinghouses, screened and selected for quality and legibility, cataloged, indexed, abstracted, and transmitted to the central ERIC Processing & Reference Facility for inclusion in the computerized data base. The time from final selection to announcement in RIE varies between two and three months.

Research in Education (RIE) is directed toward the entire educational community (e.g., school administrators, teachers and supervisors, students, school board members, educational researchers, commercial and industrial organizations, and the public); this is well evidenced by the great variability in the types and sources of documents processed for inclusion in the journal.

EDRS (ERIC Document Reproduction Service) is the document supply and distribution component of the ERIC network. All non-copyrighted documents (and any others for which reproduction permission has been obtained) announced in *Research in Education*, are forwarded to EDRS, where they are microfilmed and converted into microfiche (4" × 6" flat sheets of microfilm) according to Federal and National standards.

Interested users may obtain copies of ERIC documents from EDRS in either microfiche (at 24X reduction) or paper copy form (at 100% original size). Orders are accepted on either an on-demand or subscription basis. Subscribers may order the entire microfiche collection (monthly this amounts to about 950 titles contained on about 1400 microfiche) or subsets of the entire collection (such as all the titles input by a particular Clearinghouse). There are currently over 500 organizations that subscribe to the entire ERIC collection on a continuing basis. These are made up of Federal agencies, universities and colleges, state and local education agencies, school systems, professional associations, nonprofit groups, etc. There are over thirty subscriptions in foreign countries. Individual users consist of teachers, faculty, students, researchers, planners, administrators, counselors, therapists, and numerous other members of the educational community.

Each document announced in *Research in Education* carries with it its EDRS price (or alternate source of availability). Individual on-demand microfiche are sold at a standard price. Individual on-demand paper copies are sold on a graduated scale dependent on size. Subscription microfiche are sold at substantially less than the individual on-demand price in order to encourage subscriptions.

Announcement and distribution are coordinated so that microfiche subscribers will normally have on hand the complete month's microfiche at the time the abstract journal arrives. In this way, whenever an interesting item is detected in the journal, the user may immediately pull the item from the microfiche file and examine it without delay using a microfiche reader. The added convenience of instant feedback without having to wait for an order to be processed is another reason why prolific users tend to prefer subscriptions to on-demand procedures.

In summary, EDRS constitutes a permanent document archive for the literature of education. Research results need no longer be unobtainable after receiving their initial distribution or going rapidly out-of-print.

They need only be submitted to the ERIC system to be permanently available for future generations of practitioners and other educators.

USE OF MICROFILM IN AN
INDUSTRIAL RESEARCH LIBRARY

by Virginia L. Duncan and Frances E. Parsons

With the introduction of Chemical Abstracts *on 16mm film and the
availability of high speed reader-printers, du Pont's Lavoisier Library in
cooperation with a commercial microfilm firm, initiated a program to
microfilm basic scientific periodical sets in chemistry, physics and biology. Library user and staff reaction to the microfilm program, with
special emphasis on* Biological Abstracts, *is discussed. A brief description of space requirements for films, reader-printers and storage of
supplies is also included.*

Lavoisier Library is one of 30 libraries in the du Pont Company, and is
located at the Experimental Station, which is the major research center
for the company. The library's collection reflects all fields of the company's interests but is particularly strong in chemistry, physics, engineering and biology. There are more than 65,000 bound volumes of periodicals and books, and extensive collections of pamphlets, technical
trade literature, and government reports and documents. About 1,500
periodicals are received regularly. One copy of all important titles is
retained in the library for reference while multiple copies of about
600 journals are available for automatic circulation throughout the Experimental Station area with assistance from the IBM 360/20 computer.
Our periodical subscription program is also computer based.

Lavoisier Library has a staff of 28 people, including professionally
trained librarians and catalogers, assistants, and clerical personnel.

The library serves primarily some 1,400 technical people at the Experimental Station and to a limited extent the laboratories and plants at
other locations. The library is open twenty-four hours a day, seven days
a week. The services offered are those common to many research libraries

Reprinted from *Special Libraries*, 61: 288-90 (June 1970) by permission of the publisher. Copyright © 1970 by the Special Libraries Association.

including preparation of bibliographies and literature searches, purchase of all literature (except patents), operation of a translation service, and inter-library loan service. The library also maintains and operates a number of departmental reading rooms in the Experimental Station area. We issue two monthly bulletins, *Additions to the Library* and *Calendar of Scientific Meetings*.

Our 16mm microfilm program was begun when we acquired *Chemical Abstracts* on 16mm microfilm in September 1966. Because no other scientific journals were available in that form at the time, we enlisted the assistance of a commercial microfilm organization.

Test films were made of some basic titles in chemistry, physics, and biology. The results were very gratifying. As a result we added the follow-ing to our collection: *Annalen der Chemie* (Liebig's); *Chemische Berichte; Comptes rendus, Académie des sciences; Angewandte Chemie, Zeitschrift für anorganische und allgemeine Chemie; Biochemische Zeitschrift;* and *Zeitschrift für Physik.* These titles were filmed for the period open to public domain (through 1940); the remainder of our holdings are in hard copy. Though originally filmed for us, these titles are now commercially available from our supplier.

The American Chemical Society publications leased on 16mm film (through 1969) include *Analytical Chemistry, Chemical and Engineering News, Journal of the American Chemical Society,* and *Industrial and Engi-neering Chemistry.* The last five years of these titles are retained in hard copy also. The five-year period was chosen arbitrarily and will be adjusted as users' needs dictate.

Biological Abstracts was added in January 1969.

Four of our five reader-printers are in the Reading Room, and the fifth is on the third of our four stack levels. Having the reader-printers in the Reading Room is not a satisfactory arrangement because the machines are very noisy, especially when all four are being used at once. In addition, two of the machines in the Reading Room were returned to the factory for a modification which has reduced the time required to make a print. An adapter kit—which increased the speed of the print cycle—was installed in each machine. As a result, there has been an increase in the frequency of noise generated by the printers. To minimize the noise problem in the Reading Room, which has high ceilings and metal shelving, we have both an acoustical ceiling and deep pile nylon carpeting as well as heavy draper-ies at all the windows. Nevertheless, the four reader-printers still generate enough noise to bring complaints from our patrons. We have no separate room where these machines can be located. We are looking into the possi-bility of noise reducers.

The reader-printers receive regular routine maintenance from a member of the library staff. All solutions are flushed out at least once a day and minor adjustments made as necessary. In addition, the equipment manu-facturers provide very prompt and excellent service.

To give some idea of costs, here are estimates based on our 1968 statistics. The paper costs approximately $25/300 copies, or $0.08/copy. Developer solutions cost about $0.01/copy for a total of $0.09/copy. In addition, machine rentals average $100/month/machine.

With five reader-printers, the storage space for supplies of paper and developing solutions becomes appreciable.

The film cartridges are shelved in the stacks using a wooden strip approximately 5"D × 35½"W on the back of each shelf. The strip keeps the cartridges in a straight line at the front of the shelf. The bound volumes (1940+) of each title are shelved along with the microfilm.

Table 1. Storage Capacity: Bound Volumes vs. Microfilm

| Title | Bound Volumes | | Microfilm | |
	No. Shelves	Linear Ft.	No. Shelves	Linear Ft.
Biological Abstracts (without indexes) v. 1-49 (1926-68) 118 cartridges	11	33	3+	10½
Chemical Abstracts (including semi-annual indexes but not cumulatives) v. 1-69 (1907-68) 165 cartridges	30	90	4+	14
American Chemical Society Journal v. 1-90 (1879-1968) 123 cartridges	15+	46	3+	11

In general, microfilm has been well received by both library patrons and staff. When we acquired *Chemical Abstracts* on microfilm, we put the film and reader-printer in the Reading Room for maximum exposure. We did not remove any of our four bound sets of *Chemical Abstracts*. Nobody was forced to use the microfilm. The easy-to-use cartridge machine, quick access to individual abstracts, and high-quality photocopies helped make the selling job easier.

Some of the disadvantages are that all film is not always easy to read;

and it can be tiring to the eyes, particularly if many references are to be checked at one time. Film increases the time needed to answer reference questions if no copy is needed. Reader-printers may be temporarily inoperative because of film jams or because the printer runs out of paper and/or developing solution. Checking in the cartridges on receipt takes more time than checking in bound volumes and is more tedious. Each reel needs to be run through the machine and rewound to adjust the tension on the film. Spot checking of each reel for coding (on film) and print-outs is needed. Labels and coding on cartridges should be spot checked. This is more of a problem at present when so many sets are being acquired than it will be later when only one or two reels/year/title will be added.

We were asked to place particular emphasis on *Biological Abstracts* on microfilm when we were invited to prepare this paper for presentation at the 1969 SLA Conference. The microfilm edition became available in November 1968, and—as indicated earlier—we added it to our collection in January 1969. Since this has been such a short time, we do not have as much user reaction to report as we would like. However, we can list the following observations.

Having an abstract journal such as *Biological Abstracts* on film presents certain advantages and adds something of a new dimension to preparation of bibliographies and literature searches. For example, a client requests a list of all papers by a given author or all references on a certain subject for the last ten years. The appropriate indexes are searched and references listed, possibly several hundred. The searcher can then locate the appropriate cartridges of film and make photocopies of each abstract, or request that the copies be made for him by a library clerk. For numerical sequencing, to expedite copying, we use a 360/20 program.

With regard to the film itself, reduction appears to be about 22X. Spot checks were made for density on a few frames. The density of one title page was 2.37 and the density of another was 2.49. Density on a page of abstracts was 1.96 (films can have a density from 0.0 to 3.0). The generally accepted range for microfilm is 0.9—1.1 and the higher the density the greater the loss in resolution; 1.96 is high, yet the resolution is very good. Reader-printer copies from *Biological Abstracts* have very good quality.

On further inspection of the film, one notes frames around each page and "blips" at the bottom of each page. Double "blips" appear at irregular intervals of three to ten or more pages. The "blips" are useless as coding devices because they can not be seen when the film is run through the machine even at a reasonably low speed. Both the "blips" and the frames use up very valuable film space. One one specific frame in Abstract No. 71719 (v. 46) the name of the journal appears but the remainder of the reference is omitted. The margin was cut so close that the last line of print was lost. This is the only frame on which we have observed this defect however.

It has been suggested that reduction ratio be recorded on the cartridges, so the user will know which of three lenses to use (18X, 20X, or 23X).

In summary, we feel that good quality, high resolution 16mm microfilm of the scientific literature is a very acceptable substitute for the bound sets. The film is certainly less expensive than adding a new wing to the library building! We expect that about 50% of our periodical collection will be converted to 16mm microfilm and we can continue to live in the present building for at least the next five years.

MICROFICHE AS A MEANS OF PROVIDING STUDENTS WITH LITERATURE

by John Willemse

Introduction

Ever since the Library of the University of South Africa started investigating the possibility of providing students with their literature in microfiche form, it has received enquiries regularly from all over the world. The reason for this is, firstly, that this approach is unique because it introduces microfilm as a medium of everyday use in the study programme, instead of it being only a last resort for very infrequently used publications. Secondly, the Unisa project concerns itself with a problem which is common to most universities—the provision of books recommended for certain assignments and required by a great many students at the same time.

Unisa's special method of teletuition—mostly by correspondence— which provides roughly 30,000 people from all walks of life and living all over South Africa with the opportunity of an undergraduate or a more advanced university education, makes this problem more acute, as the process of sending books to students by post is time consuming. Moreover, possibly as much as 95% of the books are foreign publications. If, for a number of reasons, these are not ordered months in advance or not in sufficient quantities, students may be seriously hampered in their studies.

Other efforts having failed, the Unisa Library decided to try microfiche

Reprinted from the *NRCd Bulletin*, 6: 15-17 (Autumn 1973) by permission of the publisher and author.

as a solution because it has the important characteristic that an unlimited number of copies can be produced at any time and at a very low cost once the publication is available on film.

A research grant by the University led to a pilot project in 1971 with some 27 students enrolled for the third-year course on Library Science. The object was to obtain more information on three possible problem areas: the reaction of students to this method, the willingness of publishers to co-operate, and lastly the possibility of obtaining a suitable, low cost microfiche reading apparatus both acceptable to and within the financial means of the students.

Although the first results were extremely favourable, the test had so many limitations, and the general implementation of the method such serious implications, that the University agreed to invest in another 300 readers in order to extend the project to include all Library Science students.

The Second Phase

During 1972 the enrollment for the courses intended for inclusion in the second phase of the experiment showed an increase of 37.5% (from 302 to 415) over the previous year, compared to an increase of 14% for the University as a whole. This highlights the problem of estimating the correct number of copies of a book required. This occurrence, which would normally have resulted in an inadequate supply of recommended books, now led to an inadequate number of readers being available. It is therefore a prerequisite for the successful implementation of the microfiche project that sufficient quantities of microfiche readers be provided at short notice in case of such unexpected increases in the number of students. Because the Library was fortunate in having sufficient quantities of the books in stock, it was accordingly decided to exclude from the project the first year students as well as students living outside South Africa's borders.

Unfortunately the analysis of all the results of the 1972 project were not finalised at the date of writing this paper. From the information available it can, however, be concluded that the results are basically as favourable as those of the previous year. At the same time further problem areas have been indicated for which solutions will still have to be found.

A total of 333 students were automatically provided with microfiche readers after registration, together with lists of the books available on film. According to the Library's records 25.8% (86) of these students did not request any microfiches. According to the replies to a questionnaire, which was completed by 202 students taking part in the project, 13.8% (28) of those returning the questionnaires indicated that no request for fiches had been made. This is rather a large deviation from the Library's records, which may indicate some bias in the respondents. The following results based on the returned questionnaires should therefore be treated with some care.

Unfortunately 13 of the 28 students who did not request any micro-fiches did not specify any reasons. Eight students indicated that they had cancelled their studies or changed to another course, while six others mentioned the fact that they had access to other libraries. The latter is not surprising since many of the Library Science students are, in fact, working in libraries. Only in one case was the lack of adequate electrical current mentioned as a reason.

According to the questionnaire a further 35 students or 17% of the total 202 respondents stated that no actual use was made of the fiches received. In 15 cases cancellation of studies in Library Science was again the main reasons, while two students mentioned electricity problems, two found microfiche not acceptable and two gave eye strain as the reason. The other 14 students did not specify their reasons. Compared to the 1971 project when 92.1% requested microfiches, the 74.2% of 1972, although appreciably less, is still much higher than the average use made of the Library.

In total, 247 students were supplied with 3,476 books on microfiche, giving an average of 14.1 books per student—again much less than the 25 per student for 1971. This compares favourably with the average of 8 books issued per student, particularly if it is remembered that permission was received to include only 70.7% of the recommended books in the microfiche project. Furthermore, according to the questionnaire 16.8% of the students were enrolled for other courses than Library Science for which publications were only available in book form. Although further analysis is required, the available facts point strongly towards an increase in the use made of the Library with microfiche in comparison with the use made of ordinary books. The financial implications for the Library still have to be carefully computed.

Another point requiring further analysis is the use made of the various titles available on microfiche. Of the 182 titles available, an average of 19.2 copies per title were made, varying from two titles for which no copies were made, to one title which required 75 copies.

The Reaction of Publishers

There was no notable difference in the reaction of publishers compared to the findings for 1971, when 77 publishers were approached in respect of 177 books. Approval for 124 books (72.9%) was received, involving 68.8% of the publishers, while only eight publishers (10.4%) refused permission for a total of 25 books (14.7%) and 16 publishers (20.8%) did not respond in time. The 1972 project involved the use of 266 recommended books from 86 publishers and resulted in permission for 188 titles (70.6%) from

65 publishers (75.6%). Of the latter, four refused permission for some of the titles. Amongst these were the British and American Library Associations, both of whom had a great many publications intended for inclusion in the project. It is indeed interesting to note that these four publishers gave permission for 32 titles and refused permission for another 32 with a final decision on two titles being outstanding until it was too late for them to be included in the project. A further 12 publishers with 32 publications failed to react in time or at all, with the result that these titles also had to be excluded from the project. Negative answers were received from only nine publishers (10.4%) in respect of 12 titles, with a final reply on one title still being outstanding.

It should be mentioned that six of the titles for which permission was received could not be filmed in time, either because a copy could not be obtained for filming or because the quality of the publication (in stencilled form) was such that it was not suitable for filming. Thus 182 titles could be made available on microfiche, compared to 82 titles in 1971. It is a matter of some concern that only 49 out of the 82 titles for 1971 could be used for the 1972 project. Apart from 10 titles which were not again recommended in 1972, permission granted for 14 titles in 1971 was refused in 1972, while a further six titles were replaced with newer additions and three titles had to be refilmed for various reasons.

As during the previous year, delays in obtaining permission from the publishers to include publications in the project remained a problem. The majority of titles could only be filmed during March, with 14 titles following in April and the last seven titles being sent in mid-May. Further problems were encountered with delays in the actual filming of these publications, which was done outside the Library. Some of the books sent through for filming between the beginning of March and the middle of April were only received back at the end of May. Any large scale use of microfiche for other courses will therefore have to be planned well in advance.

Student Reaction

The available results of the questionnaires confirmed the surprisingly positive reaction of students involved in the pilot project for 1971. Microfiche as a means of providing literature was regarded as completely acceptable by 35.2% of the students, whilst 37.6% regarded it as acceptable and 14.4% as reasonably acceptable. Only 14.5% of the students had serious doubts about the acceptability, apart from 8.4% who did not reply to the question.

Similarly, 9.9% regarded the readability of the microfiche as excellent, 49.5% as good, 24.8% as reasonable, while 3% thought it to be poor or very poor. 12.9% failed to give their opinion. The negative microfiche used in the experiment was found to be acceptable by 67.9%, whilst 10.9% reacted negatively and 21.2% did not reply to the question.

The manageability of the material on microfiche, particularly in connection with the use of contents pages and indexes, was regarded as excellent by 6.5%, good by 28.2%, and reasonable by 36.2%, against poor 10.8% and very poor 3.5%, with 14.8% failing to reply to the question.

The most unfavourable reaction was received in respect of reading speed and eye strain. Of the students giving definite replies, 46.5% thought they read slower with microfiche, against 31.6% maintaining the same speed and 8.5% reading faster. Whereas 17.3% recorded normal eye strain while reading microfiche, only 18.4% found it unbearable, while 40.8% experienced it only after prolonged use, with a further 36.8% experiencing eye strain which was continuous, but still bearable.

Conclusion

To extend the provision of microfiches to other courses on a fairly large scale, ample time is required for preparation. With the final results of the 1972 project still incomplete, but with general indications pointing towards favourable results, it seemed logical to continue with the same courses during 1973, and to regard it as a permanent part of the Library's services. Further information on the publishers' attitude can in this way be obtained before a decision will be made about future developments.

On the basis of all the facts available at this stage, the method of supplying recommended reading in microfiche form can be considered as a qualified success. In spite of a number of actual or imagined drawbacks (lower reading speeds, greater eye fatigue, etc.) most students were willing to accept it because of its great advantages, namely the guaranteed availability and extended loan period.

A number of practical problems have to be overcome before a full-scale application can, however, be implemented. Such a step would require the compulsory acquisition of microfiche reading equipment by all 30,000 students—as it seems hardly likely that the University would consider a capital outlay of anything between R1.5—R2.5 million (£800,000-£1,300,000) to make them available free of charge. For most students the present cost of reading equipment of satisfactory quality is still prohibitive, even on a rental basis. It is even less feasible to expect the students to purchase the apparatus when only about 70% of the recommended texts can be made available on fiche. Furthermore, what would one do in the case of the few students who find microfiches completely unacceptable.

If it is remembered that the problem which gave rise to the experiment with fiche was the Library's inability in certain cases to supply copies of required books, the most logical development would be the provision in fiche form of these problem cases which arise when books are out of print or additional copies cannot be obtained in time. Such a procedure would of course raise its own problems in respect of copyright clearance, the provision of reading equipment all over the country on a loan basis, and the high cost of filming, which would be unwarranted if only a limited number of fiches are made from the master copy.

These and other implications are now being studied. If at all practical, such an approach should provide the basis for a gradual growth towards a wide application of microfiche. It is expected that developments in the next few years will definitely lead to acceptable reading equipment at low cost and, partly as a result of this, to an even greater user acceptance. Copyright clearance may, however, always remain a problem—unless an international arrangement can be established similar to that for music—through Performing Rights and other societies, whereby permission can be obtained without delay at a predetermined fee. As more publishers are starting to publish their books simultaneously in both printed and microfiche form, this idea should soon gain ground.

With the rising cost of book prices and the low cost of micro-copying, publishers may in fact find that students and other private individuals will start uncontrollable illegitimate microfiche duplication on an even larger scale than with photocopying at present—unless an acceptable means to do it legitimately is provided.

DEVELOPING A PRESERVATION MICROFILMING PROGRAM

by Pamela W. Darling

When a recent series of METRO seminars on the conservation of library materials was first proposed, there were some who wondered why microforms were being given a prominent place in the topics included. Most of the literature about conservation, as well as syllabi for courses in conservation, mention microforms only in terms of "what is the best way to store,

Reprinted from *Library Journal*, 99: 2803-809 (November 1, 1974) by permission of the author and publisher. Published by R. R. Bowker Co. (a Xerox company). Copyright © 1974 by Xerox Corporation.

preserve and repair them." Such a limited view of microforms is a pity, because several significant voices have been saying for some time that microforms, while they have certain preservation requirements of their own, can perform significant preservation functions appropriate to a broad range of library materials. The voices are growing louder—many had to be turned away from that seminar session—and there is growing recognition of the importance of microforms in a library's conservation activities. But a brief examination of the cause for this delayed recognition of the vital contribution of microforms to the solution of library preservation problems suggests a "first principle" upon which to base a preservation microfilming program.

The reluctance to apply microforms as a tool for preservation can be traced to the old stereotype that "libraries are places for books." Books have been the chief medium for storing and conveying information; and many books possess an intrinsic value-as-object due to their beauty, rarity, associational value, and so forth. But many books derive their value *only* from the information which they contain: it is the information, the intellectual content, which must be retained and made available, not always the physical book. If this distinction between books and the information they contain is not clearly made, the approach to dealing with deteriorating books tends to be "repair, rebind, restore the physical volume." But even if there developed an unlimited pool of skilled repairers, rebinders, and restorers, the costs for physical treatment (still a painstaking handcraft) are so high that it must be reserved for rare and special materials. It would be madness to spend a dollar a page to de-acidify, laminate, and rebind a dog-earred government pamphlet on poultry-raising or a crumbling city directory. We cannot hope to save our collections by physical restoration alone. We can save most of the information in our collections by transferring it to a medium more stable than paper, a medium which precludes the mutilating and tearing out of pages, takes up 90 percent less space to store, can be duplicated easily without damage to the original, and is less likely to be stolen—at least until the hardware people have their way and install microform readers next to the TV in every living room. Our "first principle," then, is that information is different than books. Microfilming must be recognized as a vital conservation technique, not because it preserves books (indeed it may hasten their destruction), but because it preserves the information for which those books were originally acquired.

Costs of microforms

Microfilm doesn't come cheap. To use it the library must invest in reading machines and reader-printers; train staff and patrons; and pay for continued maintenance and repair. Sturdy readers for library use run in the three to eight hundred dollar range; reader-printers cost several thousand dollars. One or two printers will suffice for most libraries, but half-a-dozen or more readers may be needed, especially if more than one format must be read—there are roll film readers and microfiche readers and micro-opaque readers, etc. This equipment requires a significant investment, but one which most libraries must undertake quite apart from a preservation program, as more and more materials are published in microform.

As for the costs of microforms themselves, there is no such thing as an "average." It depends, for instance, on whether film is bought from a commercial micropublisher, who can spread production costs among a number of customers, or whether it is made by the library itself. Cost depends on the format, and whether there are extensive bibliographic aids and indexes, internal and external. An example of the buy-it vs. do-it-yourself cost differential illustrates the range: for many years the New York Public Library regularly filmed a certain newspaper, at a cost of between $200-$350 per year for the master negative and one service copy. A commercial micropublisher acquired the micropublishing rights to this particular newspaper, and NYPL now buys a service copy for about $40 a year. (Binding would have cost between $30 and $75 per year, depending on the type; and the paper itself would be well on the way to the dustbin.)

A 400-page book can be bound for $4 to $12, depending on the type of binding needed and assuming that the paper does not require extensive reinforcement; Xerox University Microfilm's books-on-demand project might supply the same book in Xerox hardcopy or microfilm for $20; NYPL could film it in-house for $30; it might be available, singly or as a part of a set from a micropublisher for $3 or $4; it could be deacidified, repaired, laminated, and rebound for several hundred dollars. Are you confused? Microfilm costs and cost-benefits are confusing; they vary considerably, as do prices for physical restoration. But it is generally true that: 1) commercially-produced film is cheaper than binding; 2) in-house filming costs are higher than binding but considerably cheaper than full restoration; and 3) film has a potential life-span stretching into future centuries while most bound materials will need additional treatment or rebinding every 20-40 years, *if they last that long*—a cost factor which should not be overlooked.

Organizing for microforms

Assume that a library has agreed in principle that a preservation micro-filming program should be established, and that a reasonable sum of money is made available for this purpose. The next step must be to assign the responsibility for developing and coordinating this program to someone, somewhere within the administrative structure. In large libraries, able to support full-scale divisions devoted to all phases of the preservation of the collections, the preservation filming function is naturally located within the preservation or conservation division. In other libraries, it would make sense to locate it within the technical services department, possibly within an acquisitions or order unit, but preferably as a special office reporting to the head of technical services. "Preferably," because a comprehensive preservation microfilming program will affect acquisitions and cataloging activities, the physical processing of materials before they are added to the collections, and continuing maintenance long after materials have been turned over to the care of reading room supervisors, stack personnel, and other public service staff. The preservation microfilming officer, therefore, must have the organizational flexibility and authority to work with staff in all of these units, to develop cooperatively policies and procedures which will affect them all, with some hope that they will in fact be implemented.

Once the appropriate organizational unit has been established, someone must be found to run it. Ideally, this person should have an extensive background in microform technology, a broad acquaintance with micropublishing resources, an in-depth knowledge of the library's acquisitions and cataloging procedures, and administrative skills and experience. Since few librarians possess this range of qualifications, find a quick learner with creative organizational abilities, and lock him/her up for a couple of weeks with a good collection of microform literature. (The bibliography included in this article will provide a starting point.) The budding expert should also visit a photo lab or two, and several libraries with already-established programs; get on the mailing list (i.e., become a member) of the National Microfilm Association; and attend as many meetings of the Reproduction of Library Materials Section of ALA's Resources and Technical Services Division as possible.

The microform work

With the initial education process begun (it never finishes), attention can be turned to the actual work. The first step involves the identification of materials which might appropriately be retained on film rather than in original form. This requires adopting policies for various categories of materials, developing guidelines for distinguishing those categories, and implementing procedures for applying those guidelines. Policies might cover such materials as newspaper backfiles, long-run serials, documents and technical reports, and unbound pamphlets. Policies should also cover cataloging and recataloging; the location of film and reading machines; the types of microformats appropriate for different materials, given the library's particular needs; the disposal of originals once the film is available and the keeping of some materials in two formats (for example, maintaining current periodicals in hard copy, with back files in microform; or filming exceedingly rare materials, making the film available for general use and preserving the originals for the use of specialized scholars).

Guidelines based on such broad policies should both spell out in detail the categorical definitions and indicate the exceptions to the general policy which should be anticipated. These guidelines should take into account such things as: size, paper quality, bindability, importance of color or pictorial matter, likelihood of theft or mutilation, usability in microform (a library which circulates scores to music students might not be performing the greatest service by converting them wholesale to microfilm, unless pianos have built-in film readers, or someone can afford to feed quarters into the reader-printer all day), and criteria for weighing an item's value-as-object against present or potential deterioration and restoration costs. Policies and guidelines should address themselves both to materials being added to the collections for the first time and to things which have been quietly self-destructing in the stacks for decades. The problem must be attacked at both ends; otherwise we will either lose the bulk of our retrospective holdings by concentrating on current acquisitions, or create a whole new backlog out of current items which turn into retrospective holdings while we concentrate on the older material.

Priorities must be implicit, sometimes even explicit, in the stated policies and the day-to-day procedures, priorities which must be shaped by the library's service goals, the nature of its collections, the value, uniqueness and condition of its materials, and the availability of funds. Taken together, libraries have enough material that should be filmed to keep all the cameras in the world grinding away from now till 2001, so we'd best order our priorities lest we lose the irreplaceable whilst tending to the dispensable.

The pesky details

After the plans, the policies and guidelines, have been established, the pesky details of day-to-day procedure must be worked out. Procedures for the identification of materials which should be kept in microform might appropriately be developed for several different units within the library. Acquisition and selection officers should be alert to the possibilities of acquiring appropriate items in microform to begin with; the receiving unit should spot new materials on poor quality paper which might be converted to film before being added to the collections; at the bindery preparation stage there should be a system for determining whether things should be filmed instead; circulation staff should be trained to recognize potential microform candidates. When deteriorated titles must be replaced, the microform market should be searched along with the reprint and out-of-print markets. Shelf surveys, whether systematic or the more normal kind forced upon us by pressing space needs or the sight of crumbling pages littering the floor, should include a mechanism for identifying materials which should be converted to microform. The degree of formality which must be built into such procedures and systems will vary significantly with the size and nature of the library; but at the very least all staff should be made aware of the overall goals and of their role in meeting them.

Getting the microfilm

Along with establishing procedures for identifying materials to be kept in microform must go the simultaneous development of means for getting them in microform. There are three possibilities: buy microforms from a commercial micropublisher or another library; have your copy filmed for you by an outside filming agency; or film your copy yourself.

First, buying microforms: this is almost always preferable to getting something filmed yourself—it's much easier, and most of the time much less expensive because the production costs can be divided among a number of purchasers. You must know where to send the order, so you must search; and since bibliographic control of microforms still leaves much to be desired, this searching can be time-consuming, frustrating and inconclusive. A collection of microform bibliographies and catalogs should be set up, either in connection with the acquisition department's catalogs or in the preservation microfilming office, if there is one. The appendix lists the tools which form the core of the NYPL working collection of catalogs, and outlines the first steps in searching for various types of materials. Reasonable limits to the search should be established, both by ruling out catalogs irrelevant to the title in hand (don't search the 1969 National Register for an item published in 1972), and by limiting the time spent on each. For example, pamphlets of up to 85 or 90 pages could be put on microfiche by a microfilm service bureau for $5-$8; it wouldn't pay to spend many hours searching for such items. On the other hand, a 40-volume serial, or 25 years of a newspaper is worth a long search.

Ordering microforms

Once availability has been determined, place an order. (Depending on the library's policies, general acquisition money might be used, or special microform acquisition funds, book replacement or preservation funds, etc. If there is not a legitimate budget line to charge for such purchases, it should be fought for in the next budget.) The microfilm order should clearly specify the format and quality of film which the library will accept—that is, 35 or 16mm roll films, or microfiche or whatever, indicating maximum reduction ratios acceptable (if your reader magnifies only 20 times and you get film reduced 40 times you're in trouble), your choice of negative or positive polarity, whether you insist on silver halide film or will accept diazo or vesicular film, and a general statement to the effect that the film should conform to all appropriate national standards for archival quality and bibliographic integrity. A careful study of published standards and specifications will simplify the task of developing an order statement. Although many outside sources of film can be trusted to conform to standards without being told, there are others for whom such instructions may not be superfluous. In addition, because publisher's catalogs often give very few technical facts about the film they are offering, the instructions relating to format, reduction, and so on may be crucial.

Once the film arrives, check it carefully. Make sure that what's on the reel agrees with the box label and that both agree with the order; be sure the film is of the type specified. Study Allen Veaner's booklet, *The Evaluation of Micropublications* and do as much of the technical inspection he describes as the library has the staff and equipment for, particularly if this is the first film received from a company. Frame by frame inspection is a luxury few can afford; but examination before the invoice is paid can save a lot of trouble later on if the sixth fiche card out of 20 turns out to be missing, or if volume 5 turns up on the reel between volumes eight and nine.

Outside filming

If the material wanted is not already available in microform, consider getting your copy filmed. If there is no in-house filming laboratory, search out a microfilm service agency. The *Microfilm Source Book* and the NMA's *Buyer's Guide* list many of these firms with indications of the type of filming they can do. After locating an agency, DO NOT pack up everything and send it off to be filmed. Sit down with the company's technical director—not the sales representative—and go over in great detail the technical and bibliographic specifications for the product to be delivered. If the library has not developed such specifications tailored to its own needs, the Library of Congress specifications will cover most of the ground. When you feel confident that they understand your needs and you understand their capabilities, and if the two seem compatible, select a representative batch for a pilot project. When this comes back, examine it *rigorously*—if the library does not have all the necessary equipment for testing density, resolution, residual hypo, etc., find another lab, preferably in a library, that can do these tests. (There will probably be a fee, but it's worth it.) If the results are satisfactory, establish a schedule for sending out work and spot-testing the returns; determine an acceptable percentage of error and agree in advance on who shall pay for necessary remakes. Maintain close personal contact with the people doing the work. If the first test results are not satisfactory, sit down with the technical director again and go over the problems thoroughly. Repeat the pilot batch and again examine the results. It may take months to get the quality product needed; it may be necessary to give up on one service agency and start over with another. Many microfilm service agencies were set up to film bank checks, computer print-outs, office records-fairly uniform materials which do not present anything like the range of filming problems which library materials present, and which usually do not require the bibliographic apparatus essential for good library service. Some can learn, and learn fast, particularly if the library can muster enough technical knowledge to clearly identify the problems and explain the requirements. But be aware of the pitfalls, and plan on a significant start-up time. Whatever you do, don't sign a contract until you know the firm can produce what you want.

Do it yourself

The third alternative for getting things on film is to do it yourself. This is not an alternative available to everyone; the latest *Directory of Library Reprographic Services* lists only 242 libraries, some of which do little more than make Xerox copies. The investment in costly equipment and skilled personnel is significant and can probably be justified only if a steady volume of filming can be guaranteed for years to come. This is not the place to describe in detail the essential ingredients of a good lab; but if the library has, or can set up, an in-house laboratory, be as rigorous about inspection and quality control with yourself as you would be with an outside service agency. There are several advantages to having this in-house capability: there is less risk of damage or loss of valuable materials, much closer control can be exercised over all phases of the film process, and the laboratory staff can develop a high degree of expertise specifically tailored to the peculiarities of filming library materials. Since in-house costs tend to be higher than commercial costs, it may be well to divide the work, sending routine items outside and reserving the in-house lab for fragile, difficult-to-film materials. It will also be important to establish a balance between preservation microfilming and other kinds of photoduplication services which may be offered to readers, to the library administration, or to the world at large.

Preparing materials for film

Time and effort must go into preparing materials for filming, whether in-house or by a service agency. Every reasonable effort should be made to film a complete copy. This means a page-by-page collation to be sure that sections are in the proper order and to identify missing pages or issues. Wherever possible, such gaps should be filled before filming—by borrowing copies from other libraries, dunning publishers for missing volumes, etc. Gaps which cannot be filled must be clearly indicated on the film, through the use of contents targets, missing or mutilated page statements and other explanatory notes. The Library of Congress specifications provide excellent guidance. Unless the original is to be retained after filming, it is often better to remove the binding so that the pages can lie completely flat on the camera board. This can be done by guillotining or, if the paper is too brittle for such treatment, by carefully taking the volume apart by hand. In some cases, this will be unnecessary: newspapers, unbound single-signature pamphlets or magazines such as *Time*, or bound materials with very wide gutter margins may lie perfectly flat without cutting. In other cases the book may be so badly deteriorated that handling should be kept to a bare minimum—just get it gingerly onto the camera board or book cradle and hope that the pages will stay in one piece long enough to be photographed. Process records should be kept, like bindery process files, to facilitate the location of materials and permit follow-up on delinquents mislaid in someone's lab; and such records could be built into the next stage of cataloging procedures. Such preparation and record-keeping take time and require trained staff. The initial planning should be done at the professional level, but most of the daily routine can be carried out by library technical assistants or other nonprofessional staff.

Cooperative efforts

There is actually a fourth alternative for getting materials on film, and that is to cooperate with micropublishers who plan to market microform copies. In most such cases, the library will receive free film in return for the loan of the original material; reprint fees or royalty payments on sales are sometimes involved. Such arrangements can be of great benefit to the library, *if* they are entered into cautiously and carefully, without giving a single firm exclusive access to the library's collections and provided that such cooperation does not interfere unduly with the library's own priorities.

In most instances, once materials to be kept in microform have been identified, and in one way or another the microforms have been obtained, the original materials may then be disposed of (unless they are so valuable they should be restored and kept for restricted use in a rare book or special collection). Materials being added to the collections for the first time can be cataloged straight off as microforms. Previously cataloged materials which have not changed format may be completely recataloged, or the original records may be annotated to indicate the change. All cataloging decisions, including classification schemes or location number systems should be determined in advance, particularly if the library is having its own materials filmed rather than purchasing from outside. It may be, for instance, that the microform call number is to be included in the eye-legible header of the microfiche, or on the title target of the roll film—if so, it's much easier to build that into the initial preparation of materials for filming than to set up a labeling system for adding the number to the completed film.

If the library has filmed its own materials, and therefore owns master negatives in addition to service copies, they should be reported to the *National Register of Microform Masters* so that others will be spared the unnecessary expense of duplicate filming. It is a simple procedure (instructions appear in the introductory pages of the Register) but is too often ignored or done in a haphazard way. In the face of the gigantic tasks before us we cannot afford not to support and expand this important tool—nothing is more discouraging than to spend $1000 filming a large back file only to discover that another library filmed it years ago and could have sold a print for $100. Libraries actively seeking to sell copies of their microforms should also list them in the *Guide to Microforms in Print*, being sure there are no copyright limitations first. It is not essential to have an in-house laboratory in order to provide copies for others. Most microfilm service agencies will store masters for their customers, reproducing them on request, and duplication costs are only a fraction of the original filming costs.

Microforms can play a tremendous role in preserving the information, the intellectual contents, of a great proportion of library materials, both current and retrospective. If properly stored and handled, microforms will last as long as acid-free 100 percent rag paper—several hundred years—which is six to ten times longer than most book papers used since the mid-19th Century. If the master negative is kept under archival conditions, the material will never again be "out of print."

But a word of caution: don't be fooled into thinking that a secondhand camera and an automatic processor installed in the coat closet equal an instant preservation microfilming program. This is approximately equivalent to renting a computer terminal and calling it an automated cataloging system. The same sort of careful analysis and program development that is essential for automation is needed to establish a feasible preservation microfilming program. The technology is not as complex, of course; but it demands respect and attention to detail, both technical and bibliographic. If we plunge in thoughtlessly we may end up with miles of film which is self-destructing due to improper processing, or whose contents are inaccessible because of inadequate internal and external bibliographic control. But if we take the time to learn what it's all about and to make the technology work to meet our needs, we may yet save the millions of volumes

which will otherwise crumble to dust on our shelves before this
century is over.

ADDITIONAL READINGS

Clapp, Verner W. and Jordan, Robert T., "Re-Evaluation of Microfilm as a Method of Book
    Storage," *College and Research Libraries*, 24: 5-15 (January 1963).
Day, Melvin S., "The NASA Microform Concept," National Microfilm Association, *Proceedings*,
    1964, 13: 284-85.
Gabriel, Michael, "Surging Serial Costs," *Library Journal*, 99: 2448-53 (October 1, 1974).
Indiana University Libraries. Serials Dept. *Serials Binding and Microfilm Costs Comparison
    (July 1974-revised)*. Bloomington, 1974.
Lynden, Frederick C., "Replacement of Hard Copy by Microforms," *Microform Review*, 4: 15-24
    (January 1975).
Marron, Harvey, "The Educational Resources Information Center: Or How Educators Learned
    About Microfiche," *Journal of Micrographics*, 4: 69-71 (January 1971).
*Microform Utilization: the Academic Library Environment. Report of Conference held at Denver,
    Colorado, 7-9 December 1970*.   Denver: University of Denver, 1971.
Peele, David, "Bind or Film: Factors in the Decision," *Library Resources and Technical Services*,
    8: 168-72 (Spring 1964).
Pritsker, Alan B. and Sadler, J. William, "An Evaluation of Microfilm as a Method of Book
    Storage," *College and Research Libraries*, 18: 290-96 (July 1957).
Sajor, Ladd Z., "Preservation Microfilming: Why, What, When, Who, How," *Special Libraries*,
    63: 195-201 (April 1972).
"The Use of Audio-Visual Teaching Aids and Library Microforms in American Legal Education,"
    [Report of the AALL Audio-Visual Committee, Summer, 1972] , *Law Library Journal*,
    66: 84-87 (February 1973).

STANDARDS
AND SPECIFICATIONS

INTRODUCTION

While there are a great many standards relating to film stock and process-ing, as Veaner notes, "There are *no* ANSI[1] Standards and *no* ALA Stand-ards for microfilming library materials."[2] It is important to keep this is mind as the literature of microreproduction abounds with calls for adher-ence to "the" standard. Reichmann and Tharpe, for example, in their rec-ommendations note, "Excellent norms for controlling production have been worked out by the Copy Methods Section [sic] of the American Library Association. They have to be enforced,"[3] referring to *Microfilm Norms: Recommended Standards for Libraries*, prepared by the Library Standards for Microfilm Committee of RTSD's Copying Methods Section and published by ALA in 1966 and long out of print. Holmes found sub-stantially the same comment among persons he interviewed, "existing standards and specifications (ALA microfilm norms) should be en-forced. . . . Librarians should refuse to purchase microforms unless they meet standards and specifications."[4]

Veaner goes on to say, "while there are philosophical differences be-tween *Norms* and *Specifications* [referring to the *Newspapers* (1972) and *Books and Pamphlets* (1973) *Specifications* issued by the Library of Con-gress, both of which are reproduced in this chapter] —the *Norms* are pre-scriptive and synthetic, while the *Specifications* are empirical and prag-matic—adherence to any of these guideline documents will produce first quality film for library and research use."[5]

In my view the difference between *Norms* and *Specifications*, particu-larly the edition of *Specifications*[6] that was in force at the Library of Con-gress when *Norms* was published are more than philosophical. In addition, it is difficult to reconcile cries of enforcement of the recommended stand-ards in *Microform Norms* with the fact that ALA has let the work go out of print.

We have also the much less publicized and much more stringent micro-filming standards issued and adhered to by the National Library of Medi-cine,[7] which raises the question, "If the norms in *Microfilm Norms* are 'excellent' why did the Library of Medicine feel it had to create its own standards?"

It should be noted that the various guidelines referred to above cover only roll microfilm; none of them cover either microfiche or micro-opaques.

In addition, these guidelines do not cover diazo or vesicular films. These are films for which there are no ANSI standards but which nevertheless are being used by a number of organizations which publish microforms such as Great Britain's Public Record Office and the U.S. Government's ERIC Distribution System. It is anticipated that as the price of silver in-creases, more and more micropublishers will turn to non-silver films.

The problem that the use of non-silver films presents to libraries is that standard methods for determining the durability of these films do not exist, whereas they do for silver films. For this reaosn some libraries specify on their purchase orders "silver film only" and in a recent editorial Veaner comments, "and until such standards are developed, publicized, voted upon and promulgated *MR* [*Microform Review*] does not believe it proper to employ these materials for micropublications intended for the perma-nent collections of research libraries."[8]

ANSI has a Task Group on Stability of Diazo and Vesicular Films and at the 1975 ALA Midwinter Meeting a sub-committee of the Reproduction of Library Materials Section was established to make recommendations on needed research on non-silver film problems and standards and to initiate proposals for the funding of such research. The results of these endeavours will do much to clear up what is now at best a cloudy situation; neverthe-less, at this time the durability of diazo and vesicular films is a matter of speculation.

As the reader can see, the matter of standards for library microforms is far from simple. When one next hears or reads a call for filming to "*the*" library standard, ask, "which standard?"

References

1. American National Standards Institute, Inc., 1430 Broadway, New York, N.Y. 10018.

2. Veaner, Allen B., "Microproduction and Micropublication Technical Standards: What They Mean to You the User," *Microform Review*, 3: 82 (April 1974).

3. Reichmann, Felix and Tharpe, Josephine M., *Bibliographic Control of Microforms*. Westport: Greenwood Press, 1972, p. 32.

4. Holmes, Donald C., *Determination of User Needs and Future Requirements for a Systems Approach to Microform Technology*. July 19, 1969, ERIC ED 029 168, p. 12.

5. Veaner, *op cit*, p. 82.

6. Salmon, Steve R., *Specifications for Library of Congress Microfilming*. Washington: Library of Congress, 1964.

7. National Library of Medicine, *Roll Film Specifications for Microrecording Biomedical Literature*. Bethesda: National Library of Medicine, 1968.
   8. Veaner, Allen B., "An Ominous Trend," *Microform Review*, 4: 9 (January 1975).

MICROREPRODUCTION AND MICROPUBLICATION TECHNICAL STANDARDS: WHAT THEY MEAN TO YOU, THE USER

by Allen B. Veaner

The Significance of ANSI Standards

No industrial society can exist without national and international standards. Standards dominate every product and service of the modern world: tire sizes and inflation pressures, eggs, grass seed, drugs, screw threads, cans, wires, sockets, lamps, paper sizes, fabrics—anything which is *manufactured* as distinct from that which is handcrafted. A micropublication is a *manufactured product*, and if the producer, the seller, and the purchaser understand and accept the applicable standards, mutual satisfaction will result.

In some countries, standards are promulgated by the national government. In the United States, the national government has specified a large number of federal standards for materials and goods bought for its own use. However, in private enterprise, standards are established by the American National Standards Institute (ANSI), a non-government, voluntary association of users and manufacturers having a joint concern for standardization. It is quite important to understand that neither the government nor the Institute can compel any manufacturer to adhere to ANSI standards. Users and manufacturers are encouraged to declare their adherence to ANSI standards, but the Institute itself exists only to promote standardized practices:

An American National Standard implies a consensus of those substantially concerned with its scope and provisions. An American National Standard is intended as a guide to aid the manufacturer, the consumer, and the general public. The existence of an American National Standard does not in any respect preclude anyone, whether he has approved the standard or not, from manufacturing, marketing,

Reprinted from *Microform Review*, 3: 80-84 (April 1974) by permission of the publisher. Copyright © 1974 by Microform Review Inc.

purchasing, or using products, processes, or procedures not conforming to the standard. American National Standards are subject to periodic review and users are cautioned to obtain the latest editions.[1]

ANSI Standards are divided into numerous subject categories, and all are listed in the Institute's annual catalog (available free on request from the Institute's headquarters, 1430 Broadway, New York City 10018). The standards of chief interest to micropublication are the PH5 series, which is devoted to photographic reproduction of documents. Standards are inexpensive; the majority of the PH5 standards sell for a few dollars each. There are other important standards concerned with photographic grades of chemicals (PH4.100 and higher numbers), photographic processing (PH4.1 through PH4.34), and photographic materials (PH1 series); some or all are applicable to the micropublication industry. The following sections of this paper will attempt to outline the principal features of standards applicable to micropublications.

Choice of Film Stock

The producer must first choose a film which has characteristics suitable for archival preservation of the photographed material. Such a film must meet ANSI Standard PH1.28-1969, Specifications for Photographic Films for Archival Records, Silver-Gelatin Type on Cellulose Ester Base, or the latest revision thereof. Film manufacturers customarily indicate adherence to this standard in technical literature provided to the laboratory which processes the film. The user can easily tell for himself whether he has been supplied with a suitable film: negative and positive films conforming to PH1.28-1969 are readily identifiable by the presence of a small, solid triangle imprinted at regular intervals along one edge of the film during the manufacturing process. This mark cannot be removed. All films claimed suitable for archival use should bear this mark, which is easily visible in a microfilm reader. Positive films should bear two sets of marks, one for the positive and the copied mark from the original negative. An important note: The presence of a triangle is *not* a guarantee or warranty of "archival permanence." It merely means the film stock is *suitable* for an archival application. This suitability can, of course, be *destroyed* by improper storage conditions, or rendered useless by careless camera work or improper printing of distribution copies.

ANSI Standards for vesicular, diazo and other non-silver films do not as yet exist. The suitability of non-silver films for library applications is at this time, therefore, still a speculative matter.

Standards for Processing Chemicals

All photographic chemicals used in processing silver films must be of specified purity, as indicated in the nearly seventy standards comprising the PH4.100, PH4.200, and the PH4.300 series. Commercial or industrial grades of chemicals may have contaminants that could adversely affect film processing. Here, the risk of failure is so high that use of non-standard grades of chemicals is practically unknown. Of course, it is one thing to use the right chemicals and another to be assured that they have been properly mixed, not used beyond their capacity, nor allowed to spoil.

Processing Standards for Silver-Gelatin Films

This brings us to processing. Like many industrial processes, the chemical processing of photographic materials requires the highest degree of quality control in order to assure consistent results. The need for tight control in microreproduction is especially critical, because unlike some materials used in conventional photography, microreproduction materials are extremely sensitive to slight variations in exposure and chemical processing. Where the amateur photographer can get a picture within a wide latitude of variables (such as lens opening and shutter speed), no such opportunity exists with microreproduction materials. All modern processing is done by automatic mechanical processors, which run at preset speeds in accordance with experience and laboratory tests. In some installations, processors are computer controlled. Effective, consistent processing is dependent upon many factors: development time, strength of solutions, constancy of replenishment rate of solutions which get used up, replacement of exhausted solutions at the proper time, sufficiency of washing to remove processing chemicals, and temperature of processing solutions. If equipment is properly operated and maintained, results should consistently accord with ANSI Standards for photographic processing.

There is another significant processing variable: the film itself. Film emulsions vary slightly from batch to batch—the light sensitivity may be greater or less for one batch than for another. By proper use of sensitometric tests, the processing plant can control this variable very well. Commonly, an adjustment would be made to the lighting of the subject during exposure, while the chemical processing variables—the most difficult to control—would be held constant. A good indication of a producer's quality control is consistency in using the same brand of film, which can reduce film variables to a minimum. Less than half a dozen major brands of silver film are distributed in the U.S. The producer who changes brands often—usually for a price advantage—is asking for trouble, for he is making it more difficult for himself to maintain consistent results.

Standards for Filming Research Materials

There are *no* ANSI Standards and *no* "ALA Standards" for microfilming library materials. However, there exist three important sets of guidelines and specifications developed by the library community itself. The first is *Specifications for the Microfilming of Newspapers in the Library of Congress*, prepared in 1972 by the Photoduplication Service at the Library of Congress. The second is *Specifications for the Microfilming of Books and Pamphlets in the Library of Congress*, issued by the same unit of LC in 1973. The third is *Microfilm Norms*, issued in 1966 by the ALA's Library Standards for Microfilm Committee, then chaired by Peter Scott. A third item, *Microfiche of Documents*, was issued in 1973 by the National Microfilm Association as industry standard, MS-5. However, its scope is restricted to 8½" X 11" documents microfilmed at reductions up to and including 24X, and legal size documents "of good quality" filmed at reductions of 27X. NMA Standard MS-5 is not directly applicable to the wide variety of materials likely to be found in research libraries. Both LC *Specifications* deal with preparation of material, targeting, image placement, reduction ratio, film inspection, resolution, packaging, processing and many miscellaneous matters, such as splicing and storage of films. *Norms* covers substantially the same ground. Although there are philosophical differences between *Norms* and *Specifications*—the *Norms* are prescriptive and synthetic, while the *Specifications* are empirical and pragmatic—adherence to any of these guideline documents will produce first quality film for library and research use.

Closely related to these three documents, but not specifically directed to library materials, is PH5.3-1967, Specifications for 16mm and 35mm Silver Gelatin Microfilms for Reel Applications. This ANSI Standard directs its attention to film dimensions, winding of film, image placement, leader and trailer requirements, and other technical matters not specific to the subject being microfilmed.

The time may be right for the library community to consider merging *Norms* and LC's sets of *Specifications* into a new recommendation which could become a proposed ANSI Standard and a companion to PH5.3-1967. A useful appendix to such a document would be a "how to do it" section on actual camera technique. Unfortunately, little has been published on techniques of filming research materials, a fact that is evident to many academic users by their frustrating experiences in using micropublications. However, in the 1973 *Specifications*, a good beginning has been made in detailing techniques for books and pamphlets.

Standards for Testing Archival Qualities

For micropublication, one of the most important ANSI Standards is

PH4.8-1971, Methylene Blue Method for Measuring Thiosulfate and Silver Densitometric Method for Measuring Residual Chemicals in Films, Plates, and Papers. This document prescribes the test for excess "hypo." Hypo is a popular name for sodium thiosulfate, the chemical agent which fixes or renders permanent the silver photographic image after it has been developed. Thiosulfate is essential to chemical processing, but it must be removed from silver film immediately following processing, since its continued presence is harmful to the image. Thiosulfate is removed by washing silver film in a constantly changing supply of temperature-controlled water (flowing at a metered rate) for a prescribed period. Inadequate washing can leave a residue of thiosulfate and other harmful by-products which can fade the microimage. Finished film should contain not more than one microgram of residual thiosulfate per square centimeter of film. The Methylene Blue test is a complex laboratory procedure which cannot be carried out by a tyro.

Tests for Legibility and Sharpness

The terms "resolution" and "resolving power" are often used to describe the degree to which a reproduction system—subject, camera, film, lens, processing, reading machine, and user—can record and distinguish fine detail. Subjective factors are necessarily involved, and resolution testing is an effort to make this measurement more nearly objective.

The National Bureau of Standards has carried out extensive research in resolution testing. Its published resolution charts are widely used to obtain a numerical measure of resolution. Internationally, other techniques have been developed to assess image quality, but discussion of them is beyond the scope of this article.

The concept behind resolution measurement is simple and is based upon patterns of parallel black lines, each separated from its neighbor by a space equal to the line thickness. The idea is for the viewer to examine a graded series of line/space patterns and identify the smallest set where he can actually distinguish the lines and the spaces. To facilitate this process, the National Bureau of Standards publishes very precise resolution charts. NBS chart 1963-A has twenty-six patterns of progressively smaller line/space pairs. To use the charts, they are microfilmed at a known reduction and the resulting negative images examined through a microscope. The number identifying the smallest pattern where lines can be distinguished from spaces is then multiplied by the known reduction factor, and the resulting number is said to be the resolving power of that system in lines per millimeter. The same procedure can be applied to a positive film printed from a negative bearing an image of the chart; there is always a loss of resolution through copying.

The effect of this procedure is to impose a severe test on the producer's equipment and technical know-how. Although there is much more to resolution testing than is described in the simplified explanation given here, it is surprising how very few producers ever include resolution chart images on their films—even though both *Norms* and *Specifications* give full particulars for using the charts. The probable cause may be that producers do not wish to risk embarrassment or possible misinterpretation of the charts by uninformed laymen. Nevertheless, it is incumbent upon the micropublisher to at least assure the buying public that his film meets minimum resolution expectations, and he harms quality assurance by omitting the charts.

Microfilm Norms requires resolution of the 5.6 pattern on the NBS chart at a reduction of 14X. For books and Pamphlets the Library of Congress expects a resolution of 105 lines per millimeter in the corners of a negative frame at a reduction of 15X, which implies substantially better performance in the center of an image. This is a relatively modest expectation, and no film producer should be incapable of achieving it regularly. However, the user does not normally need a resolution chart to equate a fuzzy image with poor workmanship. Availability of the chart images would enable a film inspector to determine whether the fuzzy image was caused by equipment maladjustment or carelessness on the part of the camera operator.

Promoting Standardization

Through RTSD's Reproduction of Library Materials Section and the Committee on Micropublishing Projects, the American Library Association plays an important role in the promotion of standards affecting document reproduction and micropublication. Along with many other organizations, ALA represents the users' interests. Also contributing to this work are the American Association of Law Libraries, the American Bar Association, the American Historical Association, the American Society for Information Science, the Council of National Library Associations, the Library of Congress, The National Microfilm Association, the Society of American Archivists, the Special Libraries Association, and many other user, seller, and manufacturing organizations. Effective standards development is dependent upon good user communication to the American National Standards Institute through the user's representative organization. From the viewpoint of convenience and economy, it is unwise and disadvantageous to neglect or tamper with established standards. Ultimately, the user is responsible for evaluating the product placed before him; it is he who will decide whether standards will prevail. The user can materially aid standardization by refusing to buy sub-standard products.

References

1. This notice appears in all ANSI Standards.

Bibliography

1. Clapp, Verner W., Henshaw, Francis H., and Holmes, Donald C. "Are Your Microfilms Deteriorating Acceptably? *Library Journal*, 80: 589-95, March 5, 1955.
2. *Specifications for the Microfilming of Newspapers in the Library of Congress.* Washington: Library of Congress, 1972. 17p. ($.30).
3. *Specifications for the Microfilming of Books and Pamphlets in the Library of Congress.* Washington: Library of Congress, 1973. 16p. ($.40).
4. *Microfilm Norms.* Chicago, American Library Association, 1966. Out of print; xerographic copies available from University Microfilms.
5. Hawken, William R. *Copying Methods Manual.* Chicago, Library Technology Program, 1966. Especially the section "Microtransparencies," p. 240-287.

SPECIFICATIONS FOR THE MICROFILMING OF BOOKS AND PAMPHLETS IN THE LIBRARY OF CONGRESS

Preparation

Preliminary Collation

The entire book or pamphlet shall be collated before filming, page by page, and a complete list made of:

a. all missing pages and plates, and those out of order;
b. all imperfections, such as mutilations, tears, stains, obliterations, and missing portions. Imperfections which do not affect any text or illustration may be ignored.

Completion of the text

Every effort shall be made to obtain missing pages and replacements for

This is a reprint of the Library of Congress pamphlet, *Specifications for the Microfilming of Books and Pamphlets in the Library of Congress.* Washington: Library of Congress, 1973. Available from the Government Printing Office, order no. 3000 00068.

mutilated pages before submitting the item to the microphotographer for filming. Major research libraries and other libraries likely to have the needed material shall be contacted in an attempt to locate copies of the missing portions. If located, the material must be acquired, permanently or on loan, and inserted in the proper sequence. When this is not possible, microfilm made to the same specifications as those used for the basic volume shall be ordered from the institution concerned and later spliced into the LC negative. To avoid distortion or loss of text in the gutter of the volume, it is preferred that tight bindings be removed to permit photo-duplication of the entire content. If the integrity of the original text may be jeopardized by the removal of bindings, it is recommended that they be loosened; if this cannot be done, every effort must be made to mini-mize textual loss and to achieve the best possible copy. When pages or plates are out of order, and when it is possible to remove the bindings, rearrangement of the material into correct sequence before filming should be considered. If removal of the bindings is not practical, the question should be raised whether the item should be filmed "as is," or whether the sequence should be corrected during the filming process.

All pages of the material shall be filmed including any blank pages which figure in consecutive pagination whether actually numbered or not, but usually not including blank leaves inserted at the back or front of a volume, and not included in any pagination. It is possible, however, that these blank endpapers must be filmed if a detailed collation shows that they may serve as essential evidence to establish the authenticity of a volume, or to prove the identity of one of several editions.

Final Collation

Final collation and revision of the original item are essential before the start of filming. The complete target series outlined below must agree with this final collation in every detail, accounting for all parts included as well as noting any special circumstances in the origi-nal, such as portions and plates missing, or any physical irregularities. All targets must be made ready and inserted in the sequence before filming begins; specifically, not only those "constant" targets which are standard at the beginning and end of every item, or every reel, but also the "as needed" targets to be inserted throughout the sequence as the particular circumstances require.

Technical Guide*

Special Considerations

Although problems due to creases and wrinkles arise rarely in the case of monographs, the scattered instances of such problems cannot be ignored. No strict procedures are recommended; experienced laboratory technicians devise solutions for each case as circumstances dictate. A thin sheet of stiff backing material inserted under the page to be filmed is often adequate.

Pages stuck together must be handled with extreme caution. It is often possible to steam them apart, and, if they are not to be filmed immediately, sheets of nonadhesive material such as silicone-treated paper can be inserted between the pages to prevent further sticking.

In all such problems, if any of these prefilming treatments include elements of possible damage, particularly in the case of rare books or manuscripts, the item in question must be returned to its custodial division without filming in order that the division involved assume all responsibility for prefilming procedures of a remedial character, or for cancellation of the filming if such action seems in the best interest of preservation.

Targets

Film appropriate targets at the beginning and end of each publication, and at the beginning and end of each reel when more than one reel is needed. Film in addition the "as needed" targets throughout the film. Menu boards or titling sets are often used to make such targets (see figures 2-4).

The word "START" (figure 4, target 1) must appear in the first frame of any roll of film, and the word "END" (figure 4, target 15), in the last frame, in letters which produce images on film of at least 0.08 inch (2.032mm) high.

Following the "START" target and preceding the "END" target, there must be a bibliographic target to identify the publication filmed (figure 4, targets 2 and 14), giving the author, title, place of publication, date of publication, volume number when needed, and microfilm shelf number where appropriate (see figure 2). The height of the letters on the film in this primary bibliographic target shall also be at least 0.08 inch (2.032mm).

If the material covered by the primary bibliographic target extends over more than one reel, another bibliographic target indicating the contents of that particular reel shall be filmed immediately following the primary bibliographic target. Bibliographic data abbreviated as necessary to fit

---

*Illustrative examples in the several "figures" of this pamphlet are not drawn to scale.

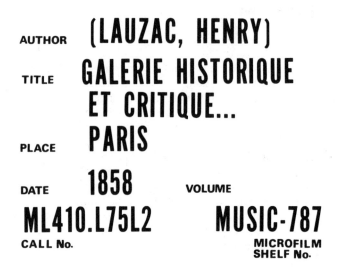

AUTHOR **(LAUZAC, HENRY)**

TITLE **GALERIE HISTORIQUE**
ET CRITIQUE...

PLACE **PARIS**

DATE **1858**   VOLUME

ML410.L75L2   **MUSIC-787**
CALL No.   MICROFILM
                                SHELF No.

Figure 2

MUSIC - 787

₍Lauzac, Henry₎
    Galerie historique et critique du dix-neuvième siècle.
₍Henry Litolff, artiste musicien. Extrait du 2ᵉ volume₎
Paris, Au bureau de la Galerie historique, 1858.
    14 p. 25ᶜᵐ.
    Author's name on cover and at end of text.

    1. Litolff, Henry Charles, 1818–1891.

                                                10–18809

    Library of Congress   ML410.L75L2

MICROFILMED   1973
LIBRARY OF CONGRESS
PHOTODUPLICATION   SERVICE

Figure 3

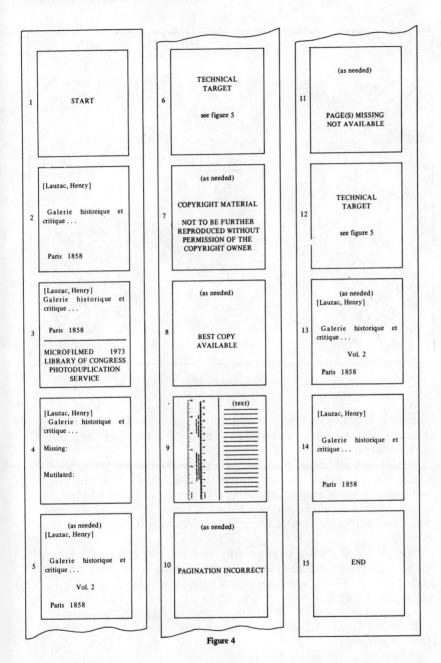

Figure 4

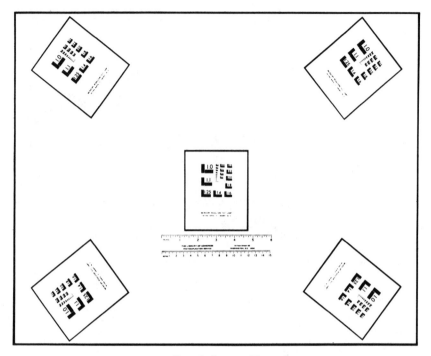

Figure 5   (not to scale)

macroscopic targets shall be in conformity with *Anglo-American Catalog-ing Rules* (Chicago: American Library Association, 1967), or the latest edition thereof.

A secondary bibliographic target consisting of a Library of Congress printed or typewritten catalog card and the Photoduplication Service credit sign (or other agency producing the microfilm) shall be filmed im-mediately after the primary target (figure 4, target 3). If another organi-zation was instrumental in planning the project, that information may be given also.

Film the list of missing pages, mutilations, etc. (see section 1.3 above) as a separate frame or frames immediately after the bibliographic targets (figure 4, target 4). If the item is fragmentary, a list of the pages filmed may be used instead.

When filming a multi-volume monographic work, a target indicating each volume shall be filmed before the pages of the volume in question (figure 4, target 5).

Following the secondary bibliographic targets, a technical target is necessary. The technical target (figure 5) shall be an assembly of five

National Bureau of Standards Microcopy Resolution Test Charts, 1010-1963A, and a 6-inch (or 150mm) paper scale, placed on a sheet of single-weight, non-glossy white paper as described below. The center resolution test chart shall be placed with the zero of the "10" pattern within 1/4 inch (6.350mm) of the center of the technical target, and with the lines of the test patterns parallel to the technical target edges. The corner test charts shall be positioned at the outermost points of the photographic field and oriented so that one edge of each chart is parallel to the diagonal of the technical target. The zero of the "10" pattern shall be within 1/4 inch (6.350mm) of the diagonal of the technical target. Depending upon the diameter or reduction ratio selected for filming, the resolution targets shall be placed in either a larger or smaller field as the document size dictates. The 6-inch (or 150mm) paper scale showing increments in both inches and millimeters shall be located under the center resolution test chart and centered on the vertical center line of the technical target. The technical targets shall be filmed on the same camera, at the same time, and under conditions which achieve the same reduction ratio as the text. To assure that this procedure has been followed, there shall be no splices between the technical targets and the adjacent 10 frames of text. These requirements apply equally to the technical targets at the beginning and end of the reel.

An indication of the reduction ratio used in the filming may also be given on one of the preliminary targets. This may be shown by filming at the same reduction ratio a section of an inch and millimeter scale, respectively, at least 3 inches (76.200mm) long; this will make possible a more accurate reconstruction of the size of the original material than would a simple statement of the reduction ratio (see figure 4, target 9). Any intervening change in reduction ratio requires the insertion of another such technical target with a ruler to show the amount of reduction or enlargement introduced.

Any of the following information must also be included on a target, when appropriate: location of the original material, a list of pages and illustrations filmed from other copies of the same title, reference to a separate index or to supplementary bibliographic data for the material being filmed, and note of any restrictions on further reproduction or use of the microfilm.

Insert targets to indicate any faults in the original so that they are not mistaken for errors in the filming. When a page is missing from the material being filmed, a space of 1 1/4 inches (31.750mm) to 2 inches (50.800mm) on the film shall be left blank to allow for splicing in missing material later. A target with the wording "page missing" or "pages missing," as appropriate, shall appear in the center of this space (figure 4, target 11).

Before a mutilated page, or if a book or pamphlet contains extensive mutilation, film a target in letters which produce images on film of at least 0.08 inch (2.032mm) in height, indicating that the following page or pages were filmed from the "Best Copy Available"; this shall also be done for illegible pages or pages otherwise faulty in the original (see figure 4, target 8). Mutilations which do not affect any printing or illustrations may be ignored. If a page has been mutilated so that a portion has been lost, the page shall be backed up with a piece of white paper, both to reveal that a portion has been lost and to prevent the filming of the corresponding portion of the ensuing leaf in faulty sequence.

Use targets 7 and 10 in figure 4 for copyright and pagination, as necessary, in letters which produce images on film of at least 0.08 inch (2.032mm) high.

Image Placement and Reduction Ratios

The position of images and the reduction ratio for a particular monographic work depend on the dimensions, type size, and legibility of the original, and the use to be made of the negative.

The four types of image placement recognized by the *USA Standard, Specifications for 16mm and 35mm Silver-Gelatin Microfilms for Reel Applications, PH5.3-1967, Section 4,* are shown at the top of figure 6. The standard specifies that the maximum permissible width of the image area (dimension A in figure 6) is 1.3 inches (33.020mm) for unperforated 35mm film, and 0.944 inch (23.980mm) for the same width film perforated on both edges. Conversely, for dimension D, a minimum of 0.038 inch (0.965mm) is specified for unperforated 35mm film and 0.216 inch (5.486mm) for perforated film. Longitudinal image (dimension B) with the lines of text arranged at right angles to the edge of the film cannot normally be extended beyond approximately 1 3/4 inches (44.450mm) with most cameras and usually must be limited to the image area occupied by the material being filmed. Dimension C shall be about 3/32 inch (2.381mm) or less. Although wider or closer spacing is allowable, it is generally advantageous to limit the interframe spacing in the interests of economy. The latter can be even better realized by the careful selection of image placement and reduction ratios. The work and its projected use must be evaluated together for optimum results, with due considerations for the capacities and limitations of the cameras, reading machines, reader-printers, etc., likely to be involved, and with special attention to compatibility.

Position 2A, as shown on the chart in figure 6, is preferred when the dimensions of the original and the type size allow it. Position 2B (the next choice) may require up to twice as much film as position 2A, as the chart indicates. (All pages shown are drawn to the same relative dimensions.) This means twice as much footage for each positive copy, of course, as well as for the negative. Position 1A (the third choice, and sometimes the

Microfilm Position Chart

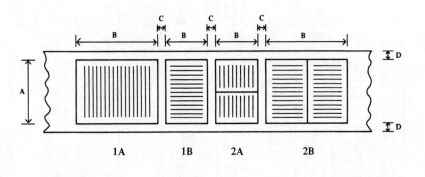

1A   **1B**   **2A**   **2B**

Positions 1A and 1B are single-page exposures; positions 2A and 2B are double-page exposures.

In positions 1A and 2A the text is perpendicular to the long axis of the film; in positions 1B and 2B the text is parallel to the long axis of the film.

For reference concerning microfilm positions, see USA Standard. Specifications for 16mm and 35mm Silver-Gelatin Microfilms for Reel Applications, PH5.3-1967, Section 4, or the latest revision thereof.

Guide to Maximum Reduction Ratios

Type size of original*: Letter height mm (lower case e)	(1-2mm)	3+mm
Maximum, Dimension A (unperf. film):	17″	25″
Maximum, Dimension A (perf. film):	13″	18″
Maximum, Dimension B:	24″	34″
Maximum reduction ratio:	16x	20x

For a discussion of type size, see William R. Hawken, Copying Methods Manual (Chicago, American Library Assn., LTP, 1966).

Figure 6

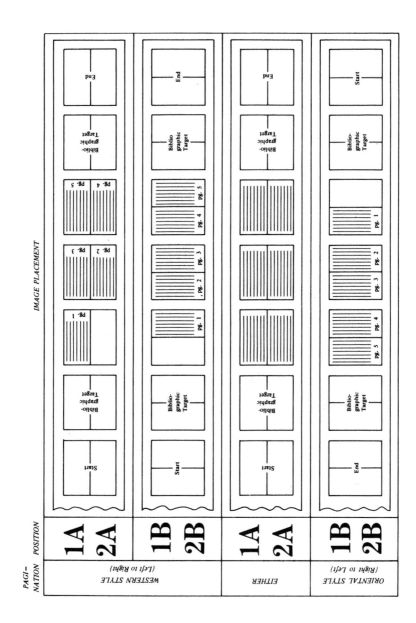

Figure 7   FILMING POSITIONS FOR PUBLICATIONS IN ORIENTAL STYLE VS. WESTERN STYLE

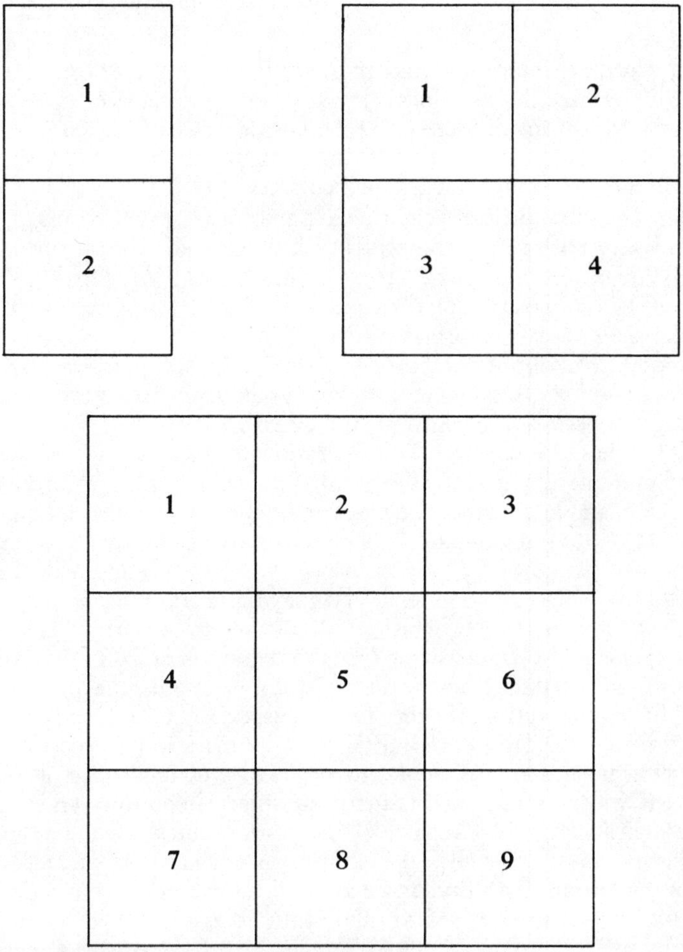

1
2

1	2
3	4

1	2	3
4	5	6
7	8	9

Figure 8

only one possible) not only may require twice the film necessary for position 2B, but also may entail, for bound material, more than twice the labor costs of position 2B because the volume must be shifted and repositioned under the camera lens after each exposure: after the recto of a page is filmed, the volume must be shifted to the right when the page is turned in order to film the verso, then to the left to film the recto of the next page, and so on.

The table in the lower part of figure 6 indicates the maximum recommended dimensions for material to be filmed in any one of the four standard positions, as well as the maximum recommended reductions for two ranges of type size; interpolations can be made for sizes not given. To use the table, determine the page height, width, and approximate type size of the material to be filmed; then, using the position chart in conjunction with the table, determine whether the material can be filmed in position 2A, or whether 2B or even 1A will be necessary.

For languages reading from right to left and for other variations from the usual Western language arrangement, the page shall be positioned to allow for the normal and logical progression of pages (see figure 7). This is accomplished by positioning the camera head so that progression of exposed film shall reflect the progression of text.

The actual reduction ratio chosen shall make the best practical use of the available film width to achieve the maximum legibility of the image. The maximum permissible width for the latter on 35mm unperforated film is 1.3 inches (33.020mm). This "permissible image width" is an important factor and must not be disregarded in making preparation for filming. An example follows: The chart and table indicate that a book 10 inches (254.00mm) high and 13 inches (330.20mm) wide (across a double-page opening) with type size of average height (2mm lower case "e", or 0.0787 inch) and good legibility, may be microfilmed in position 2A with a *maximum* reduction ratio of 20 diameters. A warning is hereby sounded, however, by emphasizing that the reduction ratios indicated in the table are maximums. These ratios must not be applied mechanically without due consideration of other factors, especially the "permissible width" dimension already noted. If the 20X specification is used for a volume with the dimensions cited, the results may be unsatisfactory: the double-page width of 13 inches reduced 20 times will produce an image width (dimension A) of 13/20 inch (16.51mm), or only half the permissible image width of 1.3 inches (33.020mm). To achieve the correct "mix" of dimension, legibility, and economy, a lower reduction ratio, around 14X, must here be used to fill up the frame, thus avoiding the waste of an undue amount of usable film along both edges, and to achieve superior legibility by using all the film area available.

If provision is to be made for the possibility of printing positive copies on *perforated* film, a reduction ratio of about 16 diameters in position 1A would be required, since the maximum permissible image width for perforated 35mm film is 0.944 inch (23.980mm).

The intended use of the negative may dictate the position as well as the reduction ratio. If other institutions or concerns will be making further reproductions, it is important to obtain their recommendations for reduction ratios and image placement before beginning the filming.

Material such as inserts and fold-outs the same size or smaller than the double-page spread of the volume in question, in which the type size and legibility are comparable to the text, shall be filmed at the same reduction ratio as the rest of the book. Where type size is smaller and legibility inferior, lower reduction ratios are indicated. Inserts and fold-outs too large to meet the specifications indicated in figure 6 must be filmed in sections, from left to right and from top to bottom as shown in figure 8. An overlap of at least one inch (25.400mm) shall be provided between adjacent sections, and the reduction ratio used shall allow for the desired number of sections with the proper overlap.

Filming shall normally be done at 14 to 20 diameters reduction, although ratios up to 24X may be used to avoid position 1A, type size permitting. For a discussion of the quality index method of determining reduction ratios, consult *NMA Standard, MS104-1972. Inspection and Quality Control of First Generation Silver Halide Microfilm, NMA. Silver Spring [Md.] 1972*, pages 19, 21, 25-26, and figure 34.

Film Stock

Use only safety microfilm stock as defined by *American Standard Specifications for Safety Photographic Film, PH1.25-1965*, or the latest revision thereof. Such film generally bears the legend "safety" along its outer edges. Microfilm intended for permanent preservation shall be made with film stock which meets the *American National Standard Specifications for Photographic Film for Archival Records, Silver-Gelatin Type on Cellulose Ester Base, PH1.28-1969*, or the latest revision thereof.

The negative film emulsion must be capable of resolving 400 lines per millimeter.

Unperforated film shall be used if at all possible; perforated film may be used only when the particular application makes it necessary.

Dimensions of the film, processed and unprocessed, shall meet the specifications set forth in *USA Standard Specifications for 16mm and 35mm Silver-Gelatin Microfilms for Reel Applications, PH5.3-1967, Section 4*, or the latest revision thereof.

Filming Procedures

Only a qualified microphotographer may perform the actual filming of library material. The camera and base support must be rigid, since any vibration will blur the film images, and the area in which the filming is done must be as free of dust as possible.

The film produced shall resolve at least the NBS 7.1 line pattern in the corners of the image at a reduction ratio of 15X (see figure 9 for more detail). In determining the resolving power of the film system, the microcopy resolution test charts available from the National Bureau of Standards or the *mire* of the International Organization for Standardization shall be used; these provide sets of precisely spaced lines of varying widths (see figure 10). The test chart shall be photographed at a predetermined reduction ratio, with a background density of 1.2 to 1.8 as measured on a densitometer. After processing, the film shall be examined under a micro-scope (not with a reading machine) and a visual determination made of the most closely spaced set of lines which can be identified as separate and dis-tinct. This reading multiplied by the reduction ratio will give the resolving power of the system in lines per millimeter. For example, if the resolution test chart is filmed at 20 diameters reduction, and the most closely spaced set of lines which can be distinguished as separate is that spaced at 5.6 lines per millimeter on the chart, the resolving power of the system is 20 X 5.6, or 112 lines per millimeter.

The film image shall be of sufficient contrast to permit easy reading and reproduction. Unless a different background density is required to produce contrast, the material to be filmed shall be lighted so that images on the camera negative normally will have a background density range of 1.0 to 1.4, with the minimum possible variation in any one frame as measured by a densitometer. To obtain correct exposure and a uniform density, ex-posure tests shall be made at the reduction ratio to be used in the filming in order to establish the level of reflected light (as determined by the light meter reading) that will produce images of a density within the required range. The intensity of the light source used shall be variable, with control by means of a rheostat or other similar device. During the filming, fre-quent light meter readings shall be taken, particularly when the color or shading of the paper changes noticeably, and the light intensity adjusted as necessary to maintain the same light meter reading. If the reduction ratio is changed significantly, new exposure tests shall be made because, even at the same light meter reading, the amount of light reaching the film is dif-ferent at various reduction ratios. The lighting shall be kept balanced at all times to ensure uniform exposure of the entire frame; when one lamp burns out, all shall be rebalanced to achieve the specified illumination. Standard filters may be used to compensate for colored inks, colored paper, or stains in the original material. The density range within an ex-posure shall not exceed .05.

Showthrough in bound originals printed on one side only shall be eliminated or reduced as far as possible by backing each page with a white opaque sheet of paper or cardboard. Showthrough in originals printed on both sides can be reduced or eliminated entirely by backing the page with a dark sheet of paper.

In turning the pages, the operator shall be certain that all page move-ment has stopped before the next exposure is made. To ensure that all parts of the image are in focus, both sides of a bound volume shall be level. An adjustable book cradle is normally used to keep the material flat and within the field of focus at all times. Photographic glass which is free of distortions may be used to hold pages flat; hands shall not be used, since they detract from the appearance of the image.

Take care to keep the material properly aligned with the camera lens and film edges through frequent use of the finder light or by aligning the

Figure 9

Microcopy Resolution Test Chart-1010

NATIONAL BUREAU OF STANDARDS-1963-A

NBS/ISO Correlation Table *

REDUCTION SCALE	ISO CHARACTER SIZE			NBS PATTERN NUMBER Numbers of line pairs per millimeter		
	1st Generation	2nd Generation	Distribution	1st Generation	2nd Generation	Distribution
1:30	90	100	112	4.5	4.0	3.6
1:24	80	90	100	5.0	4.5	4.0
1:21.2	70	80	90	5.6	5.0	4.5
1:16;1:15	56	63	70	7.1	6.3	5.6
1.12;1:10.6 1/9	45	50	56	9.0	8.0	7.1
1:7.5	35	40	45	11.0	10.0	9.0

When the National Bureau of Standards "Microcopy Resolution Test Chart" (above) is used, the pattern numbers in this table corresponding to the ISO character size (see figure 10) will give approximately the same legibility.

Note: To obtain valid results, the test charts themselves must be used. Do not use the facsimiles in figures 9 and 10 for making tests.

material with the guide marks on the copy bed.

The reel must not be overloaded; i.e., the film shall not be wound closer than 1/4 inch (6.350mm) to the outer edge of the reel, and in no case shall it exceed the diameter of the reel itself. Film shall be wound with the "START" target at the outer end.

Processing the Exposed Film

Exposed film shall be developed with an organic developing agent such as metol, hydroquinone, or glycin, compounded to produce a silver image essentially black; fixed in a thiosulfate bath; and finally washed with water to remove residual hypo (thiosulfate). Do not use so-called hypo eliminators and developers designed to produce stained or colored images. The residual hypo content of the processed film shall agree with the terms of the *American National Standard Methylene Blue Method for Measuring Residual Chemicals in Films, Plates, and Papers, PR4.8-1971,* or the latest revision thereof.

Inspection of the Film

Inspect all processed film, whether positive or negative, as soon as possible after processing has been completed. If this is not feasible, make at least a preliminary check for obvious defects resulting from faults or processing flaws, to prevent any similar defects in succeeding reels.

Extreme care must be exercised during inspection to ensure that the film is not scratched. Either a hand magnifying glass (loupe) or reading machines which have been carefully inspected to make certain that the film in motion does not make contact with the glass flats which hold it in place for reading or printing may be used. Other reading machines may be employed but only with extreme caution; a sample reel shall be tested first on the machine to make sure that the glass flats are not in contact with the image area while the film is in motion.

Inspect negative film frame by frame to determine that all volumes or parts (if more than one), pages, and targets are included and filmed in the proper order, that the images are properly aligned, and that the individual image is clear, sharp, and uniformly lighted. The background density shall be routinely checked visually, and double-checked every few feet with a densitometer. Background density shall normally be between 1.0 and 1.4, although particular applications may require heavier or lighter densities.

Pages improperly filmed shall be refilmed, together with the page preceding and the page following, in such a way that a 2-inch (50.800mm) space be allowed for splicing before and after the remake which shall consist of at least 1 foot (304.80mm) of images. The remade

MIRE

Z 43-007

CONTROLE:

AFNOR
19, rue du 4 Septembre
75-PARIS-2ᵉ

Figure 10

film shall be inspected and spliced in place of the faulty film. In the finished film, the first frame in the spliced strip will be a duplicate of the frame immediately preceding the first splice; a corresponding duplication will occur at the second splice. This arrangement ensures at each splice point one good frame unaffected by the splicing process.

Heat-weld, butt-end splices are generally stronger and less bulky than other types and will cause less trouble in printing satisfactory copies. If cemented splices are used, the cement must not contain acetic acid or other chemicals injurious to the long-term storage qualities of the film. Cellophane tape and tape of the pressure-sensitive type shall not be used.

Every effort shall be made to keep the number of splices to the minimum. Since they are potential sources of trouble when microfilm is used in reading machines, all necessary splices shall be made in the negative copy before any positive copies are printed. Splices shall not be made merely for the economy of using short ends of unexposed film.

For further discussion of inspection procedures, consult *NMA Standard. MS104-1972. Inspection and Quality Control of First Generation Silver Halide Microfilm* (see section 10, Selected References).

Intermediate Copies

Intermediate copies are used only to print many distribution (release or research) copies. The background density of a silver, second generation negative shall conform to the values listed in Appendix A.

Research Use Copies

Film Intended for the Collections of the Library of Congress

Research use copies, generally positive, which are intended for the permanent collections of the Library shall be made on a contact printer with film stock meeting the specifications of *American National Standard Specifications for Photographic Film for Archival Records, Silver-Gelatin Type on Cellulose Ester Base, PH1.28-1969,* or the latest revision thereof.

Film Specifications and Processing

Research use film must be capable of resolving at least 400 lines per millimeter.

The exposed reference film shall be processed as indicated above (see section 4) and must meet the standard for density as shown in Appendix A.

Characteristics of Research Use Films

Research use film must be without splices and have at least 18 inches (457.20mm) of leader and 18 inches of trailer.

Library of Congress Criteria for
Use in Planning Film Purchases

In purchasing research use film, the Library of Congress will test it, at least on a sampling basis, for acceptable bibliographical and technical quality. Satisfactory legibility must be uniformly present.

Safety-base film generally has the word "safety" at intervals along its outer edges. When in doubt, technicians shall test the film under procedures set forth in *American Standard Specifications for Safety Photographic Film, PH1.25-1965*, or the latest revision thereof.

Determine the residual hypo content in accordance with the *American National Standard Methylene Blue Method for Measuring Thiosulfate and Silver Densitometric Method for Measuring Residual Chemicals in Films, Plates, and Papers, PH4.8-1973*, or the latest revision thereof. Residual hypo shall not exceed 1.00 microgram/cm^2 as stated in *American National Standard Specifications for Photographic Film for Archival Records, Silver-Gelatin Type, on Cellulose Ester Base, PH1.28-1969*, or the latest revision thereof.

The technical and bibliographical quality of the film shall be in conformity with the practices outlined in sections 1, 2, and 4 above.

Since each successive generation of microfilm involves some loss of image quality, the Library of Congress shall include among other criteria in film evaluation for purchase an exact determination of the number of generations which separate the film under consideration from the camera negative.

Storage

Conditions for the storage of library microfilm shall approach, as nearly as possible, the specifications set forth in the *American Standard Practice for Storage of Processed Silver-Gelatin Microfilm, PH5.4-1970*, or the latest revision thereof, on reels made to the specifications of the *USA Standard Dimensions for 100-foot Reels for Processed 16mm and 35mm Microfilm, PH5.6-1968*, or the latest revision thereof.

Containers shall open easily and be made of durable material free from chemicals harmful to the film. Outer dimensions of the containers shall not exceed 4 inches (101.600mm) by 4 inches by 1 9/16 inches

(39.687mm) for 35mm film. Each container shall bear a lable on one end showing as much information from the bibliographical target as possible without crowding the label. If the reel is part of a set, the label shall also give the reel number and an indication of the contents of that particular reel (inclusive dates, volumes, etc.).

Rubber bands shall not be used on microfilm reels; strips of paper free from chemicals harmful to the film and furnished with strong string ties are recommended for holding the microfilm on the reels. Care shall be taken not to wind the film too tightly on the reel, since scratches on the film are likely to result.

Selected References

Ballou, Hubbard W., *ed. Guide to Microreproduction Equipment.* Annapolis, National Microfilm Association (latest edition and/or supplement).

Hawken, William R. *Copying Methods Manual.* Chicago, American Library Association, Library Technology Program, 1966.

National Microfilm Association. *Glossary of Terms for Microphotography.* Annapolis, [National Microfilm Association] 1966, or the latest edition thereof.

– – – *NMA Standard. Inspection and Quality Control of First Generation Silver Halide Microfilm,* Silver Spring, Md., National Microfilm Association [1972].

U.S. Library of Congress. *National Register of Microform Masters.* Washington, Library of Congress (latest edition).

Veaner, Alan B. *The Evaluation of Micropublications. A Handbook for Librarians.* Chicago, American Library Association, Library Technology Program, 1971 (LTP pub. no. 17).

Appendix A

The density of the background of the document image area shall be as listed below. The densities of silver films shall be visual diffuse transmission density.

Generation	Density Range
1N	1.0 to 1.4
2P	0.04 to 1.20
2N	1.0 to 1.4
3P	0.04 to 0.20
3N	0.90 to 1.5*

---

* The tolerance on distribution copy is always larger because of the variables which add up through the generations.

SPECIFICATIONS FOR THE MICROFILMING OF NEWSPAPERS IN THE LIBRARY OF CONGRESS

Preparation of the Files

Preliminary Collation

The entire file shall be collated before filming, page by page, and a complete list made of:

a. all missing issues, and issues out of order;

b. all missing pages, and pages out of order;

c. all imperfections, such as mutilations, tears, stains, obliterations, and missing portions. Imperfections,which do not affect any text or illustration may be ignored.

Completion of the File

Every effort shall be made to obtain missing issues, missing pages, and replacements for mutilated pages before submitting the file to the microphotographer for filming. Major research libraries and other libraries that may be expected to have the material shall be contacted in an attempt to locate copies of the missing portions. If located, the material shall be acquired, permanently or on loan, and inserted in the proper sequence in the files. When this is not possible, microfilm made to the same specifications as those used for the basic file shall be ordered from the institution concerned and later spliced into the LC negative. To avoid distortion or loss of text in the gutter of the volume, it is preferred that the tight bindings be removed to permit photoduplication of the entire content. Where the integrity of the original file may be jeopardized by the removal of

This is a reprint of the pamphlet, *Specifications for the Microfilming of Newspapers in the Library of Congress*. Washington: Library of Congress, 1972. Available from the Government Printing Office, order no. 3000 0055.

bindings, it is recommended that they be loosened; if this cannot be done, every effort must be made to minimize textual loss and to achieve the best possible copy. If possible, any pages or issues found out of order shall also be rearranged in correct sequence before filming.

Bibliographical Arrangement of the File and Film

Divide newspapers which require more than one roll of film on a systematic and bibliographically acceptable basis, and employ a chronological arrangement according to the Gregorian calendar. No reel should include the microfilm of more than one month or more than one year unless all months or all years contained on the reel are included in their entirety. The examples below illustrate both the acceptable and commonly used arrangements, as well as the unacceptable:

Acceptable

a. January   1-10
   January 11-20
   January 21-31

b. January   1-15
   January 16-31

c. January 1-31

d. January 1-February 28

e. January 1-March 31

f. January 1-June 30

g. January 1-December 31

h. January 1, 1960-December 31, 1961

Unacceptable

a. January   1-January 17
   January 18-February 9
   February 10-February 26
   February 27-March 15

b. January 1, 1960-January 5, 1961

c. January 6, 1961-December 25-1962

All sections and pages of newspapers shall be filmed, including any blank pages which figure in consecutive pagination whether actually numbered or not. Numbered or lettered sections shall be filmed in numerical or alphabetical order, followed by unnumbered sections such as magazine sections or comics. The principal news section, however, shall always be filmed first, regardless of its number or letter.

Final Collation

Final collation and revision of the file as necessary are essential before the start of filming, and the complete target series outlined below (see 2.2 Targets) must agree with this final collection in every detail, accounting for all items involved in the collation and noting missing issues, missing pages, and mutilations. All macroscopic targets—both those "constant" targets, standard at the beginning and end of every reel, and those "as needed," indicating variations from the norm—must be inserted in the file in their proper places before filming begins.

Technical Guide

Treatment of Creases and Wrinkles

Before filming, remove creases and wrinkles in the newspapers where possible and leave no such problems for the camera operator to resolve. If a large press is available, unbound newspaper files shall be humidified (sprinkled or sprayed lightly with water) and stacked neatly in the press with 1/4-inch (6.350mm) plywood boards of slightly larger area than the newspapers inserted in the stack at 3-inch (76.200mm) intervals. The newspapers should be free of wrinkles after pressure has been applied for 24 hours. Wrinkles and creases may also be removed with an electric iron. To prevent scorching or glazing, the iron should be set at a fairly low temperature (somewhere between the "Silk" and "Rayon" settings on most irons).

Newspapers stuck together must be handled with extreme care; they may be steamed apart if they are not to be filmed immediately. After steaming, sheets of nonadhesive material such as silicone paper can be inserted between the pages to prevent further sticking. Occasionally the center gutter of the paper will be found closed due to an excess of glue used in assembling the sheets. Especial care is needed in separating these slowly and carefully to avoid damage.

Targets

Film appropriate targets at the beginning and end of each newspaper reel, and as necessary throughout the film. Menu boards or titling sets are often used to make such targets (see figures 2 and 2a).

The word "START" must appear in the first frame of any roll of film, and the word "END" in the last frame, in letters which produce images on film at least 0.08 inch (2.032mm) high. Following the "START" target and preceding the "END" target on each reel shall be a bibliographic target identifying the work filmed. This shall contain the country (omit for U.S. newspapers), state (or province for Canadian newspapers and those of certain other countries when required to avoid ambiguity), and city of publication, the title, and the inclusive dates of the material filmed (see figure 2). The height of the letters in this primary bibliographic target shall also be at least 0.08 inch (2.032mm) high.

If the material covered by the primary bibliographic target extends over more than one reel, a secondary bibliographic target indicating the contents of that particular reel shall be filmed immediately following the primary bibliographic target. Bibliographic data shall be in conformity with the latest edition of *Newspapers on Microfilm*, published by the Catalog and Publications Division of the Library of Congress and available from the Library's Card Division, Washington, D.C. 20541.

The name of the organization or institution responsible for the actual filming and the year of the filming shall be given on one of the preliminary targets (see target 2 in figure 2a). If another organization will be handling the distribution of copies of the microfilm or was instrumental in organizing the project, that information may be given also. If it is anticipated that the master negative will not be retained by the producer, the assignment of responsibility for filming shall be amended to read "Microfilmed by (the producer) for (the expected repository of the negative)."

Film the list of missing issues, missing pages, mutilations, etc. (see section 1.4 above) as a separate frame or frames immediately after the bibliographic target. If the file is fragmentary, a list of the issues filmed may be used instead (see target 3 in figure 2a).

A target indicating the month, in letters large enough that the resulting image on film is at least 0.08 inch (2.032) high, shall precede the issues for each month. When filming several volumes, a target indicating each volume (or year, or both, as appropriate) shall be filmed before the issues for that volume or year (see target 4 in figure 2a).

An indication of the reduction ratio used in the filming may also be given on one of the preliminary targets. This may be shown by filming, at the same reduction ration used in the first issue, a section of an inch and centimeter scale at least three inches (76.200mm) long; this will make possible a more accurate reconstruction of the size of the original material than would a simple statement of the reduction ratio (see target 5 in figure 2a).

In special cases, it may be desirable to include one or more of the following items of information on a target: location of the original material,

NEW YORK NEW YORK AMERICAN MINERVA JANUARY 1 1970 THRU JUNE 30 1970

Figure 2

reference to a separate index or to supplementary bibliographic data for the material, and note of restrictions on further reproduction or use of the microfilm.

Insert appropriate targets to indicate any faults in the original so that they are not mistaken for errors in filming. When an issue or page is missing from the material being filmed, a space of 1 1/4 inches (31.750mm) to two inches (50.800mm) on the film (one half turn of the camera crank) shall be left blank to allow for splicing in missing material later. A target with the wording "issue missing," "issues missing," "page missing," or "pages missing," as appropriate, shall appear in the center of this space. (see targets 8 and 9 in figure 2a).

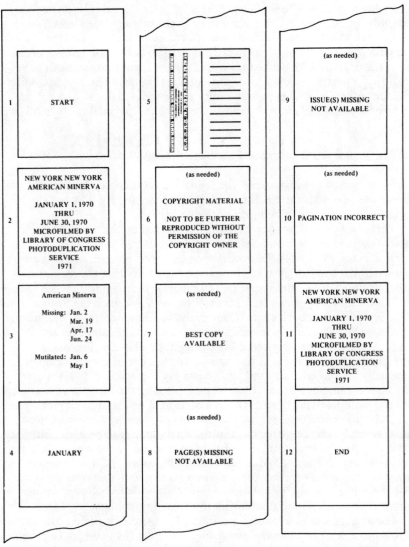

Figure 2a

Before a mutilated page, film a target indicating that the following page was filmed from the "Best Copy Available"; this shall also be done for illegible pages or pages otherwise faulty in the original (see target 7 in figure 2a). Mutilations which do not affect any printing or illustrations may be ignored. If a page has been mutilated so that a portion has been lost, the page shall be backed up with a piece of white paper, both to reveal that a portion is lost and to prevent the filming of the corresponding portion of the following page in faulty sequence.

Use targets 6 and 10, concerning copyright and pagination, as necessary.

Image Placement and Reduction Ratios

The position of the images and the reduction ratio chosen for a particular newspaper depends on the dimensions, type size, and legibility of the original, and the use to be made of the negative.

The four types of image placement recognized by the *USA Standard Specifications for 16mm and 35mm Silver-Gelatin Microfilms for Reel Applications, PH5.3-1967, Section 4,* or the latest revision thereof, are shown at the top of figure 3. The standard specifies that the maximum permissible width of the image area (dimension A in figure 3) is 1.3 inches (33.020mm) for unperforated 35mm film and 0.944 inch (23.980mm) for film perforated on both edges. Conversely, for dimension D a minimum of 0.038 inch (0.965mm) is specified for unperforated 35mm film and 0.216 inch (5.486mm) for perforated film. Longitudinal image dimension with the lines of text arranged at right angles to the edge of the film cannot normally be extended beyond approximately 1 3/4 inches (44.450mm) with most cameras and usually shall be limited to the image area occupied by the material being filmed. Dimension C shall be about 3/32 inch (2.381mm) or less. Although wider spacing or closer spacing is allowable, it is generally advantageous to limit the interframe spacing in the interests of economy. Economy can be even better realized by the careful selection of image placement and reduction ratios. The entire file and projected use must be evaluated together for optimum results, with due consideration for the capacities and limitations of cameras, reading machines, reader-printers, etc., with special attention to their compatibility.

For average-size newspapers, position 2B (figure 3) is preferred. Position 2A is possible only when the newspaper is smaller than average (e.g., tabloids). When 2A is possible, a substantial saving of film is realized. Position 1A is occasionally the only possible choice, as for older oversize newspapers or in some cases where perforated film is used. Position 1A may not only require twice as much film as is needed for position 2B but may also entail more than twice the labor costs of 2B, since the volumes must be shifted and repositioned under the camera lens after each exposure; after the recto of a page is filmed, the volume must be shifted to the right

Microfilm Position Chart

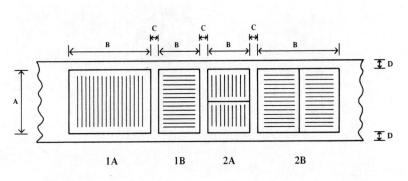

1A 1B 2A 2B

Positions 1A and 1B are single-page exposures; positions 2A and 2B are double-page exposures.

In positions 1A and 2A the text is perpendicular to the long axis of the film; in positions 1B and 2B the text is parallel to the long axis of the film.

Guide to Maximum Reduction Ratios

Type size of original:*	(2-4 pt.)	(5+ pt.)
Maximum, Dimension A (unperf. film):	17″	25″
Maximum, Dimension A (perf. film):	13″	18″
Maximum, Dimension B:	24″	34″
Maximum reduction ratio:	16x	20x

For a discussion of type size, see William R. Hawken, Copying Methods Manual (Chicago, American Library Assn., LTP, 1966).

Figure 3

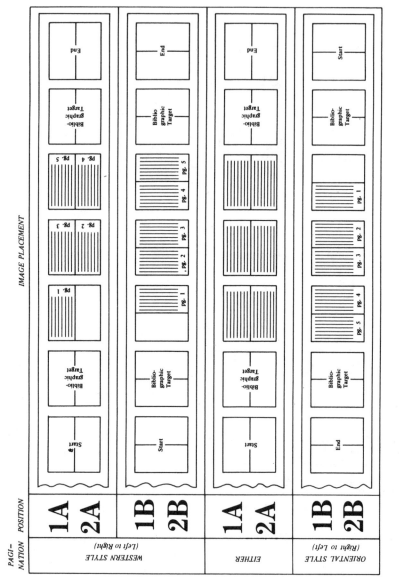

Figure 3b   FILMING POSITIONS FOR PUBLICATIONS IN ORIENTAL STYLE VS. WESTERN STYLE

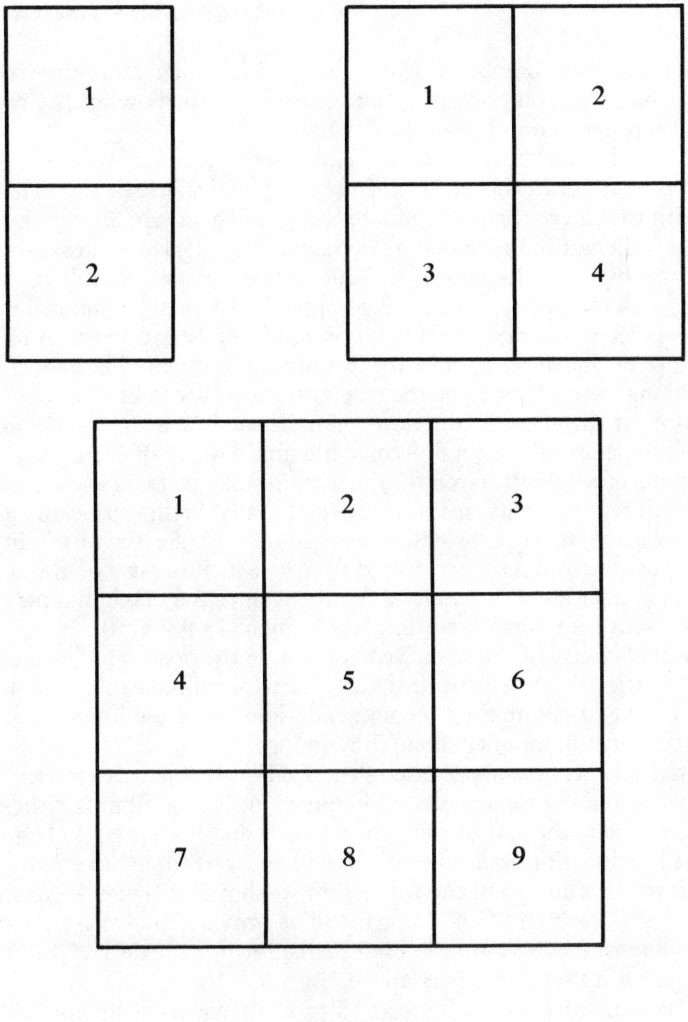

Figure 4

when the page is turned in order to film the verso, then to the left to film the recto of the next page, and so on.

The table in the lower part of figure 3 indicates the maximum recommended dimensions for material to be filmed in any one of the four standard positions, as well as the maximum recommended reductions for two ranges of type size; interpolations can be made for sizes not given. To use the table, determine the page height, width, and approximate type size of the material to be filmed; then, using the position chart in conjunction with the table, determine whether the material can be filmed in position 2B or whether 2A or even 1A.

For languages reading from right to left and for other variations from the usual Western arrangement, position the image to allow for the normal and logical progression of pages (see figure 3b).

The reduction ratios, it should be remembered, are maximums. The actual reduction ratio chosen shall make full practical use of the available film width to achieve the maximum legibility of the image. For example, the table and chart indicate that a newspaper page 23 1/2 inches (59.690cm) high and 30 inches (76.200cm) wide across a double page opening, with average type size and good legibility, may be microfilmed in position 2B with a maximum reduction ratio of 20 diameters. A reduction of 24X might be acceptable for legibility, but it would be wasteful of film along both edges, since the resultant image width on the film (dimension A) at this higher reduction will measure .979 inch (24.865 mm), considerably short of the total permissible image width of 1.3 inches (33.020 mm) for unperforated film. Use of 20 diameters, however, will satisfy both requirements: maximum use of available film space and good legibility for the image. If provision were to be made for the possibility of printing positive copies on perforated film, a reduction ratio of about 16 diameters in position 1 A would be required, since the maximum permissible image width for perforated film is .944 inch (23.980mm).

The intended use of the negative may dictate the position as well as the reduction ratio. If other institutions or concerns will be making the prints, it is important to obtain their recommendations for reduction ratio and image placement before beginning the filming.

Material such as newspaper inserts and fold-outs which are smaller than the regular spread of the newspaper in question shall be filmed at the same reduction ratio as the rest of the paper. Inserts and fold-outs too large to meet the specifications indicated in figure 3 must be filmed in sections, from left to right and from top to bottom, as shown in figure 4. An overlap of at least one inch (25.400 mm) shall be provided between adjacent sections, and the reduction ratio used shall allow for the desired number of sections with the proper overlap.

Filming shall normally be done at 16 to 20 diameters reduction, although ratios up to 24X may be used if necessary to avoid position 1 A.

Film Stock

Use only safety microfilm stock as defined by *American Standard Specifications for Safety Photographic Film, PH1.25-1965*, or the latest revision thereof. Such film generally bears the legend "safety" along its outer edges. Microfilm intended for permanent preservation shall be made with film stock which meets the *American National Standard Specifications for Photographic Film for Archival Records, Silver-Gelatin Type on Cellulose Ester Base, PH1.28-1969*, or the latest revision thereof.

The negative film emulsion shall be capable of resolving 400 lines per millimeter (see below).

Unperforated film shall be used if at all possible; perforated film may be used only when the particular application makes it necessary.

Dimensions of the film, processed and unprocessed, shall meet the specifications set forth in *USA Standard Specifications for 16mm and 35mm Silver-Gelatin Microfilms for Reel Applications, PH5.3-1967, Section 4*, or the latest revision thereof.

Filming Procedures

Only a trained operator may perform the actual filming of library material.

The film produced shall resolve at least the NBS 7.1 line pattern in the corners of the image at a reduction ratio of 15X (see figure 5 for other reductions). In determining the resolving power of the film system, the microcopy resolution test charts available from the National Bureau of Standards or the *mire* of the International Standards Organization shall be used; these provide sets of precisely spaced lines of varying widths (see figures 5 and 6). The test chart shall be photographed at a predetermined reduction ratio, with a background density of 1.2 to 1.8 as measured on a densitometer. After processing, the film shall be examined under a microscope (not with a reading machine) and a visual determination made of the most closely spaced set of lines which can be identified as separate and distinct. This reading multiplied by the reduction ratio will give the resolving power of the system in lines per millimeter. For example, if the resolution test chart is filmed at 20 diameters reduction, and the most closely spaced set of lines which can be distinguished as separate is that spaced at 5.6 lines per millimeter on the chart, the resolving power of the system is 20 x 5.6, or 112 lines per millimeter.

The camera and base support must be rigid, since any vibration will blur the film images, and the area in which the filming is done must be as free of dust as possible.

The film image shall be of sufficient contrast to permit easy reading and reproduction. Unless a different background density is required to produce contrast, the material to be filmed shall be lighted so that images on the camera negative will have a background density range of 1.0 to 1.4, with minimum possible variation in any one frame as measured by a densitometer. To obtain a uniform density and correct exposure, exposure tests shall be made at the reduction ratio to be used in the filming in order to establish the level of reflected light (as determined by the light meter reading) that will produce images of a density within the required range. The intensity of the light source used shall be variable, with control by means of a rheostat or other device. During the filming, frequent light meter readings shall be taken, particularly when the color or shading of the paper

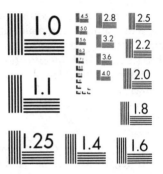

Microcopy Resolution Test Chart
NATIONAL BUREAU OF STANDARDS-1963-A

NBS/ISO Correlation Table *

REDUCTION SCALE	ISO CHARACTER SIZE			NBS PATTERN NUMBER Numbers of line pairs per millimeter		
	1st Generation	2nd Generation	Distribution	1st Generation	2nd Generation	Distribution
1:30	90	100	112	4.5	4.0	3.6
1:24	80	90	100	5.0	4.5	4.0
1:21.2	70	80	90	5.6	5.0	4.5
1:16;1:15	56	63	70	7.1	6.3	5.6
1.12;1:10.6 1/9	45	50	56	9.0	8.0	7.1
1:7.5	35	40	45	11.0	10.0	9.0

When the National Bureau of Standards "Microcopy Resolution Test Chart" (above) is used, the pattern numbers in this table corresponding to the ISO character size (see figure 6) will give approximately the same legibility.

Note: To obtain valid results, the test charts themselves must be used. Do not use the facsimiles in figures 5 and 6 for making tests.

Figure 5

changes noticeably, and the light intensity adjusted as necessary to maintain the same light meter reading. If the reduction ratio is changed significantly, new exposure tests shall be made because even at the same light meter reading, the amount of light reaching the film is different at various reduction ratios. The lighting shall be kept balanced at all times to ensure even exposure of the entire frame; when one lamp burns out, all shall be replaced. Standard filters may be used to compensate for colored inks, colored paper, or stains in the original material.

Material shall be photographed in such a way that impressions on the succeeding pages or on the recto show through as little as possible. This may be accomplished by placing a piece of black paper behind the page being filmed.

In turning the pages, the operator shall be certain that all page movement has stopped before the next exposure is made. To ensure that all parts of the image are in focus, both sides of a bound volume shall be level. An adjustable book cradle is normally used to keep the material flat and within the field of focus at all times. Photographic glass which is free of distortions may be used to hold pages flat; hands shall not be used, since they mar the appearance of the image.

Take care to keep the material properly aligned with the camera lens and film edges through frequent use of the finder light or by aligning the material with the guide marks on the copy bed.

The reel must not be overloaded; i.e., the accumulation of the film shall not be wound closer than 1/4 inch (6.350mm) to the outer edge of the reel, and in no case shall it exceed the diameter of the reel itself. Film shall be wound with the "START" target at the outer end.

Processing the Exposed Film

Exposed film shall be developed with an organic developing agent such as metol, hydroquinone, or glycin, compounded to produce a silver image essentially black; fixed in a thiosulfate bath; and finally washed with water to remove residual hypo (thiosulfate). Do not use so-called hypo eliminators and developers designed to produce stained or colored images. The residual hypo

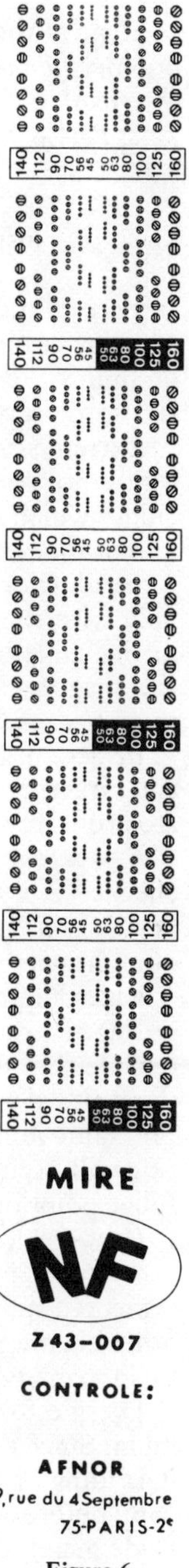

MIRE

Z43-007

CONTROLE:

AFNOR
19, rue du 4 Septembre
75-PARIS-2ᵉ

Figure 6

content of the processed film, as determined by *American National Standard Methylene Blue Method for Measuring Thiosulfate and Silver Densitometric Method for Measuring Residual Chemicals in Films, Plates, and Papers, PH4.8-1971*, or the latest revision thereof.

Inspection of the Film

Inspect all processed film, whether positive or negative, as soon as possible after processing has been completed. If this is not feasible, make at least a preliminary check for obvious defects resulting from faults or processing flaws, to prevent any similar defects in succeeding reels.

Extreme care must be exercised during inspection to ensure that the film is not scratched. Either a hand magnifying lens (loupe) or reading machines which have been carefully inspected to make certain that the film in motion does not make contact with the glass flats which hold it in place for reading or printing may be used. Other reading machines may be used only with extreme caution; a sample reel shall be tested first on the reading machine to determine whether or not the glass flats are in contact with the image area while the film is in motion, a situation to avoid lest scratches result.

Inspect negative film frame by frame to make sure that all issues, pages, and targets are included and filmed in the proper order, that the images are properly aligned, and that the image is clear, sharp, and evenly lighted. The background density shall be routinely checked visually and double-checked every few feet with a densitometer. Background density shall normally be between 1.0 and 1.4, although particular applications may require heavier or lighter densities.

Pages improperly filmed shall be refilmed, together with the page preceding and the page following, to allow adequate space for splicing. The remade film shall be inspected and spliced in place of the faulty film. In the finished film, the first frame in the spliced strip will be a duplicate of the frame immediately preceding the first splice; a corresponding duplication will occur at the second splice. This arrangement ensures at each splice point one good frame unaffected by the splicing process.

Heat-weld, butt-end splices are generally stronger and less bulky than other types and will cause less trouble in printing satisfactory copies. If cemented splices are used, the cement must not contain acetic acid or other chemicals injurious to the long-term storage qualities of the film. Cellophane tape and tape of the pressure-sensitive type shall not be used.

Every effort shall be made to keep the number of splices to the minimum. Since they are potential sources of trouble when microfilm is used in reading machines, all necessary splices shall be made in the negative copy before any positive copies of the film are printed. Splices shall not be made merely for the economy of using short ends of unexposed film.

Intermediate Copies

Intermediate copies are used only to print many distribution (release or reference) copies. The background density of a silver, second-generation negative shall conform to the values listed in Appendix A.

Reference Use Copies

Film intended for the Collections of the Library of Congress

Reference use copies, generally positive, which are intended for the permanent collections of the Library shall be made on a contact printer with film stock meeting the specifications of *American National Standard Specifications for Photographic Film for Archival Records, Silver-Gelatin Type on Cellulose Ester Base, PH1.28-1969*, or the latest revision thereof.

Film Specifications and Processing

Reference-use film must be capable of resolving at least 400 lines per millimeter.

The exposed reference film shall be processed as indicated above (see section 4) and must meet the standard for density as shown in Appendix A.

Characteristics of Reference Use Films

Reference-use film must be without splices and have at least 18 inches (45.720cm) of leader and 18 inches of trailer.

Library of Congress Criteria for Use in Planning Film Purchases

In purchasing reference-use film, the Library of Congress shall test it, at least on a sampling basis, for acceptable bibliographical and technical quality. Satisfactory legibility must be uniformly present.

Safety-base film generally has the word "safety" at intervals along its outer edges. When in doubt, technicians shall test the film under procedures set forth in *American Standard Specifications for Safety Photographic Film, PH1.25-1965*, or the latest revision thereof.

Determine the residual hypo content in accordance with the *American*

National Standard Methylene Blue Method for Measuring Thiosulfate and Silver Densitometric Method for Measuring Residual Chemicals in Films, Plates, and Papers, PH4.8-1971, or the latest revision thereof. Residual hypo shall not exceed 1.00 microgram/cm^2 as stated in *American National Standard Specifications for Photographic Film for Archival Records, Silver-Gelatin Type, on Cellulose Ester Base, PH1.28-1969*, or the latest revision thereof.

The technical and bibliographic quality of the film shall be in conformity with the practices outlined in sections 1 and 2 above.

Since each successive generation of microfilm involves some loss of image quality, the Library of Congress in film evaluation for purchase shall include among other criteria an exact determination of the number of generations which separate the film under consideration from the camera negative.

Storage

Conditions for storage of library microfilm shall approach, as nearly as possible, the specifications set forth in the *American Standard Practice for Storage of Processed Silver-Gelatin Microfilm, PH5.4-1970*, or the latest revision thereof, on reels made to the specifications of the *USA Standard Dimensions for 100-foot Reels for Processed 16mm and 35mm Microfilm, PH5.6-1968*, or the latest revision thereof.

Containers shall open easily and be made of material free from chemicals harmful to the film. Outer dimensions of the containers shall not exceed four inches (101.600mm) by four inches by 1 9/16 inches (39.687mm) for 35mm film. Each container shall bear a label on one end showing as much information from the bibliographical target as possible without crowding the label. If the reel is part of a set, the label shall also give the reel number and an indication of the contents of that particular reel (inclusive dates, volumes, etc.).

The reel must not be overloaded; i.e., the film shall not be wound closer than 1/4 inch (6.350mm) to the outer edge of the reel, and in no case may it exceed the diameter of the reel itself. Film shall be wound with the "START" target at the outer end.

Rubber bands shall not be used on microfilm reels; strips of paper free of chemicals harmful to the film and furnished with strong string ties are recommended for holding the microfilm on the reels. Care shall be taken not to wind the film too tightly on the reel, since scratches on the film are likely to result.

Selected References

American Library Association. *Microfilm Norms*. Chicago, American Library Association, Resources and Technical Services Division, 1966.

Ballou, Hubbard W., ed. *Guide to Microreproduction Equipment*. Annapolis, National Microfilm Association (latest edition and/or supplement).

Hawken, William R. *Copying Methods Manual*. Chicago, American Library Association, Library Technology Program, 1966.

National Microfilm Association. *Glossary of Terms for Microphotography*. Annapolis, [National Microfilm Association], 1966.

U.S. Library of Congress. *Newspapers on Microfilm*. Washington, Library of Congress (latest edition).

Veaner, Alan B. *The Evaluation of Micropublications. A Handbook for Librarians*. Chicago, American Library Association, Library Technology Program, 1971. (LTP pub. No. 17).

Appendix A

The density of the background of the document image area shall be as listed below. The densities of silver films shall be visual diffuse transmission density.

Generation	Density Range
1N	1.0 to 1.4
2P	0.04 to 0.20
2N	1.0 to 1.4
3P	0.04 to 0.20
3N	0.90 to 1.5*

* The tolerance on distribution copy is always larger because of the variables which add up through the generations.

ADDITIONAL READINGS

Evans, Frank, *The Selection and Preparation of Records for Publication on Microfilm.* Washington: National Archives, 1970. 14p. (free) (Also, ERIC ED 052 797).

Gaddy, Dale, "Micrographic Standards and Related Items," Appendix C of his, *A Microform Handbook.* Silver Springs, Md.: National Microfilm Association, 1974, pp. C1-C5.

Hawken, William R., "Microform Standardization: The Problem of Research Materials and a Proposed Solution," *National Microfilm Association Journal,* 2: 14-20 (Fall 1968).

Inspection and Quality Control of First Generation Silver Halide Microfilm. Silver Springs, Md.: National Microfilm Association, 1972. MS 104. 26p.

Microfilm Norms: Recommended Standards for Libraries. Prepared by the Library Standards for Microfilm Committee. Chicago: American Library Association, 1966. 48p. (Out-of-print but available from Xerox University Microfilms on microfilm or as hard-copy print-out. Order no. OP 33154).

National Library of Medicine. *Roll Film Specifications for Microrecording Biomedical Literature.* Bethesda: National Library of Medicine, 1968.

National Microfilm Association Standard, Microfiche of Documents. Silver Springs, Md.: National Microfilm Association, 1973. MS5-1973. 11p.

Veaner, Allen B., *The Evaluation of Micropublications.* Chicago: American Library Association, 1971. (LTP Publication No. 17), pp. 52-54 (Bibliography of Standards).

Veaner, Allen B., "An Ominous Trend," *Microform Review,* 4: 9 (January 1975).

USER REACTIONS

INTRODUCTION

In 1974 the Microforms Task Force of the ALA Government Documents Round Table (GODORT) sent out a survey questionnaire[1] on reactions to microforms to 8956 college, special, public and school libraries to which 487 responses were received. In the area of complaints, nearly half the respondents checked, "users feel it is difficult to use." The next major complaint was that maintenance was frequently needed for reader-printers—40 percent of the respondents checked this block and over half felt equipment was very bad or moderately severe, rather than just troublesome. The third and fourth ranked complaints were that supplies were expensive and that the differing reduction ratios necessitated many types of equipment (35 percent). The least complaints, by far, were that "film deteriorates or has measles" (10 percent) and "brittle film, cracking or breaking" (15 percent). Among the other complaints listed in the questionnaire were, "insufficient document contrast on viewer," "hard copy blowback not readable," "microfiche easily lost or misfiled," "charts, tables, and photos not readable on viewers," "microfilm difficult to thread," "scratching of film after extended use." No complaints were listed on bibliographic control, film inspection, or standards, but space was left for respondents to write in their own complaints.

Another insight into user reactions is found in the results of a 1974 survey taken by a micropublisher[2]. When the respondents (all librarians) were asked their personal opinion of microforms the results were as follows:

Like	70.25 percent
Dislike	9.50 percent
Indifferent	20.25 percent

When the same respondents were asked *their* opinion of how *others* (other library staff members, faculty, students) felt about microforms, the answers were as follows:

	Other staff members	Faculty	Students
Like	40.75 percent	16.75 percent	15.50 percent
Dislike	16.00	39.75	39.50
Indifferent	43.25	43.50	45.00

The above figures point out something that is often overlooked—that there are basically two types of users, one is the library patron who actually uses the microform and the other is the librarian whose "use" of microforms relates to the standard library functions of acquisition, reference, servicing, etc.

Patrons appear to like microforms for only one reason and that is because they make otherwise unobtainable material available to them. Except for newspapers, preference has been for hard copy. Patrons claim they dislike microforms because of: (1) eye fatigue; (2) difficulty in browsing; (3) inability to underline or otherwise mark the text; (4) embarrassment over ineptness in using reading machines ("users feel it is difficult to use" as the Microforms Task Force put it); (5) dependence upon someone to demonstrate the use of the machine; (6) having to use the machine in a specified area.

Librarians appear to dislike microforms for the reasons given in the survey, primarily the different microforms and reduction ratios necessitating a variety of machines and the frequent maintenance required by reader printers, and also for the following reasons: (1) inadequate bibliographic controls; (2) inability to inspect the product; (3) absence of a way to insure all micropublishers observe appropriate production standards; (4) storage problems due to different types and sizes of microforms.

It is well to keep in mind, however, when reading about user reactions, that most comments are based on relatively small samplings, often of librarians, not users, therefore observations about reactions to microforms should not necessarily be taken as fact.

In addition, in considering the likes and dislikes of both patrons and librarians it is important for example, to remember that whether or not, there is eye strain in using microforms (indications are that there isn't) or whether microforms are "difficult to use," is not nearly as important as the fact that patrons *feel* there is eye strain or are turned away from microforms because they *feel* they are difficult to use.

References

1. Results are available from Chet Stout, Microform Task Force, McKinley Memorial Library, Niles, Ohio 44446. (Include stamped, self-addressed envelope).

USER RESISTANCE TO MICROFORMS IN THE RESEARCH LIBRARY

by Stephen R. Salmon

Microforms enjoy only limited acceptance in research libraries, largely because of user resistance. A growing number of published studies indicate that improper production, inadequate bibliographic access, lack of standardization, defects in equipment design, maintenance problems, poor environments for microform usage, and certain inherent characteristics of the microforms themselves all combine to make their use inconvenient. Solutions to most of these problems have existed for some time, but the microform industry has been slow to correct them. Some positive developments have occurred in the last two years, but the major problems remain.

The "End of the Book"

"The millennium has already arrived," announced one observer ten years ago, as he predicted "the eventual abandonment of the physical book."[1] "Where will the books go?" asked another writer. "Already we are in the early stages of the microbook revolution."[2] This was also ten years ago, and, as such predictions go, relatively recent. For forty years, we've been getting prophecies that books are on the way out and microforms on the way in, and they're still coming; just last week I received a brochure informing me that "microfilm represents the key to fulfilling, today and in the future, the need for storage and retrieval of vast amounts of original information" and "that's just for today! For tomorrow we can look forward to microfilm readers in most households, as well as millions of

Reprinted from *Microform Review*, 3: 194-99 (July 1974) by permission of the publisher. Copyright © 1974 by Microform Review, Inc.

portable, personal-use microfilm readers. The increasing popularity of publishing on microfilm which we see today is certain to accelerate the replacement of conventional media with microfilm. The day is not far off," we're told, when microfilm will make knowledge "inexpensive, easy, and accessible to all," and we're advised to hurry and get libraries ready for "tomorrow's needs"—whatever that means.

Well, it's difficult for the research librarian to get very excited about all this. After all, it's been 133 years since microphotography was invented, so it's not particularly new. The combination of electronic technology and microforms was supposed to revolutionize everything, but the first such system was patented more than forty years ago in 1931, and scores of systems have come and gone since then. Read the list of facsimile storage and retrieval systems in existence in 1964 as compiled by Alexander in *Libraries and Automation*,[3] and then try, as Wooster suggests in a recent report, to identify those which are still in production and in use at more than one installation!

Quite obviously, the millennium has not arrived, and, equally obviously, I think, it's not about to. By and large, microforms are still limited to specialized usage in research libraries: as substitutes for crumbling and unwieldy volumes of newspapers and for out-of-print material not available otherwise.

Why hasn't the revolution taken place as predicted? Is it because such revolutions just don't happen? Clearly not. Consider another "modern" chemical and mechanical invention: fiberglass and its use for boats. People loved wooden boats as much, I suspect, as they love books, but in the last twenty years fiberglass has almost completely taken over the pleasure-boating market. The reason for this is not hidden: fiberglass is cheaper to build with than wood, and a fiberglass boat is more convenient for the user.

What Users Say About Microforms

Microfilm, on the other hand, may be cheaper, but it's definitely not easier on the user, and therein, I think, lies the reason for the delayed revolution. Quite simply, many people dislike using microforms, as indicated in some two dozen published reports and journal articles. Stevens, while still speaking of a "microform revolution," notes the "reluctance of most readers to use microfilm or other microforms."[4] Lewis notes the "overwhelming lack of enthusiasm" on the part of sixty-six users he surveyed.[5] Weber writes that "the users of libraries are dismayed by the need to use microfilm" and "instantly repelled by the thought. . . . There is a strong, conscious opposition to the microform."[6]

A recent survey by Wooster evoked stronger language.[7] Said one user: "A microfiche is in front of me now. I need the material on it. To get it in a form I can use and preserve my sanity, I will first make a print on the reader-printer. That copy is so flimsy and curly that it will be necessary to Xerox it to end up with something usable. This is progress?" Another commented that "everything about microfiche is marvelous—except reading it," while another called microfiche "an information burial system." One obviously frustrated user said, "The man who ordered the present campaign to distribute reports on microfiche should be hung, drawn and quartered"!

Kottenstette and Dailey talked to students instead of researchers and got more colorful language and more imaginative suggestions: "Destroy it!" "Get rid of it!" "Discard it!" "Bag it!" "Tell it to self-destruct!" "Give it to IBM so the computers can read in their spare time."[8]

One writer has suggested that users get such attitudes from librarians,[9] but the evidence does not really indicate this; in fact, librarians have by and large supported the use of microforms. They've formed organizations to promote it, held meetings and seminars and conferences ad infinitum, bought microforms for their libraries, and offered them to their users. After all, it saves librarians money in many cases, and they don't have to use the stuff! Their enthusiasm vanishes pretty rapidly, however, in the face of reluctance—or outright fury— on the part of users. One librarian wrote Wooster: "Daily we have an experience which breaks my librarians' hearts. Our users come in or call up for information. We research and locate it. In those instances when they are told we have it only on microfiche, the reply is 'forget it' usually accompanied by an emphatic wave of a hand."

Bibliographic Control

It appears to be in the interests of both librarians and the microform industry, then, to identify the sources of user dissatisfaction. The evidence suggests that the sources are manifold. In the first place, the user may not even know that the information he wants exists in microform because of the problems of bibliographic control, both external (cataloging)[10] and internal (indexing).[11] One writer cites the example of a project involving a large number of important regional historical works, the publisher of which neglected to provide the user with any cataloging data. The result was that every purchasing library had to do original cataloging, at great expense, on all fifty titles. As he points out, "The publication of numerous monographs in microform is not a service to scholarship if the buying library cannot economically inform its users of the fact."[12] This has become so serious a problem that a recent conference, "Microform Utilization: The Academic Environment," recommended that librarians demand cataloging information with any microform publications placed on the market and boycott those publishers which do not provide it.[13]

Even if cataloging does exist, it doesn't help if the boxes are unlabeled
or labeled with a title different from the cataloging title. Once down to the
individual fiche or reel, it also causes problems if the publisher omits an
eye-legible legend on the fiche reader or on a target at the beginning of the
reel. The situation is even worse if there are several items spliced together
on a reel, without a checklist of the contents and without numbers on the
individual frames.

Equipment: Problems with the Human Interface

Assuming that the user learns about the microform in some fashion, however, he now needs some kind of reader—and here he may start to get mad.
First of all, he may not be able to find one, and, when he does, it may turn
out not to be very portable, so he can't take it home with him, or on air-
plane trips, or wherever else he does his reading. Recently I marveled at a
library administrator who, despite other demands on his time, managed
somehow to read through *Publisher's Weekly* regularly and fire off orders
to the acquisitions department; whereupon his secretary confided that he
accomplished this feat by taking *PW* to the rest room with him every time
he went! I suspect this would have been awkward if *PW* were published
only on microfiche.

Once the user finds a reader, he may encounter another problem: the
reader and the microform don't fit. Lack of standardization, in fact, is
one of the most common complaints.[14] Veaner points out that "the
cartridge or cassette may be the answer, but, if different, incompatible
cassettes continue to proliferate, widespread use of micropublication will
certainly be inhibited. In 1969, the industry was producing at least ten
different, completely noninterchangeable cartridges and cassettes. Still
another appeared in 1970."[15] I leave it to you to update this count.

If the reader fits, it may be out of order; maintenance problems are
also a frequent complaint in research libraries. If it's working, the next
step is to load the microform on the reader—and here the user encounters more problems. Mounting a reel and threading film may be second
nature for some people, but not for most users, and they detest it.[16]
Dickinson comments that "it seems a little surprising that roll film even
survived in library usage."[17] It is particularly frustrating if the film is
improperly spooled or if the leader is so short that when the film is
mounted the user has no way to view the first frame or two. Incredibly
enough, at least one publisher insists on distributing his microfilm without
reels, on the grounds that the user can easily spool the film himself; this
has been compared to "an automobile dealer requiring the buyer of a new
car to go to a tire store, buy his tires separately and mount them himself."[18]

Moving along, let's suppose that the user has found the microform he
wants, found a reader, and somehow managed to get one mounted on the

other. Then what does he see? The answer seems to be: all kinds of things, but not necessarily what he might expect—fingers; smudges and stains; scratches; dirt and dust; text cut off in the margin; missing pages; images reversed, upside down, or out of order; and assorted blurs, caused by improper lighting, improper contrast, poor resolution, and lack of proper focus. Keep in mind that librarians can check books for production defects, but few of them can afford to go through each microform checking for such problems. This usually means that the librarian accepts the merchandise and shelves it, happy in the thought that he's providing a useful resource—until months or years later when a faculty member or student attacks him because a page is missing or illegible!

Even assuming that the microform has been produced satisfactorily, another set of problems involving some degree of physical discomfort can occur. A small but significant number of users, in fact, claim that using microforms actually makes them sick. Most of these simply refer to "discomfort," but one of Wooster's respondents mentioned "a tendency to motion sickness,"[19] Grausnick and Kottenstette had one user who complained of "headaches and a nauseous reaction,"[20] and 90 percent of the students Kottenstette and Dailey studied complained of physical fatigue, eye fatigue, or both. People who wear glasses seem especially prone to discomfort when using microform systems.[21] Reading microtext, then looking down to take notes, and then relocating one's place on the microtext is very difficult for students who use reading glasses, especially bifocals.[22] In the Kottenstette-Dailey study, it was noted that 80 percent of those who used the microform system for 10 percent or less of their study time wore corrective lenses.[23] Students with glasses or contact lenses were particularly critical of the vertical screen position on reading machines, although this is a complaint shared by other users as well.[24]

Additional problems associated with the screen include the frequent comment that the screen may not be illuminated to uniform brightness across its entire area, and the seemingly ever-present problem of focus; in a ranking of problems by Kottenstette, focus was at the top of the list.[25] Remember that focus problems include not only difficulties of getting a single image in focus across the entire area of the image, but also holding that image in focus, and maintaining the focus from frame to frame.

Complaints about reading machines also mention noise and difficulties of manipulation, including the impossibility of some machines of rotating the microform or the reading head through a right angle when a chart or an illustration is filmed at a right angle, and the difficulty in positioning some machines at a comfortable angle for note-taking.

Environments for Using Microforms

That takes us through problems associated with the microform, the microform reader, and the two used together, but there can still be problems with the environment in which microform use takes place—lighting, for example. Holmes recommends that the ambient light be kept low, yet Weber recommends that it be the same level as the screen.[26] Kottenstette and Dailey found that students "either desired high contrast between the viewer and its surround, or minimum contrast between the viewer and its surround . . . Preferences for lighting were entirely different from that anticipated: 48% preferred all lights off; 41% preferred only carrel lights on; 7% preferred only room lights on; and 4% preferred all lights on. These results indicate that microform rooms need variable lighting conditions to accommodate preferences and that further careful study needs to be made for precise ambient lighting control.[27]

Even if all of these problems were overcome, there seem to be others that are simply in the nature of the beast. The studies by Kottenstette and his associates at Denver and the survey by Wooster all turned up complaints that the use of microforms makes it difficult to take notes; that the user can't underline or write comments or notes on the fiche or film; that one can't flip pages or refer back and forth easily between different places in the text, especially between the text and an appendix; that scanning, skimming, and searching are all more difficult than with books; and that frame-to-frame interference causes distraction. In addition, Line has noted that microform systems may lack a "spatial frame of reference,"[28] it's somehow comforting to the reader to know that a particular item of information is at a fixed place in a book and disturbing not to have this fixed relationship in a microform system, particularly in those systems where the information store is isolated from the user. The sheer complexity of the more sophisticated systems may be intimidating.

Finally, there is one source of user dissatisfaction that will be the hardest to deal with, and certainly the most difficult to change. This is the fact that microforms and microform systems just don't have the same "feel" as books, to which they are inevitably compared. Books are "naturally anthropomorphic" and "matched to the hand and eye," to quote one recent description,[29] whereas the use of microforms has been said to be like kissing through a pane of glass. Kottenstette and Dailey's students complained that microform was "very impersonal" and that "you can't feel personally attached to it."[30] Someone else said that all you can do with a microfiche is read it—if you're lucky. Perhaps what's needed is the "cuddly" microfiche reader Wooster once suggested, but even then it's doubtful that anyone would want to take one to bed.

Perhaps this last category of problems is incapable of solution, but that's certainly not true of the others; the solutions, in fact, are in most cases implied by the problems. Cataloging and indexing should be adequate and available; production errors should not occur or should be caught before they reach the user; and readers should be designed to accommodate users and facilitate their work. Very little of this is beyond the state of the art: Weber, Holmes and Walkup have all provided detailed recommendations for the improvement of readers, and the American Library Association, the Library of Congress, and others have published guides to the production of satisfactory film.[31] Fussler and Rider pointed out the obvious production problems in the 1940s; in fact, Donald Holmes wrote in 1939 about the "urgent need" for the production of microfilm "of good photographic quality" and "the numerous, unfortunate defects common in microfilm," and exactly thirty years later, in 1969, he was still obliged to point out some of the very same problems![32] This does not argue for a very responsive industry; as Lewis says, "It becomes downright disheartening in reviewing the literature to find that the basic problems foreseen in the earliest trials are still the basic problems cited in our day."[33] Veaner in 1968 had harsher words: "Neglect of established guidelines and accepted good practices easily makes the librarian or scholar a victim of ignorant or careless technicians and camera operators, or of shady entrepreneurs anxious to cash in on quick profits from micro-publication schemes. Unfortunately, with the exception of the largest professional producers, malpractice is often the rule rather than the exception."[34]

Certainly many individual companies have made conscientious and vigorous attacks on these problems, but the user does not normally identify them as company problems. Two particular characteristics of the industry are at work here. In the first place, the buyer is not normally the user, and vice versa. Second, there is normally no strong brand-name association, particularly on the part of the user, so problems tend to be identified with the medium or the industry itself, rather than with particular companies. Of course, this means that so long as the problems continue to occur, they *are* problems for the industry as a whole and need to be attacked by the industry as a whole. Based on past history, however, I think most librarians are fairly pessimistic about the ability and desire of the industry to cope with them.

A business executive once told me that despite steadily rising sales, microfilm was a "mature" market; it was his judgment that unless there are fairly drastic changes in the market and the way it operates, little further growth in the industry is likely to take place. Based on the present evidence of user resistance and unhappiness with the industry's products, I think one would have to conclude that his judgment is correct.

Afterword

Since this paper was presented in 1972, several positive developments have occurred. Small, portable microfiche readers are now available; while they're not exactly cuddly, at least they are convenient for home use. The American Library Association's micropublishing committee, under the vigorous leadership of Lawrence Robinson has provided a strong and effective voice for librarians, particularly in speaking out against poor editorial and production practices in micropublishing. The National Microfilm Association has sponsored several micrographic seminars for librarians, and meetings of the NMA's Library Relations Committee and the standards committee of the ALA reproduction of library materials section have provided better communication between the industry and librarians as representatives of the user.

Briefcase readers and seminars, however, are at best minimal responses by the industry to the problems of the user. The major problems are still with us, and there is still an unfortunate defensiveness on the part of most segments of the microform industry, a tendency to deny problems rather than to solve them, a predisposition to tell librarians rather than listening to them, and a strong habit of buckpassing. Whether the leaders in this field will be able to guide their troubled business toward responsiveness rather than reaction, for their own sakes as well as the users', remains a sad but urgent question.

Notes

1. Rolland E. Stevens, "Review of Copying Methods: 1962," *Library Resources and Technical Services* 7 (Spring 1963): 161.

2. John Rader Platt, "Where Will the Books Go?" *Horizon* 5 (September 1962): 42-47.

3. Samuel N. Alexander and F. Clay Rose, "The Current Status of Graphic Storage Techniques," in *Conference on Libraries and Automation, Arlie Foundation, 1963. Libraries and Automation: Proceedings,* ed. Barbara Evans Markuson (Washington, D.C.: Library of Congress, 1964), pp. 130-135.

4. Rolland E. Stevens, "Microform Revolution," *Library Trends* 19 (January 1971): 379-395.

5. Ralph W. Lewis, "User's Reaction to Microfiche: A Preliminary Study, " *College and Research Libraries* 31 (July 1970): 260-268.

6. David C. Weber, "Specifications for a Superior Microtext Reading Machine," *American Documentation* 16 (July 1965): 246-247.

7. Harold Wooster, *Microfiche 1969—A User Survey,* AD 695-049 (Arlington, Va.: Air Force Office of Scientific Research, 1969).

8. James P. Kottenstette and K. Anne Dailey, *An Investigation of the Environment for Educational Microform Utilization. Phase II, Student Use of Classroom Microform in Support of a Content Course,* ED 050-603 (Washington, D.C.: U.S. Office of Education, 1971).

9. Donald C. Holmes, *Determination of the Environmental Conditions Required in a Library for the Effective Utilization of Microforms* (Washington, D.C.: Association of Research Libraries, 1970).

10. C. Edward Carroll, "Some Problems of Microform Utilization in Large University Collections," *Microform Review* 1 (January 1972): 22-23: Felix Reichmann and Josephine M. Tharpe, *Bibliographic Control of Microforms* (Westport, Ct.: Greenwood Press, 1972), p. 3; Suzanne Dodson, "The University of British Columbia Library's Guide to Large Collections in Microform: One Attempt to Minimize a Major Problem," *Microform Review* 1 (January 1972): 113-118; J. McRee Elrod, Review of "English and American Plays of the 19th Century," *Microform Review* 1 (October 1972): 298-300.

11. *ALA Social Responsibilities Round Table Newsletter* 18 (February 1972); D. A. Kemp, Review of "Bibliography of Astronomy, 1881-1898," *Microform Review* 2 (October 1973): 280; Albert J. Maupin, Review of "American Astronautical Society Microfiche Series," *Microform Review* 2 (January 1973): 39.

12. Allen B. Veaner, "The Crisis in Micropublication," *Choice* 5 (June 1968): 448-453.

13. *Microform Utilization: The Academic Library Environment,* Report of a conference held at Denver, Colorado, 7-9, December 1970 (Denver: University of Denver, 1971).

14. Lewis, "User's Reaction to Microfiche"; Wooster, *Microfiche 1969*; Donald C. Holmes, *Determination of User Needs and Future Requirements for a Systems Approach to Microform Technology* (Washington, D.C.: Association of Research Libraries, 1969); Carroll, "Some Problems of Microform Utilization"; *Microform Utilization*; John Webb, "Comment and News," *Microform Review* 2 (October 1973): 249.

15. Allen B. Veaner, "Micropublication," in *Advances in Librarianship* (New York: Seminar Press, 1971), 2: 180-181.

16. Homer I. Bernhardt, *An Overview of Microforms: A Report on the Role of Microforms in the University of Pittsburgh Libraries* (Pittsburgh: University of Pittsburgh Graduate School of Library and Information Sciences, 1972), p. 13.

17. R. R. Dickinson, "The Scholar and the Future of Microfilm," *American Documentation* 17 (October 1966): 178-179.

18. Veaner, "The Crisis in Micropublication."

19. Wooster, *Microfiche 1969*.

20. Robert Grausnick and James P. Kottenstette, *An Investigation of the Environment for Educational Microform Utilization. Phase I: Student Use of Classroom Microform in Support of a Survey Course*, ED 050-602 (Washington, D.C.: U.S. Office of Education, 1969).

21. Norton Goodwin, Review of "The World Through Blunted Sight," *Microform Review* 1 (July 1972): 248.

22. Grausnick and Kottenstette, *An Investigation of the Environment. Phase I.*

23. Kottenstette and Dailey, *An Investigation of the Environment. Phase II.*

24. Weber, "Specifications for a Superior Microtext Reading Room"; Kottenstette and Dailey, *An Investigation of the Environment. Phase II*; Holmes, *Determination of the Environmental Conditions*; Grausnick and Kottenstette, *An Investigation of the Environment. Phase I*; *Microform Utilization.*

25. James P. Kottenstette, *An Investigation of the Characteristics of Ultrafiche and Its Application to Colleges and Universities: An Interim Report*, ED 032-447 (Washington, D.C.: U.S. Office of Education, 1969).

26. Holmes, *Determination of the Environmental Conditions*; Weber, "Specifications for a Superior Microtext Reading Room."

27. Kottenstette and Dailey, *An Investigation of the Environment. Phase II.*

28. M. B. Line, "On the Design of Information Systems for Human Beings," *Aslib Proceedings* 22 (July 1970): 320-335.

29. B. W. Campbell, "A Successful Microfiche Program," *Special Libraries* 62 (March 1971): 136-142.

30. Kottenstette and Dailey, *An Investigation of the Environment. Phase II.*

31. Weber, "Specifications for a Superior Microtext Reading Machine"; Holmes, *Determination of the Environmental Conditions*; L. E. Walkup et al., "The Design of Improved Microimage Readers for Promoting the Utilization of Microimages," in *Proceedings of the National Microfilm Association, Annapolis, Maryland, 1962*, 11: 285; American Library Association, *Microfilm Norms: Recommended Standards for Libraries* (Chicago, 1966); *Specifications for the Microfilming of Newspapers in the Library of Congress* (Washington, D.C.: Library of Congress, 1972); *Specifications for the Microfilming of Books and Pamphlets in the Library of Congress* (Washington, D.C.: Library of Congress, 1973): Stephen R. Salmon, *Specifications for Library of Congress Microfilming* (Washington, D.C.: Library of Congress, 1964); Verner W. Clapp, Francis H. Henshaw, and Donald C. Holmes, "Are Your Microfilms Deteriorating Acceptably," *Library Journal* 80 (March 5, 1955): 589-595; William R. Hawken, *Copying Methods Manual* (Chicago: American Library Association, 1966).

32. Herman H. Fussler, *Photographic Reproduction for Libraries: A Study of Administrative Problems* (Chicago: University of Chicago Press, 1942); Fremont Rider, *The Scholar and the Future of the Research Library* (New York: Hadham Press, 1944); Donald C. Holmes, "Quality in Microphotography," *Journal of Documentary Reproduction* 2 (November-December 1939): 284-285, and his *Determination of User Needs.*

33. Lewis, "User's Reaction to Microfiche."

34. Veaner, "The Crisis in Micropublication."

USER'S REACTIONS TO MICROFICHE, A PRELIMINARY STUDY

by Ralph W. Lewis

Recent emphasis placed on the use of microfiche by large government agencies has increased the pressure on libraries supporting government research to make greater use of microfiche. Negative and apathetic user attitudes, expressed by researchers, indicate that expanded use of microfiche will have to be accompanied by concentrated efforts to overcome resistance if the great potential of microfiche is to be realized. Efforts in microphotography, expended on technical achievement in the past, should be directed toward understanding the user and his needs to discover why he avoids microforms and how to overcome his resistance to them.

The potential value offered by photographic technology in the publication, storage, and dissemination of recorded knowledge and information has been recognized for well over a century.

The use of microphotography to compress the bulk of printed material, demonstrated as early as 1853 by Rosling's experiment with microcopies of a newspaper, has made a great impact on information handling activities.[1] It has made great contributions to the advancement of scientific and humanistic studies by making rare, out-of-print, and other difficult to obtain materials available.[2] It has preserved printed materials during war and has offered countless libraries a way to improve their collections.[3]

Microfilm, microcards, microprint, and now microfiche offer potential economies in space, in acquisition and binding costs, costs in distribution of copies of materials, and library circulation costs. There are benefits, both realized and potential, in the extension of interlibrary loan services, in opportunities for individuals to obtain personal libraries of their own at little expense, and in more effective teletransmission of photofacsimiles.[4]

Still, the impact on library operations and exchange of information often prophesied for microphotography has not been realized.[5] Explanations are many for the failure of this potential to materialize, including

Reprinted from *College and Research Libraries*, 31: 260-68 (July 1970) by permission of the publisher. Copyright c 1970 by the American Library Association.

deficiencies in the quality of the mcirofilmed image, difficulties in indexing information stored on microforms, problems with bibliographic description of materials and many other aspects of microphotography. It becomes downright disheartening in reviewing the literature to find that the
basic problems foreseen in the earliest trials are still the basic problems
cited in our day.[6]

Perhaps the most basic of the problems is the reluctance of users to accept microcopies. This reluctance is caused mostly by inconvenience and
deficiencies in the quality of equipment available for reading photoreduced
materials. While many of the technical advantages originally anticipated
have been realized, the whole of these efforts have failed to realize the total potential partly because the user has not been given sufficient consideration.[7] Microfiche, despite its real and supposed advantages, might suf-
fer the same fate unless user resistance is dealt with more effectively.

Advantages and disadvantages notwithstanding, the hard fact remains
that libraries and other organizations involved in the exchange of information must expect to acquire and provide more and more information in
microforms of all varieties.

Purpose of the Study

Changes in the distribution of government technical information will make
the use of microfiche increasingly widespread, especially for libraries that
support government research. Emphasis placed on mcirofiche by the four
large governmental dispensers of technical information, as a primary medium in their technical distribution programs, began with the DDC change
of policy in July 1968.[8] Many of the technical reports in hard copy format previously available through DDC and NASA at no cost are now distributed through the Clearinghouse for Federal Scientific and Technical Information at $3.00 per copy. Microfiche copies, however, have continued to
be available at no cost. The Boulder Laboratories library has depended heavily on technical report materials for many years from both DDC and
NASA, and in both formats.

Policy changes by DDC and NASA impelled the Boulder Laboratories library to make still another significant change in policy: it could no longer
pay, because of budget restraints, for technical reports that its laboratories
requested. With the new charges, laboratories were required to buy with
their own funds all those reports that were to become the property of
their divisions or sections.

For three reasons, this change precipitated the study on microfiche user
attitudes reported here. First, it intended to increase users' awareness of
microfiche, since they would come more and more in contact with it.

Second, it intended to stimulate interest in microfiche, partly because
of the announced changes, but also because the library had accumulated a

little-used collection of more than 70,000 technical reports in microfiche form.

Third, it was expected that the change in library policy would have the initial effect of stimulating interest in microfiche on the part of the laboratory people in order to conserve funds for research activities. Knowledge of how microforms had been received in other libraries in the past and reactions by our own library users led to the belief that original enthusiasm would soon wane unless something was done to overcome negative response from laboratory people. The intent was to poll users to obtain a better idea of how they would accept the change.

The library sent out short questionnaires attached to memos explaining the new politics. The responses provided excellent information which appears to be worth reporting to a wider audience, since an extensive review of the literature produced no direct reports of user reaction to mcirotext (if one excludes the reports of librarians who report reactions of their own and their library patrons). Although the study concerns users of only one specific library, responses come directly from scientific and technical people working in the laboratories and, by-and-large, confirm and help explain reluctance to use microforms. However, there is a surprising acquiescence on the part of those responding, suggesting that some attention to their needs could overcome a considerable amount of their resistance.

There was no attempt to get a highly controlled statistical sampling. Rather, forms were sent to all people who might be concerned and everyone was provided with an opportunity to respond. No follow-up was made on unreturned questionnaires, therefore, some valid limitations may exist on the extent to which results can be applied outside this institution. Nevertheless, when results obtained in this study are considered in a broader context, that is, with other reports in the literature of similar nature, and with library experience, they appear to be valid. They may indeed be indicative of the general response to microforms.

The objective was well served, in any case, because the poll drew from those responding an indication of collective interest, as it existed, and some idea of the problems to be overcome. Of even more value were some individual comments received reflecting subjective feelings that were not evidentg in the checked responses on the questionnaires. Statistical analyses are of little practical value when the library is confronted by a single user. If he likes microfiche he must be served; if he does not, he must still be served.

Two versions of the questionnaire were distributed. The first version was sent to forty people who normally received the NASA STAR (*Scientific and Technical Aerospace Reports*) from which they selected technical reports for review. Fourteen of those, or 35 percent, were returned.

The questionnaire was later expanded by one question and sent to a much wider audience of 681 laboratory people at the Boulder Laboratories and ESSA (Environmental Science Services Administration) Research

Laboratories in Boulder, the rest of the United States, and in Peru. Of these fifty, two (or 7.5 percent) were returned. Responses (9.1 percent of all sent out) came from all of the National Bureau of Standards divisions in the Boulder Laboratories and thirteen of the seventeen ESSA Research Laboratories, giving a broad if not a perfect sample.

The results from each version of the questionnaire are differentiated in Tables 1, 2, and 3 because they originated from two different groups. The first group consisted of people whose pattern of use was somewhat known (moderate to heavy users of technical reports). The second group consisted of all "professional" laboratory employees, whose use of the library was less well known.

After the results of the first survey were received, a fourth question was added, because most of those responding thought that microfiche would be fine for the library collection as long as they could be converted to full-size, hard copy before they were used. Since such service could not be provided and because this approach to microfiche use would cost more than the purchase of the item in hard copy to begin with, the library asked how the limitation on copying would affect the general response to the first question.

Questions were structured to provide a kind of opinion scale, with the first one or two possible responses giving positive opinions, the third possible response giving a noncommittal acceptance (perhaps a lack of opinion) and the last two indicating negative opinions. They were also structured to narrow the user's perspective from a broad idea of the value of microfiche to the library's use of microfiche and finally to his own personal feelings about his use of the medium.

Table 1 illustrates the range of opinions given by respondents concerning the suitability of microfiche as a medium for the dissemination of technical information. Their responses set the tone for the rest of the study by an overwhelming lack of enthusiasm. Positive opinions were outnumbered by almost two to one. Furthermore, many of those who considered microfiche to be acceptable added significant comments that modified their acceptance. For example, many indicated that microfiche would be acceptable for materials that were to be scanned for relevance, but that materials needed for study or use in research were needed in hard copy if they were needed at all. Some acknowledged that microfiche might afford some savings in space and distribution costs, but that the user was not being considered.

For most of those responding, microfiche was merely acceptable at best, but even this opinion was reluctantly given.

Nevertheless, most thought that the library should have a significant amount of its collection in microfiche, if the microfiche was limited to technical report materials (see Table 2). Fewer than 10 percent of those responding thought that a substantial part of the collection (other than technical reports) should be in microfiche. Almost 37 percent thought

TABLE 1

Responses to Item 1 on Version 1 and 2 Questionnaires

Microfiche as a technical information medium is:	1st Version	2nd Version	Total	Percent
excellent	1	0	1	1.5
very good	0	11	11	16.7
acceptable	8	21	29	43.9
poor	2	16	18	27.3
unacceptable	2	1	3	31.8
*Other	1	3	4	6.1
Totals	14	52	66	100.0

*Responses that did not readily fit into any of these categories are represented as "other" at the bottom of each table.

TABLE 2

Responses to Question 2

The library should:	1st Version	2nd Version	Total	Percent
a. collect a substantial part of its material in microfiche	0	6	6	9.1
b. collect only reports in microfiche	6	22	28	42.4
c. acquire in microfiche only those materials available in no other form	6	18	24	36.4
d. not accept microfiche except in rare instances	1	1	2	3.0
e. not accept or collect microfiche at all	0	2	2	3.0
Other	1	3	4	6.1
Totals	14	52	66	100.0

that microfiche should be acquired only when materials were not available in hard copy. Only six people were positive toward the library collecting materials in microfiche. The great majority agreed that the library should collect some material in this form, but only items not otherwise available, or technical reports, which are considered by many laboratory people to be inferior to books and journals. Only four people, however, were against microfiche being in the library.

TABLE 3

Responses to Question 3

I, personally:	1st Version	2nd Version	Total	Percent
a. prefer microfiche copy	0	0	0	0.0
b. like microfiche very much	0	3	3	4.5
c. will use microfiche	9	21	30	45.5
d. do not like to use microfiche	2	24	26	39.4
e. will not use microfiche	2	2	4	6.1
Other	1	2	3	4.5
Totals	14	52	66	100.0

The personal preferences expressed in response to question 3 are most revealing, and they indicate the nature of the problem faced in eliciting greater use of microfiche. The pattern of response follows all past trends reported in the literature that account for the "failure" of other microforms to be accepted by the user. Table 3 is self-explanatory as far as the data are concerned, but more was received to interpret than the raw data. In answering the question, one person added to response (c) this comment: "I will use microfiche . . . reluctantly," which sums up the general attitude toward microfiche among those responding. Another added this modification to the same response, "I will use microfiche . . . if hard copy is not available." Ten others added comments indicating that they would use microfiche *if* some condition or other were met or if no alternative were possible.

As stated, data were derived from a sample that may not be statistically ideal. If they can be interpreted to apply only to respondents, and not the whole population of library users (or users of microfiche in general) at the

ESSA Research Laboratories, we must at least overcome the negative attitudes of forty-one of our users. This is significant in a local context.

The question involved here is fundamental. Microfiche, or any other microform, is intended mostly as a benefit to a library and to other information handling activities, but not necessarily to the user. The reasons usually given for the use of microforms in these activities involve the technical advantages that accrue to the library or to the distributing agency, such as less cost in distribution, the saving of space, and the preservation of deteriorating materials. Some, such as preservation of materials and making rare materials more generally available, are intended to benefit the user, too, but again through impersonal, technical advantages. As some respondents indicated, these technical advantages are of value to the user only when no other alternative is available, but users still prefer the hard copy.

If no alternative to microfilm or microfiche is provided, users can be required to use or not use them, but this approach is partly self-defeating when many dislike or refuse to use what is provided. What is desired is to generate a flow of information to individuals with the least hindrance possible. Either information is not as valuable as one is led to believe, or the technical advantages that libraries and distributors of information gain are not enough. User reluctance and antagonism have limited the use of microforms in many libraries where microtexts have proven most valuable with items that have a low probability of use. There appears to be no reason to expect any change in attitude in the case of microfiche unless there is a much greater emphasis on overcoming problems involving user comfort, convenience, personal preference, and research habits.

This assertion is further illustrated by the response received to the fourth question. The intent of agencies disseminating microfiche is that the microfiche be used without reproducing the material in hard copy. When it was explained that the library had no facilities to provide hard copies for users, their general opinions of microfiche were drastically altered, again toward the negative (see Table 4).

Within the same group of people responding to the second version of the questionnaire, the number who considered microfiche a very good medium dropped from eleven to one. The number who thought it acceptable dropped from twenty-one to nineteen. The number who considered microfiche unacceptable rose from one to seven. Negative responses increased by eleven, and none of the fifty-two respondents considered microfiche to be an excellent medium under either circumstance. Lack of facilities to reproduce microfiche in hard copy mysteriously improved the prospects for two. Eighteen responded in the same manner as they had on the first question, while twenty-four considered this condition an added detraction (see Table 5).

TABLE 4

Responses to Question 4

There are no facilities at the Boulder Laboratories for large scale reproduction of microfiche to hard copy. Only a limited number of pages from any report can be reproduced. Under these circumstances, microfiche as a medium of dissemination of scientific and technical information is:

	Total	Percent
excellent	0	0.0
very good	1	1.9
acceptable	19	36.6
poor	21	40.4
unacceptable	7	13.2
Other	4	7.7
Totals	52	100.0

TABLE 5

Effect on Acceptability of Microfiche of Limited Copying Facilities

	Number of Responses* Item 1	Item 4	Change
Excellent	0	0	0
Very good	11	1	− 10
Acceptable	21	19	− 2
Poor	16	21	+ 5
Unacceptable	1	7	+ 6

*Responses represented in this table are limited to those taken from the second version of the questionnaire.

Summary of Responses

In general, the results of the survey lean toward the negative. (Perhaps "lurch" would be a better term.) More than half of the responses indicated acceptance of microfiche, but with reservations. More than 85 percent indicated acceptance only, or a negative attitude toward the use of microfiche. Fewer than 9 percent of the answers were unmistakably positive in tone, while one-third were clearly negative (Table 6). Only five of the comments were positive in tone; twenty-four were unmistakably negative. Thirteen comments so altered the sense of the possible responses on the form questionnaire that they could not be fitted into the patterns intended.

The complaints registered in these comments are the same complaints librarians have always heard about materials in microform. The preferences indicated are no different than preferences of other scholars. The problems that have plagued the use of microforms are still very real.

TABLE 6

Total Responses Evaluated

	Number of Responses	Percent
Positive	22	8.8
Acquiescent	130	52.0
Negative	83	33.2
Other	15	6.0
Totals	250	100.0

There is some indication that the problems are not overriding, however, even in our study. The positive comments, although few, cite two instances where microfiche has been accepted without difficulty. One respondent explained that when microfiche can be checked out of the library for use, it is acceptable. Another person reported "we spend 8 to 24 hours per week reading (microfiche)." There are other examples of successful use of other microforms in the Boulder Laboratories. The most notable of these has been the use of microfilm produced directly from the computer by means of the DD 280 Microfilmer. A number of high quality microfilm reader-printers have been made available in the computer laboratory so that the computer-produced microfilm can be read at the convenience of the user and portions taken off the microfilm in hard copy at the discretion of the user. These two conveniences seem to have overcome the resistance evident in so many other situations. This last example may be somewhat misleading, however, because the materials that are filmed in this manner are very often compilations of data in the forms of tables, charts, or graphs that are not read in the same manner as narrative reports or articles.

TABLE 7

Factors Detracting from Microfiche
from Comments on Questionnaires

Factor	No. of Comments
Preference for hard copy	18
Use of materials restricted to location of readers and printers	7
Quality and number of readers available	5
Comfort lacking with equipment available	4
Light reflected from reader screen	2
Eyestrain	2
Lack of standardization in films and equipment	1
Quality of photographic copy	1

Application of Study Results

Since this study was completed, the Boulder Laboratories library has initiated a plan to make more extensive use of microfiche in its activities, including the filming of a substantial portion of its technical reports collection. In planning for this project, attempts have been made to meet as many objections to microfiche as possible. Foremost in these plans will be the liberal scattering of readers throughout the Research Laboratories with the goal of providing a reader for each small group of researchers and providing readily available reader-printers (on each floor of each building where possible) so that some of the inconveniences mentioned by respondents will be overcome. While the intent is still to promote the use of microfiche as microfiche, liberal copying privileges on readily available equipment will allow researchers to copy charts, graphs, drawings, photographs, formulae and other data that are more usable in hard copy.

The one factor that is beyond the library's control is the quality and convenience in the design of machinery available for reading microfiche, especially equipment that is inexpensive enough for purchase in large quantities. Statements abound in the literature insisting that quality viewing and copying equipment must be available in order to make effective use of microforms. They also show that such simple problems as inserting the filmed item into the viewer is an extremely important factor in acceptance by users. Even though there has been a proliferation of models available, there has been relatively little progress in the design of readers and reader-printers that are economical enough to allow most organizations to scatter them liberally where the materials will have to be used and that are of good enough quality to assure their acceptance and steady use. After the data reported here were gathered, the library arranged a display and demonstration of microfiche equipment. Machines from six manufacturers were available for viewing and use. The comments received were almost uniform: the inexpensive viewers were not acceptable. Those in the $300 to $400 range were. It is evident that the extensive use of microfiche will require considerable effort and expense.

It is difficult to understand why those engaged in the distribution of microforms and the sale of equipment for its use have not been able to overcome problems envisioned long before microphotography was extensively used in information distribution. Past experiences clearly show that the user has rejected these media when other alternatives exist, mostly because of discomfort and inconvenience. To a large extent, we are still at the point where all this began. The technical potential of microforms is still under-exploited, as much because of failure to come to grips with the needs, the desires, and the idiosyncracies of the user as of any other factor.

Whether the limitations of reader quality, user preference for hard copy, standardization needs, and deficiencies in quality of photography and reproduction can be overcome to reach full exploitation of microfiche may be doubtful for the moment at least.

Conclusions

Use of other microforms has increased greatly since the late 1930s, but it is still confined mostly to preservation of materials (newspapers and manuscripts), to distribution of materials that are available in no other form, and for storage of older materials that have comparatively little probability of use. The reluctance exhibited by users has had much to do with this limited utilization of microforms and thus could also seriously limit the use of microfiche despite the great pressures being exerted. The man who must use the material may ultimately decide the extent of the value of microfiche in research activities, the same as he has in effect determined it for microfilm and microcards. It seems logical that the needs of the user should be the next area of major concern for librarians, for the increasing number of commercial firms providing materials in microfiche, and for manufacturing firms that market reader and reader-printer equipment. Technical advancement has not completely overcome all problems in microphotography, but it has outstripped knowledge of how to get people to take advantage of microtext materials. The acquiescence exhibited in this study could possibly be directed toward acceptance and some of the negative responses could hopefully be improved.

Those who work in the information professions should do extensive market research on how services and products are received. More comprehensive studies providing closer controls and more statistically reliable data should be undertaken to determine, at first hand, what the advantages, limitations, and potentials of microforms really are. The weaknesses in available equipment should be identified and design of better ones sought, so that users will accept them. We should work on ways to introduce and acquaint users with microforms, for they will undoubtedly be a greater part of our future than they have been of our past. The great technical potential needs only to be matched by use.

References

1. Frederic Luther, "The Earliest Experiments with Microphotography," *American Documentation* 2: 167-70 (August 1951).

2. Tonnes Kleberg, "Some Uses of Microfilm in the Library at the University of Uppsala," *Journal of Documentation* 7: 244-51 (December 1951).

3. L. Moholy, "ASLIB Microfilm Service; the Story of Its Wartime Activities," *Journal of Documentation* 2: 23-31 (June 1946).

4. Charles G. LaHood, "Microfilm as Used in Reproduction and Transmission Systems," *Library Trends* 8: 338-457 (January 1960).

5. Fremont Rider, *The Scholar and the Future of the Library; a Problem and Its Solution* (New York: Hadham Press, 1944); R. R. Dickison, "The Scholar and the Future of Microfilm," *American Documentation* 17: 178-79 (October 1966); K. D. Metcalf, "Implications of Microfilm and Microscript for Libraries," *Library Journal* 70: 718-23 (1 Sept. 1945).

6. Charles Bishop, "Problems in the Production and Utilization of Microfiche," *American Documentation* 12: 53-55 (January 1961); Hubbard W. Ballou, "The Microfiche," *Library Resources & Technical Services* 8: 81-85 (Winter 1964); William G. Harkins, Fred L. Dimock, and Mary Elizabeth Hanson, "Microform in University Libraries: a Report," *College & Research Libraries* 14: 307-16 (July 1963); David C. Weber, "Specifications for a Superior Microtext Reading Machine," *American Documentation* 17: 178-79 (October 1966); Jerry McDonald, "The Case Against Microfilming," *American Archivist* 20: 345-56 (October 1950); Maurice F. Tauber, "Problems in the Use of Microfilms, Microprint and Microcards in Research Libraries," *Industrial and Engineering Chemistry* 42: 1476-78 (August 1950); Jerome Wilcox, "The Point of View of the Librarian," *American Documentation* 2: 162-66 (August 1951).

7. Alan B. Pritsker and J. William Sadler, "An Evaluation of Microfilm as a Method of Book Storage," *College & Research Libraries* 18: 290-96 (July 1957).

8. "Requests for Most 'Hard Copies' Subject to $3 Charge in July," *Defense Documentation Digest*, No. 31 (6 May, 1968).

EXCERPT FROM
*DETERMINATION OF USER NEEDS
AND FUTURE REQUIREMENTS
FOR A SYSTEMS APPROACH
TO MICROFORM TECHNOLOGY*

by Donald C. Holmes

The following data were obtained by the principal investigator and the
consultative panel from interviews conducted during November 1968-
January 1969, with eighty-five persons at twenty-six institutions.

General: Identifying and Defining the Problem

1. The survey has indicated that libraries are using microforms for a
variety of purposes. In order of importance as indicated by the interviewees, they are as follows: 1) to acquire materials not otherwise available;
2) in lieu of binding serials. Serials are generally made available to readers
in printed form while demand for them is high. When the demand decreases, the originals are discarded and microform copies are substituted;
3) to preserve deteriorating materials; 4) to store bulky materials, such as
backfiles of old newspapers, which would take a great deal of space in
their original formats; 5) to provide use copies of rare materials in order to
protect originals from loss or damage from frequent use; 6) to publish information of limited interest; 7) to produce intermediate copy necessary
to the production of facsimile copies.

2. The majority of libraries visited maintained a central microform
reading room separate from a general reading room. Other microform
reading machines were housed in branch libraries and in those areas of the
main libraries devoted to special collections.
    Staff supervision of microform reading machines was reported to be

Reprinted from Chapter III, "Findings: of Donald C. Holmes," *Determination of User Needs and Future Requirements for a Systems Approach to Microform Technology.* July, 1969. ERIC ED 029
168, pp. 6-15.

generally much less than desirable, because of insufficient staff. However, there were some reports of moderate to close supervision by the library staff of the use of reading machines.

3. Approximately one-half of the respondents believed that neither the environment nor the facilities available for the use of microforms were conducive to their proper use. A number of respondents were quite emphatic on this point. Some believed that the environment and facilities offered were partially satisfactory, while several reported they believed those provided in their institutions to be completely satisfactory.

A commercial microform producer commented that conditions for the use of microform reading machines in many customer locations are very unsatisfactory.

A second commercial microform producer commented that facilities provided in many customer microform installations are entirely inadequate for the satisfactory use of microforms.

A microform publisher stated that many of his products were used by customers in locations that are most unsuitable for reading microforms.

A well informed microform consultant commented that for every good microform reading room installation there exist ten that are poor.

It would be fair to say that a majority of the respondents to this question believed that work space provided for microform usage by many institutions is very inadequate; that reading machines are often placed near windows and in rooms where ambient light cannot be controlled; that reading machines are often placed in stack aisles where their users are often interrupted by other library patrons; and that dust and dirt are so bad in some cases that damage to both microforms and reading machines is commonplace.

4. Most users of microform reading machines are left to load and unload the machines. Initial assistance is given by the reading room attendants to those who have no experience with the machines. Only one respondent stated that microforms were always placed in reading machines by a member of the library staff.

One commercial producer commented: "Most reading machines and microforms are left to the mercy of anyone who comes along."

5. Microform readers are, in nearly all cases, used by the general public. ("General public" is here defined as the patrons of any institution using microforms.)

6. Comments concerning frequency of damage to reading machines by users ranged from "seldom" to "often." Rough handling was believed to be an important cause of damage when it appeared. It was also the opinion of some well informed librarians that many reading machines

were not adequately maintained and were permitted to gather dirt and dust. These in turn caused damage to the optics and glass flats. Advancing cables, glass flats and cracking optics are the components most frequently damaged.

7. Most of the organizations visited had in-house facilities to accomplish minor repairs of microform reading machines. When required, service men usually responded to calls within one-half to three days. One of the micro-opaque readers must be returned to the factory for repairs. Shipment and repairs normally require a month or more. Inoperative reading machines did not seem to be a cause for concern among the interviewees.

8. All microforms require more delicate handling and care than full-size library materials. Damage to microforms is caused by careless and inex-perienced users, wear from frequent use and by poorly maintained reading machines. Roll microfilm is often damaged by being incorrectly threaded in reading machines, by the use of damaged reels, by malfunctioning op-tical flats and by the accumulation of dirt and film emulsion on the flats. Some domestic and many foreign microform producers are supplying roll film with poorly fastened splices, which often break and cause tears in the film, and with scratches and abrasions. The fingerprints of users, complete with food particles, often smudge the film. Fingerprints cause the accumu-lation of "goo" on optical flats, which, in turn, accelerates the gathering of dirt and resultant film damage.

Microfiche, microcards and microprint sheets all must be individually handled while being positioned in the readers and when they are removed from the machines. Since the average microform sheet and card contain many fewer frames or pages than an average microfilm roll, they are generally handled more frequently during machine viewing. This added handling increases the hazard of contaminating the microforms and in-creases the danger of damage to both them and the machines used in viewing them.

The most repeated complaint about the use of microform sheets and cards for library materials was the inordinate amount of time required to replace them in proper order after each usage. This often results in loss or improper filing. Several complaints also were made about burn damage to micro-opaques when they are used in reading machines for prolonged periods.

9. A few interviewees believed that presently available reading machines were adequate for reading requirements. Others commented that the reading machines were reasonably adequate but they would like the over-all quality of screen images improved.

However, the majority did not believe any available microform reading machine was adequate for prolonged use.

Most respondents commented that reading machine advancing mechanisms and arrangements for positioning and removing microforms were generally clumsy and awkward. The quality of reading machine images seldom compared favorably to the original document. There were suggestions that reading machine images of microforms might be more readable if the magnification were increased to provide images slightly larger than those found in the original material.

Further, the centers and corners of screen images were often not equally sharp and most screen images were not sufficiently bright to be viewed with ease in a normally lighted room.

The usual height and angle of reading machine screens require the reader to be in a disciplined position which must be maintained with little variation for the duration of use.

10. In identifying particular types of microforms believed to be best suited for particular types of library materials, a very large majority believed that roll microfilm should be used for miniaturizing serials, monographs and manuscripts. These respondents also thought that microfiche was ideal for miniaturizing report literature. There was a general consensus that roll film, installed in cassettes for use in a suitable reading machine, would be highly desirable if the cost were not prohibitive.

A librarian, who has used microforms extensively to supplement full-size materials and as a substitute for them in rounding out the collection of a new library, stated that he does not believe it possible to solve the problems of administering collections of fiche, cards and microprint for general library use because of the problems of damage, loss, misfiling, etc. He has found roll microfilm reasonably satisfactory and believes that it could be made much more manageable if installed in cassettes and used in a reader designed for their specific use.

Several respondents believe that both fiche and aperture cards might be useful in very special library applications.

A director of a university library, who has been closely associated with the development and use of microforms for many years, commented that roll microfilm would become more generally acceptable if offered in a reasonably priced cassette, provided a satisfactory reading machine were offered to accommodate the cassette. Cassettes would eliminate direct handling of the microform and would go a long way toward eliminating mechanical problems of threading and damage now associated with roll film. He further observed that if fiche and cards were generally and freely used, the bibliographic integrity of library materials would often be violated. Such violations, he thought, should be permitted only when there is an overwhelming reason for them.

Another respondent commented that if a standard cassette for roll microfilm could be agreed upon and if a satisfactory reader for it were developed, roll microfilm would be preferred for a large majority of library applications where microforms are indicated.

Holdings and Acquisition Policy

1. 35mm roll film has been, and is presently, being used extensively for acquiring a variety of library materials, with some emphasis on newspapers. Government documents, republished series, and special collections of monographs offered by microcard publishers account for large holdings of microcards and microprint. Microfiche acquisitions have generally been limited to scientific and report literature obtained from the Department of Commerce Clearing House in Springfield, Virginia.
    The average growth rate of microform collections is reported to be from 10% to 15% per year.

2. The acquisition of microforms by libraries is reported to be both planned and incidental. The acquisition of microfilm copies of newspapers is planned, while the acquisition of government documents and of scientific material obtained from the Department of Commerce Clearing House is thought to be incidental because this material is available only in microform. It was reported that the largest portion of library budgets for microforms is used for planned acquisitions.

3. There was general agreement among the interviewees that publishers' lists and catalogs and news releases were useful in determining what is available in microforms. However, a number commented that it would be most helpful if all of the data on available microforms could be combined in a single publication, which would be kept current and which would be published with full bibliographic annotations. There were complaints about the practice of microform publishers announcing projects which depended upon a sufficient number of subscriptions for implementation. This practice causes librarians to obligate funds which may be lost if the publishing project is delayed and the money is not actually spent during a specified period of time.

4. Most respondents indicated that if a desired title is not available in original format at a reasonable cost, purchase in microform is considered.
    All interviewees stated that 35mm roll film is preferred for newspapers.

Quality, Maintenance and Servicing of Collections

1. All libraries visited had facilities for making facsimile prints from microforms. Only three rely exclusively on reader-printers for these prints.

All respondents complained about difficulty with reader-printers. All institutions offered prints to their patrons upon payment of a fee.

2. Most libraries either do not inspect microforms for bibliographic and technical quality or do so in a most casual way. With such a lack of proper inspection practices, readers discover deficient microforms at a future time, generally too late for the library to do anything about them. Some libraries do devote considerable time to inspecting microforms and find both bibliographic and technical quality wanting.

3. Few libraries have the staff time to inspect microforms after each use. Inspections that have been made revealed that occasionally pieces of roll microfilm had been cut out and taken by library patrons. Five institutions reported this phenomenon. Further, fingerprints, replete with the aforementioned food particles, were often found on the surfaces of microcards, microfiche and microprint.

4. A majority of institutions visited stored reels of microfilm, microfiche, and microcards in specially designed slide-drawer cabinets. Others stored microfilm, housed in cardboard boxes, on regular library stack shelves and used a variety of wooden and metal slide-drawer cabinets for storing microfiche and microcards. Microprint sheets are placed on regular library shelves, housed in the special boxes supplied by the publishers.

   Most, but not all, areas in which microforms were stored were air-conditioned. However, no special temperature and humidity controls were provided for microforms.

5. Master negatives were housed in separately designated stack areas or in juxtaposition to those stack areas housing use copies. Consequently, they experience the same temperature and humidity as other library materials.

6. Master negatives are normally reserved for reproduction purposes. However, some libraries find it necessary, in the absence of positive copies, to provide master negatives for reading machine use.

7. The use of specially designed slide-drawer cabinets by a number of institutions has reduced some of the problems of storing microforms. Comments concerning the shelving of microforms were as follows: 1) when stack shelves are filled, some microforms are pushed to the rear and subsequently lost; 2) the storage of roll microfilm is not difficult, but other microforms are often misfiled, which means they are lost; 3) microforms are sometimes difficult to shelve because they cannot be marked easily; 4) boxes containing film and film cassettes are not as difficult to house as fiche with their envelopes; 5) microforms are lost and misshelved because readers have access to them; 6) specially designed stack shelving would be

useful in housing the various types of microforms.

Production and Processing of Microforms

1. Most of the libraries visited had facilities for exposing 35mm roll microfilm and 16mm roll microfilm with the use of an adapter kit. None had a step-and-repeat camera in regular use.

2. Practically all institutions that had camera facilities had facilities for in-house film processing.

3. Twelve institutions had facilities to produce 35mm film copies and five had facilities to produce film copies of microfiche.

4. A large majority of institutions reported that up to 98% of their microform acquisitions is purchased from microform publishers. Four institutions reported that in-house produced microforms accounted for 96%, 80%, 35% and 35%, respectively, of their total microform acquisitions.

Bibliographic Control and
Access to Microforms

1.   There were a variety of answers to "What problems are experienced in cataloging microforms?" The range of answers included the following: There are no problems; There are no problems except markings; The need to use a reading machine slows cataloging; Problems in descriptive cataloging result from having to describe sheets, frames and rolls; Irregular quality of targets requires added time for verification; Cataloging microforms is a "snake pit" with many unsolved problems; Catalogers put microforms on bottom of pile; Limited number of personnel experienced with microforms causes delays; There are not enough catalogers to keep up with the work load; Catalogers real or imagined problems in working with microforms cause them to put microforms aside, resulting in a constant backlog.

2. Most respondents stated that there has been gradual improvement in the arrangement of material before it is committed to microform. However, they thought constant pressure must be exerted to further upgrade the bibliographic quality of microforms. All agreed that the cataloging of large microform projects should be the responsibility of the producer.
     Some pertinent comments on this subject were as follows: The bibliographic data provided is often inconsistent; existing standards and specifications (ALA microfilm norms) should be enforced; foreign

produced projects often present real problems; librarians, acting through ALA and ARL, should cooperate in requiring improved microform quality; librarians should refuse to purchase microforms unless they meet standards and specifications; librarians should organize a corporation to undertake large scale microform projects; there should be a cooperative agency for cooperative testing of the quality of all microforms.

3. Microform collections were generally separated from other library collections but were most often shelved in adjoining stacks. Most, but not all, institutions gave their microforms full cataloging and most assigned a sequential number for convenience in shelving.

Reader Habits and Attitudes

1. There were individual preferences expressed for reading machines with translucent type screens and for those with the opaque, reflective type. The majority of those interviewed who were in charge of microform reading rooms believed the opaque, reflective type of screen was preferred by most users because the screen image is brighter and it provides better contrast between background and text. Individuals who wear bifocal eyeglasses or strong magnifying reading glasses have a definite preference for translucent screens because of the focal distance requirement imposed by the eyeglass lenses.

Several researchers who are working with early American newspapers expressed a preference for the Recordak, Model C, library reader (manufacture has been discontinued) because of its ability to enlarge the screen image text to a size greater than the original.

2. There were some complaints about eye strain associated with using microforms and reading machines. Most complaints are made by the casual user. Experienced microform users seldom complain.

3. When given a choice, readers choose hard copies in preference to microforms (newspapers excepted).

4. Whenever feasible and when they are not personally responsible for the cost, readers do demand blowup prints. By a margin of two to one, respondents indicated that blowups from reader printers do not satisfy reader requirements. It was regularly reported that trial exposures were required and high wastage was normal when working with library microforms.

5. Readers seldom expressed a preference for particular types of microforms. They use whatever is available. They have no choice.

General Response to Microform Usage

1. There were a variety of responses to the question of the general
evaluation of microform usage. Some of them:

There should be more cooperative filming of newspapers in order to
fill gaps in backfiles.

There should be an information clearing house which would report
on microfilm projects being undertaken.

Microform projects should be completed regardless of the number of
purchasers.

There is a need for a "universal reader" which would accommodate
microfilm reels, cassettes, fiche and opaques.

Readers should be improved so that they would not damage microforms.

Reading equipment should be generally and greatly improved with
more attention given by producers to finding aids.

There is a need for a good portable reading machine which could be
loaned along with microforms.

In the future there will be increased use of microforms as an intermediate for hard copy and in the machine retrieval of information.

There is a real need for a rapid and inexpensive means of providing
printouts from microforms.

There must be adequate optics and engineering to provide first
quality printouts.

A reader-printer should be developed which would produce full-size
facsimile prints of text and pictorial materials.

Microforms are invaluable for the acquisition of materials not available in other forms.

Microforms should be used to provide the widest dissemination of
library materials.

A breakthrough is needed in automation as applied to production
and use of microforms.

The future use of microforms should provide for automatic retrieval.

Microfiche is valuable because it can be made available for loan.

Microforms are valuable because they mitigate the space problem in
libraries and are less expensive to acquire and preserve than hard copies.

Microforms should facilitate the development of a comprehensive
system of information identification and retrieval.

There may be developed a means of using television screens in the
homes for reading various types of microforms.

Microforms have a real role to play in the publication of research
tools and for the storage of data which can be located and retrieved via
computer.

Microforms could be used to speed up the availability of current
materials.

Many information systems not in use today could be viable with improved hardware and quality microforms.

Color microfilm for maps and works of art would be very helpful.

2. There are complaints from readers because desired library materials are available in microform only. Everyone seems to prefer hard copy, except for newspapers. However, most readers are happy to have the material they require and do not complain.

3. Complaints are not uncommon with regard to all of the problems mentioned in the interviewing guide, for example, images which are either too dark or too light or too fuzzy, text in gutters of volumes not readable, etc. There are far more complaints about foreign produced microforms than about those produced in the United States.

4. There were some complaints about improper reduction ratios used in the production of microforms. However, they were infrequent.

5. Except for newspapers, readers do not find microforms satisfactory for browse searching.

6. There were a number of interesting overall observations expressed. For example, a number of respondents stressed the importance of a microform reader carrel that would be a complete module. It should possess all of the requirements for ambient light control; it should provide auxiliary work space for note-taking and for a limited number of reference books; and the screen should be easily adjustable to the requirements and comforts of an individual.

There was a consensus that microform readers are generally inadequate as substitutes for reading hard copy. Manufacturers should give much more attention to user habits and requirements and to eliminating the many mechanical operations, such as threading, inserting and positioning microforms.

Much more attention should be given by producers of microforms to the bibliographic and technical quality of microforms. There was general support for an inspection and certifying agency, available to all libraries, which would pass on the suitability of any microform. This agency would go a long way toward improving the quality of microforms.

EXPERIENCES WITH SCIENTIFIC
JOURNALS ON MICROFILM IN
AN ACADEMIC READING ROOM

by Ann M. De Villiers and
Barbara Frick Schloman

Experiences with chemistry and biology journals on 16mm microfilm in a reading room which serves chemistry faculty and graduate students are reviewed. Surveys in 1971 and 1972 indicate that the users have accepted the microfilm as a satisfactory replacement for hardcopy; in some instances they even find it preferable to hardcopy. The reactions of both the staff and users are, however, that both the microfilm machines and the micropublishing criteria need to be improved.

The MIT Ford Reading Room has been in operation as an official part of the MIT library system since April 1970. The Reading Room provides convenient access to a basic core collection of research journals and monographs in chemistry and biology, duplicating material in the more comprehensive Science Library collection. The room is located in the Camille Edouard Dreyfus Chemistry Building and is open to the entire MIT community Monday through Friday, 9 am-5 pm; faculty and graduate students in the Chemistry Department and researchers with related interests can obtain keys to the room for use after hours. It is presently staffed by one librarian and an assistant, who work a combined total of 40 hours per week in the facility.

In planning for the room, the decision was made that backfiles of the more highly used journals would be kept on 16 mm microfilm only. This decision was instigated by several faculty members who were aware of a successful film operation in an industrial chemical library. For the library staff there were two immediate advantages to the use of microfilm: 1) the possibility of acquiring complete backfiles of journals that might not otherwise be available from book dealers; and 2) the ability to store lengthy sets.[1]

Reprinted from *Special Libraries*, 64: 555-60 (December 1973) by permission of the publisher. Copyright © 1974 by the Special Libraries Association.

The complete reliance on microfilm for journal backruns has given the staff of the Ford Reading Room a unique opportunity to observe both user and staff reactions to the microfilm.

Contrary to an earlier impression that microforms would not find acceptance in academe,[2] the limited experience of this reading room indicates that a microfilm facility can successfully be integrated into an academic library system.

A user survey has shown a general acceptance of the microfilm, rather than the frequently mentioned reluctance of patrons to use microforms.[3, 4] The survey results were comparable to the experiences of industrial chemistry libraries which have reported general satisfaction with using chemistry journals on microfilm and increased ease and efficiency in doing a literature search in *Chemical Abstracts*.[5, 6, 7, 8]

User and staff criticisms of this microfilm experiment have largely been directed at problems with the available microfilm readers and printing attachments and the shortcomings in film quality. The dry-process reader-printer was a significant improvement over the wet-process machine initially employed; but both staff and users look forward to a more flexible machine, such as the reader described by Stevens[9].

Although the quality of the microfilm acquired has been improving, the staff strongly agrees with Veaner that micropublishing has to be recognized as a complex manufacturing process and that standards need to be established.[10] Patrons rightfully expect to find microfilm journal editions to contain what is present in hardcopy.

The Collection

The present book collection contains approximately 1,800 volumes. The chemistry faculty participated in the initial selection of monographs and serial titles. The 100 journal titles under regular hardcopy subscription were chosen entirely by the faculty and represent the basic journals in the field, as well as specialty journals for specific research.

The microfilm plan for the journals has been to acquire complete back-files in 16 mm cartridges for 40 of the most frequently used titles (including *Chemical Abstracts*) and to update these film runs yearly. For another 30, the film backfiles date only to 1970 because of cost considerations, but are updated yearly. Also due to cost, there are no microfilm plans for the remaining 30 journals, and they are accumulating in hardcopy at this time. The Appendix lists the journals in these three groups.

The microfilm is all 16 mm negative and is loaded in cartridges. The hardcopy journal volumes are removed when the microfilm editions arrive. As of Feb 30, 1973, there were over 1,700 cartridges in the collection, representing approximately 1,600 cumulative years of journal volumes.

Film Acquisition and Quality Control

As much film as available was ordered commercially. To insure long-term stability of the microfilm after its receipt, an MIT micro-reproduction facility has made spot checks for residual thiosulfate; there has been a minimum amount of rejection due to this.

When the cartridges are received in the reading room, the staff checks the film for image quality, proper film exposure and contrast, complete pagination, and proper labeling. The majority of the film cartridges have been found to be satisfactory, although enough have been returned to make an initial check worthwhile.

In addition, all reels are checked for an index, and the label is marked indicating the presence of an index and its location on the reel. To the dismay of staff and users, many indexes, as well as supplementary material, have been omitted from the microfilm journal editions although they exist in hardcopy. Also, publishers generally do not indicate the presence or position of special material on the reel.

Film Costs and Space Savings

As expected, purchasing journals on microfilm in addition to having hard-copy subscriptions is a strain on the budget. As part of the MIT library system, the reading room does not directly benefit from hardcopy sales to dealers since the money goes into a general fund.

Unfortunately, many titles are not yet commercially available on film; and custom filming is almost prohibitively expensive. For those journals that are available on microfilm, the film costs for the recent year can be as high as the hardcopy subscription although this is not usually the case. Several publishers have offered to trade the microfilm edition for the hard-copy volumes—either on an even exchange basis or at a sizeable discount. Hopefully, the market for microfilm will increase sufficiently to induce publishers to make the journals available on film to their hardcopy sub-scribers at a cost dramatically lower than the hardcopy subscription rate.

The reading room still has adequate room for a moderate growth in the collection. This freedom is entirely due to the reliance on microfilm for journal backfiles; comparable backfiles in hardcopy could never have been accommodated. For example, the hardcopy volumes for the *Journal of the American Chemical Society* from volume 1, 1879, to volume 94, 1972, occupy about 60 feet of shelf space; each volume measures 11½ inches tall. The comparable film run uses about 12 feet of shelf space, and the cartridges are only 4 inches tall.

Microfilm Machines

During the operation of the reading room, both Recordak Lodestars and Recordak Microstars have been used. The Lodestar, which has a wet-process printer, is being phased out by the manufacturer. It is being replaced by the Microstar which, among its several improvements, has an optional dry-process printer.

The room now has two Microstar readers and two Microstar reader-printers. Equipment costs remain high and have restricted the number of machines it is possible to have in the reading room. It should also be noted that, because cartridges of different manufacturers are presently not compatible in competitors' machines, the initial choice of equipment has to be recognized as a long-term commitment.

The staff performs basic machine maintenance, including changing the toner every 300 prints and replacing the paper and projection lamps when needed. The wet-process printer required periodical flushing of the system and changing of the fluid, a messy and unpleasant task.

Also, the staff has become adept at troubleshooting for machine problems and at correcting some difficulties which previously required a service call. Nonetheless, the staff feels strongly that service contracts are indispensable. Servicing is periodically needed to readjust the optical system, to check for mechanical wear, and to correct printer difficulties.

Copy charges are passed on to the patron. With the wet-process printer it was necessary to charge $.10 a copy if cash was paid (and $.15 if charged to an account to cover the copy plus bookkeeping). However, since the dry-process printing attachments were installed in September 1972, the print cost has been lowered to $.05 for a cash copy.

User Response

The most pleasant surprise has been the ease with which our users have accepted microfilm despite machine problems and gaps in film holdings. Since the opening of the reading room, during the public hours, the staff has kept an hourly count of the total number of people in the room and of the specific number using the microfilm machines, with a breakdown by the type of machine used. These figures have consistently shown that both the room and the film receive active use. There is no reliable measure of the extent of use the room and/or machines receive in the evenings or on weekends. In addition, it was noted that when there was a choice between using a Lodestar or a Microstar reader, the Microstar was invariably selected.

TABLE 1.
Users' Response to Journals and
CA on Microfilm 1971 and 1972

1971 Survey*

Response	Journals Users	%	CA Users	%
Prefer	54	59%	71	76%
Accept	17	19%	3	3%
Dislike	20	22%	20	21%
Total	91		94	

1972 Survey**

Response	Journals Users	%	CA Users	%
Prefer	59	62%	67	87%
Accept	15	16%	8	10%
Dislike	21	22%	2	3%
Total	95		77	

*Machines included 3 Microstar readers and 3 Lodestar reader-printers.
** Machines included 2 Microstar readers and 2 Microstar reader-printers.

Another measure of user reaction was made in September 1971, and again in September 1972. Machine users were asked to indicate their reactions ("prefer," "accept," or "dislike") to using both journals and *Chemical Abstracts* on film. A copy of the questionnaire was placed by each machine for a period of a week; written comments were also solicited. The results of the two surveys are shown in Table 1.

The percentage of users who preferred using the microfilm editions of the journals and particularly of *Chemical Abstracts* increased in 1972. Many users said they prefer doing a literature search in *Chemical Abstracts* on film because they find it more efficient and less exhausting physically. Other comments indicated that the accessibility of all journal volumes of a given title make searching more convenient. Enthusiastic users are quite so, giving such comments as "great," "excellent quality," and "hooray for microfilm."

In both the 1971 and 1972 surveys, the written comments directed criticism toward machine inadequacies. The Lodestar had been a particular target for criticism. Patrons indicated the Microstars were preferred because of: 1) the zoom attachments (optional on the machine) which make reading easier and reduce eyestrain; 2) a more sensitive advance/rewind knob that improves scanning; and 3) the dry-process printer for its cleaner, faster, and more inexpensive copies. Several patrons wished the Microstar had a surface on which to place a notebook while taking notes from the screen. Also, there was an expressed interest in a more horizontal or an adjustable screen.

Conclusion

Based on operating experience in the MIT Ford Reading Room and on the results of two user surveys, it is apparent that a retrospective journal collection on microfilm can be a substitute for a comparable hardcopy collection. While the results of the 1971 and 1972 surveys discussed here indicated strong support for the use of microfilm, it must be recognized that there is no available measure of the attitudes of faculty and student nonusers who may have a basic resistance to using microfilm, or who may have tried it at one time and found it unsatisfactory.

While users have recognized and appreciated recent improvements in microfilm readers and printer attachments, there remain valid criticisms of the quality of commercially available microfilm. Editorial and technical criteria for the preparation of microfilm journal editions must be established to make them as acceptable as hardcopy editions. Despite present shortcomings, user and staff responses have been very positive. In the short time the reading room has been in existence, some machine and film improvements have been noted, and it remains our feeling that journal collections on microfilm do have a future.

Appendix

Journal holdings in the Ford Reading Room

I. Current subscriptions in hardcopy; complete backruns on microfilm:*

Accounts of Chemical Research	Archives of Biochemistry and Biophysics
Acta Chimica Scandinavica	Biochemical and Biophysical Research
American Chemical Society Journal	Communications
Analytical Chemistry	Biochemical Journal
Angewandte Chemie	Biochemistry

* The last part of this appendix lists the suppliers' names, addresses, and phone numbers.

Canadian Journal of Chemistry
Chemical Abstracts
Chemical Reviews
Chemical Society, London, Journal
Chemische Berichte
Coordination Chemistry Reviews
Faraday Society. Transactions
Helvetica Chimica Acta
Immunochemistry
Inorganic Nuclear Chemistry Letters
Inorganic Chemistry
Inorganica Chimica Acta
Journal of Biological Chemistry
Journal of Chemical Education
Journal of Chemical Physics
Journal of Chromatographic Science
Journal of Molecular Biology
Journal of Organic Chemistry
Journal of Organometallic Chemistry
Journal of Physical Chemistry
Justus Liebigs Annalen der Chemie
Macromolecules
Nature (all sections)
Organometallic Chemistry Reviews (A and B)
Quarterly Reviews
Royal Society of London, Proceedings
    (A and B)
Societe de Chimie. France. Bulletin
Tetrahedron
Tetrahedron Letters

II. Current subscriptions in hardcopy; back-
     runs from 1970 onward on microfilm:

Acta Crystallographica (A and B)
Biochimica et Biophysica Acta (all sections)
Biophysical Journal
Canadian Journal Research
Experimental Cell Research
European Journal of Biochemistry
FEBS Letters

Federation Proceedings
Genetics
Journal of Bacteriology
Journal of Biochemistry (Japan)
Journal of Cell Biology
Journal of Experimental Biology
Journal of Immunology
Molecular Pharmacology
National Academy of Science. Proceedings
Physiological Review
Quarterly Reviews of Biophysics
Science
Scientific American
U.S. National Cancer Institute. Journal
Virology

III. Current subscriptions and backruns dating
      from 1970 in hardcopy:

Applied Physics Letters
Canadian Journal of Physics
Chemical Physics Letters
Current Contents: Physics & Chemistry
Developmental Biology
Journal of Applied Physics
Journal of Molecular Spectroscopy
Journal of Physics (A-F)
Journal of Statistical Physics
Molecular Physics
Physica
Physical Reviews (A-D)
Physical Society, Japan. Journal
Physics Abstracts
Physics Letters A, B, C,
Physics of Fluids
Progress in Theoretical Physics
Reviews in Modern Physics
Soviet Physics J.E.T.P.
Studies in Applied Mathematics
Zeitschrift fur Physik

Micropublisher	Address	Phone
American Chemical Society	1155 16th St. N.W. Washington, D.C. 20036	202/737-3337
American Institute of Physics	335 E. 45th St. New York, N.Y. 10017	212/685-l940
Chemical Abstracts Service	Ohio State University Columbus, Ohio 43210	614/422-5022
Maxwell International Microforms Corporation	Fairview Park Elmsford, N.Y. 10523	914/592-9141
Princeton Microfilm Corporation	Alexander Rd. Princeton, N.J. 08540	800/257-9502 (toll free)

Micropublisher	Address	Phone

University Microfilms	300 N. Zeeb Rd.	313/761-4700
	Ann Arbor, Mich. 48106	
Williams & Wilkins Co.	428 Preston St.	301/727-2870
	Baltimore, Md. 21202	

Literature Cited

1. Stevens, Rolland E. / The Microform Revolution. *Library Trends* 19: 379-395 (Jan 1971).
2. Veaner, Allen B. / Reprography and Microform Technology. In *Annual Review of Information Science and Technology,* v.4. Chicago, Encyclopedia Britannica, 1969. p. 193.
3. Stevens, Rolland E. / The Microform Revolution. *Library Trends* 19: 379-395 (Jan 1971).
4. Lewis, Ralph W. / User's Reaction to Microfiche: A Preliminary Study. *College & Research Libraries* 31: 260-268 (Jul 1970).
5. Weil, B. H., et al. / Esso Research Experiences with Chemical Abstracts on Microfilm. *Journal of Chemical Documentation* 5: 193-200 (Nov 1965).
6. Starker, Lee N. / User Experiences with Primary Journals on 16 mm Microfilm. *Journal of Chemical Documentation* 10: 5-6 (Feb 1970).
7. Kaback, Stuart M. / User Benefits from Secondary Journals on Microfilm. *Journal of Chemical Documentation* 10: 7-9 (Feb 1970).
8. Duncan, Virginia L., and Frances E. Parsons / Use of Microfilm in an Industrial Research Library. *Special Libraries* 61 (no.6): 288-290 (Jul/Aug 1970).
9. Stevens, Rolland E. / The Microform Revolution. *Library Trends* 19: 379-395 (Jan 1971).
10. Veaner, Allen B. / Whither Micropublishing? *Micrographics News & Views* 2: 2, 6-7 (May 15, 1971).
11. Starker, Lee N. / User Experiences with Primary Journals on 16 mm Microfilm. *Journal of Chemical Documentation* 10: 5-6 (Feb 1970).

ADDITIONAL READINGS

Baldwin, Thomas S. and Bailey, Larry J., "Readability of Technical Training Materials Presented on Microfiche vs. Offset Copy," *Journal of Applied Physics,* 55: 37-41 (1971).

Carroll, C. Edward, "Some Problems of Microform Utilization in Large University Libraries," *Microform Review,* 1: 19-24 (January 1972).

Christ, C. W., "Microfiche: A Study of User Attitudes and Reading Habits," *Journal of the American Society for Information Science,* 23: 30-35 (January 1972).

Gardner, J. J. and Canfield, M. P., "User Preference Study," in *Project Intrex Semi-Annual Activity Report March 15, 1972-September 15, 1972.* Cambridge: Massachusetts Institute of Technology, Sept. 15, 1972, p. 54-57.

Gardner, J. J. and Keator, C. L., "User Preference Study," in *Project Intrex Semi-Annual Activity Report, September 15, 1971-March 15, 1972.* Cambridge: Massachusetts Institute of Technology, March 15, 1972, p. 95-99.

Greene, Robert J., "Microform Attitude and Frequency of Microform Use," *Journal of Micrographics,* 8: 131-34 (January/February 1975).

Holmes, Donald C., *Determination of the Environmental Conditions Required in a Library for the Effective Utilization of Microforms.* Washington: Association of Research Libraries, 1970. ERIC ED 046 403. 44p.

Holmes, Donald C., "The Needs of Library Microform Users," National Microfilm Association, *Proceedings,* 1969, pp. 256-61.

Kaback, Stuart M., "User Benefits from Secondary Journals on Microfilm," *Journal of Chemical Documentation,* 10: 7-9 (February 1970).

Lee, Thomas, "Microfilm Use by Secondary School Students in Michigan," in *Microform Utilization: The Academic Library Environment. Report of Conference Held at Denver, Colorado 7-9 December 1970.* Denver: University of Denver, 1971, pp. 225-26 (Also, ERIC ED 048 071).

Microforms Task Force, Government Documents Round Table, American Library Association, *Summary of the Survey Questionnaire, 1974.* (Available from Chet Stout, Microform Task Force, McKinley Memorial Library, Niles, Ohio 44446. Include stamped, self-addressed envelope).

Svobodny, Dolly D., *A Program to Demonstrate the Uses of an Inexpensive Microfiche Reader and the Resources of ERIC and other Microform Information Collections. Final Report.* New York: Modern Language Association, March 25, 1971. (Also, ERIC ED 048 744).

Wooster, Harold, *Microfiche 1969—User Survey,* Arlington, Va.: Air Force Office of Scientific Research, July, 1969. AD 695 049.

SELECTED
BIBLIOGRAPHY

"A Basic Microfilm Bibliography," *Microfilm Source Book*, 1972. New York: Microfilm Publishing, Inc., 1972. To be updated in the 1975/76 edition.

"Bibliography of Micrographics," *Journal of Micrographics*, 6: 119-22 (January 1973).

Born, Lester K., "The Literature of Microreproduction, 1950-55," *American Documentation*, 7: 167-97 (July 1956).

Gaddy, Dale, "Bibliography," in his *A Microform Handbook*. Silver Springs, Md.: National Microfilm Association, 1974, pp. 57-66. Approximately 130 items arranged by subject. Annotated. This is a reprint of "Resource Report RR2-1974" issued by the National Microfilm Association.

Library Resources and Technical Services. Annual coverage of significant micrographic activities. Articles for the past five years are cited below:

Sullivan, Robert C., "Developments in Reproduction of Library Materials, 1969," 14: 189-230 (Spring 1970).

Sullivan, Robert C., "Developments in Photo Reproduction of Library Materials, 1970," 15: 158-90 (Spring 1971).

Spreitzer, Francis F., "Developments in Copying, Micrographics, and Graphic Communications, 1971," 16: 135-54 (Spring 1972).

Spreitzer, Francis F., "Developments in Copying, Micrographics and Graphic Communications, 1972," 17: 144-67 (Spring 1973).

Spreitzer, Francis F., "Developments in Copying, Micrographics and Graphic Communications, 1973," 18: 151-70 (Spring 1974).

"Microfilm Bibliography," in *Microfilm Source Book*. New York: Microfilm Publishing, Inc. Lists and annotates "books which deal extensively with, were largely related to, or had key sections on Microfilm." The 1974/75 edition lists forty-two books.

"Microform Reading Devices: A Selective Chronological Bibliography," *Microform Review*, 3: 134-36 (April 1974).

Microform Review, 1972-. Each issue of this quarterly journal includes a list of "Recent Articles in Micropublishing."

The Micrographics Index 1974. Rita Tatis, editor. Silver Springs, Md.: National Microfilm Association, 1974. 172pp. An author, title, and keyword index to NMA's, *Journal of Micrographics*, 1967-, and its annual conference, *Proceedings*, 1952-, with some coverage of books, pamphlets, and other periodicals (of approximately 900 entries, 770 were published by NMA). Reviewed in *Microform Review*, 4: 71-73 (January 1975).

Micrographics Newsletter, 1968- (formerely, *Microfilm Newsletter*). Most issues of this semi-monthly "news report for executives who use or market microfilm services and equipment" contains a section titled, "Micrographics in Magazines" which consists of brief annotations of articles appearing primarily in business oriented magazines.

Reichmann, Felix and Tharpe, Josephine. *Bibliographic Control of Microforms*. Westport: Greenwood, 1972. This book contains two major bibliographies. The first, "A Microform Bibliography," is annotated and in four parts: (1) "Catalogs and Lists," pp. 60-110, items 1-169; (2) "Collections and Series," pp. 112-65, items 170-313; (3) "Manuscripts and Archival Collections," pp. 168-230, items 314-482; "References," pp. 232-35, items 483-93. The second is, "Bibliography of Literature Used," pp. 250-56, is not annotated and consists of approximately 260 items.

Spigai, Frances G., *The Invisible Medium: the State of the Art of Microform and a Guide to the Literature*. March, 1973. ERIC ED 75 029. 31p.